# HOW TO STUDY IN COLLEGE

# How to Study in College

## SIXTH EDITION

## WALTER PAUK
Cornell University, Emeritus

Houghton Mifflin Company　　Boston　New York

Cover Design: Judy Arisman, Arisman Design
Cover Image: Emblems, 1913 oil on canvas by Roger de la Fresnaye, The Phillips Collection,
Washington, D.C.

Printed in the U.S.A.

Library of Congress Catalog Card Number: 96-76945

Student Edition ISBN: 0-395-83062-1
Instructor's Edition ISBN: 0-395-83063-X

456789–CS–00 99

*72235*

# Contents _____

**v**

# Part II   Your Memory

# Part IV   Your Lecture Notes

## Part V   Your Textbooks

# *To the Instructor of the Sixth Edition* _____

Time after time, students have told me that by learning a particular technique for taking useful notes or reading and retaining a textbook assignment they have achieved major breakthroughs. Moreover, these breakthroughs in a particular subject often jump-start the entire learning process and extend to all other subjects.

Students who are seeking help are not primarily interested in theory, and most of them have little patience with merely inspirational talk. They want practical instruction on how to succeed academically. They want something that they can readily understand and apply and that works. After a week of classes, they discover that the hit-or-miss tactics that got them through high school are grossly inadequate and inefficient at the competitive college level. So they turn to us for help.

Let's then teach these students proven techniques for studying and learning.

*How to Study in College* is brimming with exciting techniques, based on widely tested educational and learning theory, that have already helped myriad students. But the tail of theory is never allowed to wag the practical, feet-on-the-ground dog. While theory is always implicit and is sometimes given in enough detail to explain the rationale behind a particular technique or reassure the skeptic, it is never presented without explicit applications and never used simply as exhortation. After all, the person who needs penicillin is hardly cured by learning the history of antibiotics!

Because it is so crucial that students learn for the long term, I am wholeheartedly against techniques that stress mere memorization. Such techniques fill the mind with "knowledge" that melts away after a test and leaves learning still to be done. The techniques presented in this book result in real learning. And real learning, like a real diamond, lasts.

Finally, no textbook—no matter how complete or current—is truly useful if it is boring, confusing, or excessively difficult to read. I have therefore tried to write in a conversational tone so that reading this book is like having a sincere, person-to-person chat.

## WHAT'S NEW OR DIFFERENT IN THE SIXTH EDITION?

- The "To the Student" introduction has been reoriented. It starts by bringing in the personal concept of "the will to learn" and there's a ten-item self-assessment inventory, which greatly aids students in identifying their basic learning style.

- "Setting Goals—A Self-Management Skill" is a brand-new chapter on a vital subject, the importance of which, like a last will and testament, is unarguable. Nevertheless, goal setting is subject to intense procrastination. Two quotations from Norman Vincent Peale's *Positive Imaging* provide convincing wisdom not only for drawing up one's goal or goals but also for taking vigorous action to achieve them. Then there are about twenty question-and-answer paragraphs and illustrations to aid students in formulating their academic and lifetime goals.

- The chapter "Improving Your Reading Speed and Comprehension" was brought back from the Fourth Edition. It is packed with so much great research and so many classical approaches to better reading and better comprehension that every new class of college students should have the chance to benefit by reading, thinking, and applying the techniques that best fit their individual learning styles.

- "Understanding and Using Key Concepts" is not only a brand-new chapter; it is a brand-new concept. As many of you know, almost all sound learning systems incorporate at least three principles to make learning understandable and memorable: recitation, reflection, and questioning. Obviously, during the actual presentation of, say, the Cornell Notetaking System, it takes too much time and space to explain fully any one of these principles. However, with a separate chapter to explain the importance of these principles, students will gain a thorough understanding of them in advance, so when the words *recite, reflect,* and *question* are mentioned in any system, understanding will be swift and complete.

- Part IV, "Your Lecture Notes," comprises two chapters, "Listening to Take Good Notes" and "Taking Good Notes." Notetaking is too important to discuss in one chapter; therefore, we have back-to-back chapters.

- Part V, "Your Textbooks," consists of three important chapters: "Learning from Your Textbook," "Noting What's Important in Readings," and "Thinking Visually." Students' academic success hinges upon mastering their inevitable textbook assignments, and these three chapters provide the principles and techniques for achieving success with efficient certainty.

- Three things are different in this edition regarding vocabulary development. First, I have reassembled the vocabulary chapter, "Improving Your Vocabulary," as a unit rather than distributing the topic throughout the book. My approach allows students to see and read the components of the chapter in full context. Second, at the end of each chapter you will find a vocabulary exercise composed of twenty-five words taken from (1) the chapter itself, (2) *Time*, (3) *Forbes*, (4) *New York Times*, (5) *Wall Street Journal*, and (6) Elizabethan poetry. These words are practical and can be used by students in writing term and research papers, as well as in their speech. Third, the last component in Chapter 6, "Vocabulary Development," features *word origins*, which frequently creates in many students a permanent interest in words. In the section "To the Student" students are encouraged to use a 3 × 5 card system for gathering words supported by word histories.

- The chapter "Studying Literature With the *Evoker* System" is mentioned here because of several strong requests to include it in this text. As one professor has noted, "The fundamental nature and the practicality of the *Evoker* does for literature what the Cornell Notetaking System does for lectures and the Questions-in-the-Margin System does for textbook assignments." The big advantage of the *Evoker* system is that it provides a systematic, step-by-step way for students to begin breaking down a literary passage to see how the author put it together in the first place.

- In this book, the principles, systems, and techniques are the vital determinants that will enable students to succeed academically. When these determinants are mentally absorbed, students can then use and adapt them to fit their learning styles. It is *not* the end-of-the-chapter exercise that will have a permanent effect on the students. It is the basic, sound principles, systems, and techniques. This is why the chapters are not diluted but rather kept crisp and compact, and uncluttered. I think we all agree that for a program to be successful, it must have basic soundness. Actually, no one knows what is the best way for any individual student to learn. Therefore, our mission should be to present clearly the best principles, systems, and techniques and then let students use them in their own personal and unique ways.

- Each "Have You Missed Something?" chapter quiz includes questions to reinforce students' understanding of key concepts. The rationale for these questions is NOT to test but rather to teach. If the chapter is read with care and understanding, then any student should achieve a perfect score.

- The "concept map" technique has been continued in this edition. It would be good to remind the students that much can be gained from these maps, both before reading the chapter and, perhaps even more, AFTER reading the chapter. Before reading the students can gain *advance organizers*, which, according to David P. Ausubel, can help them learn and remember material they encounter in the chapter itself. After reading the chapter, the concept maps provide a bird's-eye view of the entire chapter when the main concepts are shown with linking lines that establish relationships.

- Chapter 18, "Studying Mathematics," has been revised by Dr. Susan Piliero who now teaches the same course in mathematics at Cornell University that Dr. Harrison A. Geiselmann, the original author of the chapter, taught for more than thirty years.

- Chapter 19, "Learning With the Computer," has been extensively revised.

## ACKNOWLEDGMENTS

Warm and sincere words of thanks go to those who are permanently linked to this book: the late Henry F. Thomas and Ian D. Elliot.

My sincere thanks also go to the contributors of material in previous editions: Dr. Harrison A. Geiselmann and Professors Kenneth A. Greisen and Jane E. Hardy, all of Cornell University; Professor William G. Moulton of Princeton University; Professor James A. Wood and Dr. Nancy V. Wood, both of the University of Texas at El Paso.

I am very pleased that the original work done by a valued friend, John Rethorst, and my esteemed colleague Professor H. Dean Sutphin, both of Cornell University, still forms the basis of the revised Chapter 19, "Learning with the Computer." Professors Mike Radis and Ron Williams of The Pennsylvania State University prepared the "Questions for Further Study and Discussion" that first appeared in the Instructor's Resource Manual for the Fourth Edition. Professor Carol Kanar of Valencia Community College assisted with the updating and revising of Chapter 1 in that edition. I thank them all for their valuable assistance.

Now for a very special acknowledgement: I am very grateful to my friend Ross James Quirie Owens, whose experience as a writer, newspaper editor, director, cinematographer, and, currently, managing editor of *InfoWorld* (a publication devoted to computers) prepared him to take full charge in revising, editing, and improving the Fifth Edition. His talents are still particularly apparent in the Sixth Edition—in the mini-overviews and concept maps at the beginning of each chapter and in the quizzes at the end of each chapter. He also revised the quizzes and questions in the Fifth and Sixth Editions of the Instructor's Resource Manual.

I would also like to thank the reviewers of the Sixth Edition for their fine suggestions:

Richard Bremer
Napa Valley College

Arlene Carroll
Wichita State University

Patricia Davis
San Francisco Community College

Dom Garino
Irvine Valley College

Faith Heinrichs
Central Missouri State University

Dr. Carolyn Hopper
Middle Tennessee State University

Pauline Levine
Corning Community College

Dr. Larry Ludewig
Kilgore College

Teresa Lullo
University of New Mexico

Janet Pelletier
Modesto Junior College

Dr. Sara Lee Sanderson
Miami-Dade Community College

Finally, I am eternally grateful to my many students who have taught me much—so that I may pass on a little more to others.

W.P.

# To the Student _____

How did Helen Keller learn to read and communicate, in spite of being blind and unable to hear? Why did Abraham Lincoln walk twenty miles to borrow a book? How did Booker T. Washington, born in slavery, travel five hundred miles to a high school where he could get the education he craved? Each was motivated by the will to learn. Each so desired learning for its own sake that he or she allowed few things to interfere with that goal.

Perhaps you know people like Keller, Lincoln, or Washington. Perhaps you are such a person yourself. If you are, you have already discovered that the desire to learn can give you the strength to start projects, see them through during difficult spots, and finish them with satisfaction. In college, you are likely to find that the will to learn—perhaps more than any other single factor—will help you the most, particularly when you falter from time to time. On a cold winter morning, it's far easier to get out of bed if you want to ace a midterm than if you don't really care about your performance!

## USING THIS BOOK

No matter what academic goals you've set for yourself, this book can help you achieve them. In theory, there is no limit to learning and no limit to how you can improve your natural abilities to understand the material you study. By applying the techniques presented here, you will quickly begin to improve as a student, making your college experience a rewarding one.

## HOW TO USE THE "HAVE YOU MISSED SOMETHING?" QUESTIONS

The end-of-chapter questions are designed to teach, not test; you'll find no trick questions and no traps to lead you to an incorrect answer. Take each question at face value and answer it to the best of your ability. Use any incorrect answers you give as opportunities to reread the pertinent portion of the chapter. By rereading and rethinking the question and answer, you will greatly strengthen your understanding of the entire concept.

## A SECOND CHANCE

The Nine-Dot Problem not only demonstrates a point; it is also an excellent learning device. For instance, though very few students have solved the

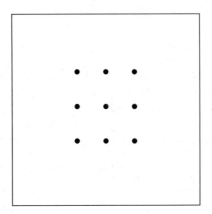

**FIGURE 1   The Nine-Dot Problem**
Connect these dots by drawing four straight lines without taking your pencil from the paper and without retracing any lines. The solution appears on page xxv.

puzzle, they nevertheless have learned to break out of the conventional-thinking mold and let their minds rove more freely, which leads to more innovative and imaginative approaches to solving problems.

To prove that you, perhaps, have learned a great deal from this one puzzle, apply your new-found knowledge to the following problem.

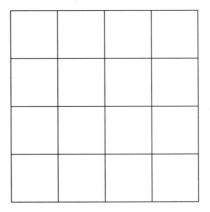

**FIGURE 2   The Puzzle of Squares**
How many squares are there in this figure? The solution appears on page xxvi.

## DISCOVER YOUR OWN RESOURCES

"Know thyself" is wise advice for a student poised at the path that leads to an academic goal. Development of your skills begins with understanding your personal learning style and study skills. By identifying your preferences and strengths, you can zero in on the best study skills techniques for you.

The following list can help you identify your basic learning style. For each item, circle the letter that best matches your style. Keep your responses in mind as you read this book.

## Learning Styles Self-Assessment

1. I study better   (a) by myself;   (b) in groups;   (c) in a combination of the two.
2. I remember best when   (a) I've *heard* something;   (b) I've *read* or *seen* something;   (c) I've *done* something active, like problem solving.
3. I think I'm   (a) better with facts, such as names or dates;   (b) better with concepts, ideas, or themes;   (c) about the same with both.
4. I learn better when I read   (a) slowly;   (b) quickly;   (c) either way.
5. I study more efficiently in   (a) one solid study period;   (b) small blocks of time.
6. I work   (a) well under pressure;   (b) poorly under pressure.
7. I work   (a) quickly, for short periods of time;   (b) at a steady, slower pace for longer periods of time.

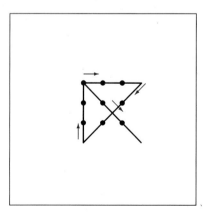

**FIGURE 3   Answer to the Nine-Dot Problem**
Begin at the top left corner and follow the arrows.

**8.** I   (a) do learn best in a structured setting, such as a classroom or laboratory;   (b) do not learn best in a structured setting.
**9.** I think that the greatest strength of my learning style is _____.
**10.** I think that the greatest weakness of my learning style is _____.

You'll improve your chances of success if you balance this knowledge
of your learning style with a willingness to remain flexible. For example,
you may be thinking, "It's true. I'm a sprinter who begins working with a
burst of energy and then slacks off. That's the way I've always been. How
can I possibly change?" Or you may believe that studying all night is an
effective way of coping with a tight schedule and that you have no need for
a more conventional strategy. These ways of thinking probably feel comfortable but they may have created blind spots in your view of studying. To get
a sense of how blind spots can limit you, try to solve the problem shown in
Figure 2. Odds are that a blind spot will prevent you from solving it. Yet
once you see the solution, you'll probably say, "How easy! Why didn't I
think of that tactic myself?"

## TAKE ADVANTAGE OF YOUR SCHOOL'S RESOURCES

**College Catalog**   General information about your college's requirements,
policies, programs, and services appears in the college catalog. Make sure
you have a copy and use it often during the first weeks of classes to remind
yourself of requirements and deadlines to be met.

**Student Handbook**   The student handbook provides information about
your school's procedures, regulations, and code of conduct. It may also
describe the school's requirements for good academic standing and graduation. For details or for specific department requirements, consult your department office or your academic advisor.

1 × 1 squares .....................................16

2 × 2 squares ......................................9

3 × 3 squares ......................................4

4 × 4 squares ......................................1
_____

Total squares .....................................30

**FIGURE 4   Answer to the Puzzle of Squares: 30 squares.**

**Admissions or Registrar's Office**   You can find answers to questions about grades, transcripts, and college requirements in the admissions or registrar's office. Admission to college and registration for courses begin with this office.

**Office of Financial Affairs**   For answers to questions about scholarships, loans, and grants, contact the financial affairs office. You will come here to pay fees and fines and to pick up your checks if you are in a work-study grant or program. If you want a part-time job on campus for which you must qualify on the basis of your financial status, you will fill out application forms in this office.

**Career Development and Placement Office**   If you want help choosing a major or setting a career goal, contact the career development and placement office. People in this office can administer various interest, personality, and skills assessment tests to help you determine the kind of work for which you are best suited. They can help you find jobs on and off campus. Some career development centers sponsor on-campus recruitment, inviting businesses to interview prospective graduates and aiding them in submitting applications and résumés. After graduation, you can file a résumé in the placement office if you want your school's help in landing a job.

**Academic Advising Office or Counseling Department**   Academic and guidance counselors can help you with everything from choosing the right course to solving personal problems that prevent you from meeting your academic goals. The academic office or counseling department may be part of the admissions office, or it may be a separate department. In many colleges students are assigned to an advisor or a counselor who follows their progress throughout their college careers.

**Student Health Center**   If you become ill, you can go to a doctor at the health center. The health center may have a pharmacy and may provide a limited amount of hospital care. Some mental health services may be available through this center, through the office of a school psychologist or psychiatrist, or through a peer counseling group. The health center may also refer students to an agency outside the college.

**Student Government Association**   Working with the dean of students, the student government association sponsors student activities such as intramural events, dances, special-interest organizations and clubs, and other social and academic events. (Joining a club or taking part in campus events is a good way to meet other students who share your interests.) In addition, your student government may publish a weekly bulletin or a student hand-book that summarizes college requirements and resources.

**Student Publications**   The college newspaper or literary magazine offers contributors unique opportunities for self-expression and provides readers with information and entertainment. Serving on the editorial staff of one of these publications may also fulfill some journalism or English requirements.

**Learning Lab or Skills Center**   You may turn to the learning lab or skills center for help in improving your study, reading, writing, math, or computer skills. Whether you are required to spend time in a lab because of your performance on a college skills assessment test or you choose to go on your own, take full advantage of the opportunity to gain the skills you need.

**Special Student Services**   Veterans, students with physical or learning disa-bilities, minority students, international students, and students who are eco-nomically disadvantaged may need the special assistance of a trained support group to meet their academic goals. If you think you qualify for these services, ask your counselor or advisor about them. Your college may also offer services such as off-campus residence listings.

**Athletics Office**   A listing of the college's athletic programs and events is available in the athletics office. This is the office to visit if you are interested in participating in sports.

**Resident Assistant**   For on-campus students, resident assistants (RAs) can be a great source of information about campus services. Although RAs are not professional counselors, they have recently been through many of the experiences you're undergoing and can probably direct you to the campus office best suited to your needs.

## A FINAL THOUGHT

To state in one sentence what I try to do in this book, let me rely on the words of Ralph Waldo Emerson: "The best service one person can render another person is to help him help himself."

## VOCABULARY DEVELOPMENT USING THE WORD ORIGINS SYSTEM

Thirty college-bound seniors placed in the highest percentile on their final standardized vocabulary test after using the Word Origins System for only six weeks.

The improvement in vocabulary came about because of a genuine *interest* in words, developed by perusing at least one of the books listed:

Holt, Alfred H., *Phrase and Word Origins*, 1961, Dover Publications, Inc.

*Morris Dictionary of Word and Phrase Origins.* New York: Harper & Row, Publishers, 1977, 654 pages. By William and Mary Morris. Ask the librarian for other books or dictionaries on word origins.

*Oxford English Dictionary,* 20 volumes, ed. J. A. Simpson & Edmund S. Weiner, 22,000 pages, 1989. Not in all libraries, but try this classic dictionary when you find time.

These students were told as they read the word histories to picture in their minds how they would illustrate each word as if they were artists. The theory is, of course, that a mental picture of a word created this way would be implanted in their long-term memory.

## HOW WORDS TURNED ONE MAN'S LIFE AROUND

Malcolm X developed a powerful vocabulary while in prison. He said, "A prisoner has time that he can put to good use. If he's motivated, he can change his life."[1] In an interview with Alex Haley, Malcolm X said:

People don't realize how a man's whole life can be changed by *one* book." He came back again and again to the book that he had studied when in prison. "Did you ever read *The Loom of Language?*" he asked me and I said I hadn't. "You should. Philology, it's a tough science—all about how words can be recognized, no matter where you find them."[2]

Malcolm X went on to become an outstanding preacher and public speaker. With a wide and exact vocabulary, he was able to express his thoughts and ideas forcefully and intelligently. He earned and commanded respect.

## HOW TO USE THE WORD ORIGINS SYSTEM IN THIS BOOK

An interest in words, which I hope you will gain from this book, supplies the motivation and natural desire to look at words, not as common coins, but as something special, usually provoking the question, "I wonder where

---

[1] *The Autobiography of Malcolm X with the Assistance of Alex Haley.* A One World Book published by Ballantine Books, copyright 1964 by Alex Haley and Malcolm X, pp. 453–4.
[2] Ibid.

that word came from?" Once you're interested, your vocabulary will quickly and naturally grow in both size and precision. Words become a joy.

How can you capitalize on this opportunity? As you work your way through the twenty-five words on the vocabulary quiz, an occasional word or two might appeal to you as *your type of word*. This is a word you'd like to master so that you can use it in your speaking, writing, and thinking.

Take a 3 × 5 card (which you can easily carry for study in spare moments) and write on one side the phrase in which the word is embedded. You want context. Underline the target word.

After you've collected five or six of these words, find time for some library work with dictionaries.

On the front of the card, make sure that you write the word in syllables, including accent and diacritical marks so that you can pronounce it correctly.

The reverse side belongs to the word's history. However, at the very bottom of the card write the present definition, which you can get from any good "collegiate" or unabridged dictionary. (See illustration for form.)

**(FRONT)**                                    **(REVERSE)**

| |
|---|
| Don Quixote and his faithful <u>companion</u>, Sancho Panza |
| |
| com-pan'ion |

| |
|---|
| <u>companion</u>: one who shares bread with another. |
| "Breaking bread" together is an ancient rite of friendship. |
|     com = with |
|     panis = bread |
| Now: one who accompanies another with no longer a reference to sharing bread. |

**(FRONT)**                                    **(REVERSE)**

| |
|---|
| <u>escape</u> from Alcatraz was impossible. |
| |
| es-cape' |

| |
|---|
| <u>escape</u>: to slip out of one's cape. The word gives us a picture of a prisoner, held by his cape or coat, who suddenly slips out of the garment and flees. |
|     Latin: <u>ex cappa</u> = out of one's cape or cloak |
| Now: to break loose from confinement; get free. |

# Setting Goals—
# A Self-Management Skill

*Always have a plan and believe in it. Nothing good happens by accident.*

—CHUCK KNOX, NFL football coach

Do you believe in your goal? If you believe, you'll know it by the strong desire from within that drives you. You'll need this inner drive especially during hard times—times bordering on failure. A true goal will do even more. It will keep you focused. Unfocused, like water on a flat surface, your efforts will be spread too thinly. But focus your efforts, and, like focused water, your planned goal can etch its way to make a mile-deep Grand Canyon. In this chapter, the focusing of your life can begin as you read and think about

- Shaping your future through goals
- Making a plan
- Writing your goals
- Taking action

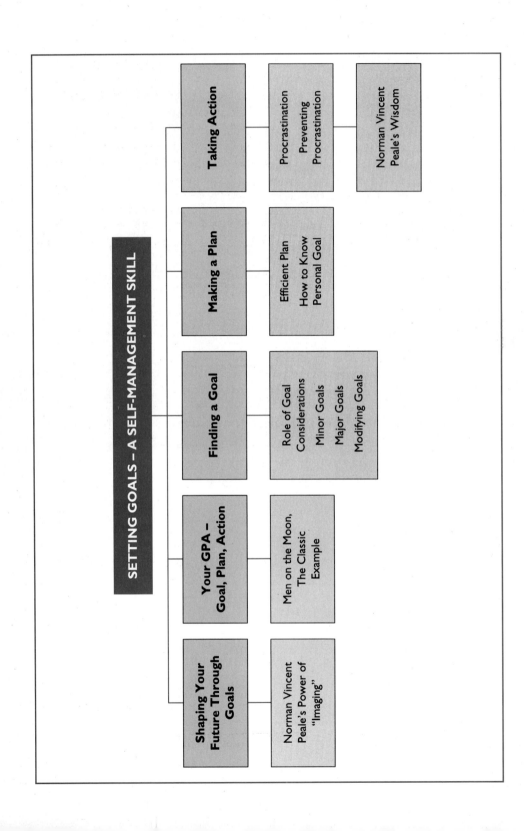

# SETTING GOALS – A SELF-MANAGEMENT SKILL

**Shaping Your Future Through Goals**

Norman Vincent Peale's Power of "Imaging"

**Your GPA – Goal, Plan, Action**

Men on the Moon, The Classic Example

**Finding a Goal**

Role of Goal
Considerations
Minor Goals
Major Goals
Modifying Goals

**Making a Plan**

Efficient Plan
How to Know
Personal Goal

**Taking Action**

Procrastination
Preventing
Procrastination

Norman Vincent
Peale's Wisdom

I was recently startled by a full-page picture of a yawning baby in a CIGNA ad, which appeared in the *Wall Street Journal*. What struck me were these big, bold-faced words at the top of the page: **"ONLY 22,463 DAYS UNTIL RETIREMENT."**[1]

My immediate reaction was "Oh, no! Life is not so short. We have more working days than this." I quickly pressed 22,463 into my calculator and divided by 365. Sure enough, the figure confirmed the advertisement's point: "The average retirement age is now 61.5, not 65. And it's getting even lower." If you're already 18, you have only 15,163 days until retirement—and you're not through college yet!

But don't race breathlessly through your days. Rather, make the most of them by planning for college, for work, for fun, and for retirement. Plan so that you have control over your life. It is all up to you.

## SHAPING YOUR FUTURE THROUGH GOALS

A goal is far more than a word. Actually, it's a dream that has been mentally acted and reenacted. What lawyer hasn't first imagined presenting a closing argument to judge and jury? What business executive hasn't imagined outlining an exciting plan to a staff seated around the board of directors' table?

Up to this point, the word *imagined* has been used to denote imagination; however, in all the excerpts in this chapter from Norman Vincent Peale's book *Positive Imaging*, the word *imaged* is used to convey a much deeper concept, which is as follows:

> Imaging consists of vividly picturing, in your conscious mind, a desired goal or objective, and holding that image until it sinks into your unconscious mind, where it releases great, untapped energies.[2]

So, if we think deeply enough and image vividly enough about what we want to do with our lives, our whole being can be energized by it. Norman Vincent Peale, one of the most widely read inspirational writers of all time, goes on to say:

> There is a powerful and mysterious force in human nature that is capable of bringing about dramatic improvement in our lives. It is a kind of mental engineering. . . . In imaging, one does not merely think about a hoped-for goal; one "sees" or visualizes it with tremendous intensity. Imaging is a

---

[1]Reprinted by permission of CIGNA.
[2]Norman Vincent Peale. *Positive Imaging.* Copyright © 1982. Published by Fleming H. Revell, a division of Baker Book House. Used by permission.

kind of laser beam of the imagination, a shaft of mental energy in which the desired goal or outcome is pictured so vividly by the conscious mind that the unconscious mind accepts it and is activated by it. This releases powerful internal forces that can bring about astonishing changes in the life of the person who is doing the imaging.[3]

To set the stage for imaging, I believe that you can find and clarify your goal through the following questions and answers.

## What Is the Best Way to Become a Success?

"If you want to make it in college, your GPA is the key." Students who tell you this are talking about your grade point average, your report card, the

---

### A FAMOUS GOAL, PLAN, AND ACTION

#### The Goal

*First, I believe that this nation should commit itself to achieving the goal, before this decade is out, of landing a man on the moon and returning him safely to earth.*

> President John F. Kennedy
> before a joint session of Con-
> gress
> May 25, 1961

#### The Plan

| | |
|---|---|
| The Mercury Program: | Each rocket would send a single astronaut into space. |
| The Gemini Program: | Each rocket would send two men into space to orbit the earth, to practice docking with other spacecraft, and to test human beings' ability to withstand prolonged periods in space. |
| The Apollo Program: | Each rocket would send three men into space in order to leave the earth's orbit, to orbit the moon, and eventually to land on the moon and explore it. |

#### The Action

The United States sent twenty manned flights into space between May 1961 and June 1969. In July 1969, eight years and two months after President Kennedy set the country's original goal, astronauts Neil Armstrong and Edwin "Buzz" Aldrin set foot on the moon and returned safely to earth.

---

[3]From Norman Vincent Peale, *Positive Imaging.* Copyright © 1982. Published by Fleming H. Revell, a division of Baker Book House. Used by permission.

number of A's and B's you get in relation to the number of C's, D's and F's. There's no question that grades can be important, but they aren't as important as another GPA: your Goal, your Plan and the Action that you take. If you really want to make it, then *that's* the GPA you should strive for. If you are able to set a specific Goal in your life, if you can come up with an efficient Plan for that goal, and finally, if you have the discipline required to take Action, there's an excellent chance you will be headed down the road to success.

## What Is the Role of a Goal?

Where are you headed? That's the question that your goal is designed to answer. Imagine throwing ingredients into a mixing bowl without any idea of what you are making. Think of running around on the basketball court with no knowledge of the object of the game. The best cooks and the best basketball players know both what they are doing and why they are doing it. They have a clear idea of where they are headed. In short, they have a goal in mind.

## What Kinds of Things Could Be Considered Goals?

Although winning a basketball game and baking a cake can both be seen as goals, it can be easier to look on your goal as a kind of destination. A lot of our common expressions make use of this idea. "Making it to the top," "climbing the corporate ladder," and even "reaching for the stars" portray the goal as a place in the distance that you are trying to reach. Of course, some goals really are destinations. When American pioneers declared that their goal was "Pike's Peak or Bust" and tacked the sign to their wagons, they were talking about an actual destination hundreds of miles to the west and more than fourteen thousand feet above sea level. When President Kennedy made the moon the country's goal in 1962, he was aiming for a destination that was about 238,900 miles out into space.

## Do Smaller Goals Have Any Use?

Your life should be full of goals both major and minor. Most of us are aware of minor goals; we set them all the time. Passing a test can be seen as a minor goal. So can completing a homework assignment or even finishing a chapter before dinnertime. It can be a great help to have minor goals. Each time we reach one we get a small sense of victory that helps to spur us on toward something even bigger. Notice in a basketball game how the crowd cheers and the scoring team's pace quickens each time a basket is made. Everyone knows that one basket by itself won't win the game, but when the score is added up, each basket can prove to be crucial. The same is true in school. Although no one has gained success by virtue of a single test or paper, these little victories will add up and help you move toward your major goal. In the meantime, minor goals provide the encouragement you need to cheer yourself on and to quicken your pace.

## How Do You Choose Your Major Goal?

Choosing a major goal will come naturally for some, while it may be an agonizing decision for others. For every person who says "I've always wanted to be a doctor" or "I know that teaching others is what really matters to me," there are those who complain, "There's really nothing I'm interested in," or perhaps "I'm interested in practically everything; how am I ever going to choose?" Although goals may vary widely from person to person, they all grow out of the same source: the things we want and need. Therefore, choosing your goal means deciding what you value most in life.

## How Large Should a Major Goal Be?

Your major goal should be large and distant. It should act as a target you can aim for, something you can think of to inspire you. Don't let short-term minor goals like finishing an assignment, passing an exam, and simply getting through the day mark the limits of your dreams. Aim high but at the same time be sure that the goals you set are specific and distinct. Health, happiness, security, love, and money are all ideals that people aim for, but they are far too vague to be considered goals. On the other hand, "discovering a cure for cancer" and "becoming the best possible parent" are both admirable and specific goals that can help you to approach the broad ideals we share as well.

## What Should You Do with Your Goal Once You've Chosen It?

If the goal you have chosen is a clear one, you should have no trouble writing it down. Goals that stay only in your head have too great a chance of remaining vague. Furthermore, once you write down your goal, that documentation can act as a constant reminder. If you're feeling discouraged, a quick look at your goal can serve to inspire you. (That's what the signs on the covered wagons did.) And if for some reason you forget your goal, a written description can refresh your memory.

## Are You Stuck with a Goal until You Reach It?

The purpose of a goal is not to force you on a course that you don't want to follow; it is to give you a target so that your efforts can be more focused than they would be if you had nothing to aim for. Time and fate have a way of shifting our priorities. People change, and so do the things they view as important. If the goal you once wrote down no longer matches your ambition in life, come up with another goal to replace it.

## MAKING A PLAN

### What Is a Plan?

If you think of your goal as your destination, then a plan can be seen as the route that will take you there. Coming up with a plan is like drawing a map. You need to know where you are starting, where you are heading, and where you plan to stop along the way. Most goals will have several plans. The challenge comes in choosing the best route to take.

### How Can You Choose the Most Efficient Plan?

An efficient plan is a balancing act between what you need and want and what you are able to pay. Paying, as far as a plan is concerned, doesn't always mean money. It can mean time and energy as well. For example, a one-week plan for reviewing your notes is "too expensive" if the test is only two days away. In the same way, a plan that forces you to stay up all night will often be too costly, because what you gain in knowledge you will lose in sleep. The most efficient plan will meet your goal without costing too much.

## Shouldn't It Be Easy to Tell which Plan Is the Most Efficient?

Although it might seem as though efficient plans should be easy to find, the best ones are not always so obvious. For example, during an exam, many students begin answering questions as soon as they've got the test in their hand. At first that may sound like a pretty good plan. After all, a typical exam has a time limit, and so it would seem to make sense to begin working on it right away. Actually this plan is a bad idea. Although it might seem as though you are wasting precious time, you should read the exam directions, look over all the questions, and even come up with a time plan before you write down a single answer. The first plan is fast but reckless, whereas the second is steady and dependable. When you use a systematic plan of this type, you will usually gain more benefits than you would from a plan that seems to be best at the outset.

## Shouldn't It Be Easy to Know when You've Used Logical Thinking in Drawing Up Your Plan?

No! It is neither easy nor certain. For example, it seemed very logical for commercial airlines to take the "Mediterranean route" when flying from Amsterdam to Tokyo. The plan made sense. Navigators felt that the shortest way to go to the Far East was to fly in an easterly direction. Now flights from Amsterdam take the "Polar Route." Instead of heading east, they go north over the Pole to Alaska, and then west to Tokyo—for a savings of roughly 1,500 miles!

The lesson to draw from this example is, after you've decided on a goal, work vigorously to accomplish it, but in the meantime let your mind dart off in different directions to see how you might achieve the goal more efficiently, perhaps from a different angle.

## Is There a Single Plan that Will Work for Every Goal?

No plan will work for every goal, and only a handful of plans are flexible enough to work for several goals. The secret is to find the right plan to match the goal you have in mind. Using the wrong plan can be inefficient and sometimes even comical. Perhaps you remember the old story of the boy who followed his mother's directions exactly, irrespective of circumstances, when sent to market to buy a lamb. His mother directed him to carry the lamb back on his shoulder. She meant, of course, a lamb already slaughtered.

Instead, the boy bought a live lamb at a bargain price, and true to his mother's directions, he carried it back home on his shoulder rather than leading it back on a leash. Although his mother's plan was a good one, it would work only when used in the right circumstance. The same idea applies to your study plans. For example, if you are studying your textbook, putting your notes in your own words and in complete sentences is normally an excellent plan. But if you used the same plan for taking lecture notes, you'd move so slowly that you'd miss most of what the speaker said.

## What Are the Best Plans for Your Own Personal Goal?

Good plans may not work for every goal. In the same way, systems that work for most people may not work for you. That's why the best way to come up with a plan for success is to balance wise advice with your own personal experience. This book is full of plans for success and tricks of the trade.

All these systems have been proven to work, and most of them will work for you. You can decide which systems work and which do not through trial and error—in other words, from your own personal experience.

## Is a Good Plan Guaranteed to Work?

Even the best plans won't work all the time, so you and your plan should have some built-in flexibility. Flexible plans are specific without being too detailed. Students who plan their days right down to the second are on a collision course for almost certain failure. It pays to allow a little extra "breathing room" in case things don't go as smoothly as you had hoped. In addition to making your plans flexible, you should try to be a little flexible yourself. When things go wrong, don't give up. Adjust and keep on going.

## TAKING ACTION

## What Is Action?

Goals and plans won't do you any good unless you take some action. Action is the spark that brings your goal and plan to life. Without action, goals and plans are pointless. You can decide you want to finish a book, and you can even plan the pages that you need to read each day, but until you actually start reading, all your preparations will be pointless. In the same way, the United States' goal to reach the moon and the plans for the spacecraft were both impressive, but they didn't come to life until the first rocket left the launch pad and headed into space.

## What Prevents People from Taking Action?

Once you do have a goal and a plan, that's no guarantee that you will take action. Procrastination is what stops many people from taking action. It is the tendency to put things off, to write that paper the night before it is due, to cram for a test instead of studying for it right from the start. Although procrastination is just one of many common bad habits, it may be the single greatest obstacle to success. It is also, as we'll see in chapter 3, a prime source of tension.

## What Causes Procrastination?

Experts on procrastination can find no single cause for this roadblock to success. Sometimes it is prompted by a fear of failure; at other times, as strange as it may seem, it can be brought on by a fear of success. Other factors like family responsibilities as well as personal triumphs and tragedies can contribute to a habit of procrastination. Although the experts can't pin down a single cause of procrastination, most agree that procrastination is a compulsion: once you begin procrastinating, it's easy to continue. But like any bad habit, the self-destructive circle of procrastination can be broken.

## How Can You Prevent Procrastination?

The first step in fighting procrastination is to develop a goal and a plan. If you do have a goal and a plan but you're still procrastinating, you should take aim at the excuses you have given for not getting your work done. Dream up reasons why you can instead of why you can't. That will often be all it takes to pull yourself out of the vicious circle of inactivity and low self-esteem and put you on the road to progress and success.

CONFRONTING PROCRASTINATION

| Negative excuse | Positive response |
|---|---|
| My effort might not be good enough. | I realize that it won't be perfect, but if I start right now, I'll have time to make some changes. |
| There's a good program on TV tonight. I'll do my work later. | I've still got some time until the show starts. I can squeeze in some work before then. |
| I don't have the right materials to get the job done. | I know I don't have everything I need, but I'll see how much I can accomplish with the materials I do have. |

THE GPA OF SUCCESS

GOAL—should reflect your wants and needs. Make it large and ambitious without being vague. Write it down!

PLAN—lists the route you plan to take in order to reach your goal. It should be efficient and specific. Good advice and personal experience combine to create the most effective plans.

ACTION—brings your goal and your plan to life. Requires confidence, self-discipline, and a power over procrastination.

This chapter would not be complete without more wisdom from Norman Vincent Peale, who tells about the vital importance of *taking action*—taking action throughout the entire process of personal goal setting.

*I suggest that you write down what you want to do with your life. Until you write a goal, it is only a wish; written, it becomes a focused objective. Put it down on paper. When it is on paper, boil it down to a single sentence: what you want to do, exactly when you intend to start (which should be right now), exactly when you plan to achieve your goal. Nothing fuzzy or hazy. Everything sharp and clear and definite. No reservations or qualifications. Just one strong, simple, declarative sentence. . . . I want you to make half a dozen copies of that sentence and put them where you'll see them at least three times a day. I want that pledge to sink down through all the levels of your conscious mind and deep into your unconscious mind, because that is where it will unlock the energies that you will need to achieve your goal.*

*If setting worthy goals is the first step on the road to success, the second is the belief—the conviction that you are capable of achieving those goals. There has to be in your mind the unshakable image of yourself succeeding at the goal you have set yourself. The more vivid this image is, the most obtainable the goal becomes.*

*Great athletes have always known this. The high jumper "sees" himself skimming over the bar; the place-kicker in football keeps his head down as he kicks, but in his mind's eye he holds the mental picture of what he wants to happen in the next few seconds. . . . The more intensely he images this before it happens, the higher his confidence in himself and the better his chances of making it happen.*[4]

I hope that by now you are ready to pick up your pencil and begin writing your goal or goals. The following format-examples and four sequential steps are designed to help you in this thinking-writing process.

*Step 1.*   On a clean sheet of $8\frac{1}{2} \times 11$ paper, brainstorm about your goals. Jot down possible goals and words about them that come to mind, and do so quickly and freely. Use brainstorming as an opportunity to explore any aspects of any goals you choose. Do not stop writing to correct your spelling, polish a phrase, reorganize your notes, or analyze a thought. Just keep going until you've jotted down all that you can think of about your possible goals. Now look over your notes and group together similar items. Formulate each group into a goal by writing a summarizing sentence that states the main idea of each group. Select any one of these goals, and write it in your own $8\frac{1}{2} \times 11$ version of block 1 of Figure 1.1.

*Step 2.*   On a separate sheet of paper, list in chronological order the steps you'll need to take to reach one of your goals. Transfer this list to your own block 2.

*Step 3.*   On another sheet, jot down those academic and personal strengths that will help you achieve this goal. List them in your own block 3.

*Step 4.*   Identify any academic weaknesses (such as difficulty with writing papers) or personal obstacles (such as financial, family, or health problems) that you will have to overcome to reach this goal, and list them in your own block 4. Repeat steps 2 to 4 for each goal you wrote in step 1.

---

[4]From Norman Vincent Peale, *Positive Imaging.* Copyright © 1982. Published by Fleming H. Revell, a division of Baker Book House. Used by permission.

**FIGURE 1.1  Shaping Your Future**

With the completed Shaping Your Future sheets in hand, expand your resources. Talk with your academic advisor or with a counselor in your school's career center. Don't underestimate the value of discussing your goals and your plans for achieving them. Get as much feedback as you can. Then, if necessary, modify your goals and plans into realistic, attainable maps for your future.

```
Date _____

Book _____

Starting page _____

Ending page _____

No. of pages _____

Time allotment _____

Time started _____

Time to finish _____

Time finished _____

Page reached _____

Goal achieved   yes—no

Reason (if no) _____

_____

No. min. worked _____

No. of pages read _____

Atmosphere:  interruptions
             no interruptions

Work location _____

_____
```

**FIGURE 1.2   Reading Assignment Card**


You can also develop plans to achieve short-term goals such as completing textbook assignments. After writing out his academic goals, one college student enthusiastically said, "I now do almost everything in terms of goals, even my textbook assignments. I feel I'm in control of every day."

He then gave me a copy of a card that keeps him focused on his assignments (see Figure 1.2). "Using this card," he explained, "I waste no time. I comprehend better and remember more."

With this format as a guide, you can design your own Reading Assignment Card. Try it, refine it if necessary, and then reproduce the final version so you'll have a ready stack.

By getting into the goal-setting mode, you can put yourself in control not only of your academic life but also of your life after college.

## SUMMARY

**In regard to goals, what does GPA stand for?**

"G" stands for Goal, "P" for Plan, and "A" for Action. All three are necessary for success.

**What's the primary purpose of a goal?**

Its purpose is to keep your thinking and your actions focused.

**Do smaller intermediary goals get in the way of the primary goal?**

No. Achieving small goals on the way to the primary goal is like being a marathon runner who makes the first mile on time, then the second mile, and so forth.

**Is it a danger to set a goal that's too ambitious?**

No. You can always downsize your goal and the effort made is not wasted. You'll be further ahead than if you worked originally for a much lesser goal. Best of all, you never know your full potential unless you shoot for the stars. Don't sell yourself short.

**What is within the concept of "imaging" as put forth by Norman Vincent Peale?**

According to Norman Vincent Peale, the visualizing and imaging of your goal permeates your entire mind and body, thus releasing powerful internal energy that almost guarantees the successful attainment of your goal.

**What is the most common fault that dooms the attainment of many goals?**

Without question, it's procrastination. Procrastinators are always going to start tomorrow, once they get the small tasks out of the way, and there are a multitude of other excuses.

**What's the main message for achieving your goal put forth by Norman Vincent Peale?**

He says, in effect, "Write it on paper in one concise, clear sentence. Then, keep it before you so you'll roll out of bed early, attend classes eagerly, do your homework energetically, always with that goal, like a moving picture, plainly in your mind."

**How does goal setting affect a person psychologically?**

Very favorably. It gives you a sense of control over your life. Goals also prevent you from drifting into situations, then finding yourself at the mercy of circumstances. Goals help you to develop a sense of inner peace, which gives you physical and mental poise.

## HAVE YOU MISSED SOMETHING?

*Sentence completion.*  Complete the following sentences with one of the three words listed below each sentence.

   **1.** Having a goal constantly in mind usually keeps you ———————— .
   tensed      hurried      focused

   **2.** Goals should be looked upon as ————————————— .
   routes      destinations   motivations

*Matching.*   In each blank space in the left column, write the letter preceding the phrase in the right column that matches the left item best.

———— **1.** Imaging                a. Remains fuzzy and hazy

———— **2.** GPA                    b. Deals with short-term items

———— **3.** Minor goal             c. Usually begins with brainstorming

———— **4.** Procrastination        d. Provides a good sounding board

———— **5.** Unwritten goal         e. Consists of vividly picturing desired
                                      goal

———— **6.** Deciding on a goal     f. Stands for goal, plan, and action

———— **7.** Academic advisor       g. Are usually career goals

———— **8.** Primary goals          h. Means finding ways to delay getting
                                      started

*True-false.*   Write *T* beside the *true* statements and *F* beside the *false* statements.

———— **1.** Imaging by itself can lead one to achieve goals successfully.

———— **2.** Once a goal has been set, action follows almost naturally and automatically.

———— **3.** Smaller goals are necessary on the way to a major goal.

———— **4.** Choosing a goal is always an agonizing decision.

———— **5.** Good career goals can be health, happiness, security, and love of money.

———— **6.** Aiming high can often be a mistake.

———— **7.** A short-term goal takes into consideration the expenditure of time and energy to achieve it.

_____ **8.** The original goal, once set, should not be modified.

_____ **9.** It is easy to kick the habit of procrastination.

_____ **10.** Writing down what you want to do with your life is a sound way to establish your major goal.

*Multiple choice.* Choose the phrase that completes the following sentence most accurately, and circle the letter that precedes it.

**1.** The overriding objective in choosing a goal should be the
   a. satisfaction in attaining it.
   b. professional esteem in which it is held.
   c. personal interest in it.
   d. monetary rewards it brings.

**2.** The meaning of the quotation "Stupidity is sticking to your guns when you're firing blanks" is
   a. Stick to your goal no matter what happens.
   b. Work even harder to achieve successfully your goal.
   c. Don't let a few failures discourage you.
   d. Change or modify your goal if it isn't working out right.

*Short answer.* Supply a brief answer for each of the following.

**1.** Explain how Norman Vincent Peales' "powerful and mysterious force in human nature" is brought about.
**2.** Discuss the role of minor goals.
**3.** Describe one way in which you would go about overcoming the habit of procrastination.

## VOCABULARY BUILDING

DIRECTIONS: Make a light check mark (√) alongside one of the three words (choices) that most nearly expresses the meaning of the italicized word in the phrases that are in the left-hand column. (Answers are given on p. 433.)

|   | | **1** | **2** | **3** |
|---|---|---|---|---|
| 1. | easy to *procrastinate* | complete | postpone | spoil |
| 2. | procrastination is a *compulsion* | vocation | choice | impulse |
| 3. | self-destructive *cycle* | pattern | result | force |
| 4. | no *reservation* or qualification | withholding | arrangement | characteristic |

|     |                            | **1**          | **2**        | **3**       |
|-----|----------------------------|----------------|--------------|-------------|
| 5.  | one *declarative* sentence | tentative      | explicit     | false       |
| 6.  | *rejuvenate* the plan      | alter          | improve      | restore     |
| 7.  | escape *debilitating* outcomes | weak       | unplanned    | unprofitable |
| 8.  | this *amorphous* mess      | enormous       | foul         | shapeless   |
| 9.  | level of *sophistication*  | simplicity     | naturalness  | refinement  |
| 10. | ought to *emulate*         | imitate        | exceed       | win         |
| 11. | clear *coherent* message   | organized      | forceful     | loud        |
| 12. | abrupt *innovation*        | invention      | newness      | decision    |
| 13. | usual *egregious* example  | common         | repetitive   | offensive   |
| 14. | feel *patronized*          | condescended   | flattered    | elated      |
| 15. | *apex* of his career       | end            | middle       | top         |
| 16. | *scrutinize* your plans    | inspect        | refurbish    | reorganize  |
| 17. | no *whimsical* plan        | expensive      | fanciful     | modern      |
| 18. | *portentous* plans         | ponderous      | evil         | foreboding  |
| 19. | particularly *ominous*     | threatening    | overbearing  | profitable  |
| 20. | Edison was *legendary*     | famous         | mythical     | wealthy     |
| 21. | a timely *mandate*         | authorization  | document     | manuscript  |
| 22. | *propitious* signs         | favorable      | unfavorable  | clouded     |
| 23. | to *mollify*               | soothe         | fortify      | enlarge     |
| 24. | *manifold* plans           | exhaustive     | multiple     | failed      |
| 25. | how *strait* the gate      | narrow         | uniform      | direct      |

# Managing Your Time

*Perhaps the most valuable result of all education is the ability to make yourself do the thing you have to do, when it ought to be done, whether you like it or not.*

—THOMAS HUXLEY (1825–1895) English biologist

Time flies, but that's no reason for you to go through each day simply "winging it." Through conscientious use of time and commonsense planning, you can make the most of your day. This chapter ticks off the important elements of time management, including

- Saving time
- Using a master schedule
- Using a weekly schedule
- Using a daily schedule
- Using a task-based schedule
- Using a weekly schedule based on assignments
- Using a things-to-do list

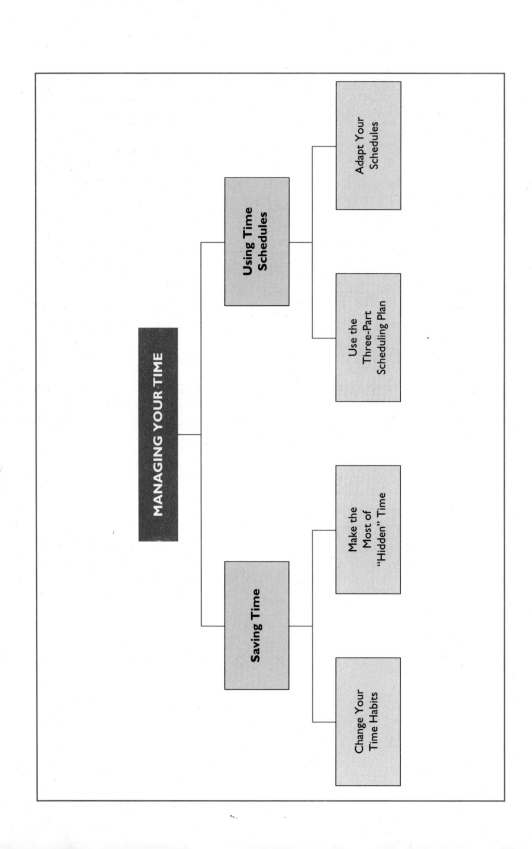

Time is a precious and irreplaceable commodity. Few have noted that fact more convincingly and succinctly than Queen Elizabeth I of England (1533–1603). As she lay dying, she wished, "All my possessions for a moment of time."

How you use time can determine your success or failure in college. If you use time wisely, you'll prosper. If you use it poorly, you'll fail in the job you came to do. That's why the management of time is the number-one skill to master in college.

Yet students frequently squander time. A survey conducted at Fordham University in 1987 found that college freshmen spent roughly one-third of their waking hours during a typical weekday engaged in social activities or idle leisure. This "free time" amounted to nearly twice the time the students spent studying. And on the weekend the ratio of social and idle leisure time to study time for the same group was almost six to one!

Although the students in the survey seemed to waste time routinely, you needn't put yourself in the same position. You can gain extra time in two ways: (1) by doing a job in less time than usual and (2) by using small blocks of time that you usually waste. The first way requires you to study more efficiently, and this book provides a great many techniques to help you do just that. The second way requires you to save time by changing your habits and making the most of "hidden" time, and to manage your time by using a three-part scheduling plan. This chapter offers a number of suggestions that can enable you to use time more productively.

## SAVING TIME

All of us have claimed that we don't have enough time to accomplish what we need to do. But the fact is that everyone is allotted the same amount of time: twenty-four hours a day. It's our day-to-day habits, activities we no longer notice, that save time or waste it. You can put your time to better use by eliminating the bad habits that waste time, cultivating good habits that save time, and pinpointing areas of "hidden" time.

A good way to begin is by keeping a daily activities log. From the time you wake up to the time you go to sleep, note all your major activities, the time you started and finished each, and the time each activity consumed. With your day itemized on paper in this way, you can gain a clearer picture of where your time is being spent and where it's being wasted. The activities log in Figure 2.1 shows one student's daily routine and how he decided to put his time to better use.

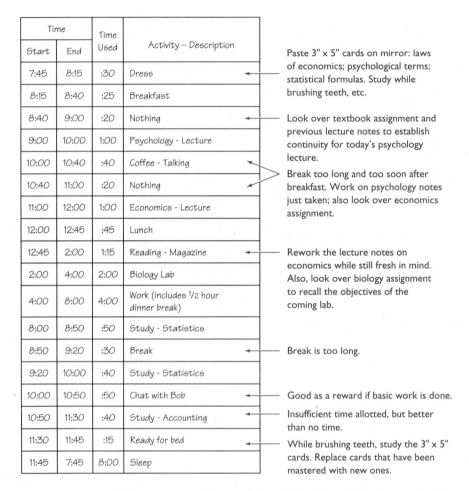

| Time | | Time Used | Activity – Description |
|------|-----|------|------------------------|
| Start | End | | |
| 7:45 | 8:15 | :30 | Dress |
| 8:15 | 8:40 | :25 | Breakfast |
| 8:40 | 9:00 | :20 | Nothing |
| 9:00 | 10:00 | 1:00 | Psychology - Lecture |
| 10:00 | 10:40 | :40 | Coffee - Talking |
| 10:40 | 11:00 | :20 | Nothing |
| 11:00 | 12:00 | 1:00 | Economics - Lecture |
| 12:00 | 12:45 | :45 | Lunch |
| 12:45 | 2:00 | 1:15 | Reading - Magazine |
| 2:00 | 4:00 | 2:00 | Biology Lab |
| 4:00 | 8:00 | 4:00 | Work (includes 1/2 hour dinner break) |
| 8:00 | 8:50 | :50 | Study - Statistics |
| 8:50 | 9:20 | :30 | Break |
| 9:20 | 10:00 | :40 | Study - Statistics |
| 10:00 | 10:50 | :50 | Chat with Bob |
| 10:50 | 11:30 | :40 | Study - Accounting |
| 11:30 | 11:45 | :15 | Ready for bed |
| 11:45 | 7:45 | 8:00 | Sleep |

Paste 3" x 5" cards on mirror: laws of economics; psychological terms; statistical formulas. Study while brushing teeth, etc.

Look over textbook assignment and previous lecture notes to establish continuity for today's psychology lecture.

Break too long and too soon after breakfast. Work on psychology notes just taken; also look over economics assignment.

Rework the lecture notes on economics while still fresh in mind. Also, look over biology assignment to recall the objectives of the coming lab.

Break is too long.

Good as a reward if basic work is done.

Insufficient time allotted, but better than no time.

While brushing teeth, study the 3" x 5" cards. Replace cards that have been mastered with new ones.

**FIGURE 2.1   Record of One Day's Activities and Suggestions for Making Better Use of Time**

## Change Your Time Habits

Once you have the concrete evidence of a daily activities log before you, you can see where to save time. The way to begin doing so is to eliminate common time-wasting habits and to develop time-saving habits.

**Defy Parkinson's Law**   *Parkinson's Law* says that work expands to fit the time allotted.[1] To avoid running out of time, work Parkinson's Law in reverse:

---

[1]C. Parkinson, *Parkinson, the Law* (Boston: Houghton Mifflin, 1980).

For each task, set a deadline that will be difficult to meet, and then strive to meet that deadline.

Each time you achieve your goal, reward yourself with some small but pleasant activity. Take a break. Chat with a friend. Stroll around the room. Have a special snack, such as a bag of peanuts (keep it in your desk, to be opened only as a reward).

If you fail to meet a deadline, don't punish yourself. Just hold back your reward and set another goal. It is *positive* reinforcement that is powerful in effecting a change in behavior.

**Obey Your Alarm Clock**  How many times do you hit the snooze button on your alarm clock before you finally get out of bed? Even once is too many. Set your alarm for the time you want to get up, not for the time you want to *start* getting up. If you can't obey your alarm, you'll have a hard time sticking to your time schedule. After all, it doesn't even buzz.

**Take "Time Out"**  Reward yourself with regular short breaks as you work. Learning in several small sessions, rather than in one continuous stretch, actually increases comprehension. In one study, students who practiced French vocabulary in three discrete sessions did 35 percent better on an exam than those who tried to learn the words in one sitting.[2] So take a breather for ten minutes every hour, or spend five minutes resting every half-hour. Whichever method you choose, keep your breaks consistent. This way, you'll study with more energy and look forward to your regular rests. And when you return to your desk, you'll find that you feel more refreshed.

**Jot Down Thoughts on a Notepad**  Keep a memo pad or a plain sheet of paper by your side, and write down any obligations or stray ideas that occur to you as you're studying. By putting them on paper, you'll free your brain to focus entirely on the task before you. You will work more efficiently, and as a result you'll save time.

If the thoughts you've written down don't relate to your studies, you can deal with them when your work is done or even while you're taking a break. If your jottings do relate to your work, you can use them to get the jump on the subject they pertain to. Often the hardest part of shifting from one activity to another is just getting started. Your jottings may provide an impetus to overcome the inertia that seems to characterize the outset of a new activity. If so, they may save you some valuable time. Here is an example

---

[2]Kristine C. Bloom et al., "Effects of Massed and Distributed Practice on the Learning and Retention of Second-Language Vocabulary," *Journal of Educational Research* 74, no. 4 (March–April 1981): 245–248.

from the notepad of one student who, while working on a calculus assignment, came up with a topic for an upcoming paper. As soon as she finished her calculus, she was able to begin doing preliminary research on the topic without delay.

> Call Mr. Soames about make-up test.
>
> Check Campbell book for discussion of brain laterality.
>
> What about "Earthquake Prediction" as possible paper topic?
>
> Look up definitions for leftover vocab. cards.
>
> Tennis at 6 tonight, not 7!

## Make the Most of "Hidden" Time

Another way you can gain time is by tapping into "hidden time" that goes unused because you don't recognize it as available.

**Carry Pocket Work**   Many situations may leave you with a few moments of unexpected free time—a long line at the bank or supermarket, a delayed bus or train, a wait at the doctor's office, a lunch date who arrives late. If you make a point to bring along a book, a photocopied article, or 3 × 5 cards carrying key concepts or formulas, you'll be able to take advantage of otherwise frustrating experiences.

**Use Your Mind When It's Free**   Some activities may still afford the opportunity for studying if you're prepared. For example, if you're shaving, combing your hair, or washing dishes, there's no reason you can't be studying at the same time. Attach small metal or plastic clips near mirrors and on walls at eye level. Place a note card in each clip. Or do a problem or two in math or master some new vocabulary words as you eat a sandwich at work.

**Put Information on Audiocassettes**   Another way of using hidden time is by listening to information you've recorded on audiocassettes. Recorded information enables you to keep studying in situations where you're moving about or your eyes are otherwise occupied, such as when you're getting dressed or driving. In addition, recorded information can provide a refreshing change from written material.

**Employ Spare-Time Thinking**   You can make the most of the moments immediately before or after class by recalling the main points from the last lecture as you're heading to class or by quickly recalling the points of a lecture just completed as you're leaving class.

**Use Your Subconscious**   At one time or another, you have awakened during the night with a bright idea or a solution to a problem that you had been thinking about before bedtime. Your subconscious works while your conscious mind is resting in sleep. If you want to capture the ideas or solutions produced by your subconscious, write them down as soon as you wake up; otherwise, they'll be lost. Many creative people know this and keep a pad and pencil near their beds. For example, Nobel Prize winner Albert Szent-Györgyi said, "I go to sleep thinking about my problems all the time, and my brain must continue to think about them when I sleep because I wake up, sometimes in the middle of the night, with answers to questions that have been eluding me all day."[3]

## USING TIME SCHEDULES

A time schedule is a game plan, a written strategy that spells out exactly what you hope to accomplish—for a day, a week, or even the entire term—and how you plan to do it. Committing yourself to planning and keeping to a schedule can seem a bit frightening at first, but following such a schedule soon becomes a source of strength and a boon to your life. There are several benefits to a schedule.

*A schedule provides greater control.* A thoughtfully constructed time schedule can increase your sense of control in four ways. First, because your schedule is written down, your plans seem more manageable. You can start working without delay. Second, you know you'll study all your subjects— even those you dislike—because you've allotted time for them in your schedule. There's less of a temptation to skip disliked subjects when study time has already been allotted for them in your schedule. Third, a schedule discourages you from being lazy. You've got a plan right in front of you, and that plan says, "Let's get down to business!" Fourth, you can schedule review sessions right from the start and avoid last-minute cramming for tests.

*A schedule encourages relaxation.* At the same time, because your plan is written down instead of floating around in your head, your mind is freed for other things. There's no time wasted worrying about what to do next. It's all there on paper. There's no guilt either. Both work and play are written

---

[3]Originally published in *Some Watch While Some Must Sleep,* by William C. Dement, as a volume in The Portable Stanford series published by the Stanford Alumni Association. Copyright © 1972. Reprinted by permission of the Stanford Alumni Association.

your schedule. This means that when you take a break, you know you deserve it.

Despite these benefits, many students are reluctant to start using a time schedule. They feel not only that a schedule will do them little good but also that keeping track of time will turn them into nervous wrecks. Neither worry is warranted.

*A schedule saves time.* Yes, it takes time to devise a schedule, but that time is rewarded. You will be able to shift smoothly from one activity to the next, without the pauses and panics involved in wondering what to do next.

*A schedule provides freedom.* Scheduling frees you from time's control. The people you see dashing from class to library to gym, or eating lunch on the run, are slaves to time. The students who schedule time, who decide how it will be used, are the masters of time.

*A schedule increases flexibility.* Disorganized people often waste so much time that there's no room for flexibility. People who do scheduling free their time for a variety of activities and are therefore more flexible.

## Use the Three-Part Scheduling Plan

If you're attending classes full time, your best strategy for scheduling is to use a three-part plan. The three schedules—a *master schedule,* a *weekly schedule,* and a *daily schedule*—work in concert to help you manage each day as well as the term as a whole. If you are balancing your studies with the extra responsibilities that come with working at a job, participating in a time-consuming extracurricular activity, or raising a family, the basic principles that underlie the plan are still valuable, but you may want to tailor them to your particular needs.

The three-part scheduling plan provides a system for handling the assignments and activities that make up your daily life. The master schedule serves as a basic structure for organizing your activities. The weekly schedule adds specific details to the master schedule, and the daily schedule puts the weekly schedule in a portable form. Although each schedule performs a different function, all three follow the same scheduling guidelines:

1. *Plan your time in blocks.* A father once tied a bundle of small, thin sticks together with a strand of twine, handed the bundle to his youngest son, and said, "Son, break these sticks in half." The boy used his hands and knees but could not break the bundle. Sadly, he handed it back to his father. Without a word, the father untied the twine and, using only his fingers, snapped each stick one by one.

When the sum total of your obligations and academic assignments seems overwhelming, it helps immensely to split them up into small, manageable units. By dividing each day into blocks, time schedules provide you with a method for breaking up your responsibilities and dealing with them one by one. Assigning a block of time to each activity ensures that you will work at peak efficiency.

When you're faced with an assignment, particularly a long-term one, remind yourself right from the start that you do not intend to accomplish everything in one sitting. The "divide and conquer" tactic applies to academic assignments just as it does to military campaigns.

2. *Don't waste big blocks.* There's a strong tendency to say, "I'm going to clean up the several little assignments so that I can devote uninterrupted time to a big assignment." This is a poor decision. Instead, save these small assignments for the little slivers of time.

3. *Study during prime time.* For most of us, prime time is daytime. In fact, research has shown that each hour used for study during the day is equal to one and a half hours at night. Even so, you may find that you have dead hours during the day when you are less productive than you'd like to be. Schedule less-demanding tasks for these hours.

4. *Study before recitation classes and after lecture classes.* A study session before a recitation or discussion class (a foreign language course or a psychology seminar, for example) helps warm you up. When you walk into class, the material is fresh in your mind. For lecture classes, use the time immediately after class to fill in any gaps in your notes and to review the information you've just learned.

5. *Schedule your time effectively.* Account for all your time, but do so without being overly detailed. The time you'd take to make an over meticulous schedule can be better used in studying a subject directly, and the chances of your following such a plan are slim.

6. *Include nonacademic activities.* Always set aside time for food, sleep, and recreation as well as the other activities of your life. Cheating yourself out of a meal, a good night's sleep, a swim, a family get-together, or a meeting with friends won't save you time in the long run. In fact, this may cost you time because all these activities are necessary for your overall mental and physical wellness. Make your plan for living, not just for studying.

**Lay a Foundation with a Master Schedule**   A master schedule provides a schedule of fixed activities around which your varying activities are arranged.

Unless changes occur in your basic program, you need to draw up a master schedule only once per term.

A master schedule grid lists the days of the week at the top and the hours of the day down the left side. The boxes within the grid are filled in with all your required activities: sleep, meals, job, regular meetings, community activities, sports, and, of course, classes. The empty boxes that remain represent your free time. Figure 2.2 provides an example of a typical master schedule.

Such a master schedule, on a 5 × 8 card taped over your desk or carried in your notebook, unclutters your mind. More important, it enables you to visualize the blank boxes as actual blocks of time into which you can fit necessary activities.

**Account for Changing Details with a Weekly Schedule**   The weekly schedule takes over where the master schedule leaves off. To construct it, photocopy your master schedule and then fill in the empty blocks with the activities you have planned for the upcoming week. If you have a math test on Friday, for example, you will need to schedule a little extra study time for math. Next week you may be assigned a research paper. If so, you'll probably want to leave space in your schedule for library research. The weekly schedule helps you adapt your time to your changing priorities. Keep it posted by your desk or pasted on the inside cover of your notebook.

A sample weekly schedule is shown in Figure 2.3. The lists that follow show how the guidelines for scheduling were used to set it up.

*Monday Through Friday/Saturday*

| | |
|---|---|
| 7–8 A.M. | Avoid the frantic dash and the gobbled (or skipped) breakfast by getting up on time. |
| 12–1 P.M. | Take a full, leisurely hour for lunch. |
| 5–6 | Relax before dinner—your reward for a day of conscientious work. |
| 7–9 | Keep up with current notes and assignments through systematic studying. |
| 9–10 | To forestall cramming at quiz and examination times, give some time every day to a review of previous assignments and ground covered to date. |
| 10 | A cease-study time of 10 P.M. provides an incentive for working hard during the day and early evening. |
| 10–12 | Devote some time every day to reading books that truly interest you. Recreational reading and conversation help you unwind for a good night's sleep. |

| | Mon. | Tues. | Wed. | Thurs. | Fri. | Sat. | Sun. |
|---|---|---|---|---|---|---|---|
| 7-8 | ← Dress and Breakfast → | | | | | | |
| 8-9 | Bio-Sc | | Bio-Sc | | Bio-Sc | Dress & Breakfast | |
| 9-10 | | P.E. | | P.E. | | P.E. | Dress & Breakfast |
| 10-11 | History | | History | | History | | |
| 11-12 | | Spanish | | Spanish | | Spanish | |
| 12-1 | ← Lunch → | | | | | | |
| 1-2 | Math | Computer Lab. | Math | Computer Lab. | Math | | |
| 2-3 | English | | English | | English | | |
| 3-4 | | Work-study Prog. | | Work-study Prog. | | | |
| 4-5 | Work-study | | Work-study | | Work-study | | |
| 5-6 | | | | | | | |
| 6-7 | ← Dinner → | | | | | | |
| 7-8 | | | | | | | |
| 8-9 | | | | | | | |
| 9-10 | | | | | | | |
| 10-11 | | | | | | | |
| 11-12 | ← Sleep → | | | | | | |

**FIGURE 2.2  A Master Schedule with Work**

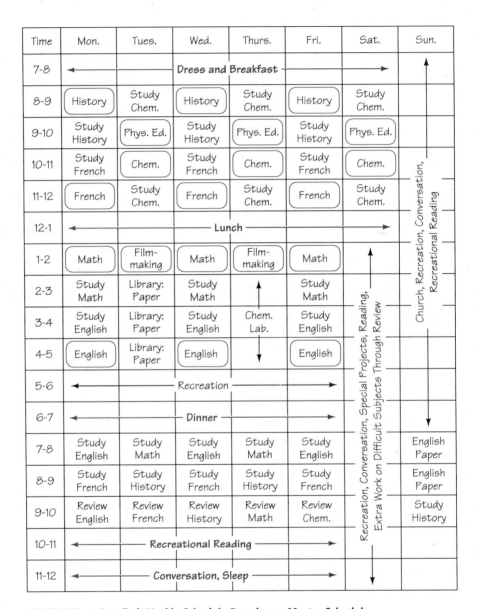

| Time | Mon. | Tues. | Wed. | Thurs. | Fri. | Sat. | Sun. |
|---|---|---|---|---|---|---|---|
| 7-8 | Dress and Breakfast → | | | | | | |
| 8-9 | History | Study Chem. | History | Study Chem. | History | Study Chem. | |
| 9-10 | Study History | Phys. Ed. | Study History | Phys. Ed. | Study History | Phys. Ed. | Church, Recreation, Conversation, Recreational Reading |
| 10-11 | Study French | Chem. | Study French | Chem. | Study French | Chem. | |
| 11-12 | French | Study Chem. | French | Study Chem. | French | Study Chem. | |
| 12-1 | Lunch → | | | | | | |
| 1-2 | Math | Film-making | Math | Film-making | Math | Recreation, Conversation, Special Projects, Reading, Extra Work on Difficult Subjects Through Review | |
| 2-3 | Study Math | Library: Paper | Study Math | | Study Math | | |
| 3-4 | Study English | Library: Paper | Study English | Chem. Lab. | Study English | | |
| 4-5 | English | Library: Paper | English | | English | | |
| 5-6 | Recreation → | | | | | | |
| 6-7 | Dinner → | | | | | | |
| 7-8 | Study English | Study Math | Study English | Study Math | Study English | | English Paper |
| 8-9 | Study French | Study History | Study French | Study History | Study French | | English Paper |
| 9-10 | Review English | Review French | Review History | Review Math | Review Chem. | | Study History |
| 10-11 | Recreational Reading → | | | | | | |
| 11-12 | Conversation, Sleep → | | | | | | |

**FIGURE 2.3   A Detailed Weekly Schedule Based on a Master Schedule**

*Tuesday/Thursday/Saturday*

8–9 A.M.          Because chemistry (10–11) is your hard subject, build your morning study program around it. An hour's study before class will make the class period more meaningful.

11–12 P.M.       Another hour's study immediately after chemistry class will help you remember the work covered in class and move more readily to the next assignment.

*Special*

Tuesday          2–5 P.M., library: paper
Sunday           7–9 P.M., English paper
                 For some assignments you will need to schedule blocks of time to do research or to develop and follow up ideas.

Saturday         From noon on, Saturday is left unscheduled—for recreation, for special projects to which you must devote a concentrated period of time, for extra work on difficult subjects, for thorough review.

Sunday           This is your day until evening. Study history before you go to bed because it is the first class you'll have on Monday morning.

**Provide a Portable Game Plan with a Daily Schedule**   A daily schedule is a brief yet specific list of the day's tasks and the time blocks you plan to accomplish them in. You should be able to fit all this information on a 3 × 5 index card that you can carry around with you all day. Make up your daily schedule each night before you go to bed. Once you have put your worries and concerns on paper, your mind will be free for sleep. You will also have thought through your day and will be better prepared when the morning comes. Figure 2.4 shows one student's daily schedule and explains why it is effective.

## Adapt Your Schedules

If you have a job, a family, or some other commitment that requires a great deal of your attention, the predictable time blocks that characterize traditional time schedules may not be as useful for you. You may need a system that helps you use scattered bits of time instead. And if you are faced with a long-term assignment, your schedules and scheduling strategies may require some adjustment as well.

FOR MONDAY

| | |
|---|---|
| 8-9 | Psychology - Review Chapter V and Lecture Notes |
| 9-10 | Psychology Lecture |
| 10-11 | Economics Lecture |
| 11-12 | Economics - Fix Up Notes, Begin Chapter VII |
| 1-2 | Campus Store - Pick Up Paper and Binder, Pen, Lead, Calculator |
| 2-5 | Engineering - Work on Assignment |
| 5-6 | Exercise - Tennis Court with Joan |
| 7-10 | Accounting and Math |

Review: Just before class is a good time to review the high points of chapters previously studied. Also review the previous lecture for continuity.

Fix up notes: The very best time to fix up lecture notes, and review them simultaneously, is immediately after the lecture.

After lunch: This is a good time to give yourself a semi-break from academic work and do some necessary errands.

2-5 block: This a valuable block of time during which you should be able to read the assignment and work out the assigned problems without losing continuity.

Exercise: After an entire day with the books, some exercise and a shower will help put an edge on your appetite, as well as make a definite break between study during the day and study during the evening.

Breaks: Breaks are not listed. You judge for yourself when a break is best for you. Also, the break should be taken when you arrive at a good stopping point.

After dinner: Both subjects need unbroken time for efficient production. Use the block of three hours to do a balanced amount of work for each, depending on the assignments.

**FIGURE 2.4  A Daily Schedule**

**Develop When Necessary a Task-Based Master Schedule**  A task-based master schedule enables you to keep track of one or more assignments or goals over an extended period of time. Figure 2.5 provides an example of a task-based master schedule. Across the top of the schedule, instead of the days of the week, list the major goals you hope to accomplish or the assignments you plan to complete. Deadlines for subgoals may be written down the left-hand side where the hours of the day would normally be written in a standard master schedule.

Now divide up each goal or long-term assignment into manageable subgoals. List these in a column beneath the task they refer to. For example,

| | Psychology Research Paper April 21 | Train for Amateur Triathlon May 1 | Self-Paced Computer Course |
|---|---|---|---|
| Feb. 7 | ~~Select Three Topic Ideas~~ | ~~Up Minimum to 60 Laps~~ | ~~Complete Ch. 1-3~~ |
| Feb. 10 | Do Preliminary Research | Try Ride Up Satyr Hill | |
| Feb. 14 | Make Final Topic Choice | Run 30 Miles Per Week | Complete Ch. 4-6 |
| Feb. 18 | Complete Bibliography | | |
| March 15 | Finish First Draft | | Mid-term Exam |
| March 18 | Begin Rewriting | | |
| April 21 | Paper Due | | Final |

**FIGURE 2.5   A Task-Based Master Schedule**

if you've been assigned a research paper, you may arrive at the following subgoals: Do preliminary research, choose topic, plan outline, conduct research, complete first draft, and revise first draft. As you reach each milestone on the way to completing your assignment, cross it off your schedule. As you do, you provide yourself with visual evidence and positive feedback of the progress you've made.

**Use the Task-Based Principle of Ivy Lee**   Although the following example pertains to business, you, as a student, can use the Ivy Lee principle in your academic scheduling to get things done.

Charles Schwab, then-chairman of the Bethlehem Steel Company, went to management consultant Ivy Lee with the challenge, "Show me a way to get more things done with my time, and I'll pay you any fee within reason." Lee thought for a while, then said:

- Every *evening* write down the six most important tasks for the next day in order of priority.
- Every *morning* start working on Task #1 and continue until you finish it; then start on Task #2, and so on. Do this until quitting time and don't be concerned if you have finished only one or two tasks.
- At the end of each day, tear up the list and start over.

When Charles Schwab asked how much he owed for this advice, Ivy Lee told him to first use the plan for a few weeks, then to send in a check for whatever he thought it was worth. Three weeks later, Lee received a check for $25,000, which is equal to about $250,000 in today's dollars![4]

Several other efficiency experts have given similar advice:

- Leboeuf says, "*Efficiency* is doing the job right; whereas, *effectiveness* is doing the right job."[5]
- Pareto says that 80 percent of our successes come from 20 percent of our studies; therefore, students should spend more time on high priority subjects and less time in low priority subjects.[6] (More on the Pareto Principle later.)

By using good judgment, you can allot the bulk of your time to getting top-priority tasks done yet be mindful not to ignore other tasks with due dates.

---

[4]T. W. Engstrom and R. A. Mackensie, *Managing Your Time* (Grand Rapids, MI: Zondervan, 1967).
[5]M. Leboeuf, *Working Smart: How to Accomplish More in Half the Time* (New York: Warner Books, 1979).
[6]C. Parkinson, *Parkinson, the Law* (Boston: Houghton Mifflin, 1980).

**Make Your Weekly Schedule Assignment Oriented** If the span of your goal or assignment is a week or less, you can use an assignment-oriented weekly schedule as a supplement to your master schedule. Figure 2.6 shows such a schedule. The format is simple. Draw a horizontal line to divide an $8\frac{1}{2} \times 11$ sheet of paper in half. In the top half, list your subjects, assignments, estimated study times, and due dates. Then, with the due dates and estimated times as control factors, check your master schedule for your available time.

| Subject | Assignment | Estimated Time | Date Due | Time Due |
|---|---|---|---|---|
| Electronics | Chapter V - 32 pp. - Read | 2 hr. | Mon. 13th | 8:00 |
| English | Paper to Write | 18 hr. | Mon. 20th | 9:00 |
| Math | Problems on pp. 110-111 | 3 hr. | Tues. 14th | 10:00 |
| Industrial Safety | Make Shop Layouts | 8 hr. | Fri. 17th | 11:00 |
| Computer Graphics | Generate Slide Presentation (2-4 slides) | 6 hr. | Fri. 17th | 1:00 |
| Electronics | Chapter VI - 40pp. - Read | 2 1/2 hr. | Weds. 22nd | 8:00 |

| Day | Assignment | Morning | Afternoon | Evening |
|---|---|---|---|---|
| Sun. | Electronics - Read Chap V<br>English - Find a Topic | | | 7:30-9:30<br>9:30-10:30 |
| Mon. | English - Gather Notes<br>Math - Problems | | 2:00-6:00 | 7:00-10:00 |
| Tues. | English - Gather Notes<br>Industrial Safety | 8:00-10:00 | 3:00-6:00 | 7:00-10:00 |
| Wed. | English - First Draft<br>Computer Graphics | | 2:00-6:00 | 7:00-10:00 |
| Thurs. | Industrial Safety<br>English - Paper<br>Computer Graphics | 8:00-10:00 | 3:00-6:00 | 7:00-10:00 |
| Fri. | English - Final Copy<br>Electronics | | 2:00-6:00 | 7:00-9:30 |
| Sat. | | | | |

**FIGURE 2.6   A Weekly Schedule Based on Assignments**

```
1. Basic Math
    - 5 problems to solve
2. Geology
    - Look over specimens
3. Accounting - definitions
- - - - - - - - - - - - - - - - - - - - - -
Bread - 2
Eggs - 1 doz.
Margarine - 1 lb.
```

**FIGURE 2.7   A Things-to-Do List**

Choose enough hours to do the job, and write them on the appropriate line on the bottom half of the sheet. Stick to your schedule. As long as you give study hours top priority, your remaining hours will be truly free.

If your available time is unpredictable, your daily study schedule should simply be a list of things to do arranged in order of priority on a 3 × 5 card. In this case, assigning specific times is likely to lead only to frustration.

Figure 2.7 shows a typical daily list. To be successful, you need a sense of urgency about referring to your list and studying whenever an opportunity presents itself. Then cross off the tasks as you complete them.

Use the *Pareto Principle* to help you draw up your list. Named after Vilfredo Pareto (1848–1923), an Italian economist and sociologist, the Pareto Principle states that the truly important items in any given group constitute only a small number of the total items in the group. This principle is also known as the *80/20 rule*.

For example, in almost any sales force, 80 percent of the business is brought in by 20 percent of the salespeople. In any committee, 80 percent of the ideas come from 20 percent of the members. In a classroom, 80 percent of the teacher's time is taken up by 20 percent of the students.

In any list of things to do, 80 percent of the importance resides in 20 percent of the list. In a list of ten items, 80 percent of the list's value lies in two items, which constitute 20 percent of the list. Because of Pareto's Principle, in your lists of things to do always put the most important items first. Then, if you accomplish only the first few items, you will have accomplished the most important tasks on the list.

Keep the Pareto Principle in mind whenever you make up a list or a schedule or must decide which subject to study first. Apply the principle by listing first things first.[7]

---

[7]Reprinted with the permission of Scribner, a division of Simon & Schuster from *Getting Things Done*. Revised and Updated Edition by Edwin C. Bliss. Copyright © 1976, 1991 Edwin C. Bliss.

## SUMMARY

**How can you gain time?**

You can gain time by changing your time habits and by finding hidden time throughout your day.

**What time habits can you change?**

If you defy Parkinson's Law and obey your alarm clock, you can break time-wasting habits and add time to your day. You can save time by taking regular breaks when you study and by jotting down distracting thoughts on a notepad.

**How can you take advantage of hidden time?**

You can carry pocket work to do for unexpected free time, use your mind when it's free, listen to audiocassette versions of your notes, think in your spare time, and draw on your subconscious.

**What is the value of using a time schedule?**

A time schedule enables you to plot out and manage your time. Using a time schedule can increase your control over your life, leave you feeling more relaxed, and add to your freedom and flexibility.

**How do you choose the right type of schedule?**

If you're attending classes full time, you can use a three-part scheduling plan with separate master, weekly, and daily schedules. If you have additional demanding commitments, you may want to use schedules that emphasize the tasks you want to accomplish.

**What general guidelines should you follow in making up a master, weekly, or daily schedule?**

All three schedules should be made up of separate time blocks that enable you to tackle your tasks in manageable units. Schedule most of your important activities for daylight hours. For recitation classes, study before the class; for lecture classes, study after class. Schedule your time effectively—list all your tasks, but not in daunting and unrealistic detail. Finally, schedule nonacademic activities (meals, sleep, recreation) as well as those that relate to your schoolwork. Your schedule should serve as a plan for living, not just for studying.

**What are the purpose and content of a master schedule?**

A master schedule provides you with a basic framework for a term's activities. Written on a grid, this schedule includes those obligations that stay the same week in and week out. The blocks that are left blank signify the time you have available for scheduling weekly and daily activities.

**What is a weekly schedule?**

A weekly schedule picks up where the master schedule leaves off, filling in the blanks with your daily activities as they vary from week to week.

**What is a daily schedule?**

A daily schedule is a portable game plan, showing your day's schedule on a 3 × 5 card.

**How can you adapt schedules to your life outside school?**

If you have a job, a family, or other time-consuming demands, or if you are faced with a long-term assignment, set up your schedules to emphasize the tasks you need to accomplish instead of the time when you will do them. Devise a special master schedule that focuses on long-term goals. Make your weekly schedule more assignment oriented, and turn your daily schedule into a list of things to do.

**What is a task-based master schedule?**

A task-based master schedule is a list of the major goals you hope to accomplish and the deadlines you set on the way to reaching those goals.

**What is an assignment-oriented weekly schedule?**

An assignment-oriented weekly schedule budgets your week's school-related activities. It begins with a list of your upcoming assignments and a time estimate for each and then shows a time block for each.

**What is a list of things to do?**

A daily list of things to do is an outline in order of priority of what you plan to accomplish.

## HAVE YOU MISSED SOMETHING?

*Sentence completion.*  Complete the following sentences with one of the three words listed below each sentence.

1. To take control of your life, you must take control of your _____ .
   personality     principles     time

2. How we spend or waste time is largely a matter of _____ .
   habit     procrastination     priority

*Matching.* In each blank space in the left column, write the letter preceding the phrase in the right column that matches the left item best.

_____ **1.** Pocket work

_____ **2.** Weekly schedule

_____ **3.** Master schedule

_____ **4.** "Free time"

_____ **5.** Pareto Principle

_____ **6.** Subconscious

_____ **7.** Parkinson's Law

_____ **8.** Daily schedule

a. Says a task expands to fit the time allotted

b. Consumes a large portion of a typical freshman's weekday

c. Continues working even while you sleep

d. Provides a basic structure for organizing the term's activities

e. Puts your schedule in a portable form

f. Lets you keep track of activities that vary throughout the term

g. Supplies study material for unexpected free time

h. Explains why the most important items on a list should be completed first

*True-false.* Write *T* beside the *true* statements and *F* beside the *false* statements.

_____ **1.** Taking regular breaks wastes valuable time.

_____ **2.** Free time can often occur unexpectedly.

_____ **3.** The master, weekly, and daily schedules all follow the same basic guidelines.

_____ **4.** Time schedules can make you feel like a slave to time.

_____ **5.** Scheduling saves time that might otherwise be wasted.

_____ **6.** Most of us work more efficiently in the daytime.

*Multiple choice.*   Choose the word or phrase that completes the following sentence most accurately, and circle the letter that precedes it.

1. The three-part scheduling plan is particularly helpful for

   a. working parents.
   b. full-time students.
   c. student athletes.
   d. none of the above.

2. A time schedule functions as a

   a. game plan.
   b. computer.
   c. punishment.
   d. reward.

3. All your time should be accounted for, but without too much

   a. hesitation.
   b. recreation.
   c. detail.
   d. interest.

4. Energy is increased and efficiency is improved when you

   a. work or study continuously.
   b. take brief but regular breaks while studying.
   c. do most of your studying at night.
   d. use only one schedule instead of three.

5. The master schedule provides

   a. an alternative to a weekly schedule.
   b. an excuse for increased recreation.
   c. a framework of fixed activities.
   d. a solution to the problem of hidden time.

6. The best approach to a long-term assignment is

   a. increase and multiply.
   b. divide and conquer.
   c. meals and recreation.
   d. rules and regulations.

7. An assignment-oriented weekly schedule is appropriate

   a. as a supplement to your master schedule.
   b. when you face an unusual or long-term assignment.

c.  if you don't have big blocks of uninterrupted time.
d.  for all of the above.

**8.**  Unlike a daily schedule, a list of things to do

a.  works efficiently.
b.  is only 80 percent useful.
c.  has no time blocks.
d.  is written on an index card.

*Short answer.*  Supply a brief answer for each of the following items.

**1.**  What is the purpose of keeping a daily activities log?
**2.**  How does a time schedule increase your sense of control?
**3.**  In what ways does a schedule promote relaxation?
**4.**  What is the advantage of scheduling your time in blocks?
**5.**  Discuss how to prepare a task-oriented master schedule.

## VOCABULARY BUILDING

DIRECTIONS: Make a light check mark (√) alongside one of the three words (choices) that most nearly expresses the meaning of the italicized word in the phrases that are in the left-hand column. (Answers are given on p. 433.)

|  |  | 1 | 2 | 3 |
|---|---|---|---|---|
| 1. | *discrete* sessions | proper | separate | short |
| 2. | overcome *inertia* | speed | movement | unchanging |
| 3. | a *meticulous* schedule | precise | neat | overloaded |
| 4. | psychology *seminar* | debate | meeting | examination |
| 5. | students are *reluctant* | eager | repetitious | unwilling |
| 6. | such a view proved *prescient* | profitable | foretelling | appropriate |
| 7. | a federal government *behemoth* | enormity | agency | building |
| 8. | the now *ignominious* trader | successful | disgraced | ignored |
| 9. | the *allegations* sent tremors | evidence | assertions | proofs |
| 10. | carried out *unorthodox* trades | improper | universal | conventional |
| 11. | smudged *parodies* of ourselves | heroics | imitations | accomplishments |

| | **1** | **2** | **3** |
|---|---|---|---|
| 12. an *eclectic* environment | favorable | stormy | combined |
| 13. *quixotic* battler | idealistic | undecided | quiet |
| 14. *ubiquitous* delivery trucks | large | common | swift |
| 15. is a *euphemism* | substitution | record | accomplishment |
| 16. an *anemic* average | acceptable | well-earned | weak |
| 17. a *plethora* of diversifications | abundance | scarcity | balance |
| 18. his investment *prowess* | record | wealth | skill |
| 19. selling under *duress* | oath | coercion | contract |
| 20. against *litigious* greed | literary | legitimate | lawsuit |
| 21. the *indolent* sinking sun | lazy | hot | glaring |
| 22. with the *lustrous* star | fading | sinking | radiant |
| 23. *myriad* daffodils | beautiful | countless | yellowish |
| 24. its *melancholy* roar | sparkling | gloomy | cheerful |
| 25. *perfidious* wrongs | correctable | dangerous | treacherous |

# 3

# Managing Stress

*Life is a journey, not a guided tour.*

—ANONYMOUS

Stress, writes Dr. Hans Selye, a pioneer in the study of stress, is "the spice of life or the kiss of death—depending on how we cope with it."[1] Unfortunately, most of us cope with it badly. We worry too much, criticize too much, get angry too often, and become too tense. But if you can learn to deflect the stress that comes your way, you can thrive, as a student and as a human being. This chapter helps you manage stress by focusing on

- Developing a positive mental attitude
- Following a healthy physical routine
- Reducing stressors

---

[1]Hans Selye, "How to Master Stress," *Parents* 52 (November 1977): 25.

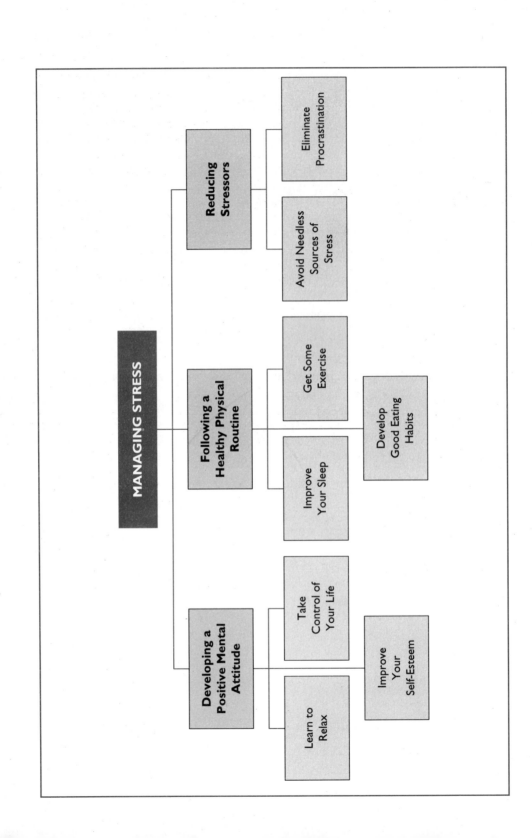

**M**ere mention of the word *stress* is enough to make most people anxious. It brings to mind images of frayed nerves, shortened tempers, and rising blood pressure. But being under stress isn't always a bad thing. In fact, stress can prompt us to respond effectively to a tough situation, to rise to the occasion when a paper comes due or a test is handed out. According to Marilyn Gist, a professor at the School of Business Administration of the University of Washington, "A certain amount of stress is healthy and beneficial; it stimulates some to perform, makes them excited and enthusiastic."[2]

"Stress," according to Hans Selye, "is the nonspecific response of the body to any demand made upon it."[3] In other words, it is the body's attempt to adjust to a demand, regardless of what the demand may be. You undergo stress when you run or walk at a brisk pace. Your body responds to the demand for more oxygen by increasing your breathing and causing your heart to beat faster. Yet most people view exercise, not as a source of stress, but as a means of stress relief. Likewise, watching a quiz show or doing a crossword can both be considered stressful. In each case, the brain responds with increased mental activity. Yet most people undertake these activities specifically for relaxation.

The problem is that we don't always respond to the sources of stress (known as *stressors*) in such a positive fashion. If instead of running for exercise, you're racing to catch a bus, or instead of solving a crossword puzzle, you're struggling with a math test that you didn't study for, your reaction is apt to be quite different. Rather than experiencing the exhilaration of exercising or the stimulation of solving a puzzle, you may wind up feeling exhausted or intimidated.

That's the two-sided potential of stress. Instead of compelling us to rise to the occasion, stress can sometimes plunge us down into a sea of anxiety, worry, hostility, or despair. The way we respond to stress, whether we use it as a boon or a burden, depends on two major factors: our overall approach to life and the number of stressors we face at any one time. These two factors can for the most part be controlled, which means you can basically decide whether stress will have a positive or negative effect on your life. To improve the chance that stress will affect you positively, you are wise to adopt a positive mental attitude, follow a healthy physical routine, and limit the number of stressors that confront you at any one time.

---

[2]Pam Miller Withers, "Good Stress/Bad Stress: How to Use One, Lose the Other." *Working Woman* (September 1989): 124.
[3]Hans Selye, *Stress Without Distress* (New York: J.B. Lippincott, 1974), p. 27.

## DEVELOPING A POSITIVE MENTAL ATTITUDE

Although you can't turn away disaster simply by keeping a smile on your face, there are now abundant indications that your overall attitude can have a powerful influence on the outcome of potentially upsetting or stressful situations. The first evidence was offered around the turn of the century, when American philosopher and psychologist William James and Danish psychologist Carl Lange simultaneously developed a remarkable theory of emotion. You don't cry because you're sad, they suggested. You're sad because you cry. This revolutionary reversal of the apparent cause and effect of emotions briefly sent the scientific community into an uproar. As the twentieth century progressed, this controversial proposal, known as the James-Lange theory, was scoffed at by most members of the mainstream scientific community and was advocated instead by "inspirational" writers and speakers such as Dr. Norman Vincent Peale, who championed the virtues of "positive thinking." Now the James-Lange theory has been vindicated, and Peale's ideas, bolstered by recent scientific evidence, have garnered mainstream defenders.

As part of a study conducted in 1983 by Paul Ekman, Robert W. Levenson, and Wallace V. Friesen at the Department of Psychiatry of the University of California, San Francisco, subjects were given specific instructions for contracting various facial muscles to imitate six basic emotions: happiness, sadness, disgust, surprise, anger, and fear.[4] Instead of being told, for example, to "look scared," the subject was instructed to "raise your brows and pull them together, now raise your upper eyelids and stretch your lips horizontally, back toward your ears."[5] Expressions were held for ten seconds, while electronic instruments measured the subjects' physiological response.

The results were fascinating. Simply imitating an emotional expression was enough to trigger the physiological changes normally associated with that emotion. The most interesting contrast was between expressions for anger and for happiness. The average subject's heart rate and skin temperature increased more with anger than they did with happiness. Yet the subjects weren't truly angry or happy: they were just imitating the expressions associated with these two emotions.

We can conclude from this study that simply putting on a happy face may make you feel happier and that taking a dim or overly pessimistic view can lead to the discouraging outcome you expected. But managing stress

---

[4]Paul Ekman, Robert W. Levenson, and Wallace V. Friesen, "Autonomic Nervous System Activity Distinguishes Among Emotions." *Science* 221 (1983): 1208–1210.
[5]Ibid., p. 1208.

shouldn't simply be a fuzzy-headed smile-at-all-your-troubles strategy. Improving your attitude should be done systematically by learning to relax, by improving your self-esteem, and, above all, by *taking control of your life*.

## Learn to Relax

The regular use of relaxation techniques, according to studies at the Mind/ Body Medical Institute of Harvard Medical School, reduces stress and the prevalence of stress-related illness.[6] But many of us don't consider using such techniques because we misinterpret what the word *relaxation* means. Relaxation doesn't necessarily mean you're about to fall asleep. In fact, some World War II pilots used relaxation techniques, not to prepare themselves for sleep or to "take it easy," but to stay alert and avoid fatigue during bombing missions.[7]

Nor is relaxation a synonym for lethargy. "Relaxation," write psychologists Edward A. Charlesworth and Ronald G. Nathan in *Stress Management*, "simply means doing nothing with your muscles."[8] Relaxation therefore is relief from wasted effort or strain, an absence of tension. Indeed, explains author Emrika Padus, "tenseness wastes energy; tenseness causes anxiety. . . . The best performances come when the mind and body are *floating*, enjoying the activity just as we did when we were young children, completely absorbed in the experience and unaware of any consequences of the actions. This is true relaxation."[9]

There's nothing mystical about relaxation. Two simple techniques— breathing deeply and using progressive relaxation—can help you get the hang of this life-sustaining practice.

**Breathe Deeply**    There's a strong connection between the way you breathe and the way you feel. When you're relaxed, your breaths are long and deep, originating from your abdomen. When you're anxious, your breathing is often short and shallow, originating from high in your chest.

This link between breathing and emotion operates in both directions. Just as the way you feel affects the way you breathe, changing your breathing alters your emotional response. A handful of experiments have established

---

[6]Stephanie Wood, "Relax! You've Earned It." *McCall's* 118 (July 1991): 50.
[7]Edward A. Charlesworth and Ronald G. Nathan, *Stress Management* (New York: Atheneum, 1984), p. 41.
[8]Ibid., p. 42.
[9]Emrika Padus, *The Complete Guide to Your Emotions & Your Health* (Emmaus, Penn.: Rodale Press, 1986), p. 490.

this connection. Dr. James Loehr found that when a relaxed group of subjects was asked to take short, rapid, and irregular breaths for two minutes—in other words, to pant—nearly everyone interviewed felt worried, threatened, and panicky.[10] Simply by imitating the response of an anxious person, the subjects had actually made themselves anxious.

Luckily, this principle can be used to encourage relaxation as well. By breathing slowly, steadily, and deeply and by beginning your breaths in your abdomen instead of up in your chest, you can encourage a feeling of relaxation. So just before an exam, an interview, or a dental appointment, when your palms are sweating, your body is tense, and your breath is short and shallow, try the count-of-three method to induce a more relaxed state. Count slowly and calmly through each step:

1. Inhale slowly through your nose while silently counting to three.
2. Hold your breath for the count of three.
3. Exhale slowly through your nose while silently counting to three.
4. With your breath expelled, count to three.
5. Repeat the cycle (steps 1 to 4) several times. (Once you have the rhythm, you need not continue counting; but maintain the same timing and the same pauses.)

**Use Progressive Muscle Relaxation**    A big advantage of the count-of-three method is that it can be done inconspicuously almost anywhere, including in an exam room. But if you have some time, a quiet place, and a little privacy, you may want to try progressive muscle relaxation (PMR), a method for systematically tensing and relaxing the major muscles in your body.

PMR was developed more than seventy years ago by Edmund Jacobson, a doctor who saw the connection between tense muscles and a tense mind. PMR works by helping you become aware of the difference between how your muscles feel when they're tensed and how they feel when they're relaxed.

Start PMR by assuming a comfortable position, either sitting or lying down, and by closing your eyes. Make a tight fist in your right hand, and at the same time tense your right forearm. Hold this position for five seconds, feeling the tension in both your hand and arm, and then slowly release that tension, letting it flow out of you as you unclench your fist. Repeat the procedure with your left hand, noting the difference between how this hand feels tensed compared with your right hand and arm, which are now relaxed. Continue by separately tensing your shoulder muscles, your neck, and the

---

[10]James E. Loehr and Peter J. McLaughlin, with Ed Quillen, *Mentally Tough* (New York: M. Evans and Company, 1986), pp. 141–142.

muscles in your face. Then start with your feet and toes, moving up each leg; finish by tensing the muscles in your abdomen and chest. Once you've tensed and released every muscle group in your body, take a moment to savor the overall feeling of relaxation. Then open your eyes and end the exercise.

## Improve Your Self-Esteem

*Self-esteem* is your personal assessment of your own value. Unfortunately, many of us are our own toughest critics. We overlook our positive attributes and forget our successes, emphasizing our shortcomings instead and providing ourselves with a silent but constant stream of discouraging dialogue. The stress that results from these inner discouragements is far worse than any criticism we might receive from a nagging parent, an insulting instructor, or an overly demanding boss.

A healthy level of self-esteem is crucial to keeping stress at bay. If your self-esteem needs improvement, rewrite the potentially destructive inner dialogue that haunts you throughout the day, and take some time out to dwell on your successes.

**Rewrite Your Inner Dialogue**    You can't rewrite your inner dialogue unless you've seen the script. Therefore, the first step in eliminating the destructive thoughts that undermine your self-esteem is to become aware of them.

Most of us talk silently to ourselves almost continually. Psychologists commonly refer to this inner conversation as *self-talk*. Although you may have learned to ignore the sound of your self-talk, the effect it has on your overall attitude can still be damaging. So when you enter a new situation or are faced with a difficult challenge, take a moment to express your apprehensions to yourself. Then listen to your self-talk. Whenever you have a negative thought, counteract it with a positive one. Remember that the thoughts you have are your own and they're under your control. You can open the door of your mind to whatever thoughts you want. Admit only the positive ones, and leave the negative thoughts out in the cold.

**Build on Your Success**    All of us have experienced success at one time or another. When you feel your self-esteem slipping, remember when you did a job you were proud of, when you overcame an obstacle in spite of the odds, or when everything seemed to go smoothly. It helps to congratulate yourself from time to time, to put yourself in an achieving frame of mind so that you can manifest success again.

## Take Control of Your Life

One of the results of increased self-esteem is an increased sense of control, a quality that both medical doctors and psychologists are finding can have a measurable effect on your physical well-being and state of mind. According to the *Wellness Letter* from the University of California, Berkeley, "A sense of control may, in fact, be a critical factor in maintaining health."[11] When you're in control, you act; you set your own agenda instead of reacting to the wishes or whims of others or resigning yourself to what we often call "fate."

**Control Time, and You Control Stress**　Stress intensifies when you feel you're running out of time. The solution: get things done! A vigorous, aggressive approach must become a way of life in the classroom, the laboratory, the library, and elsewhere. Get what you came for! During a lecture, for example, you must be alert and work hard to capture the lecturer's ideas and put them down on paper.

In the library, some students wander about aimlessly or spend time watching other students coming and going. If your purpose is to gather data for your research paper, then move on to the computer to gather your references, secure the books, and begin reading and taking notes. Get something done according to plan!

The intelligent use of time plays a large part in keeping stress from becoming a way of life. Plan your time wisely, then be sure to follow the plan.

**Appreciate the Significance of Control**　In the early 1960s, writer and magazine editor Norman Cousins was stricken with a painful and terminal illness. Determined not to let the illness control his life and sentence him to death, Cousins fought back. He watched movie comedies, one after another. The laughter the films elicited made the sleep that had eluded him come more easily and ultimately reversed the crippling illness.[12] In fact, the results were so impressive to the medical community that Cousins, who had no medical background, was awarded an honorary degree in medicine from the Yale University School of Medicine and was appointed adjunct professor in the School of Medicine at the University of California, Los Angeles.

Norman Cousins is not the only person who has demonstrated the importance of a sense of control. Author Richard Logan investigated the lives

---

[11]"Healthy Lives: A New View of Stress," *University of California, Berkeley, Wellness Letter* 6, no. 9 (June 1990): 4.

[12]*Managing Stress—From Morning to Night* (Alexandria, Va.: Time-Life Books, 1987), p. 21.

of people who were able to survive extreme stress—such as imprisonment in a concentration camp—and found that they all had at least one quality in common: a belief that their destiny was in their own hands. In other words, they had a sense of control.[13]

The importance of control was reinforced in a study that provided a physiological insight into the phenomenon. When your body is under stress, your adrenal glands release *cortisone,* a hormone that in small doses can fight allergies and disease but that in larger amounts can impair the body's ability to fight back. When the two groups of employees who made up the study worked almost to the point of exhaustion, only one group experienced a significant increase in cortisone production. Those employees with high levels of cortisone had jobs that allowed them very little control. Those employees who experienced no increase in cortisone held positions with a high level of control.[14]

A lack of control can result in a sense of helplessness almost guaranteed to bring about the frayed nerves, tense muscles, and overall feeling of panic normally associated with short-term stress. If these conditions persist, they can have an adverse effect on your body's immune system, making you more susceptible to illness. Robbed of your sense of control, you not only react instead of acting but you also overreact. Turned outward, this overreaction may surface as anger. Turned inward, it can lead to fear, anxiety, and general depression.

In *The Joy of Stress,* Dr. Peter Hanson describes an experiment in which two groups of office workers were exposed to a series of loud and distracting background noises. One group had desks equipped with a button that could be pushed at any time to shut out the annoying sounds. The other group had no such button. Not surprisingly, workers with the button control were far more productive than those without. But what's remarkable is that no one in the button group actually pushed the button. Apparently the knowledge that they could shut out the noise if they wanted to was enough to enable them to work productively in spite of the distractions. Their sense of control resulted in a reduction in stress and an increase in productivity.[15]

**Understand How Attitude Affects Control**    Dr. Hanson's story of the control button underscores an important element of control: Taking control is primarily a matter of adjusting your attitude. As a student, you can achieve a sense of control by changing the way you view your courses, assignments, and exams.

---

[13]Mihaly Csikszentmihalyi, *Flow: The Psychology of Optimal Experience* (New York: Harper & Row, 1990), p. 203

[14]Robert M. Bramson, *Coping with the Fast Track Blues* (New York: Doubleday, 1990), p. 217.

[15]Peter Hanson, *The Joy of Stress* (New York: McMeel & Parker, 1985), pp. 15–16.

Taking control of your classes and assignments means viewing them as choices instead of obligations. The stressed-out, overwhelmed student looks to the next lecture or reading assignment with dread, seeing it as a burden he or she would rather do without. The student who feels in control (and feels confident as a result) understands that he or she attends lectures and completes assignments as a matter of choice and that the benefits derived from both are not only practical but also enjoyable. According to psychologist Mihalyi Csikszentmihalyi, "Of all the virtues we can learn, no trait is more useful, more essential for survival and more likely to improve the quality of life than the ability to transform adversity into an enjoyable challenge."[16]

Even students who feel they have their assignments under control can feel swamped by the prospect of an exam or a paper assignment. But by shifting their attitude, they can transform a dreaded paper or final into a challenge. Although the pressure is still on, students who take control prepare with confidence and relish the opportunity to demonstrate what they know.

**Learn to Cope with Out-of-Control Circumstances**   Clearly, a great many situations in life are out of your control. But even in unavoidable or unpredictable situations, you can still exercise some degree of influence. Psychologists have found that as your coping resources increase (both in number and in variety), so does your sense of control. Thus, a person with multiple coping strategies, instead of just one plan, is better able to adapt to the inevitable surprises that can accompany almost any undertaking.

For example, you have no control over whether an upcoming exam will be made up of essay or multiple-choice questions. If the instructor doesn't tell you which type it will be, you can increase your coping resources by preparing for both types of questions. Then regardless of what type the instructor chooses, you'll be ready. You'll have a feeling of control.

The same strategy can be applied to a number of mundane situations that often generate unwanted stress. An unexpected line at the bank or the grocery store can leave you feeling helpless and anxious. You can't make the line disappear or move more quickly, but you can put the situation back in your control by reading a book or reviewing a set of vocabulary cards while you wait. As you can see, even a small degree of control can be used to minimize a large amount of stress.

---

[16]Csikszentmihalyi, *Flow*, p. 200.

## RECOGNIZING THE MAJOR CAUSE OF STRESS

Individual stress, in most cases, is self-inflicted—not purposefully, but because of procrastination, that is, by (a) lack of control over one's actions and (b) disguised laziness. Here's how stress is self-inflicted:

> One evening, Harry promised himself, "Okay, I'm going to make a fresh start. I'll set the alarm for 6:30, which will give me time to shower and shave, get over for a good breakfast, then go on to Goldwin-Smith Hall, where I'll have time to look over the notes of the previous lecture and get set for Professor Larson's lecture on Scandinavian epics."
>
> Next morning: Alarm clock buzzes, a hand slaps the "off" button, and Harry's groggy, sleep-drugged mind rationalizes, "I'll take five more minutes. I set the alarm too early anyway."
>
> An hour later, Harry springs out of bed like a jack-in-the-box, muttering, "I must have *really* fallen asleep again." Then, bolting for the bathroom and splashing some water on his face, he mumbles, "I'll shave when I get back."
>
> By now, the pituitary gland is injecting its third dose of adrenalin directly into his bloodstream as the harried Harry streaks for Goldwin-Smith Hall. All eyes follow the perspiring and hyper student to his seat, where he fumbles for his notebook and pencil. Yes, he hears words, but the fast lub-dub, lub-dub of his heart makes it difficult to attach any meaning to them. By now the heat from his face has clouded his glasses, so with his shirttail, he wipes the lenses. By the time he's settled, he feels lost, so he just slumps in his seat, thinking, "I'll borrow Dick's notes when I get back to the dorm."
>
> The first student out of the lecture room, Harry heads for the vending machine and gurgles down a 12-ounce can of cola, which is sweetened by at least eight full teaspoons of sugar. This sugar is quickly absorbed into the bloodstream, which, now overloaded, triggers the pancreas to secrete insulin. As usual, the emergency secretion is too large, thus neutralizing more sugar than Harry ingested from the can of Coke. His lowered-blood-sugar condition would normally leave Harry feeling "washed-out," but the insulin keeps him hyper and going. A day thus started is likely to continue to bedtime, interfering with sound sleep. What a day! What a self-inflicted condition of stress! All for that extra "five minutes" of sleep.

Pulling an all-nighter to study for an exam or to beat the deadline for writing a term paper is a prime example of inflicting a condition of stress upon oneself, because of procrastination. To eliminate the need for an all-nighter, all we need to do is study for the exam from the first day of class and begin the term paper on the day the assignment is announced by the professor.

## FOLLOWING A HEALTHY PHYSICAL ROUTINE

Stress isn't all in your head. It has a noticeable effect on your body and can often be avoided through changes in your physical routine. If you make a concerted effort to improve your sleep, develop good eating habits, and get some exercise, you'll make yourself more stress resistant and decrease your chances of being subjected to stress in the first place.

## Improve Your Sleep

If your morning starts with the sound of an alarm clock, then you're probably not getting the sleep you need. According to Dr. Wilse Webb, a psychologist at the University of Florida, Gainesville, "If that's how you wake up every day, you're shortening your natural sleep pattern."[17] And yet an alarm clock is a part of most people's lives. Does that mean *all* of us are cheating ourselves on sleep? Perhaps not all, but most Americans are getting less sleep than they actually need. In fact, according to an article in the *New York Times,* "sleep scientists insist that there is virtually an epidemic of sleepiness in the nation."[18]

The image of a nation filled with semiconscious citizens may seem comical, but in reality the effects of this widespread sleep deprivation are seldom humorous and sometimes deadly. The U.S. Department of Transportation estimates that up to two hundred thousand traffic accidents each year are sleep related.[19] Furthermore, the worst nuclear power emergency in this country's history, at Three Mile Island, occurred at night, when workers were most susceptible to the effects of insufficient sleep.[20] Also, lack of sleep was implicated in the Exxon *Valdez* oil spill and the space shuttle *Challenger* disaster.

Although the consequences of sleep deprivation are not normally deadly, college students still suffer from them. Dr. Charles Czeisler, director of circadian (the daily rhythmic sleep and wake-up cycle) and sleep disorders medicine at Brigham and Women's Hospital in Boston, has outlined some of the penalties that people pay for getting too little sleep: "Short term memory is impaired, the ability to make decisions is impaired, the ability to concentrate is impaired."[21] Clearly, a student who can't remember, can't make decisions, and has trouble concentrating will have a tough time surviving in an academic setting. Furthermore, the struggle to overcome the disabilities that sleep loss creates frequently leads to an even more pervasive problem: stress.

---

[17]Natalie Angier, "Cheating on Sleep: Modern Life Turns America into the Land of the Drowsy," *New York Times,* May 15, 1990, pp. C-1, C-8
[18]Ibid., p. C-1.
[19]Anastasia Toulexis, "Drowsy America," *Time,* December 17, 1990, p. 80.
[20]Angier, "Cheating on Sleep," p. C-8.
[21]Ibid.

"Weariness corrodes civility and erases humor" read an article in *Time* magazine. "Without sufficient sleep, tempers flare faster and hotter at the slightest offense."[22] The day-to-day challenges and inconveniences of going to school and of living in the modern world are potentially stress inducing. Add in habitual sleep loss, and you turn a chronic problem into an acute one. Dr. Ernest Hartmann's study of "variable sleepers" (patients whose sleep and wake-up times are not consistent) revealed that people under stress tend to need more sleep than those who lead a life relatively free of anxiety and change. Yet stress often triggers insomnia, which leads to less sleep and the chance for even more stress.[23] The results can be a vicious circle of stress and sleeplessness.

**Get the Right Amount of Sleep**    Sleep loss: You cannot escape the penalty that sleep loss imposes upon your ability to think creatively during an exam the next day. "Sleep loss affects divergent thinking, or the ability to think creatively, flexibly, and spontaneously."[24]

If an adequate amount of sleep is so important, then how much sleep should you be getting? Sleep experts have no easy answer to this basic question. The amount of sleep a person requires is based on a number of factors, including age, heredity, and day-to-day stress, and it may vary widely. Sleep researchers generally agree that the average person needs between six and nine hours of sleep each night.[25] But college students aren't necessarily average people. A study done by Dr. Mary Carskadon, director of chronobiology at the E. P. Bradley Hospital in Providence, Rhode Island, found that teenagers may require more than nine and a half hours of sleep each night to feel sufficiently rested.[26] And indeed, another study seems to add credence to Carskadon's findings. When healthy college students were allowed to lie down in a darkened room in the daytime, 20 percent of them feel asleep almost instantaneously, even though all of them were averaging seven to eight hours of sleep per night.[27]

How can you be sure that you are getting the right amount of sleep? In general, your overall alertness should serve as a good indicator. If you are getting the right amount of sleep, you should be able to stay awake through twenty minutes of darkness at midday. Students in art history and film

---

[22]Toulexis, "Drowsy America," p. 80.

[23]Lynne Lamberg, *The American Medical Association (Straight-talk, No-nonsense) Guide to Better Sleep*, Rev. (New York: Random House, 1984), p. 35.

[24]J. A. Horne, "Sleep Loss and "Divergent" Thinking Ability," *Sleep* 11 (1988):528–36.

[25]Milton K. Erman and Merrill M. Mitler, *How to Get a Good Night's Sleep* (Phillips Publishing, 1990), p. 5.

[26]Toulexis, "Drowsy America," p. 81.

[27]Angier, "Cheating on Sleep," p. C-1.

courses, where slides or movies are commonly shown, often complain that a darkened auditorium or classroom makes them sleepy. These situations don't *create* sleepiness. They simply reveal a problem of insufficient sleep and should serve as a warning to get more rest. Sleep behavior experts tell us that on the average, most people fall short of their needed length of sleep by sixty to ninety minutes each night.[28] Aggravating this daily deficit is the fact that sleep loss is cumulative; it adds up. If you feel tired on Monday morning, you're apt to feel even more so when Friday rolls around.[29]

Although sleep loss adds up, sleep does not. You can't stash away extra hours of sleep like money in the bank. You need to get sufficient sleep seven nights a week. Just as so-called weekend athletes engage in strenuous exercise only on Saturday and Sunday and thereby jeopardize their hearts and their overall health in their effort to "stay fit," people who "sleep in" on weekends don't eliminate the effects of a week of sleep deprivation. In fact, they complicate the problem by disturbing their rhythm of sleeping and waking.

**Keep to a Schedule**    Achieving full alertness isn't simply a matter of getting enough sleep. It's equally important to do your sleeping at the right time of day.

The body has its own internal clock, a natural pattern of wakefulness and sleep that roughly follows the rising and setting of the sun. These cycles of waking and sleeping are known as *circadian rhythms.* Thanks to your circadian rhythms, when morning arrives you instinctively become more alert in anticipation of the day that lies ahead. With the advent of evening, signals in your brain begin preparing you for needed sleep. You go to sleep, and when you wake up the process is repeated.

The way to make the most of these circadian rhythms is to maintain a regular sleep-wake schedule. Sleeping late on the weekends or going to bed at widely varying times throws your circadian rhythms out of whack. You find yourself feeling drowsy when you should be alert and wide awake when you should be fast asleep.[30]

If you've ever traveled a great distance by air, you may have experienced a feeling known as *jet lag,* which was prompted because your body's internal clock, "set" in the place where you started, didn't match the clocks of the place where you landed. A person who flies from New York to San Francisco, for example, may find herself feeling drowsy at 8 P.M. Pacific time because

---

[28]Ibid.
[29]Ibid., p. C-8.
[30]Richard M. Coleman, *Wide Awake at 3:00 A.M.* (New York: W. H. Freeman, 1986), p. 149.

her sleep-wake cycle was set out East. where the time is already 11 P.M. And at 4 A.M., when the rest of the West is sleeping, she may be feeling wide awake. But she will soon synchronize her internal clock with Pacific time.

People who stay at home but go to sleep at widely varying times are not so fortunate. They are often plagued by chronic drowsiness and insomnia, a sort of stay-at-home jet lag. If you go to bed at 11 P.M. one night and at 2 A.M. the next, you may wake up the next day and feel as though you've flown across the country. In these situations, even getting the right amount of sleep won't be enough. Your rest will be reduced because you'll be going against the beat of your body's natural rhythms.

If you consistently arise at the same time regardless of when you went to bed, you'll keep your circadian rhythms on tempo.[31] Furthermore, an unwavering wake-up time should help discourage you from staying up too late.

Students who cheat themselves out of sleep feel they're adding extra hours to their day. They are, of course, but in increasing the quantity of their waking hours, they are reducing the quality. A well-rested student is usually more productive than one who is sleep deprived, even though the latter student may have more hours of study time available.

**Recognize the Truth About Naps** Students and others who have flexible schedules often see naps as the solution to sleep deprivation. Unfortunately, naps fall far short of their reputation and actually create a number of problems: They're impractical, they adversely affect learning, they harm both sound sleep and the sleep cycle, and they act as a convenient excuse for chronic procrastinators.

As we have discussed, your circadian rhythm is operated by an internal clock in your brain. It is set in motion by the light-dark cycle. But in taking naps, we need to know about the vital role of the hormone melatonin in maintaining our health.

"Melatonin is the sleep-inducing hormone secreted by the pineal gland. . . . Melatonin not only helps us to sleep, but also may help to prevent tumors since it stimulates our tissues to destroy oxidants, chemical pollutants that produce cancer."[32]

"Melatonin levels are high at night when it's dark and we're resting, and low in the daytime when it's light and we're active. Normally, there's

---

[31]Cooper, *The Performance Edge*, p. 222.
[32]Dr. Alexander Grant's *Health Gazette* 18, no. 2 (February 1995). Published by Alexander Grant, M.D. and Associates. P.O. Box 1786, Indianapolis, IN 46206.

at least five times more melatonin in your blood at night than during the day."[33]

In addition, naps generally deprive you of two of sleep's more important components: dream, or rapid eye movement (REM), sleep, the period in which all our dreaming occurs, and deep sleep (also called *delta sleep*), which many sleep experts believe recharges our batteries and increases our overall alertness.[34] Therefore, if you take a nap, you may be adding to the quantity of your sleep but not to the quality of it because you will probably be lacking the dream and deep sleep that your body requires. "There is no doubt that this deep sleep is essential to health. Muramyl peptides, which are vital to tissue renewal and immune enhancement, are only released during deep, slow-wave sleep."[35]

As you might expect, naps also interfere with your sleep-wake cycle. Unless you take a nap every day at the same time and for the same duration, you will probably wind up with stay-at-home jet lag and have difficulty falling asleep at night.

Finally, the temptation to misuse naps can be great. Many students give in to the urge to sleep, rationalizing that when they awake they will feel refreshed and perform more productively. Unfortunately, few students report this happy result. The harsh reality is that if you try to escape a mountain of work by taking a nap, you will wake up to face the same amount of work, and you'll have less time to do it in. It is far better to combat the desire to sleep, get the work done, and go to bed at your usual time with a clear conscience. You'll get the sleep you need, you'll minimize disruptions to your body's circadian rhythms, you'll feel healthier and more alert, and you'll be less susceptible to the potentially corrosive effects of stress.

**Take Solid Steps for Better Sleeping**     Optimal sleep promotes not only a more alert, energetic, zestful life but also, according to some studies, a longer life. If you're not concentrating, if you're dozing off in class and at your desk, or if you're feeling dragged out, take steps to put yourself on the right track.

*Schedule something active during your post-lunch slump.* Sitting in a dark room between 2:00 and 4:00 in the afternoon can be risky. If you're planning on taking a class where slides or movies are shown, try to avoid scheduling it during this time. If you don't have any class at this time, do something

---

[33]Dr. Marcus Laux, *Naturally Well* 2, no. 10 (October 1995): 4. 7811 Montrose Road, Potomac, MD 20854: Phillips, Inc.
[34]Dianne Hales, *The Complete Book of Sleep* (Menlo Park, CA: Addison-Wesley, 1981), p. 18.
[35]William Campbell Douglass, MD. Published by *Second Opinion* 4, no. 12 (December 1994): 7. Published by Second Opinion Publishing, Inc., Suite 100, 1350 Center Drive, Dunwoody, Georgia 30338.

energetic, like running errands, sorting papers, practicing a musical instrument, or exercising to pull yourself through this daily dull period. If your energy seems to flag at other times, take frequent five-minute breaks, or slowly pace the floor while you read a book or recite a lesson.

*Don't use caffeine after 4 P.M. or alcohol after 8 P.M.* The effects of caffeine can often result in insomnia and thus throw your sleep-wake schedule off.[36] Alcohol, although it has a reputation for making you drowsy, actually upsets your body's sleep pattern, first by reducing your REM sleep and then by triggering a "REM rebound," which can result in excessive dreaming and/or nightmares.[37]

*Reserve your bed for sleeping.* Eating, doing coursework, and even worrying in bed can scramble your body's contextual cues. If your bed becomes a multipurpose area, you may find it more difficult to fall asleep when the time comes.

*Exercise!* In addition to the benefits it provides to your heart, muscles, and self-esteem, exercise also enhances both the waking and sleeping phases of your circadian rhythms. Twenty minutes or more of vigorous aerobic exercise will boost your alertness in the daytime and improve the quality of your sleep at night. People who exercise regularly have been found to enjoy more deep sleep than people who don't.[38]

## Avoid Caffeine and Coffee

Caffeine will keep you awake at night. If you are one of the many people who are sensitive to caffeine, even one cup of coffee toward evening will prevent you from falling asleep easily. Laboratory studies show that from 200 to 500 milligrams of caffeine per day may produce headaches, nervousness, and gastrointestinal disturbances in some people. Coffee is not the only substance that contains caffeine. There's also caffeine in tea, some soft drinks, chocolate, and nonprescription drugs.

Coffee apparently may do more damage than simply keeping you awake. It has been linked to diabetes, heart attack, and cancer of the colon, urinary tract, and stomach. In addition, Harvard University researchers have found a statistical link between coffee and cancer of the pancreas, which is virtually incurable. After admitting that the pancreatic link needs further study, Dr. Brian MacMahon, the leader of the Harvard research team and a three-cupa-day man himself, nevertheless stopped drinking coffee.

---

[36]Erman and Mitler, *How to Get a Good Night's Sleep.*
[37]Coleman, *Wide Awake at 3:00 A.M.,* p. 124.
[38]Ibid., p. 146.

## Caffeine: A Poor Substitute for Sleep

Caffeine is the most widely used drug in the United States. Many people drink a cup of coffee or a can of caffeinated soda to produce the feeling of alertness normally associated with sound sleep. Ironically, though, caffeine can actually lead to sleepiness.

- Although morning coffee can mean morning alertness, afternoon coffee may cause afternoon blahs.
- Regular use of caffeine reduces its ability to stimulate alertness.
- Large quantities of caffeine can induce behavioral depression, which results in sleepiness and decreased performance.
- Caffeine burns calories (energy) as it stimulates insulin production, leading to a sudden drop in blood sugar and feeling of lethargy.
- Drinking only 250 mg. of caffeine can produce symptoms associated with clinical anxiety.

Sources: Richard M. Coleman, *Wide Awake at 3 a.m.* (New York: W.H. Freeman & Co., 1986); Susan Perry and Jim Dawson, *The Secret Our Body Clocks Reveal* (New York: Rawson Associates, 1988); Jere E. Yates, *Managing Stress* (New York: AMACOM, 1979).

## Develop Good Eating Habits

One aspect of a healthy physical routine is developing good eating habits. That means taking time out for meals and eating the right foods.

**Take Time Out for Meals**   Stress can diminish or deplete certain vitamin and mineral supplies. An erratic meal schedule can help to aggravate this problem. According to nutritionist Jane Brody:

> Millions of Americans have fallen into a pattern of too-late-for-breakfast, grab-something-for-lunch, eat-a-big dinner, and nibble-nonstop-until-bed-time. They starve their bodies when they most need fuel and stuff them when

they'll be doing nothing more strenuous than flipping the TV dial or pages of a book. When you think about it, the pattern makes no biological sense.[39]

The simplest way to put some sense back into your eating routine is by beginning each day with breakfast. Breakfast stokes your body's furnace so you have energy to burn for the rest of the day. Lunch and dinner simply throw a few coals on the fire; breakfast gets that fire burning.

Meals not only provide needed nutrients; they also supply you with a necessary break from the stresses of school or work. Here are some stress-relieving suggestions for mealtime:

*Don't work as you eat.* Time will have been wasted, and you won't have gained the break you deserved when you sat down to eat. As a result, you'll probably feel more stressed than you were before you ate.

*Eat quickly, but don't rush.* There's a difference. If you have a lot of work to do, you won't have time to while away the afternoon with a leisurely lunch. But if you keep one eye on your sandwich and the other on the clock as you eat, you'll increase your chances of getting indigestion and stress without significantly speeding up your meal.

**Eat the Right Foods** Dieting advice varies widely, from the prudent to the downright absurd. Nevertheless, there are some basic principles most nutritionists agree on. A recent report from the U.S. Department of Health and Human Services confirmed what nutritionists have long suspected: Americans eat too much protein and fat and not enough carbohydrates. You can improve your diet by eating proteins sparingly but strategically, reducing your intake of fats and simple sugars, and increasing your intake of complex carbohydrates.

***Eat proteins sparingly but strategically.*** Although few nutritionists would dispute the necessity of protein as part of a healthy diet, the importance of protein has been blown out of proportion, while its shortcomings have been downplayed. Protein plays an integral role in your body's upkeep. It builds, maintains, and repairs muscle tissue. Protein also appears to have at least one psychological benefit: alertness. Among the amino acids that make up many proteins is *tyrosine,* which activates two hormones that nutritionist Dr. Judith Wurtman refers to as "alertness chemicals." When the brain produces these chemicals, there is "a tendency to think more quickly, react more rapidly to stimuli, and feel more attentive, motivated, and mentally energetic."[40]

---

[39]Jane E. Brody, *Jane Brody's Good Food Book* (New York: Norton, 1985), p. 187.
[40]Judith I. Wurtman, *Managing Your Mind & Mood Through Food* (New York: Harper & Row, 1986), p. 13.

Because protein isn't stored in the body (as sugar and fat are), you need to eat it every day. The National Research Council asserts that a diet that derives 8 percent of its total calories from protein should be adequate for 98 percent of the population. In a similar study, the Food and Nutrition Board came up with a figure of 6 percent. Yet the average American gets a whopping 17 percent of his or her calories from protein.

What happens to all that excess protein? It is stored as fat and sugar and used as an energy reserve. Unfortunately, the chemical process of turning protein into energy yields by-products that must be absorbed by the liver and kidneys and then excreted as waste. The task of absorbing those protein by-products puts a strain on the organs. And when the waste is excreted, needed minerals such as calcium, magnesium, and potassium are eliminated as well. All three of these minerals influence your ability to handle stress.

According to Dr. Michael Lesser in *Nutrition and Vitamin Therapy*, "Calcium shortage may result in a grouchy, irritable, tense disposition."[41] Even a moderate calcium deficiency can prompt symptoms that resemble an anxiety attack. Magnesium, considered a natural sedative by some researchers, was found to be deficient in subjects who exhibited aggressive behavior. Finally, potassium has long been known to moderate the body's level of sodium, which can trigger hypertension if not kept in check.

*Reduce your intake of fats and simple sugars.*   The primary nutritional purpose of fat is to store energy. But you need very little fat to meet your body's requirement for it. Researchers from the National Institutes of Health recommend that we limit fat to roughly 25 percent of our daily calories. Because a gram of fat contains more than twice the calories that a gram of protein or carbohydrates does, meeting or even exceeding your daily requirement for fats is alarmingly easy. Eat a plate of macaroni and cheese, a dinner roll with butter, and a slice of pecan pie for dessert, and you've satisfied your body's fat requirement for the entire day!

Excess fat is even more dangerous than excess protein. Not only does consumption of too much fat lead to obesity, which places undue stress on the body's ability to function properly; it also results in a marked increase in blood cholesterol, which has been linked to a number of life-threatening cardiovascular diseases.

According to one nutritionist, simple carbohydrates such as white flour, refined sugar, and alcohol constitute more than 20 percent of the calories in a typical American diet. What nutritional benefit is derived from these caloric treats? None. With most of their fiber and nutrients removed in processing, these foods provide virtually empty calories—that is, short-lived

---

[41]Quoted in Padus, *The Complete Guide to Your Emotions & Your Health*, p. 11

## Fat: Where to Find It

A surprising number of common foods derive over 50 percent of their calories from fat. Unfortunately, most of these foods do little to meet the body's need for carbohydrates.

| Food | Calories from Fat | Calories from Protein | Calories from Carbohydrates | Total Calories |
|---|---|---|---|---|
| Vegetable oil | 100% | 0% | 0% | 122 |
| Butter (1 T) | 100 | 0 | 0 | 108 |
| Margarine (1 T) | 100 | 0 | 0 | 108 |
| Mayonnaise | 98 | 1 | 1 | 101 |
| Bacon/fried crisp (1 strip) | 92 | 8 | 0 | 49 |
| Cream cheese (1 oz.) | 89 | 3 | 8 | 101 |
| Bologna (1 slice) | 86 | 14 | 0 | 88 |
| Frankfuter (beef) | 83 | 14 | 3 | 145 |
| Peanut butter (1 T) | 75 | 12.5 | 12.5 | 96 |
| Cheddar cheese (1 oz.) | 72 | 25 | 3 | 112 |
| Egg, boiled (1 med.) | 69 | 31 | 0 | 78 |
| Ricotta cheese (1/2 c.) | 67 | 7 | 26 | 216 |
| Pork chop (3.5 oz.) | 66 | 34 | 0 | 354 |
| Tuna in oil (4 oz.) | 66 | 34 | 0 | 285 |
| Potato chips (3.5 oz.) | 62 | 3 | 35 | 580 |
| Hamburger (1 patty) | 61 | 39 | 0 | 224 |
| Roast chicken with skin intact (3.5 oz.) | 56 | 44 | 0 | 243 |
| Broiled tenderloin steak | 54 | 46 | 0 | 149 |
| Bass, striped, broiled (3.5 oz.) | 51 | 35 | 14 | 229 |

Source: Adapted from *The Mount Sinai School of Medicine Complete Book of Nutrition*, Victor Herbert and Genell J. Subak-Sharpe, eds. (New York: St. Martin's Press, 1990), pp. 64-65.

energy with no long-term food value. In addition, they can take your blood sugar on a roller-coaster ride, leaving you up one minute and down the next. Finally, because simple carbohydrates often cause your blood sugar level to dip so dramatically, eating them can sometimes evolve into an addiction as you constantly seek to boost your energy level as quickly as you can.

*Increase your intake of complex carbohydrates.*    Complex carbohydrates, which we commonly call *starches*, are chains of sugars. Rice, whole grains, beans, and pasta are all examples of complex carbohydrates. Unlike simple carbohydrates, complex carbohydrates are valuable sources of nutrients and fiber. And because they occur in chains, complex carbohydrates take longer to digest, thus releasing their energy gradually instead of all at once.

## SAFEGUARDING YOUR HEALTH

Before you came to college, you had already formed many habits. Now that you are a college student, you are likely to drop some, modify others, and add a few new ones. Take a minute to think about the consequences of the habits that affect your health. If you believe they're good for the long pull, keep them. If not, consider changing them.

In a study of seven important health habits performed by the Human Population Laboratory of Alameda County, California, 6,928 adults were chosen as a cross section of the general population. The habits studied and the conclusions drawn from the research were these:

| *Habit* | *Conclusion* |
|---|---|
| **1.** Smoking | Never smoke. |
| **2.** Exercise | Engage in some physical activity daily. |
| **3.** Alcohol | Use alcohol very moderately or not at all. |
| **4.** Sleep | Get from seven to eight hours of sleep regularly. |
| **5.** Weight | Maintain the proper weight. |
| **6.** Breakfast | Always eat a balanced breakfast. |
| **7.** Snacking | Do not eat between meals. |

The results of the study were startling. Women who followed six or seven of these conclusions lived more than *seven years longer* than women who followed from none to three. Men who followed six or seven of these conclusions lived more than *eleven years longer* than men who followed from none to three.

Those seven conclusions are so easy to follow that you might wonder who would value life so little as not to follow them. You might think that no person would trade a year of life for any amount of money; yet, for no money at all, many people may be shortening their lives by getting too little sleep, smoking, and drinking too many alcoholic beverages.

## Don't Smoke

When asked how long it takes for a cigarette to harm you, one California doctor answered, "About three seconds." In just three seconds, your heart begins to pound an extra fifteen beats per minute, raising your blood pressure about twenty points. And that's just the short-term effect of smoking. The long-term effects on your lungs, heart, mouth and throat, and even your skin are well known and documented. Find out these facts before you consider taking up smoking, and take up something else instead (hiking, tennis, and crafts all offer the opportunity for companionship and give you something to do with your hands).

If you already smoke, for your health's sake quit. Get help on the first step toward quitting by visiting the campus health center and asking about cessation programs, or find the trainer at the gym and ask for help and advice. If you want to work with someone who knows you already, talk to your doctor about quitting. Recognizing why you smoke is often the first and most important part of a quit-smoking program. Many people have quit successfully; you can, too. Remember that every nonsmoking day adds to the length and quality of your life.

## Get Some Exercise

According to respected American cardiologist Dr. Paul Dudley White, "Vigorous . . . exercise is the best antidote for nervous and emotional stress that we possess."[42] In study after study, experts are corroborating that exercise decreases stress and anxiety. Many other researchers report that regular exercise raises self-esteem and well-being and decreases depression. A study of forty-eight students who had been suffering from test anxiety found that their anxiety was reduced after meditative relaxation and exercise.[43] In another study, both prisoners and prison guards took part in a carefully

---

[42]Robert K. Cooper, *Health and Fitness Excellence* (Boston: Houghton Mifflin, 1989), p. 100.
[43]Kenneth H. Cooper, *The Aerobics Program for Total Well-Being* (New York: Bantam Books, 1982), p. 186.

monitored exercise program. After a regimen of aerobic exercise, participants on both sides of the law found that they were able to sleep better, that their sense of well-being and self-esteem often improved, and that they experienced less tension and depression.[44]

The relationship between exercise and depression, one of the most damaging emotional outgrowths of prolonged stress, led psychologist William Morgan, recent president of the American Psychological Association's Division of Exercise and Sport Psychology, to suggest "that running should be viewed as a wonder drug, analogous to penicillin, morphine and the tricyclics [drugs used to treat depression]. It has a profound potential in preventing mental and physical disease and in rehabilitation after various diseases have occurred."[45] And the most effective exercise is that done regularly and aerobically.

**Exercise Regularly**   You don't have to be an Olympic athlete to reap the benefits of exercise. Exercising three or more times per week is usually enough to improve your overall conditioning, although many students who follow an exercise routine look forward to their time away from their desks and exercise between five and seven times per week. Aside from its well-documented benefits, one of the reasons that exercise is so effective in reducing stress is a simple one. Like eating, sleeping, or any other type of recreation, it provides a welcome break from your studying and recharges your mental and physical batteries.

**Exercise Aerobically**   Although all exercise can provide *relief* from stress, only aerobic exercise can actually *prevent* the harmful effects of negative stress. The word *aerobic* means "relating to oxygen." Aerobic exercise is any activity that causes a steady, prolonged increase in your breathing and heart rate. A quick sprint across a football field or a dash from home plate to first base is certainly exercise, but it isn't aerobic exercise. You are inhaling lots of oxygen and speeding up your heart, but you are doing so only for a few seconds, probably not at a steady rate, and definitely not for a prolonged period of time. If, however, you swim twenty-five laps or so, pedal your bike steadily for several miles, or take a brisk thirty-minute walk, in each case you are getting aerobic exercise.

Perhaps the greatest benefit of aerobic exercise is that it lowers your heart rate. Once your heart muscle has been strengthened through exercise, it acts more efficiently, beating fewer times to circulate the same amount of blood. And if anxiety should strike, the increase in the heart rate of an

---

[44]Ibid.
[45]Keith W. Johnsgård, "Peace of Mind" *Runner's World* 25, no. 4 (April 1990): 81.

aerobically fit person is not as drastic as it is in someone who gets little or no aerobic exercise. Furthermore, if your heart rate remains comparatively low when subjected to stress, you are less likely to overreact emotionally. The result not only discourages overreaction to stress but also may save your life. A person in poor health who is subjected to unexpected stress can die from the sudden strain the excitement puts on his or her heart.[46]

Exercise provides a perfect example of good stress. It works as a stimulant to release the hormone *norepinephrine,* which promotes enhanced awareness, and *endorphins,* morphinelike hormones that provide the euphoric feeling commonly referred to as "runner's high." Exercise leaves you feeling simultaneously alert and relaxed, a nearly ideal state for efficient, prolonged, and stress-free study. According to Dr. Kenneth Cooper, if you exercise at the end of the day when stress levels are traditionally highest, "you can continue to work or play much later into the evening than might be possible otherwise."[47]

## Be Sensible About Your Relationships

It's not the purpose of this book to tell you everything you should know about protecting yourself from sexually transmitted diseases. It's worth saying, however, that such information—accurate and reliable—is essential to your health and well-being, both in college and after. Make sure you take the opportunity offered by the campus health center to learn what you need to know; it's readily available. Once you have good information, use it wisely.

## REDUCING STRESSORS

The number of stressors you encounter can be reduced by sidestepping unnecessary sources of stress and by avoiding procrastination.

## Avoid Needless Sources of Stress

Some stressful elements in life must be faced head-on. But others can be avoided; here are some suggestions for doing so:

---

[46]Cooper, *The Aerobics Program for Total Well-Being,* p. 189.
[47]Ibid., p. 191.

*Wake up a half-hour earlier.*   If you find yourself skipping breakfast or taking your last bite just as you race out the door, then you're starting your day on a stressful note. Although getting an adequate amount of sleep is crucial, waking up a half-hour earlier than usual won't significantly affect your sleeping habits but can do wonders to ease the pace of your morning preparations.

*Allow yourself plenty of travel time.*   High-strung travelers are easily aggravated by slow drivers or long traffic lights. But slow drivers and long lights are facts of every driver's life. Factor them into your travel time.

*Never wait empty-handed.*   The stress that comes from standing in line or waiting in traffic stems from boredom and from irritation about wasting time. Both problems have the same easy solution: Have a book to read or some notes to review ready for the next time you're kept waiting, and you'll find that the time will fly by. Simply listening to the radio while waiting may be relaxing for some, but in general it won't provide the same sense of accomplishment.

*Keep a note pad handy.*   Needless stress and aggravation can accumulate if you spend your time trying not to forget what tasks you want to accomplish. Jot down reminders, and you'll free up your mind so that what you need to remember will no longer function as a stressor.

*Eat dinner early.*   If you eat at a college dining hall, it's usually wise to get there early. The trivial but real stress that comes from waiting in line, searching for a seat, or racing to get a second helping before the kitchen closes can be eliminated if you show up soon after the dining hall opens. Whether you eat your meals at home or at school, an early dinner gives you more time before bed to be productive.

*Don't take your work to bed with you.*   Your bed is for relaxation. Don't mix your mind's signals by turning your bed into an auxiliary workspace. If you establish a clear boundary between where you work and where you sleep, your work will become more productive, and your sleep will be more restful. And both activities will tend to improve your approach to life's stressors.

## Eliminate Procrastination

"Nothing [is] so fatiguing as the eternal hanging on of an uncompleted task." These words by William James, distinguished American psychologist, strike at the hearts of us all. Every one of us has had many bouts with procrastination. The best ways to avoid future bouts is to learn why people procrastinate and what you can do to prevent procrastination.

**Learn Why You Procrastinate**   There's no single explanation for why people procrastinate. Nevertheless, many of the stressors already discussed in this chapter can trigger procrastination. Here's a list of the major sources:

*Fear of failure.*   Many students hesitate to even begin a task because they're afraid they won't be able to successfully complete it. Have some faith in yourself. Think back to past successes, and realize that if you've achieved success before, you can achieve it again. If you've failed in similar situations in the past, think of times when you've succeeded in other areas, and apply the confidence you gained then to the present.

*Fear of success.*   Some students put tasks off because they are afraid of succeeding. A person might be afraid of success for at least two reasons. First, successful people are a minority. There is a kind of loneliness in success. Some students unconsciously procrastinate because they want to remain part of the group. They don't want to be resented by people who aren't as successful. Second, success brings on responsibility and choices. When a person succeeds, doors suddenly open. That should be good news, but some students view these opportunities as threats and burdens instead of challenges and choices.

*Lack of time.*   If you used all the time you've been spending worrying about the time you don't have, you'd be well on your way to completing the task you've been putting off. This is a problem of control. Realize that how you budget your time is up to you. If you feel in control, you'll find it easier to complete the jobs that need to be done.

*Shortage of energy.*   Claiming a lack of energy can hide the real reason for not doing something. If you truly don't have the energy, sleep, food, and exercise may be the root of your problem. Make sure you're getting enough regularly scheduled sleep, that you're eating a balanced diet, and that you're promoting good health and alertness through exercise. If you still feel tired, then some other cause is responsible. It may be a medical problem, in which case you should make a point to see a doctor. Or it may be a psychological problem masquerading as fatigue. In either case, find the cause and take care of it—right away!

*Poor organization.*   Perhaps you begin each day determined to get started on that task you've been putting off. But when nighttime comes, you find that despite your best intentions, you didn't get around to it. If that's your trouble, then the cause may be a lack of priorities and/or poor organization. If you organize what you plan to do each day into a schedule and list your activities in order of priority, then you should be able to accomplish those important tasks.

William James would agree, I'm sure, that not getting started on a report the day the assignment is made is a prime example of that daily nagging thought, "I gotta get started on that report." The "Peanuts" cartoon graphically illustrates this type of procrastination.

**Devise Ways to Prevent Procrastination**   Although the roots of procrastination are varied, the methods that follow for preventing procrastination should work regardless of the cause.

**Source: PEANUTS reprinted by permission of United Features Syndicate, Inc.**

*Make your plans a part of the public record.*   When you have a job that has to be completed or a goal that you want to reach, resist keeping your objective as a loggy, easy-to ignore idea in your head. Write down your plan. Once you've preserved it on paper, the job will be harder to ignore. Or announce your intentions to close friends or family members. For example, "I plan to finish the bibliography for my research paper this weekend." Once you've made your intentions official, you're less likely to put them off. Procrastinators commonly fall into the habit of deceiving themselves, but they are less likely to deceive the people around them.

*Step back and check your progress from time to time.*   One way many people procrastinate is by getting entangled in the details of their work. If you plan on finishing an entire chapter assignment in a single evening but then find yourself spending most of your time reading, rereading, and fine-tuning your notes for a single section, you may not be looking for increased understanding. You may simply have found a way to procrastinate. If, however, you periodically step back and measure your progress, you'll realize that you've gotten bogged down, and you'll be able to pick up your pace so you can reach your goal in the allotted time.

*Let your momentum work for you.* If you've successfully completed a task you were anxious to finish, let your momentum carry over to an activity that you aren't as enthused about. This extra energy can help you get started on the dreaded task, and once you've begun (the hardest part), completion will become much easier.

*Use the five-minute plan.* William J. Knaus, author of *Do It Now: How to Stop Procrastinating,* recommends what he calls the "five-minute plan."[48] Tackle a long-neglected task by agreeing to work on it for only five minutes. When the five minutes are up, decide whether you want to keep going. You usually will. The hardest part of almost any job is simply getting started. The five-minute plan takes the sting out of that painful first step.

*Be specific.* A task is almost always more intimidating when it looms large and undefined. For most students, the research paper is a classic example of this nebulous source of anxiety. Instead of constantly telling yourself, "I've got to start writing that research paper," zero in on a specific aspect of your paper, such as choosing the topic or compiling a working bibliography. Suddenly your goal becomes more concrete, more doable, and thus much easier to complete. Or as James R. Sherman, author of *Stop Procrastinating* puts it. "A job well-defined is a job half done."[49]

*Verbalize your excuses.* You may think you've got perfectly good reasons for putting off what needs to be done. If you let your excuses see the light of day by writing them out or explaining them to a friend, you'll often find that your reasoning isn't nearly as logical as you'd thought.

*Visualize success or completion.* Take a moment to imagine yourself accomplishing a task, passing a test, or achieving a goal. Through visualizing, you chart a course in your mind's eye. That course gives you a tangible game plan. The positive outcome you've imagined provides an incentive to follow that course until you reach the point of completion.

---

[48]William J. Knaus, *Do It Now: How to Stop Proctrastinating,* quoted in Padus, p. 393.
[49]James R. Sherman, *Stop Proctrastinating* (Los Altos, Calif.: Crisp Publications, 1989), p. 38.

## SUMMARY

**What can you do to relax?**

Try the relaxation techniques suggested in this chapter—deep breathing and progressive muscle relaxation—or others you're familiar with.

**How can you improve your self-esteem?**

Changing the script of your internal dialogue from words of discouragement to words of encouragement and building on your past successes should do a lot to boost your sense of your own value.

**How do you take control of your life?**

Taking control of your life involves shifting your attitude so that you are able to view threats as challenges and obligations as choices. It also means acknowledging and accepting those situations you are unable to control.

**How can regular mealtimes discourage stress?**

Regular mealtimes can alleviate some of the effects of stress by providing you with a consistent rest from your work and by replenishing some of the energy and nutrients that stress may have consumed.

**How does your diet affect your response to stress?**

Adequate nutrition can make you more resistant to stress, whereas poor nutrition can make you less stress resistant and can actually increase your susceptibility to stress.

**How can exercise help reduce stress?**

Regular exercise provides a needed rest from your work and improves the quality of your sleep and your general attitude.

**What is the benefit of aerobic exercise?**

Aerobic exercise builds up your heart muscle. (Most steady, sustained exercise, such as distance running, swimming, and brisk walking, is aerobic.) When you exercise aerobically, you increase your heart rate and your intake of oxygen. Your heart responds by getting stronger and working more efficiently.

**How can you reduce the number of stressors you face?**

You can minimize stressors by avoiding needless sources of stress and by eliminating the damaging habit of procrastination.

**What can you do to avoid needless sources of stress?**

You can deflect or avoid many potentially damaging sources of stress by getting into the habit of developing backup plans and by learning to use time more efficiently. You can also identify the causes of procrastination and then find ways to prevent them.

## HAVE YOU MISSED SOMETHING?

*Sentence completion.* Complete the following sentences with one of the three words listed below each sentence.

1. The body's response to demands that are made on it is known as

   _____ .

   stress     tension     deviation

2. The desire to attain perfection in all that you do usually leads to

   _____ .

   failure     success     cooperation

*Matching.* In each blank space in the left column, write the letter preceding the phrase in the right column that matches the left item best.

| | | |
|---|---|---|
| _____ **1.** Jacobson | a. | Has silent impact on self-esteem |
| _____ **2.** Panting | b. | Developed progressive muscle relaxation |
| _____ **3.** Aerobic | c. | Should be eaten sparingly but strategically |
| _____ **4.** Proteins | d. | Dip in energy, usually in midafternoon |
| _____ **5.** Self-talk | e. | Means "relating to air" |
| _____ **6.** Circadian trough | f. | Has been shown to cause feelings of panic |

*True-false.* Write *T* beside the *true* statements and *F* beside the *false* statements.

_____ **1.** Your body undergoes stress when you walk at a brisk pace.

_____ **2.** Experts don't all agree on how much sleep you require.

_____ **3.** Fear of success is one possible cause of procrastination.

_____ **4.** It is difficult to meet your daily nutritional requirement for fat.

_____ **5.** "Sleeping in" should eliminate the effects of sleep deprivation.

_____ **6.** Your attitude can have a powerful effect on your sense of control.

*Multiple choice.* Choose the word or phrase that completes the following sentence most accurately, and circle the letter that precedes it.

**1.** Relaxed breaths usually originate from the

   a. chest.
   b. waist.
   c. abdomen.
   d. neck.

**2.** Complex carbohydrates are chains of

   a. fats.
   b. starches.
   c. proteins.
   d. sugars.

**3.** One of the greatest benefits of aerobic exercise is that it

   a. takes only ten minutes to do.
   b. lowers your heart rate.
   c. burns only fats, not carbohydrates.
   d. builds up your arm muscles.

**4.** Common aerobic exercises include

   a. swimming.
   b. running.
   c. bicycling.
   d. all of the above.

**5.** Logan found that a group of survivors of extreme stress all

   a. believed in God.
   b. had a strong sense of control.
   c. avoided fats and sugars.
   d. had lowered heart rates.

**6.** Your learning may be impaired if you try to study right after

   a. exercise.
   b. a large meal.
   c. a brief nap.
   d. a final exam.

**7.** Taking control involves turning

   a. proteins into carbohydrates.
   b. threats into challenges.
   c. choices into obligations.
   d. food into calories.

*Short answer.* Supply a brief answer for each of the following items.

\_\_\_\_\_ **1.** Explain the "two-sided potential of stress."

\_\_\_\_\_ **2.** What is the James-Lange theory?

\_\_\_\_\_ **3.** What makes an exercise aerobic?

## VOCABULARY BUILDING

DIRECTIONS: Make a light check mark (√) alongside one of the three words (choices) that most nearly expresses the meaning of the italicized word in the phrases that are in the left-hand column. (Answers are given on p. 434.)

| | | **1** | **2** | **3** |
|---|---|---|---|---|
| 1. | James-Lange theory *vindicated* | attacked | cleared | disproved |
| 2. | to transform *adversity* | misfortune | work | pleasure |
| 3. | *exhilaration* of exercising | exhaustion | futility | invigoration |
| 4. | a *regimen* of exercise | lack | system | excess |
| 5. | *euphoric* feeling | pessimistic | neutral | happy |
| 6. | cigar *connoisseurs* | smokers | judges | merchants |
| 7. | to *affluent* baby boomers | retired | mobile | wealthy |
| 8. | his political *pragmatism* | realism | judgment | experience |
| 9. | *contemptuous* of idle thinking | approving | scornful | encouraging |
| 10. | last week's *tumultuous* trading | furious | misguided | irrational |
| 11. | to restore the *equilibrium* | balance | losses | assets |
| 12. | Morgan's *hubris* is a memory | humanity | humbleness | arrogance |
| 13. | the *effervescent* economy | bubbly | heavy | lagging |
| 14. | the odds are not *auspicious* | negative | favorable | overwhelming |
| 15. | the *temerity* to do so | boldness | skill | experience |

|     |                              | **1**        | **2**          | **3**       |
| --- | ---------------------------- | ------------ | -------------- | ----------- |
| 16. | one *serendipitous* discovery | tremendous   | valuable       | chance      |
| 17. | usually *innocuous*          | harmless     | unseen         | mild        |
| 18. | selling was *exacerbated*    | controlled   | worsened       | balanced    |
| 19. | economy slowed *perceptibly* | gently       | tremendously   | visibly     |
| 20. | entirely too *sanguine*      | troublesome  | optimistic     | pessimistic |
| 21. | such *jocund* company        | nimble       | departing      | merry       |
| 22. | for *transient* sorrows      | forgotten    | passing        | anticipated |
| 23. | my *sylvan* home             | country      | village        | woodland    |
| 24. | sound of *vernal* showers    | spring       | summer         | autumn      |
| 25. | strains of *martial* music   | wedding      | military       | symphonic   |

# 4

# Concentrating and Focusing

*Consider the postage stamp. It secures success through its*
*ability to stick to one thing until it gets there.*

—JOSH BILLINGS (1818–85), pen name of
Henry Wheeler Shaw, American humorist

Everyone—from astronauts to athletes, from merchants to musicians—appreciates the value of concentration. Yet few of us know how to attain and then sustain it. Although concentration does not appear at the snap of the fingers, there are ways you can improve the conditions for concentration. To aid you in learning the art of concentration, this chapter deals with

- Reducing external distractions
- Finding a place to study
- Overcoming internal distractions
- Adopting strategies for concentration
- Coping with fatigue

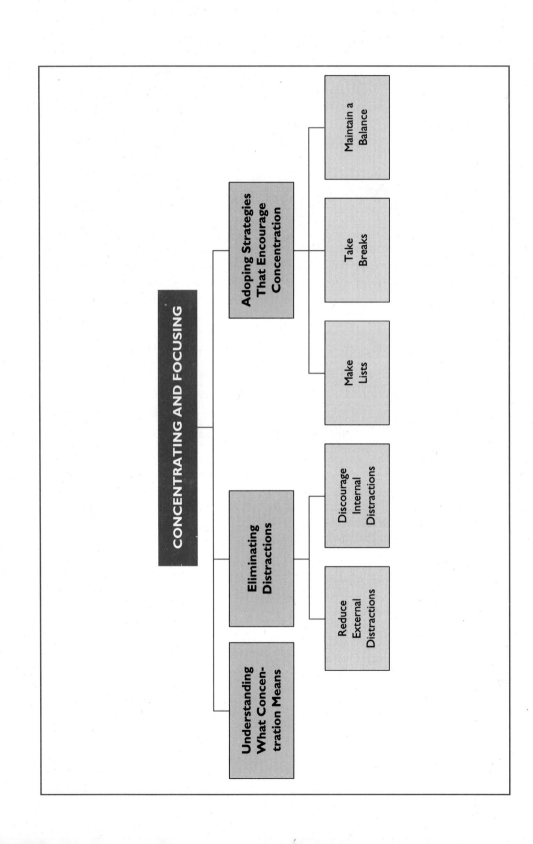

Concentration is focused thinking. During our waking hours we are, with varying degrees of intensity, thinking all the time. We never run out of things to think and worry about. Thoughts and ideas bang, rattle, and knock on the door of our consciousness trying to gain entry.

## UNDERSTANDING WHAT CONCENTRATION MEANS

Watch a good bowler as she takes her position and directs all her thoughts on knocking down the pins at the end of the alley. Watch a quarterback as he focuses entirely on getting a pass to an open receiver, even while linebackers rush in on him from several directions. That's concentration!

Imagine becoming so absorbed in your textbook that you find yourself "talking" to the author: "That's not proof enough," or "Other writers explain it differently," or "I never thought about the problem that way before." Imagine studying your notes so intently that when you finally look up, you see that it's been two hours since you last checked the clock. That's concentration!

Just as light waves can be focused into a single powerful beam—a laser—concentration can focus the power of your thoughts, enabling you to think with greater precision and penetrate difficult ideas. But powerful as it can be, concentration has an elusive quality. In fact, concentration comes only when you don't think about it. Ironically, if you were thinking deeply about a subject and suddenly realized that you were concentrating, at that moment you would have broken your concentration. Such prolonged, undivided attention can be difficult to achieve. After all, in normal circumstances there are dozens of things competing for your attention.

Figure 4.1 provides a vivid illustration of the natural tendency to divide attention. As you gaze at this picture, you'll probably discover that your visual focus is shifting every few seconds so that you first see a goblet, then two profiles, and then the goblet again. Once you're aware of both images, it is difficult for your eyes to focus on one and ignore the other. Similarly, it is hard for your mind to focus on one idea at a time. People who *can* focus exclusively on the task before them have a much better chance of completing that task more quickly and accurately than those who divide their attention even when they don't mean to do so.

Because you can't strive for concentration directly, you must instead try to improve the conditions that promote concentration. That involves eliminating distractions and adopting strategies to enhance concentration.

**FIGURE 4.1  A Goblet or Two Profiles?**

## ELIMINATING DISTRACTIONS

Trouble in concentrating may come from external distractions, such as sights or sounds that compete for your attention, or from internal distractions, such as worries or daydreams. Once recognized, these obstacles to concentration can be overcome.

## Reduce External Distractions

Anything that stimulates your senses and in the process disrupts your concentration can be considered an external distraction. Study halls and living quarters are overflowing with such distractions, everything from banging doors to baking bread. To work in a way that is compatible with concentration, you need the proper environment as well as the right equipment.

**Select the Right Environment**  Your study environment should be used exclusively for study. In addition, it should be quiet and well lighted. You can take your work to a place that is already designed for study, or you can create your own study environment.

*Find a workshop.*  You'd be hard pressed to find an environment more suitable for high-quality concentration than a library. It offers a minimum of nonacademic distractions, a quiet atmosphere (usually as a matter of policy), and sufficient lighting. Get in the habit right away, on the first day of class, of studying at the library. Even the walk to the library can be used productively as a review session or a refreshing break.

Whether you choose to work in the library or somewhere else, make sure your study area is reserved only for studying. Psychologists emphasize that a conditioning effect is created between the desk and you: If you nap or daydream a lot while sitting at the desk, then the desk can act as a cue for napping or daydreaming. By the same token, if you read or work in bed, you make it difficult to work energetically and to fall asleep easily. To avoid this negative conditioning, use your desk only for studying. When you feel the urge to nap or daydream, leave your desk to nap or daydream elsewhere.

Your study area should be your workshop, a place where you feel secure and comfortable. You can ensure that you have the proper environment for study and concentration if you minimize visual distractions, avoid or eliminate distracting noises, refrain from playing music, control the impulse to register distractions, and provide the area with plenty of light.

*Minimize visual distractions.* A sheet of notes or a page from a textbook can seem dull compared with a glimpse of a softball game being played on a nearby diamond or a view of gently falling snow. To improve your chances of concentration, avoid competition for your eyes' attention. Study by a window so you can take advantage of the natural light, but keep your head turned away from the potentially distracting view.

Of course, not all visual distractions lie on the other side of a window pane. If your study area contains photographs you're liable to look at, gadgets you're likely to fiddle with, or books you'll be tempted to pick up and read, remove them until you have completed your work.

*Eliminate noise.* If you need a quiet spot for efficient study, do your utmost to find one. Noise can be one of the most serious obstacles to effective study. Nothing is more wasteful than going over the same paragraph again and again because there is too much noise for you to absorb what you are reading. If the library is the right place for you, then make an effort to study there whenever you can. If you study at home, achieving quiet can sometimes be as simple as closing a door or inserting ear plugs.

*Tune down the loud music.* When studying, loud music, especially vocal music, can break your concentration. To keep your concentration from bouncing between the music and your books, you expend energy that could be put to better use. However, some students can tolerate music better than others. If you find music nonintrusive, then soft instrumental music could form a pleasing background, and such a background can actually muffle some of the external, intermittent noises.

*Try the spider technique.* A vibrating tuning fork held close to a spider's web sets up vibrations in the web. After the spider makes a few hurried investigations and finds no fly in the web, it learns to ignore the vibrations.

The next time you are studying in the library and the door opens, don't look up. Controlling your impulse to look up will disturb your concentration the first few times. But very soon, like the spider, you'll learn to ignore these external disturbances.

**Use the Right Equipment**   Because proper lighting is an important component of your study environment, the right light should head the list of the equipment you need to promote concentration and reduce external distractions.

*Find the right light.*   Whether it comes from conventional light bulbs, fluorescent tubes, or the new compact fluorescent bulbs, the best light for study is bright, even, and steady (remember B, E, and ST).

*Bright.*   The emission of light is measured in lumens. For studying, you need at least 2,500 lumens. Two standard 100-watt bulbs (1,750 lumens each) will meet that requirement. So will a double-tube fluorescent lamp; it provides the same amount of light as two 100-watt incandescent bulbs and can last up to one hundred times longer!

*Even.*   Shadows in your work area or "hot spots" caused by glare will tire out your eyes and make concentration difficult. Get rid of glare by shielding your lamp with a shade and by using a light-colored, nonglossy blotter on your desk. Eliminate shadows by using two lamps, fluorescent light, or diffuse light.

*STeady.*   A constant flicker will undermine concentration. If you use fluorescent light, try a double- or triple-tube lamp. These multitubed fixtures eliminate the natural strobe of fluorescent light. If you are using conventional (incandescent) light, make sure the bulb is screwed in properly.

Good lighting makes for good studying. By contrast, poor lighting makes for eyestrain, general tension, headaches, and sleepiness—irritations that interfere with concentration. If you study under good light but your eyes still bother you, have them examined by an ophthalmologist or optometrist. Clear and comfortable vision is essential to good studying.

*Use a pencil to catalyze concentration.*   A technique that has never failed any student over the past many years is the simple, humble *pencil technique.* The technique is this: *Whenever you are working to learn, study with a pencil in hand. And use it!* For example, if you are reading a textbook chapter, stop after several paragraphs and very briefly, in your own words, write down the key points made by the author. If, after reading several paragraphs, you find no words come to you, then you have no recourse but to go back and read the passage again. This time, read with determination and concentration, to make sure that you learn the key points. The secret: Activity promotes and almost ensures concentration. The pencil provides the activity!

*Find a comfortable seat.*   More ink and more words have been wasted extolling the virtues of a straight-backed, hard-seated hickory chair than on any other single piece of study equipment. Forget it: Use a comfortable, well cushioned chair. Keeping awake or falling asleep does not depend on your chair, rather, it depends primarily on the method of study, on your attitude and self-discipline, the light, and the room temperature. A hard, straight-backed chair can't take the place of these basic requirements.

*Use a bookstand.*   An extremely practical piece of equipment is a bookstand. I don't mean a bookshelf or bookends; I mean a stand that is placed on your desk to hold the book in a tilted position with the pages held down so that they do not flip over. It can work for you in many ways: First, and very important, it can give you a feeling of readiness to study—a feeling of being a scholar in the traditional sense. This alone is worth many times the price of a stand. Second, the stand provides physical freedom. It eliminates the strain of continually holding the book open, pressing down on two sides to keep the pages from flipping over, tilting the book to avoid the glare, and trying to find something heavy enough to hold the book open so you can free your hands to make notes. It permits you to sit back with arms folded, to contemplate and reflect on the meaning of what you are reading.

*Keep other equipment nearby.*   Other basic equipment that can help you study without interruption includes an up-to-date dictionary, a calculator, a clock, a calendar, paper, notebooks, paper clips, tape, rubber bands, pencils, pens, erasers, and note cards. If you make it a habit to keep your desk well stocked, you won't derail your concentration with unplanned emergency trips to obtain necessities.

## Discourage Internal Distractions

Internal distractions are distractions that *you* create: daydreams, personal problems, anxiety, indecision, forgetfulness, and unrealistic goals. These distractions are as disruptive as the sights, sounds, and smells that make up the external variety, even though in this case the only one who is aware of them is you. Because internal distractions come from within, you have the power to eliminate or at least control them.

**Use a Concentration Scoresheet**   Keep a sheet of paper handy by your book. Then whenever you catch your mind wandering, keep score by putting a check mark on the sheet. The mere act of doing this reminds you to get back to work. Students report that when they first tried this system, they accumulated as many as twenty check marks per textbook page, but after one or two weeks, they were down to one or two check marks per page.

The concentration scoresheet encourages self-observation. Taking note of your breaks in concentration—when they happen, how often they occur, and what triggers them—will make you realize just how intrusive the lapses are and will enable you to gradually eliminate them.

**Put Stray Thoughts on a Worry Pad**   Although pleasant plans and diverting daydreams are major sources of internal distraction, nagging worries and obligations can also take your mind off your work. The concentration scoresheet will alert you to these breaks in your attention, but it won't address the problems that prompted the distraction. To prevent the same worries from interfering with your concentration again and again, you must address them. A worry pad provides an excellent short-term solution to the problem.

When an intrusive thought disrupts your concentration, write it down on your worry pad with the idea that you will attend to it just as soon as you get the chance. Then with your conscience clear and your bothersome thought recorded on paper, you can get back to the business of concentration. After you have finished studying, read over your list and give these concerns your full attention. If you cannot alleviate them yourself, get the help of friends or counselors.

## ADOPTING STRATEGIES THAT ENCOURAGE CONCENTRATION

Although the best way of encouraging concentration is usually to discourage distractions, you can also take positive actions to improve your concentration. Get into the habit of making lists, taking regular breaks, and maintaining a balance between the challenge of a particular assignment and the level of your skill.

## Make Lists

As we have seen, keeping random thoughts and information in your head instead of writing them down is a primary impediment to concentration.

Use lists to remind yourself of day-to-day obligations, and catalogue all the study equipment you're likely to need.

**Use a Reminder List** To avoid worrying about the possibility of missing personal appointments and forgetting those things you've set out to do, write them down on your daily schedule (see Figure 2.4, page 32). As a result, you will be able to shift smoothly from one activity to the next without breaking your concentration.

## Take Breaks

If you allow physical energy to build up unabated, your mind will race. If you keep repressing concerns that compete for your attention, those concerns will eventually triumph and scuttle your concentration. And if you persist in denying such a basic instinct as hunger, all you'll be able to think of is food.

If, however, you take a few minutes to defuse these distractions, stand up and stretch, address a problem you've been avoiding, or grab a healthy snack to tide you over, you can return to your work ready to concentrate.

## Maintain a Balance Between Your Goal and Your Skills

Psychologist Mihaly Csikszentmihalyi believes that the most intense and rewarding kind of concentration (which he calls "flow") comes when you develop a balance between the challenge of the work you are doing and the level of skills you possess.[1] If the challenge of an assignment overwhelms your skill level, then anxiety—not concentration—is likely to result. Conversely, if your skills are high but the assignment isn't challenging, then you're apt to become bored and easily distracted. Finally, if both your skill level and the challenge of an assignment are low, then you'll probably become apathetic and have no desire to concentrate.

Here are some strategies for boosting your skills and raising your interest level.

**Find a Tutor** If you find yourself struggling with a subject, don't procrastinate. Before you reach the point of anxiety—or worse, apathy—get a tutor. Either go to the campus learning skills center or tutoring office, or find a

---

[1] Richard Flaste, "The Power of Concentration," *New York Times Magazine,* (October 8, 1989), p. 26.

classmate who has time to help you. In most cases, it won't take long before a tutor will pinpoint your problem, help you work it out, and send you off to tackle the rest of the term on your own.

**Join a Study Group**   Get together regularly with a small group of students to discuss specific assignments and the course as a whole. During the give-and-take of the discussions, you are bound to learn a great deal, and the subject may come alive, or the enthusiasm of some of the members may rub off on you. As you grow more familiar with the subject, your interest level will rise. The only prerequisite for a group meeting is that all members do their homework. Only then can each member become an active contributor.

**Pick Out an Alternate Textbook**   If you're struggling with a course, the textbook, not the subject, may be at the root of your problem. A little investigating at a library or bookstore may turn up books in which other authors discuss the same topics in ways you may find more accessible. After you have consulted some alternative books, read the material in your assigned textbook. The two texts may discuss the same topic, but your class will probably be focusing on aspects and approaches specific to the assigned text.

**Use Programmed Materials and Workbooks**   If your skills don't seem to match the requirements of a course, you may need some extra practice. Programmed materials furnish questions and problems closely followed by their answers, thereby enabling you to teach yourself every incremental step of each lesson. Workbooks provide exercises that apply the ideas explained in your textbooks. Either of these study aids can help minimize the anxiety that arises from feeling uncertain about putting newly learned ideas to use. They can also stimulate your interest by helping you take what you've learned a step further.

Also, try the computer center for programmed materials that are interactive. Drills, practice tests, and simulations are available for many subjects.

**Set Realistic Study Goals**   In some cases when the challenge of your work outstrips your skills, the problem lies with you and is easily remedied. For instance, don't expect to acquire a term's worth of skills in a few marathon study sessions. If up to now you have done little or no studying, change your habits gradually. Start by studying for only two hours on that first evening; then work up to longer sessions in which you'll be able to achieve increasingly large goals.

## SUMMARY

**What is concentration?**

Concentration is thinking that is focused. It occurs when nearly all your thinking energy is devoted to a single subject instead of to a variety of scattered ideas.

**How do distractions affect concentration?**

Distractions compete for your mind's attention. External distractions, such as loud noises or interesting scenery, or internal distractions, such as nagging worries or vivid daydreams, divert your attention and destroy your concentration.

**What is the proper environment for concentration?**

The proper environment is a place you use only for studying and use consistently. The area should be relatively free of visual distractions and noise, including music. The area should be brightly and evenly lit to discourage fatigue and prevent eyestrain.

**What equipment aids concentration?**

Good lights head the list of equipment that encourages concentration. A comfortable chair is important as well. A bookstand can free your hands and keep your textbook in a position that encourages active, focused thinking. Well-stocked and accessible supplies help you keep your mind on your work.

**What is a concentration scoresheet?**

A concentration scoresheet is a tally of the times when your concentration is broken. To keep score, put a check mark on a sheet of paper each time you realize you are no longer concentrating. The check marks will motivate you to keep your mind on your work.

**What is a worry pad, and how do you use it?**

A worry pad acts as a holding tank for stray thoughts that divert your attention from your studying. Putting these thoughts on paper takes them off your mind until you have the time to focus on them.

**What strategies encourage concentration?**

Strategies that help promote concentration and reduce the chance that distractions will arise in the first place include making lists, taking breaks, and maintaining a balance between your skills and the level of the material you're learning.

| | |
|---|---|
| **What is the value of taking a break?** | Taking a break can help defuse the distractions—hunger, fatigue, boredom—that commonly accumulate during study sessions. |
| **What is meant by "maintaining a balance"?** | This phrase means matching your personal skills to the level of challenge of a particular task. Otherwise, if the challenge overwhelms your skills, you may become anxious. If your skills exceed the challenge, you may become bored. And when both challenge and skills are low, you will probably feel apathetic. |
| **What techniques allow you to maintain a balance and concentrate?** | If you find yourself off balance, you have several strategies from which to choose. Find a tutor to help raise your level of skills. Study in a small group to boost the challenge of a course. Search out alternative texts that challenge you if your assigned text seems boring or that set your mind at ease if the text seems intimidating. Use programmed materials and workbooks to test your skills if you're feeling unsure of yourself or to provide an extra challenge when the course seems too easy. Finally, set realistic study goals, which will help keep the challenge within the range of your skill level. |

## HAVE YOU MISSED SOMETHING?

*Sentence completion.* Complete the following sentences with one of the three words or phrases listed below each sentence.

1. When you realize you're concentrating, your concentration will be

_____ .

intensified　　　broken　　　habitualized

2. You'll probably find the best atmosphere suitable for concentration in _____ .

your room　　　the study hall　　　the library

3. To keep awake during studying, it is important to have _____ .
a hard-seated chair    self-discipline    a private room

*Matching.* In each blank space in the left column, write the letter preceding the phrase in the right column that matches the left item best.

_____ 1. "Flow"

_____ 2. Boredom

_____ 3. Spider technique

_____ 4. Reminder list

_____ 5. Self-observation

_____ 6. Check mark

_____ 7. Worry pad

_____ 8. Programmed materials

a. Technique for tuning out external distractions

b. Encouraged by the concentration score-sheet

c. Used to promote interest and raise skill levels

d. Can serve as a signal for broken concentration

e. Stopgap measure for dealing with internal distractions

f. Enables you to shift smoothly from one task to the next

g. Term that describes an especially rewarding kind of concentration

h. Results when skills exceed the challenge of the task

*True-false.* Write *T* beside the *true* statements and *F* beside the *false* statements.

_____ 1. You can't realize you're concentrating while you're concentrating.

_____ 2. Loud music provides a suitable background for studying.

_____ 3. In normal circumstances, there are dozens of things competing for your attention.

_____ 4. Most internal distractions are beyond your control.

_____ 5. The best way of achieving concentration is by striving for it directly.

_____ 6. Your study environment will be more effective if you use it for recreation as well.

_____ **7.** Concentration involves achieving a balance between challenges and skills.

*Multiple choice.* Choose the word or phrase that completes the following sentence most accurately, and circle the letter that precedes it.

**1.** Trouble in concentrating is due primarily to

    a. internal and external distractions.
    b. boredom.
    c. anxiety.
    d. poor eyesight.

**2.** To promote concentration, your work area should be

    a. quiet.
    b. well lighted.
    c. used only for studying.
    d. all of the above.

**3.** When you're studying, music should be considered

    a. a help.
    b. a reward.
    c. noise.
    d. an internal distraction.

**4.** Internal distractions are

    a. disruptions that you create.
    b. caused by such problems as headaches and indigestion.
    c. a by-product of concentration.
    d. encouraged by a comfortable study area.

**5.** Although concentration is powerful, it is often

    a. unnecessary.
    b. elusive.
    c. underestimated.
    d. time consuming.

**6.** When the challenge is high but your skill level is low, you will probably experience

    a. concentration.
    b. boredom.
    c. anxiety.
    d. apathy.

*Short answer.*  Supply a brief answer for each of the following items.

1. What are the two general ways in which concentration can be promoted?
2. How will a tutor help minimize your anxiety and apathy?
3. Explain the conditioning effect that occurs when you use your desk only for studying.
4. What are some ways you can eliminate noise?
5. Discuss how you can use lists to encourage concentration.

## VOCABULARY BUILDING

DIRECTIONS: Make a light check mark (√) alongside one of the three words (choices) that most nearly expresses the meaning of the italicized word in the phrases that are in the left-hand column. (Answers are given on p. 434.)

|     |                              | 1            | 2            | 3          |
|-----|------------------------------|--------------|--------------|------------|
| 1.  | a *conditioning* effect      | negative     | association   | favorable  |
| 2.  | at least 2,500 *lumens*      | candles      | watts        | units      |
| 3.  | *incandescent* light         | hot          | bright       | luminous   |
| 4.  | you'll become *apathetic*    | spiritless   | apologetic   | athletic   |
| 5.  | every *incremental* step     | level        | proven       | added      |
| 6.  | the *juggernaut* that is Asia | novelty     | force        | rebirth    |
| 7.  | the *inexorable* lifting     | relentless   | inexcusable  | illegal    |
| 8.  | will soon *abate*            | increase     | arise        | end        |
| 9.  | I'll be *touting* this company | praising   | avoiding     | inspecting |
| 10. | stubbornly *inept*           | alert        | awkward      | working    |
| 11. | has *ominous* implications   | foreboding   | favorable    | great      |
| 12. | strategic *ambiguity*        | ambition     | clarity      | uncertainty |
| 13. | the *succinct* message       | wordy        | concise      | coded      |
| 14. | develop *intractable* problems | obstinate  | puzzling     | solvable   |
| 15. | a *debilitating* disorder    | remedial     | gradual      | weakening  |
| 16. | a *vulnerable* market        | powerful     | assailable   | falling    |
| 17. | as most *pundits* forecast   | authorities  | salesmen     | buyers     |
| 18. | investors' historical *aversion* | greed     | revision     | dislike    |
| 19. | the firm *ostensibly* belongs | inevitably  | doubtfully   | apparently |
| 20. | invincible *surmise*         | promise      | guess        | contract   |
| 21. | bosom of the *palpitating* air | rising     | pulsating    | stormy     |
| 22. | looked *wistfully* at the day | thoughtfully | energetically | hopefully |
| 23. | chart *deciphered* in the skies | etched     | depicted     | unravelled |
| 24. | the *turbid* ebb and flow    | murky        | smooth       | swift      |
| 25. | with *tremulous* cadence     | noisy        | wavering     | harsh      |

# 5

# Forgetting and Remembering

*Those who cannot remember the past are condemned to repeat it!*

—GEORGE SANTAYANA (1863–1952). Spanish-born American philosopher

Forgetting is like an ocean wave steadily washing away what you've learned. You can't stop forgetting any more than you can stop a wave. But you *can* reinforce what you've learned and strengthen your memories in the face of the incoming tide. To aid you in doing so, this chapter focuses on

- Theories about forgetting
- Pseudo-forgetting
- Principle of selectivity
- Silver Dollar System
- Organizing information
- Remembering with mnemonics
- Value of recitation
- Memory consolidation
- Distributed practice

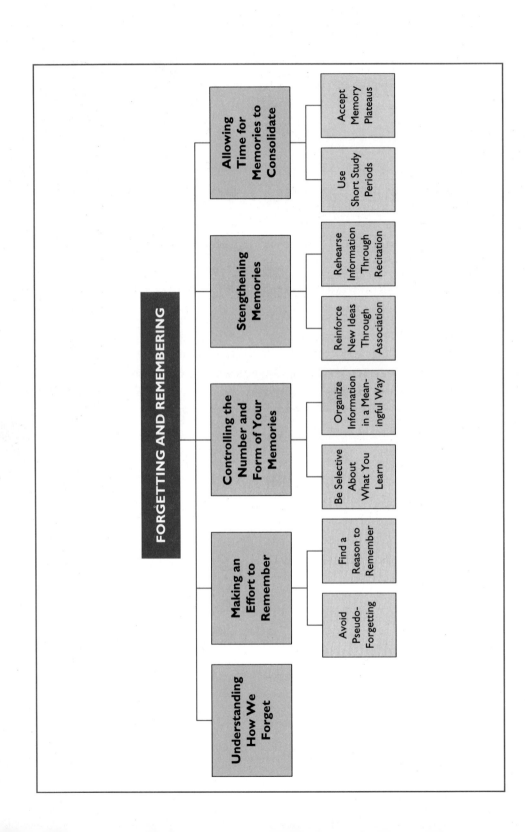

**M**ost of us become annoyed when we realize we've forgotten something crucial or when something "we should have known" has managed to slip our minds. But just how big a problem is forgetting? In the hierarchy of academic woes, forgetting holds sole possession of the summit. It is the biggest single problem you will encounter in school.

## UNDERSTANDING HOW WE FORGET

Memory is under constant assault from forgetfulness. Forgetting works both massively and rapidly to undo the work that learning has done. Unfortunately, forgetting's acts of sabotage are extremely successful. After you learn something new, you will forget most of it by the end of the day. Numerous studies and experiments have shown how quickly we forget what we read and what we hear.

In one experiment, people who read a textbook chapter forgot 46 percent of their reading after one day, 79 percent after fourteen days, and 81 percent after twenty-eight days. In other words, subjects could remember only slightly more than half of what they'd read the previous day; after less than a month, the information they were able to retain from their reading had dwindled down to 19 percent. Therefore, 80 percent of what they had originally read was now lost.

Not surprisingly, remembering what you have heard is even more difficult than recalling what you have read. After all, as you read you are able to slow down, pause, reflect, and, if necessary, reread. Listeners have no such luxuries; they usually have just one chance to catch the words and ideas being spoken.

For instance, in a classic experiment researchers secretly recorded a seminar held by the Cambridge Psychological Society.[1] Two weeks later, the society members who had attended the seminar were asked to write down all they could recall of it. The results were shocking. More than 90 percent of the points from the lecture had been forgotten or confused with the passage of time. The average proportion of specific points each member correctly recalled was 8.4 percent! Much of what members recalled was at odds with what had actually been said. Events were mentioned that never took place; casual remarks were embellished; points were reported that had only been hinted at. This learned group of psychologists forgot 91.6 percent of the specific points made in the seminar.

---

[1]See Ian M. L. Hunter, *Memory: Facts and Fallacies* (Baltimore: Penguin, 1957), p. 83.

How does this devastating forgetting occur? Although the experts are divided on the answer, they have formulated a number of interesting and plausible theories to explain forgetting (Figure 5.1).

*Use it or lose it: Fading theory.*   According to fading theory, the trace or mark a memory etches in your brain is like a path you make when you walk across a meadow. If you don't continue to walk over the path, grass will grow up and obliterate your trail. In the same way, a fact that's learned but never used will become fainter until it is obliterated completely by forgetfulness.

*I know it's here somewhere: Retrieval theory.*   Unlike proponents of fading theory, some psychologists believe that once a fact or idea is thoroughly learned, it remains a memory for life. According to this retrieval theory, a forgotten fact hasn't faded; it has been misfiled in the vast storehouse of your mind. Whether the information has disappeared completely or has

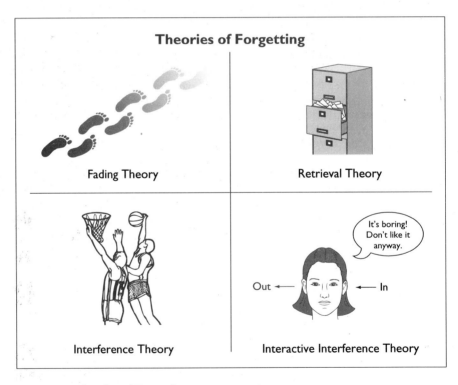

**FIGURE 5.1  Theories of Forgetting**

simply been lost, the net result is the same: Information you once learned and remembered has now been forgotten.

*Fighting for a spot: Interference theory.* According to interference theory, limited space puts old and new memories at odds. Memories become like a bunch of competitive basketball players fighting for a spot beneath the basket. Old memories and facts elbow out new information (forward interference), thereby causing us to forget what we've recently learned. Meanwhile, new facts and ideas battle for a coveted position by forcing out facts that we've known for a while (backward interference). The result is a constant battle, with old and new memories both jockeying for position. Some win and some lose.

*Caught in a crossfire: Interactive interference theory.* Imagine you have learned three facts at three different times. For example:

Oldest:  *Photosynthesis* is the process whereby plants employ sunlight to turn chemicals into food.

Middle:  A *photomicrograph* is a picture taken through a microscope.

Newest:  *Phototropism* is the movement of a plant in response to light.

According to interactive interference theory, you'll lose the middle fact rapidly because it will be bombarded by the oldest learning and the newest learning. To complicate things, the middle fact, fighting for survival, will do its best to bombard the newest and the oldest learning (fighting both frontal and rear attacks). In the course of this fighting, the middle fact, while going down in defeat, will inflict some damage (forgetting) to both the oldest and the newest learning.

*Tuning out what you don't like: Reactive interference theory.* According to reactive interference theory, your general attitude toward the facts you learn plays a crucial role in whether you will recall them. Facts related to a subject you don't like or find boring can be difficult to understand and even harder to remember. The implications of this theory are clear: Attitude has a noticeable effect on what you are able to learn and remember.

## MAKING AN EFFORT TO REMEMBER

To remember something, you have to make a conscious effort to learn it. If you don't learn new information in the first place, it isn't really yours to forget. And even if you do learn new information, it won't last very long unless you're convinced that it's worth hanging onto. The effort you initially make determines whether you'll remember for a lifetime what you've heard or read or forget it in a matter of seconds.

## Avoid Pseudo-Forgetting

Whenever you cannot remember a name, a telephone number, a fact, an idea, or even a joke, it's quite natural to say, "I forgot." Yet forgetting may not have anything to do with your problem. You may never have learned the information in the first place. As the poet Oliver Wendell Holmes succinctly put it, "A man must *get* a thing before he can *forget* it."

If you are introduced to someone but don't hear that person's name, it's only natural that the name will slip your mind. You didn't forget it. You pseudo-forgot it. The word *pseudo* means "false" or "phony." Thousands of instances we blame on forgetting are actually a result of this "phony forgetting."

If an idea or a fact is to be retained in your memory, it must be impressed on your mind clearly and crisply at least once. A record of that idea or fact must be laid down in your brain before you can truly recall or forget what you've learned.

## Find a Reason to Remember

If you can find a reason for holding onto information you've learned, you have a much better chance of remembering it. In a carefully designed study, researchers showed how intention can influence the life span of a memory. Two groups of students were given identical material and asked to master it. The only difference was that the first group was told it had to remember the material for only a single day, whereas the second group was instructed to master the material for recall after two weeks.[2] The difference in intention had a noticeable effect. Although the two groups studied the same material in a similar fashion, after two weeks the students who had intended to remember over the long term retained more than the students who had intended to hang on to what they had learned for only a day.

Psychologists agree that to learn something thoroughly, you have to be properly motivated. Indeed, a strong motivation can have a surprising effect on your memory. A basketball coach at Cornell University recalled that

[2]H. H. Remmers and M. N. Thisted, "The Effect of Temporal Set on Learning," *Journal of Applied Psychology* 16 (June 1932), 257–268.

although as a student at DePauw University he had first found physics uninteresting, his attitude changed when he encountered material dealing with angles, trajectory, and force. He used this information to better understand how basketballs carom off the backboard. Because of his newfound interest, he was able to raise his grade from a C to an A by the end of the semester. What was his reason for remembering? Information from physics, a subject he had once dreaded, could be applied to basketball, a sport he loved.

Of all the sources of motivation, interest is the strongest. If you could study every one of your subjects with motivated interest, you would not have to worry about your final grades. When you are naturally interested in a subject, you have no problem. If, however, you are not naturally interested, try to combat boredom by artificially creating interest. Once you begin to learn something about a new subject, the chances are great that you will find it genuinely interesting. Use the power of interest to work *for* you, not against you.

Whether genuine interest or simple academic survival serves as your motivation, when you hear or read information you want to hold onto, there are ways to strengthen your intention to remember, so that what you've learned will be recalled:

*Pay attention.* If you're distracted while you're trying to learn, it's unlikely you'll remember anything. Therefore, make a point to minimize distractions as you read your assignments or listen to lectures.

*Get information right the first time.* False ideas and misunderstood facts can hang on as tenaciously as information you learn correctly. Therefore, it pays to be attentive when you learn something new. For example, many people incorrectly pronounce the word *nuclear* (NEW-clee-er) as "NEW-cue-ler." One look at the word shows you that this pronunciation is incorrect. But if you learn a word incorrectly, you'll have difficulty replacing the old memory with the correct pronunciation. If you learn something correctly in the first place, you'll have no bad habits to break.

*Make sure you understand.* Ideas that aren't clear to you when you read or hear them won't miraculously jell and become clearer in your memory. You cannot fashion a lucid, correct memory from a fuzzy, poorly understood concept. Therefore, don't hesitate to ask the instructor to explain any point that you are not clear on. And don't be reluctant to read and reread a passage in your textbook until you're sure you fully grasp its meaning.

Interestingly, the same motivation that enables you to remember can also help you forget. Recall that reactive interference theory suggests we have a tendency to "tune out" information that bores or bothers us. But motivated forgetting can be used positively to clear your mind of information you no longer need to retain.

This conscious intention to forget is well demonstrated by servers in restaurants. They exhibit a remarkably good memory for what their customers have ordered up to the moment the bill is paid. Then experienced servers jettison the entire transaction from their minds and give their full attention to the next customer. Just as they intend to remember, so they intend to forget.

Dr. Hans Selye, a pioneer in stress management, explains how he used motivated forgetting to help minimize the anxiety caused by an overburdened memory:

> I make a conscious effort to forget immediately all that is unimportant and to jot down data of possible value (even at the price of having to prepare complex files). Thus, I manage to keep my memory free for facts which are truly essential to me. I think this technique can help anyone to accomplish the greatest simplicity compatible with the degree of complexity of his intellectual life.[3]

This idea of intending to forget explains why Albert Einstein, unquestionably one of the great minds of the twentieth century, was nonetheless unable to provide his home telephone number from memory. Although the famous physicist's forgetfulness may have seemed like absent-mindedness to some, it was usually deliberate. Einstein used his exceptional brain as the incubator for ideas and theories that fundamentally changed the way we view the world. He saw no point in clogging his mind with simple numbers that could easily be stored in an address book, and so he purposely forgot them.

## CONTROLLING THE NUMBER AND FORM OF YOUR MEMORIES

The forgetting that many of us practice instinctively seems to imply that there is a limit to how much we can remember at once. In 1956 psychologist G. A. Miller produced scientific support for this notion. In his article "The Magical Number Seven, Plus or Minus Two," Miller points out that most people are able to hold only seven items in short-term memory at one time. The size of each item, however, can be virtually unlimited as long as the information in it is meaningfully organized. For example, you couldn't expect to remember the following thirty-one items:

---

[3]Hans Selye, *The Stress of Life* (New York: McGraw-Hill, 1956), p. 269.

aabceeeeeeeilmmmnnnoorrrssttuvy

But if you organized these items in a meaningful way—as words—you could reduce the number of items to seven and increase your odds of remembering them:

You    can    learn    to    remember    seven    items.
 1      2       3       4        5          6        7

As Miller explains, "Our language is tremendously useful for repackaging material into a few chunks rich in information."[4]

The lesson to be learned from Miller's research is this: Improve your chances of remembering by being selective about what you learn and by making sure that what you do choose to remember is meaningfully organized.


## Be Selective About What You Learn

Long before Miller's "magical number seven," Herman Ebbinghaus (1850–1909), a German psychologist, had spent more than twenty years investigating forgetting and the limits of memory. In his most famous experiment, Ebbinghaus counted the number of trials required to learn a series of six nonsense syllables (such as *bik, luf, tur, pem, nif,* and *wox*). He then counted the number of trials required to learn a series of twelve such syllables. Ebbinghaus's tabulations yielded surprising results: The number of trials required to memorize the twelve syllables was fifteen times greater than the number required to learn the six syllables.[5] So, for example, if it took four minutes to memorize six syllables, it would take an hour to memorize twelve.

Although Ebbinghaus dealt only with nonsense syllables, his careful research teaches us a valuable lesson that can be applied to both textbook and lecture material: To improve your chances of remembering what you've learned, you must condense and summarize. In practical terms this means picking out the main ideas from your lecture and textbook notes and leaving the supporting materials and examples aside. Once you have selected the important points from what you've read, you should be able to memorize them in a manageable amount of time.

---

[4]G. A. Miller, "The Magical Number Seven, Plus or Minus Two: Some Limits on Our Capacity for Processing Information," *Psychological Review* 63 (March 1956): 81–97.
[5]Matthew High Erdelyl, 1994. "Commentary: Integrating Dissociations Prone Psychology," *Journal of Personality* 62(4): 669–680.

Of course, reducing pages and pages of notes down to just a handful of main ideas is often easier said than done. If you need a painless method of extracting the highlights from your notes, consider the *Silver Dollar System.*

### The Silver Dollar System

Read through your notes and make an *S* in the margin next to any idea that seems important. Depending on the number of pages of notes you read, you'll probably wind up with several dozen *S*'s.

Now read only the notes you have flagged with an *S.* As you go through these flagged notes for a second time, select the ideas that seem particularly important, and draw a vertical line through the *S*'s that are next to them. Your symbol will look like this: **$**.

Make a third and final pass through your notes, reading only those ideas that have been marked $. Out of these notes, mark the truly outstanding ideas—there will be only a handful of them—with another vertical line so your markings look like dollar signs: $

The Silver Dollar System shows you at a glance which ideas are crucial to remember and which are not. The $ sign alerts you to the truly important ideas, the "Silver Dollar" ideas that should receive most of your attention. Next come the $ ideas; they are worthy but shouldn't clutter up your memory if you have a lot to remember in a limited amount of time. Finally, the *S* ideas can be ignored. Although you flagged these as potentially important ideas, since then you've twice marked ideas that were even more important.

In normal circumstances, deciding what's important can be a time-consuming and even frightening experience. It requires real courage to select just a few ideas from pages and pages of notes and ignore the rest. With this system, you can select the Silver Dollar ideas gradually and relatively easily.

## Organize Information in a Meaningful Way

The papers on your desk are easier to keep track of if you organize them into groups and put them into several file folders. A textbook is easier to understand because the information in it has been divided into chapters. A single item is easier to find in a supermarket because the products have been grouped together and arranged in different aisles. If you had to look for a jar of peanut butter in a supermarket where the items were randomly placed, you might give up the search.

The same idea applies to memories as well. If the material you try to remember isn't well organized, you'll have trouble remembering it. But if you organize information in a meaningful way, you'll have a much easier time recalling it.

When you have a large list of items to remember, try to cluster similar items around a natural heading or category. Once clustered and categorized, the items will resist the decaying power of forgetting. Just as the stem holds together the individual grapes, so categories and clusters hold together individual facts and ideas.

This hanging together is especially useful during an exam: Remembering one item from a cluster is usually the key to remembering all the items. For example, it would take a long time to memorize by rote the following words, which you might encounter in a geology course:

| | | |
|---|---|---|
| slate | diamond | sapphire |
| bronze | lead | aluminum |
| iron | marble | silver |
| emerald | steel | brass |
| gold | limestone | ruby |
| granite | platinum | copper |

But when these words are organized into categories and are clustered as shown in Fig. 5.2, memorization is relatively easy and remembering is strong.[6]

## STRENGTHENING MEMORIES

The stronger a memory is, the longer it lasts. If you reinforce new ideas by connecting them to ones already in your memory, and if you conscientiously rehearse what you've learned, that result should be strong enough to stand up to forgetting.

### Reinforce New Ideas Through Association

That famous saying "No man is an island" applies to memories as well. An idea that stands alone is not likely to be recalled because the ideas you remember are woven into a network that connects a single memory with

---

[6]Figure from *Psychology: An Introduction*, Fourth Edition by Jerome Kagan and Ernest Havemann, copyright © 1990 by Harcourt Brace & Company, reproduced by permission of the publisher.

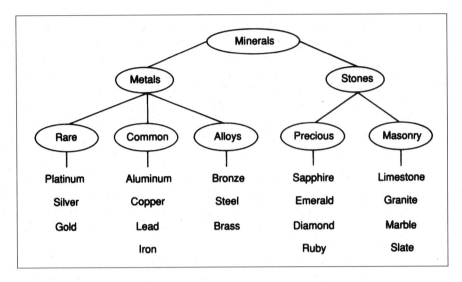

**FIGURE 5.2 The Category and Cluster System of Organizing Items**

hundreds and often thousands of other memories. The more connections there are in the network and the stronger those connections are, the better the chance for recall is.

Sometimes these connections are made automatically. Most people easily recall, for example, where they were and what they were doing when President Kennedy was assassinated in 1963 or when the space shuttle *Challenger* exploded in 1986. In these cases, you instantly connect the memory of the event with the memory of where you were.

But in normal circumstances, relying on your memory to automatically make these connections is risky. If you want to improve your chances of remembering something, you must make a real effort to link what you've learned to your memory network. You can strengthen the staying power of information when you add it to your memory by consciously making either logical or artificial connections.

**Make Logical Connections**   Consider how you can recall the written directions to a friend's house by keeping in mind a map you once saw of the location or strengthen your memory of the bones of the body by recalling a diagram of a human skeleton. These are examples of logical connections you make to improve your recall. The best ways of strengthening your memory network through logical connections are building on your basic background and using images to support what you're trying to remember.

*Build on your basic background.*    The principle behind basic background is simple but powerful. Your understanding and memory of what you hear, read, see, feel, or taste depend entirely on what you know, on what you already have in your background. Some of this information has been with you for years, whereas other parts of it may be just seconds old. When listening to a speaker, you understand his or her points as long as you can interpret them in light of something you've already learned. When you make connections this way, you increase the power of your memory.

Here are some concrete steps to help you build a solid background:

*Give basic courses the attention they deserve.*    Many students make the mistake of thinking that the basic courses they take in their freshman year are a waste of time. Yet these introductory courses create the background essential for all the courses that follow. Indeed, each student's professional life begins with freshman courses.

*Make a conscious attempt to link what you learn to what you already know.* When you learn something new, ask yourself questions such as "How does this relate to what I already know?" and "How does this *change* what I already know?"

*Ask an instructor to explain what you don't understand.*    At times an entire class can hinge on a single point. Miss that and you miss the purpose of the class. Don't feel hesitant or shy about asking an instructor to go back over a point you can't quite get a fix on. After all, the instructor is there to help you learn.

*Strengthen memories with pictures.*    Another way of reinforcing what you've learned is by creating a picture of it. Whether you draw the new information on paper or simply visualize it in your mind, you add an extra dimension to your memory. After all, only one-half of your brain thinks in words; the other half thinks in pictures. When you convert words into pictures, you are using both sides of your brain instead of just one.

A student who attended a lecture on amoebas included a sketch of this one-celled organism in her notes (see Figure 5.3). The combination of words and picture gave her a clearer understanding of the subject than she would have gained from relying exclusively on written information. When a question about amoebas appeared on a test, the student handled it easily by recalling the picture she had drawn.

Even when material doesn't lend itself to drawing, you can still devise a mental image. According to Dr. Joseph E. Shorr of the Institute of Psycho-Imagination Therapy in Beverly Hills, California, "The human memory would be worthless without the capacity to make mental pictures." Almost any memory can be turned into a mental image. If you need to remember,

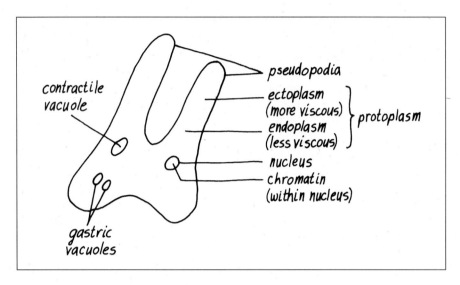

**FIGURE 5.3    Structure of the Amoeba**

for example, that Abraham Lincoln was born in 1809, you can picture a log cabin with "1809" inscribed over the doorway. The image you recall doesn't have to be especially detailed; it only has to be strong enough to jog your memory. (Chapter 13 provides a detailed discussion of how to tap into your natural ability to think visually.)

**Make Artificial Connections**   Strong connections don't always have to be logical ones. They can be completely artificial. After all, what natural link is there between the word *face* and a group of musical notes? Yet many beginning music students rely on this word to help them recall the notes written in the spaces of the treble clef (F, A, C, E). These connections are by no means limited to music.

Suppose you have just been introduced to a man named Mr. Perkins. To remember his name, you immediately associate it with a coffeepot *perking.* You even visualize the perking pot and smell the aroma of freshly brewed coffee.

What you have done is tie *new* information (Mr. Perkins) to *old* information (perking coffeepot) that is already well established in your memory. When you meet Mr. Perkins at some future time, you will recall the perking coffee pot, which will prepare you to say, "Hello, Mr. Perkins. Nice to see you again."

The majority of memory tricks (known as *mnemonic devices*) rely on such artificial connections.

**Use classic mnemonic devices.**   Nearly everyone employs at least one or two mnemonic devices to recall specific hard-to-remember facts and information. Probably the most widely used mnemonic device is the old jingle by which many of us keep track of the irregularities in the calendar:

> Thirty days hath September,
> April, June, and November.
> All the rest have thirty-one,
> Except February alone.

Rivaling this days-in-the-month mnemonic is one for spelling:

> *i* before *e* except after *c*
> or when sounding like *a*
> as in *neighbor* and *weigh*

Many people have their own personal mnemonics, such as "Surround the *r* with *a* for the word *separate.*"

As we've already learned, the cardinal rule for dealing with masses of information is to make sure that information is organized in a meaningful way. A mnemonic device is an organizational system pure and simple. It is an ordinary means to an important end. Gerald R. Miller conducted a study to evaluate the effectiveness of mnemonic devices as aids to study.[7] He found that students who used mnemonics raised their test scores by as much as 77 percent!

Miller recognizes that the use of too many mnemonics can overload the memory. Nevertheless, he argues that learning a large number of mnemonics well creates no greater hazard for a student than learning a large amount of material in the traditional way. Here's a sampling of some classic mnemonics that you may have encountered:

*Spelling.*   The greatest number of mnemonic devices are aids to spelling. Here's how to remember the correct way to spell two words that confuse many students:

> A princip<u>al</u> is a p<u>al</u>.
>
> A princip<u>le</u> is a ru<u>le</u>.

If you use classic mnemonic devices to help you recall information, make certain you memorize the sentence, word, or jingle thoroughly. The slightest

---

[7]Gerald R. Miller, *An Evaluation of the Effectiveness of Mnemonic Devices as Aids to Study,* Cooperative Research Project no. 5-8438 (El Paso: University of Texas, 1967).

error can throw you off completely. For example, some algebra students use the FOIL method to remember the order for multiplying a binomial: First, Outer, Inner, Last. But if you recall the wrong word instead, say FILE, you wind up hopelessly confused.

*Biology.* The first letters of the words in the following sentence stand for the major categories and subdivisions of the animal world—kingdom, phylum, class, order, family, genus, species, variety:

Kings Play Cards On Fairly Good Soft Velvet.

*Geography.* Remembering the names of the Great Lakes is easy if you keep HOMES in mind, but recalling the lakes in a particular order is not so easy. Here's a mnemonic device that organizes them from west to east (Superior, Michigan, Huron, Erie, Ontario):

Super Machine Heaved Earth Out.

*History.* The royal houses of England (Norman, Plantagenet, Lancaster, York, Tudor, Stuart, Hanover, Windsor) are difficult to remember without the help of a mnemonic device:

No Plan Like Yours To Study History Wisely

*Medicine.* Even doctors and pharmacists use memory systems to help keep certain chemicals straight. To distinguish between cyanates, which are harmless, and cyanides, which are extremely poisonous, they use this device:

*-ate,* I ate; *-ide,* I died.

Medical students are expected to remember massive amounts of information. Often, a mnemonic comes to the rescue. Some med students use the word SKILL to help them recall the body's excretory organs:

Skin Kidneys Intestines Liver Lungs

**Devise your own mnemonics.** Associating new information logically is generally better than doing so artificially, and truly knowing something is always better than using a system to remember it. But if you're required to learn facts that you can't connect with your memory network and that have no classic mnemonic, you may want to invent your own mnemonic device to help you remember.

*Keyword mnemonic.*[8] Connecting a man named Perkins with a perking coffee pot provides a good example of a *keyword mnemonic* in action. The

---

[8]The keyword mnemonics section is based on a discussion in K. L. Higbee, *Your Memory: How It Works and How To Improve It,* 2/e (New York: Prentice-Hall, 1988).

procedure for devising a keyword mnemonic has two steps, a verbal step and a visual step.

1. *The verbal step.* Find a familiar word or a phrase that sounds like the word you are trying to remember. This is your keyword. For the name *Perkins* the keyword is *perking.*
2. *The visual step.* Connect your keyword with what you want to remember. For example, form a mental image of Mr. Perkins' face on a perking coffeepot. Then when you see him again, you'll recall that image which will remind you of his name.

The keyword system isn't limited to helping you remember the names of people you meet. It also comes in handy for remembering vocabulary words from a foreign langauge. For example, if you want to recall the French word for butter, *beurre,* connect it with a keyword like *burr,* or *brrr,* and then link the two with a visual image, a pat of butter covered with burrs or a stick of butter wearing a parka and shivering (brrr!).

*Create-a-word mnemonic.* The letters of a "created" word can be used to help you remember important information in the same way the classic mnemonics FACE and FOIL are used. Here's an example: The task is to devise a mnemonic that will enable you to recall five guidelines for preventing heart attack and stroke.

1. After <u>age</u> 40, get a medical checkup every year.
2. Do not <u>smoke</u>.
3. Keep your <u>weight</u> down.
4. <u>Exercise</u> moderately and wisely.
5. Get sufficient <u>rest</u>.

To devise a *create-a-word mnemonic,* proceed as follows:

1. Underline the key word in each item (as has been done in the previous list).
2. Write down the first letter of each key word. (Here we have A, S, W, E, and R.)
3. Create a word or several words from the first letters of the key words. Change the order of the letters as necessary to do so. (Here we can make SWEAR, which will help us recall the five key words: <u>S</u>moke, <u>W</u>eight, <u>E</u>xercise, <u>A</u>ge 40, <u>R</u>est.)
4. If possible, make a link between your key word and the idea for which it acts as a mnemonic. ("If you want to reduce your risk of heart attack or stroke, you must *swear* to do the following.")

Your mnemonic may be a real word or a word you just made up. If you use a made-up word, be sure you will be able to remember it.

*Create-a-sentence mnemonic.* This is a variation on the create-a-word mnemonic. In fact, most of the steps are the same. A *create-a-sentence mnemonic* is devised as follows:

1.  Underline the key word in each main point in your notes.
2.  Write down the first letter of each key word.
3.  Construct an easy-to-remember sentence using words whose first letters are the same as the first letters of the key words.
4.  Devise a sentence that relates to the information you're trying to remember.

As an example, here are eight main points taken from a long article about what to do if you are in a building that is on fire. The key words have been underlined.

1.  Feel the <u>door</u> with your hand. If it is hot, the room or hall on the other side is on fire.
2.  If the door is cool, check the <u>air</u> coming under the door. If it is cool, then there's probably no fire on the other side.
3.  Even so, don't take chances. Open the door just a <u>crack</u> while kneeling with your face turned away. Listen and smell for fire and smoke.
4.  When you leave, <u>shut</u> all doors and windows.
5.  If your room is smoke filled, <u>crawl</u> with your nose about one foot from the floor.
6.  Never use an elevator; use a <u>stairway</u>.
7.  If you are trapped, use <u>wet</u> cloths to protect your face, hands, and breathing passages.
8.  <u>Hang</u> something out of a window to attract attention.

The first letters of the key words are D, A, C, S, C, S, W, and H. An easy-to-remember sentence using words beginning with the first letters of the key words is

<u>D</u>ry <u>A</u>ir <u>C</u>reates <u>S</u>parks, <u>C</u>ausing <u>S</u>moke <u>W</u>ithin <u>H</u>ouses.

The letters need not appear in the same order as the key words. But in this case, the sequence of steps was considered important, so the original order was retained.

In general, creating a simple sentence is easier than taking the first letters from your key words and turning them into a word or two, especially if the order of the points has to be maintained. Of course, if the initial letters are mainly consonants, both methods can be difficult. To circumvent the problem of having too many consonants, choose some key words (or synonyms of the key words) that begin with a vowel.

*Employ commercial memory methods.* Most commercial memory courses rely on *the peg.* This system for memorizing items in sequence employs a master list of words that act as hooks or pegs on which to hang the information you want to remember. A peg word often rhymes with the number it stands for. For example, one is bun, two is shoe, three is tree, and four is door. To remember a group of items, you associate them with the peg words, often by employing bizarre images.

For example, if you want to remember a shopping list consisting of butter, sugar, and sausage, you might visualize a pound of butter melting atop a gigantic bun, a shoe filled with loose sugar, and a sausage as tall as a tree. Then when you arrive at the supermarket, you run through the peg words in sequence (bun, shoe, tree) and recall the words with which each is associated.

The peg may work for buying groceries but not for doing schoolwork because the system assumes you'll be able to memorize the original list. When you are unable to do this, the entire system falls apart. In addition, the peg works with only one list at a time, it may cause interference, and it does little to reinforce information in your long-term memory. Commercial memory courses do have some value, and peg words can help out in a pinch, but in general the cost of the courses outweighs their usefulness, and the techniques are better for survival than success.

## Rehearse Information Through Recitation

No single activity is more important in strengthening your memory than recitation. That's because recitation forces you to think seriously about what you've read or heard. This deep thinking (experts call it *deep cognitive processing*) is the key to making memories last.

To reap the benefits of recitation, you need to know how to recite. But it also helps to understand how reciting strengthens your memory and why reciting is more effective than rereading.

**Learn How to Recite** Most students have only a vague idea of what reciting involves. Others more familiar with reciting incorrectly assume that there is only one method of doing so. Although there is a traditional method of reciting, if you follow some basic guidelines, you can recite in several ways. In fact, the best method of reciting is not the best known.

*Do traditional reciting.* Traditional reciting involves restating information out loud, in your own words, and from memory. For example, if you read a paragraph from a textbook, look away, and then explain the meaning of what you have just read, then you are reciting.

Unfortunately, not all students are keen on this kind of reciting. Some feel that the process is strange or unnatural, like talking to themselves. Others are reluctant to recite in a quiet place where people are studying. Still others are embarrassed to be heard reciting no matter what. As a result, many students don't recite. But there are other ways to recite that avoid such embarrassments. The trick is to stick to the basics of reciting.

***Understand the process of reciting.***   All reciting follows three basic steps: You *read*, you *convert* what you've read, and then you *test* yourself on what you've learned. A simple way to recall these steps is to think of the consonants in the word *recite*. The *R* stands for read, the *C* for convert, and the *T* for test.

1. *How to read.* Read one paragraph at a time if you're reciting from your textbook or one note at a time if you're reciting from your note sheets. In each case, extract the main idea as you do so. If you're reciting from your notes, your job is a breeze: The main idea is the note you wrote down. If you're reading from your textbook, remember that each paragraph typically contains just one main idea, which all the other sentences support.
2. *How to convert what you've read.* Once you've read the paragraph or note and extracted the main idea, convert this main idea into a key word or two that hint at the idea or a question that uses the idea as its answer.
3. *How to test yourself.* Use the key words or the question you've devised to demonstrate out loud or on paper your knowledge of the main idea.

***Recite by writing out questions and answers.***   The best way to recite is by converting what you've read into questions, reading those questions, and then writing down answers. Converting ideas into questions is usually more effective than coming up with a key word or two. In addition, writing down answers on paper provides better practice than simply stating those answers out loud.

The difference between using key words and asking questions is basically the difference between recognizing and recalling. Recognizing a correct answer is always easier than recalling one without any clues. Key words "cheat" by enabling you to recognize part of the answer, whereas questions emphasize recall. With no clues to go on, if you can answer your question, you have probably recalled the right answer and not simply recognized it. And because most of the answers you'll be asked to give in tests and quizzes will be written, not spoken, this kind of reciting provides excellent practice for test taking.

When done properly, reading out loud can be an excellent way of reciting. But some students who are reluctant to recite out loud either skip the reciting step altogether or mumble instead of speaking clearly. Reciting under your breath makes it too easy to convince yourself that you know the correct answer when you don't. But when you do your reciting by writing, you have solid proof that you can answer your questions.

**Understand Why Recitation Works**   Whether you recite by speaking or by writing, the effect on your memory is basically the same. Recitation strengthens the original memory trace by prompting you to think actively about the new material. The physical activity of thinking, pronouncing, and hearing your own words involves your body as well as your mind in the process of learning. The more physical senses you use in learning, the stronger the memory in your brain will be. In addition, recitation provides a number of psychological benefits that improve your ability to learn and remember.

*Recitation gets you involved.*   Reading is not the same as comprehending. It's possible, for example, to read a book aloud to a child without paying attention to the story. Likewise, if you're having a tough time concentrating, you can read every word on a page and still not recall what you've read. To truly comprehend what you've read, you need to know both what the words *say* and what they *mean.* When you recite, you make yourself stop and wonder, "What did this just say?" You're transformed from a detached observer into a participant.

*Recitation provides feedback.*   Reciting not only gets you involved in your reading, it also demonstrates how involved you are. Rereading can give you a false and dangerous sense of confidence. It takes a lot of time and leaves you with the feeling that you've been hard at work, yet it provides no concrete indication of what you're learning. When test time comes, you may blame your mental blanks on test anxiety or on unfair questions when the real culprit is ineffective studying.

Unlike rereading, reciting lets you know right away where your weaknesses lie. You find out at the end of every paragraph whether you understand what you've just read. This gives you a chance to clarify and solidify information on the spot, long before you're tested on it.

*Recitation supplies motivation.*   Because it gets you involved and checks your progress regularly, recitation provides motivation for studying. And motivated interest promotes stronger memory.

If you struggled to extract the information from a paragraph you just read, you may be motivated to get the point of the next paragraph more easily. If you had no trouble finding the meaning in that paragraph, then the momentum of your reading may serve as a motivation.

**Recognize the Difference Between Reciting and Rereading**  Students who don't recite usually reread their notes or chapter assignments until they feel they "know it." They do this in the hope that repetition will lead to comprehension. Unfortunately, any real learning that takes place through rereading usually occurs by accident. This all-too-common study method really does little to strengthen memory.

Recitation, however, works in several ways at once to help improve the chances that you'll remember what you've learned. Recitation gets you involved. It provides immediate feedback so you can test yourself and check your progress. It motivates you to keep on reading.

## ALLOWING TIME FOR MEMORIES TO CONSOLIDATE

The fact that recitation helps new information to jell hints at another aspect of memory: New ideas don't instantly become a part of your memory. Your memory needs time to consolidate what you've learned.

A dramatic illustration of the memory's need to consolidate comes in a story of a mountain climber who fell and hit his head. Although the man was not permanently injured, he couldn't remember falling. In fact, he couldn't recall anything that had happened to him in the fifteen minutes *before* the accident. Why not? According to the principle of consolidation, the climber's memories before the accident had not had a chance to consolidate. As a result, when the climber hit his head, those unfinished memories were lost.[9]

This principle helps explain why in most cases the most effective way to study is in short blocks of time instead of in one long stretch. An understanding of consolidation will help you live through those frustrating times when you don't seem to retain what you're studying.

## Use Short Study Periods

In *distributed practice*, you engage in relatively short study periods broken up by rest intervals. In *massed practice*, you study continuously until the task is

---

[9]R. S. Woodworth and H. Schlosberg, *Experimental Psychology,* rev. ed. (New York: Holt, Rinehart, and Winston, 1954), p. 773.

completed. A number of studies have demonstrated that several short "learn-ing sprints" are more productive than one grueling, long-distance study session.

In an extensive experiment, researchers Krug, Davis, and Glover exam-ined the effects of massed and distributed practice on a reading comprehen-sion task and found that distributed practice lead to better performance.[10]

Bertram Epstein used two experimental groups to find out whether distributed practice had an effect on retention.[11] One group studied in bite-sized stretches with rest periods in between (distributed practice) while the other worked in one long session with no rests (massed practice). Both groups were tested immediately after studying as well as two weeks and then ten weeks later. Epstein concluded that distributed practice was superior to massed practice for both immediate and long-term retention.

The memory's need to consolidate information seems to play a key role in explaining why distributed practice is superior to massed practice. But there are other advantages as well that support these bite-sized study sessions:

Periodic "breathers" discourage fatigue. They refresh you both physically and emotionally.

Motivation is stronger when you work within short blocks of time. The end of each session marks a minivictory that provides momentum and a sense of accomplishment.

Distributed practice wards off boredom. Uninteresting subjects are easier to take in small doses.

In spite of all the advantages of distributed practice, massed practice is superior in a few cases. For instance, when you are writing the first draft of a paper, massed practice is often essential. You have organized your notes in stacks, discrete bits of information are waiting in your mind like jigsaw puzzle pieces to be fitted together, and the organizational pattern of your paper, though dimly perceived, is beginning to take shape. To stop working at this point would be disastrous. The entire effort would collapse. So in such a circumstance, it is far more efficient to overextend yourself—to com-plete that stage of the process—than to take a break or otherwise apply the principle of distributed practice.

---

[10]D. Krug, T. B. Davis, and J. A. Glover, "Massed versus Distributed Repeated Reading: A Case of Forgetting Helping Recall?" *Journal of Educational Psychology* 82 (1990): 366–71.
[11]Bertram Epstein, *Immediate and Retention Effects of Interpolated Rest Periods on Learning Performance,* Contributions to Education no. 949 (New York: Bureau of Publications, Teachers College, Columbia University, 1949).

## Accept Memory Plateaus

No two people learn at exactly the same rate, yet the learning patterns of most people are quite similar. We all experience lulls in our learning. Progress is usually slow and steady at first, but then for a period of time there might be no perceptible progress even though we are making a genuine effort. This "no-progress" period is called a *plateau*. After days, weeks, or even a month of effort, suddenly a surprising spurt in learning occurs and continues until another plateau is reached.

When you reach a plateau, do not lose heart. Plateaus are a normal part of learning. You may not see any progress, but learning is occurring nevertheless. Once everything is in place, you'll be rewarded for your effort.

## SUMMARY

**How powerful is forgetfulness?**

Forgetting works quickly and thoroughly to rob you in less than a day of much of the new information you've read or heard. As time goes on, the forgetting continues.

**What causes forgetting to occur?**

Experts propose several theories about why we forget. Fading theory says that rarely used information fades away. Retrieval theory argues that forgotten information is misplaced. Interference theory contends that old and new memories interfere with each other. Interactive interference theory suggests that middle memories are squeezed out by older and newer memories. Reactive interference theory maintains that you tune out and consequently forget information you don't want to know.

**What is pseudo-forgetting?**

Pseudo-forgetting is false forgetting. It occurs when you fail to learn something in the first place.

**Does having a reason to remember affect your memory?**

Yes. A study showed that simply intending to remember can significantly increase the life span of a memory. There are numerous examples of people who are motivated to remember and then do so. Of these motivations, the most effective one is interest.

**How can you strengthen your intention to remember?**

Start by paying close attention. If you're distracted, you aren't as likely to remember. When you learn something new, be sure that you understand it and that you learn it correctly. If you confuse or fail to understand the original information, you aren't going to miraculously correct it in your memory.

**How do the number and form of your memories affect your ability to retain information?**

Limiting what you try to learn and organizing it in a meaningful way will improve your ability to retain this information. The Silver Dollar System can aid you in memorizing information. Organizing such information into meaningful categories further improves recall.

**Why is it crucial to connect what you learn with what you already know?**

Linking new, individual memories to a memory network improves recall. Sometimes you make these connections automatically, but consciously establishing connections (either logical or artificial) between new information and a memory network ensures greater remembering.

**What is the principle of basic background?**

The principle of basic background says that what you are able to learn and remember is based on what you already know.

**How do pictures strengthen your memory?**

By connecting new information to something you've drawn or visualized, you add a new dimension to that memory by getting the visual side of your brain involved.

**How do you make artificial connections?**

You make artificial connections by using memory tricks, or mnemonic devices, to link new information with old information.

**How do you recite?**

The most common method of reciting involves repeating information out loud, from memory, and in your own words. There are, however, other ways to recite. All can be effective if you follow the basic process of reciting.

**What is the basic process of reciting?**

The basic process comprises three steps: (1) read, (2) convert what you've read, and (3) test yourself on what you've learned.

**What is the best method for reciting, and why?**

The best way of reciting is by transforming what you've read into questions, reading them, and then answering them. This is the best method because when you convert a main idea into a question, you force yourself to remember what you've just read. Reciting by writing causes no embarrassment, creates no disturbance, and provides you with written evidence of whether you've understood what you've read. And because most tests are written, reciting by writing provides excellent practice in taking tests.

**How does reciting strengthen your memory?**

Reciting holds information in your short-term memory long enough for the material to jell and then move on to long-term memory.

**How does distributed practice aid consolidation?**

Distributed practice aids consolidation because memory needs time to coalesce what you've learned and the breaks in this practice provide that time.

**What are some advantages of distributed practice?**

In addition to allowing time for consolidation, distributed practice provides breathers that discourage fatigue and burnout, increases motivation by creating a sense of accomplishment, and wards off boredom by dividing dull or intimidating subjects into more manageable pieces.

**Are there times when it's better to study continuously?**

Continuous studying, or massed practice, is appropriate for doing prolonged creative work, such as writing a paper or preparing an oral report. In these situations it's usually best to keep working while you have ideas and information in your mind so they have time to interact and jell.

**What are memory plateaus?**

Memory plateaus are periods when you appear to be making no progress even though you are making an effort. During these lulls, your mind is consolidating what you've learned thus far.

## HAVE YOU MISSED SOMETHING?

*Sentence completion.*  Complete the following sentences with one of the three words listed below each sentence.

1. According to interactive interference theory, the fact that is most likely to be lost is the _____ .
   oldest     newest     middle

2. Reactive interference theory generally applies to information that is

   _____ .

   complicated     old-fashioned     disliked

*Matching.*  In each blank space in the left column, write the letter preceding the phrase in the right column that matches the left item best.

| | | |
|---|---|---|
| _____ **1.** Pseudo-forgetting | a. | Primary cause of reactive interference |
| _____ **2.** Basic courses | b. | Suggests that memories fight each other for space |
| _____ **3.** Memory network | c. | Failure to recall what you never really learned |
| _____ **4.** Plateaus | d. | Method for selecting key ideas from your notes |
| _____ **5.** Negative attitude | e. | No-progress periods that occur during learning |
| _____ **6.** Interactive interference | f. | Study sessions divided by regular breaks |
| _____ **7.** Silver Dollar System | g. | Connects and strengthens related memories |
| _____ **8.** Distributed practice | h. | Lay the foundation for basic background |

*True-false.*  Write *T* beside the *true* statements and *F* beside the *false* statements.

_____ **1.** In creative work, massed practice is often preferred over distributed practice.

_____ **2.** In general, it's easier to recall what you've read than it is to remember what you've heard.

_____ **3.** Rereading does very little to strengthen your memory.

_____ **4.** Gerald Miller found that mnemonics had no effect on learning.

_____ **5.** New information is automatically transferred to long-term memory.

*Multiple choice.*   Choose the word or phrase that completes the following sentence most accurately, and circle the letter that precedes it.

**1.** Memory acquires an extra dimension when information is

   a. written on note cards.
   b. drawn or visualized.
   c. reread or recited.
   d. condensed or reduced.

**2.** The most valuable facts from your notes are known as

   a. Silver Dollar ideas.
   b. mnemonic devices.
   c. memory traces.
   d. none of the above.

**3.** According to fading theory, old memories are like a(n)

   a. basketball court.
   b. filing cabinet.
   c. underused path.
   d. oil slick.

**4.** In general, mnemonic devices supply

   a. visual cues.
   b. an organizational system.
   c. consolidation time.
   d. interference insurance.

**5.** No single activity is more important to strengthening memory than

   a. recitation.
   b. rereading.
   c. revising.
   d. none of the above.

*Short answer.* Supply a brief answer for each of the following items.

1. What does retrieval theory suggest about memory?
2. What is the nature of G. A. Miller's notion of memory?
3. Explain the three steps used in all types of reciting.
4. Explain why in recitation questions are preferable to key words.
5. List some of the advantages of distributed practice.

## VOCABULARY BUILDING

DIRECTIONS: Make a light check mark (√) alongside one of the three words (choices) that most nearly expresses the meaning of the italicized word in the phrases that are in the left-hand column. (Answers are given on p. 434.)

| | 1 | 2 | 3 |
|---|---|---|---|
| 1. a *lucid* memory | firm | clear | hesitant |
| 2. *jettison* previous orders | discard | retain | rehearse |
| 3. it seems to *imply* | state | question | suggest |
| 4. items *randomly* placed | haphazardly | precisely | squarely |
| 5. *mnemonic* devices | Greek | mindful | trick |
| 6. modern-day *archetype* | printer | publishers | model |
| 7. somewhat *impudent* suggestion | helpful | insolent | direct |
| 8. a *sea* of lawsuits | scarcity | time | multitude |
| 9. a *conglomerate* company | cluster | specialty | fundamental |
| 10. people *coalesce* around tax cuts | talk | walk | unite |
| 11. to the *chagrin* | humiliation | humor | novelty |
| 12. the familiar *colossus* | giant | market | conclusion |
| 13. Kane's *beguiling* arrogance | deceptive | masculine | charming |
| 14. his *suave* partner | selfish | polished | arrogant |
| 15. an *ebullient* doomed man | enthusiastic | enormous | aged |
| 16. gained a *spate* of attention | start | modicum | rush |
| 17. lulled into *complacency* | action | planning | satisfaction |
| 18. *obsolete* manufacturing rigs | outmoded | reinforced | expanded |
| 19. *contemporaneous* relationship | scornful | mutual | simultaneous |
| 20. at *unprecedented* levels | expected | unexampled | deficit |
| 21. lead to gold *transmute* | transmit | transfer | transform |
| 22. memory of that *insolence* | arrogance | attempt | decision |
| 23. in a *doleful* son | wealthy | sad | venturesome |
| 24. to *lament* a tale of wrong | remember | forget | mourn |
| 25. in *secluded* recesses | mountainous | secret | hidden |

# Improving Your Vocabulary

*The difference between the right word and the almost right word is the difference between lightning and the lightning bug.*

—MARK TWAIN (1835–1910), pen name of Samuel Clemens, author of *Huckleberry Finn*

Numerous research studies in both the academic and the business worlds show a close relationship between a good vocabulary and success. A vocabulary that is large and precise can lead you to a wealth of knowledge. This chapter explains why building a vocabulary can be a worthwhile investment. It discusses the importance of

- Using a dictionary
- Recognizing word roots and prefixes
- Becoming interested in the origin of words
- Mastering difficult words
- Using the Frontier Vocabulary System
- Testing your vocabulary

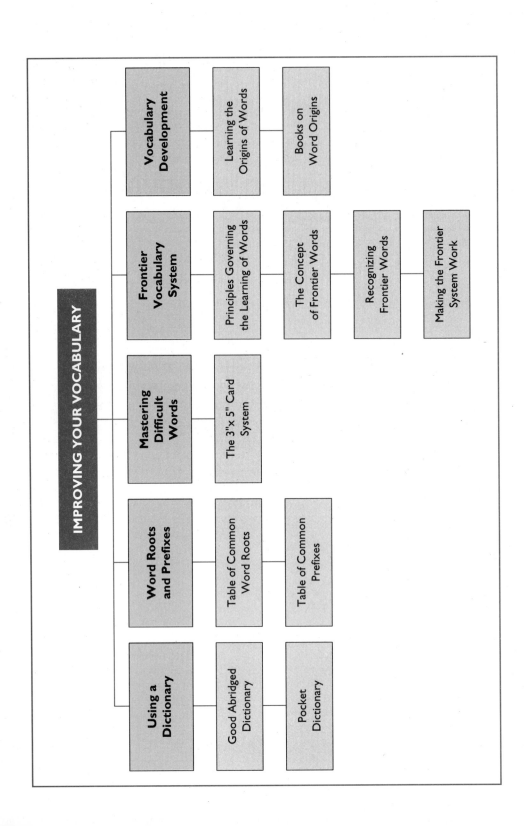

# IMPROVING YOUR VOCABULARY

**Using a Dictionary**
- Good Abridged Dictionary
- Pocket Dictionary

**Word Roots and Prefixes**
- Table of Common Word Roots
- Table of Common Prefixes

**Mastering Difficult Words**
- The 3" x 5" Card System

**Frontier Vocabulary System**
- Principles Governing the Learning of Words
- The Concept of Frontier Words
- Recognizing Frontier Words
- Making the Frontier System Work

**Vocabulary Development**
- Learning the Origins of Words
- Books on Word Origins

Throughout your college years, new words will be flooding into your consciousness. Many of them are the keys to ideas and information that will be new to you. When students have trouble in a course, the trouble can often be traced back to their imperfect comprehension of terms that are essential to an understanding of subject matter. A first-year science or social science course may introduce you to almost as many new words as a first course in a foreign language—for example:

| Chemistry | Geology | Psychology | Sociology |
|-----------|---------|------------|-----------|
| kinetic | syncline | decenter | ethnocentrism |
| colloid | moraine | synapse | sociometry |
| adsorption | diastrophic | receptor | superorganic |
| isomer | Pleistocene | mesomorph | mana |

Then there are also words like *base* in chemistry and *accommodation* in psychology, which may not literally be new to you, but which have specific meanings within the context of a specific course and, therefore, must be learned as if they were new words.

For a college student, a large, wide-ranging vocabulary is not just something "nice" to have. It is a necessary medium for grasping fundamental ideas and facts. Words are the instruments of communication, learning, and thinking. Like a mechanic with an inadequate tool kit, a student with an inadequate vocabulary cannot function effectively and efficiently. Because, you cannot go to a hardware store and buy new words to complete your kit of communication tools, as you listen and read you must be on the lookout for words to add to your vocabulary. When you find such words, gather them in immediately. Write them down, in the sentence in which you found them, so you'll have their context. Then, as soon as you can, look them up in a good dictionary.

## USING A DICTIONARY

The best way to learn new words is to keep a good dictionary close to your elbow and use it. Gliding over a word that you don't quite know can be costly. Consider this sentence: "The mayor gave *fulsome* praise to the budget committee." What does *fulsome* mean? If you think it means "full of praise," you're mistaken. Look it up in your dictionary.

Sometimes, you can get some idea of the meaning of a new word from its context—how it is used in your reading material. Use context when you can, but be aware that it has its limitations. Lee C. Deighton of Columbia University points out three: (1) Context provides only the meaning that fits that particular situation. (2) You often end up with a synonym, which is not quite the same as a definition. (3) When you have to infer the meaning of a word, you can be slightly (or greatly) in error.[1] Your safest bet is to avoid all the guesswork and go straight to your dictionary.

As you study, consult your dictionary whenever you come to a word that you don't know precisely. Find the exact meaning you need; then go back to your textbook and reread the paragraph, with the *meaning* substituted for the word. If you become interested in a particular word, write it on a 3 × 5 card. Later, go back to the dictionary and investigate it. Write its meanings on the card, and keep the card and other like cards to look through and study occasionally. But don't break into your studying for a long session with the dictionary; save that for later.

Many scholars and business people rely on a pocket dictionary as a handy source of definitions. Eddie Rickenbacker (1890–1973), auto racer, ace fighter pilot in World War I, and businessman who left school when he was only twelve years old, made it a habit to carry a small dictionary in his pocket. In his autobiography, he recalled:

> Though much of my association was with mechanics and other drivers, I also had the opportunity to converse with men in higher positions, automotive engineers, and company officials. . . . I listened carefully and marked well the way such men constructed and phrased their thoughts. I carried a dictionary with me always and used it. I have never slackened in the pursuit of learning and self-improvement.[2]

Follow the example of thousands of successful people. Get yourself a pocket dictionary such as *Webster's II New Riverside Pocket Dictionary* and always carry it with you. Instead of reading the print on cereal boxes, or looking at advertising placards on buses and subways, or staring into space, take out your dictionary and *read* it. Its definitions will be terse, consisting mainly of synonyms, but its value lies in its ability to spark a lifelong interest in words as well as increase your vocabulary. Of course, a pocket dictionary is no substitute for a larger, desk-size dictionary, but as a portable learning tool, the pocket dictionary is worth at least its weight in gold.

To illustrate how a dictionary is read, let's study Figure 6.1, which is a page from a pocket dictionary.[3] You open to page one and as your eyes drift

---

[1]Lee C. Deighton, *Vocabulary Development in the Classroom* (New York: Teachers College Press, 1959), pp. 2–3.
[2]Edward V. Rickenbacker, *Rickenbacker* (Englewood Cliffs, NJ: Prentice-Hall, 1967), pp. 65–66.
[3]*Webster's II New Riverside Pocket Dictionary* (Boston: Houghton Mifflin Company, 1991), p. 1.

# A

**a, A** (ā) *n*. The 1st letter of the English alphabet.

**a** (ə; *emphatic* ā) *indef. art*. One; any.

**a•back** (ə-băk´) *adv*. —**take aback.** To startle; confuse.

*The Japanese used this device from ancient times* → **ab•a•cus** (ăb´ə-kəs) *n., pl.* **-cuses** or **-ci**. A manual computing device with rows of moveable beads.

**a•ban•don** (əbăn´-dən) *v*. **1.** To give up; forsake. **2.** To desert. —*n*. A complete surrender of inhibitions. —**a•ban´-doned** *adj*. —**a•ban´don• ment** *n*.

*Strong, simple word* → **a•base** (ə-bās´) *v*. **abased, abasing.** To humble; humiliate. —**a•base´ment** *n*.

*Somewhat similar to abridge* → **a•bate** (ə-bāt´) *v*. **abated, abating.** To reduce; lessen. —**a•bate´ment** *n*.

**ab•bey** (ăb´e) *n., pl.* **-beys.** A monastery or convent.

**ab•bre•viate** (ə-brē´vē-āt´) *v*. **-ated, -ating.** To make shorter. —**ab•bre´vi•a´tion** *n*.

*King Edward VIII Throne of England* → **ab•di•cate** (ăb´dĭ-kāt´) *v*. **-cated, -cating.** To relinquish (power or responsibility) formally. —**ab´di•ca´tion** *n*.

*Preferred accent on 3rd syllable* → **ab•do•men** (ăb´də-mən, ăb-dō´mən) *n*. The part of the body between the thorax and the pelvis. —**ab• dom´i•nal** *adj*.

*"Exception" to the rule* → **ab•duct** (ăb-dŭkt´) *v*. To kidnap. —**ab• duc´tion** *n*. —**ab•duc´tor** *n*.

**ab•er•ra•tion** (ăb´ə-rā´shən) *n*. Deviation or depature from the normal, typical, or expected. —**ab•er´rance** , **ab•er´ran•cy** *n*. —**ab•er´rant** *adj*.

*In law: to "aid & abet"* → **a•bet** (ə-bĕt´) *v* . **abetted, abetting. 1.** To encourage; incite. **2.** To assist. —**a•bet´tor, a•bet´ter** *n*.

**a•bey•ance** (ə-bā´əns) *n*. Temporary suspension.

**ab•hor** (ăb-hôr´) *v*. **-horred, -horring.** To dislike intensely; loathe. —**ab•hor´rence** *n*. —**ab• hor´rent** *adj*.

**a•bide** (ə-bīd´) *v*. abode or abided, abiding. **1.** To wait. **2.** To tolerate; bear. **3.** To remain; last. —**abide by.** To conform to; comply with. —**a•bide´ing** *adj*.

**a•bil•i•ty** (ə-bĭl´ĭ-tē) *n. pl.* **-ties. 1.** The power to perform. **2.** A skill or talent.

**ab•ject** (ăb´jĕkt´, ăb-jĕkt´) *adj*. **1.** Contemptible; base. **2.** Miserable; wretched. —**ab•jec´tion** *n*. —**ab•ject´ly** *adv*.

*Looks like object but far off*

**ab•jure** (ăb-joor´) *v*. **-jured, -juring.** To renounce under oath; forswear.

*In unabridged dictionary: "He abjured all titles, preferring 'Mr.'"*

**a•ble** (ā´bəl) *adj*. **abler, ablest. 1.** Having sufficient ability. **2.** Capable or talented. —**a´bly** *adv*.

**ab•ne•gate** (ăb´nĭ-gāt´) *v*. **-gated, -gating.** To deny to oneself; renounce. —**ab´ne•ga´tion** *n*.

*Personal rights. Abdicate – national power*

**ab•nor•mal** (ăb-nôr´məl) *adj*. Not normal; deviant. —**ab´nor•mal´i• ty** *adv*.

**a•bode** (ə-bōd´) *v*. p.t. & p.p. of **abide.** —*n*. A home.

**a•bol•ish** (ə-bŏl´ĭsh) *v*. To put an end to; annul. —**ab´o•li´tion** *n*. —**ab´o•li´tion•ist**. *n*.

*Usually connected to Snowmen of the Hymalayas*

**a•bom•i•na•ble** (ə-bŏm´ə-nə-bəl) *adj*. Detestable; loathsome. —**a•bom´i• na•bly** *adv*. —**a•bom´inate´** *v*. —**a•bom´ina´tion** *n*.

**ab•o•rig•i•ne** (ăb´ə-rĭj´ə-nē) *n*. An original inhabitant of a region. —**ab•o•rig´i•nal** *adj. & n*.

*Usually applied to original people of Australia*

**a•bort** (ə-bôrt´) *v*. To terminate pregnancy or full development prematurely. —*n*. Premature termination of a rocket launch or space mission. —**a•bor´tive** *adj*.

**a•bor•tion** (ə-bôr´shən) *n*. **1.** Induced premature termination of pregnancy or development. **2.** Something malformed. —**a•bor´tion•ist** *n*.

**a•bound** (ə-bound´) *v*. To be great in number or amount; teem.

*"The mosqui-toes abound in swamps"*

**a•bout** (ə-bout´) *adv*. **1.** Approximately. **2.** Toward a reverse direction. **3.** In the vicinity. —*prep*. **1.** On all sides of. **2.** Near to. **3.** In or on. **4.** Concerning. **5.** Ready. —*adj*. Astir.

**a•bove** (ə-bŭv´) *adv*. **1.** Overhead. **2.** In a higher place, rank, or position. —*prep*. **1.** Over. **2.** Superior to. **3.** In preference to. —*n*. Something that is above. —*adj*. Appearing or stated earlier.

**a•bove•board** (ə-bŭv´bôrd´, -bōrd´) *adv*. Without deceit. —**a•bove´board´** *adj*.

**ab•ra•sion** (ə-brā´zhən) *n*. **1.** A wearing away by friction. **2.** A scraped or worn area. —**a•brade´** *v*. —**a• bra´sive** *adj. & n*.

*Rubbing, scraping as in friction*

**a•bridge** (ə-brĭj´) *v*. **abridged, abridging.** To condense; shorten. —**a• bridg´ment, a•bridge´ment** *n*.

*Big dictionary – unabridged*

**a•broad** (ə-brôd´) *adv*. **1.** Out of one's own country. **2.** Out of doors. **3.** Broadly; widely.

**FIGURE 6.1   Random and Spontaneous Thoughts about Words**
Copyright © 1991 by Houghton Mifflin Company. Reproduced by permission from *Webster's II New Riverside Pocket Dictionary, Revised Edition.*

down the column of words an internal conversation takes place: You think about what you already know about the word, you think about the other aspects of the word such as the syllable that must be accented, the precise definition of the word, and how it could be used in your writing and speaking.

For your study periods, buy and use the best abridged dictionary that you can afford, but be aware that no word is ever fully defined even by a good abridged dictionary. The dictionary meaning is only an operational meaning that will solve your immediate problem. Words have multiple shades of meaning that add richness to our language. These various shades will become apparent to you as you keep reading, listening, and trying to use words in a variety of contexts.

Good abridged desk dictionaries include the following:

> *The American Heritage Dictionary* (Houghton Mifflin Company)
>
> *Webster's New Collegiate Dictionary* (G. & C. Merriam Company)
>
> *Webster's New World Dictionary of American English* (Silver Burdett)

For intensive word study, however, there is no substitute for an unabridged dictionary. Locate the unabridged dictionaries in your library—usually they are in the reference room—and use them to supplement your own abridged desk dictionary. An unabridged dictionary gives more definitions, more about the derivations of words, and more on usage. Good one-volume unabridged dictionaries include *Webster's Third New International Dictionary of the English Language,* and the *Random House Dictionary of the English Language. The Oxford English Dictionary,* in twenty volumes plus supplements, is indispensable for the historical study of words but is more detailed than you will need for most purposes.

The reference librarian can help you find specialized dictionaries on various subjects. They list technical terms not always found even in un-abridged dictionaries. However, your textbooks are usually the best sources of the definitions for such terms.

## RECOGNIZING WORD ROOTS AND PREFIXES

Using the dictionary is an excellent way to increase your vocabulary one word at a time. However, if you would like to learn whole clusters of words in one stroke, you should get to know the most common roots and prefixes in English. A word *root* is the core of a word, the part that holds the basic meaning. A *prefix* is a word beginning that modifies the root. Table 6.1 lists some common word roots, and Table 6.2 lists some common prefixes.

It has been estimated that 60 percent of the English words in common use are made up partly or entirely of prefixes or roots derived from Latin and Greek. The value of learning prefixes and roots is that they illustrate the way much of our language is constructed. Once learned, they can help you recognize and understand many words without resorting to a dictionary. With one well-understood root word as the center, an entire "constellation" of words can be built up. Figure 6.2 shows such a constellation, based on the root "duct," from the Latin *ducere* ("to lead"). Notice that it makes use of twenty common prefixes and of other prefixes and combining words as well as various word endings. It does not exhaust all the possibilities, either; you should be able to think of several other words growing out of "duct."

### TABLE 6.1   Common Word Roots

| Root | Meaning | Example | Definition |
|------|---------|---------|------------|
| agri | field | agronomy | *Field*-crop production and soil management |
| anthropo | man | anthropology | The study of *humans* |
| astro | star | astronaut | One who travels in interplanetary space (*stars*) |
| bio | life | biology | The study of *life* |
| cardio | heart | cardiac | Pertaining to the *heart* |
| chromo | color | chromatology | The science of *colors* |
| demos | people | democracy | Government by the *people* |
| derma | skin | epidermis | The outer layer of *skin* |
| dyna | power | dynamic | Characterized by *power* and energy |
| geo | earth | geology | The study of the *earth* |
| helio | sun | heliotrope | Any plant that turns toward the *sun* |
| hydro | water | hydroponics | Growing of plants in *water* reinforced with nutrients |
| hypno | sleep | hypnosis | A state of *sleep* induced by suggestion |
| magni | great, big | magnify | To enlarge, to make *bigger* |
| man(u) | hand | manuscript | Written by *hand* |
| mono | one | monoplane | Airplane with *one* wing |
| ortho | straight | orthodox | Right, true, *straight* opinion |
| pod | foot | pseudopod | False *foot* |
| psycho | mind | psychology | Study of the *mind* in any of its aspects |
| pyro | fire | pyrometer | An instrument for measuring temperatures |
| terra | earth | terrace | A raised platform of *earth* |
| thermo | heat | thermometer | Instrument for measuring *heat* |
| zoo | animal | zoology | The study of *animals* |

**TABLE 6.2   Common Prefixes**

| Prefix | Meaning | Example | Definition |
|--------|---------|---------|------------|
| ante- | before | antebellum | *Before* the war; especially in the U.S., before the Civil War |
| anti- | against | antifreeze | Liquid used to guard *against* freezing |
| auto- | self | automatic | *Self*-acting or *self*-regulating |
| bene- | good | benefit | An act of *kindness;* a gift |
| circum- | around | circumscribe | To draw a line *around;* to encircle |
| contra- | against | contradict | To speak *against* |
| de- | reverse, remove | defoliate | *Remove* the leaves from a tree |
| ecto- | outside | ectoparasite | Parasite living on the *exterior* of animals |
| endo- | within | endogamy | Marriage *within* the tribe |
| hyper- | over | hypertension | *High* blood pressure |
| hypo- | under | hypotension | *Low* blood pressure |
| inter- | between | intervene | Come *between* |
| intra- | within | intramural | *Within* bounds of a school |
| intro- | in, into | introspect | To look *within,* as one's own mind |
| macro- | large | macroscopic | *Large* enough to be observed by the naked eye |
| mal- | bad | maladjusted | *Badly* adjusted |
| micro- | small | microscopic | So small that one needs a microscope to observe |
| multi- | many | multimillionaire | One having *two* or *more* million dollars |
| neo- | new | neolithic | *New* stone age |
| non- | not | nonconformist | One who does *not* conform |
| pan- | all | pantheon | A temple didicated to *all* gods |
| poly- | many | polygonal | Having *many* sides |
| post- | after | postgraduate | *After* graduating |
| pre- | before | precede | To go *before* |
| proto- | first | prototype | *First* or original model |
| pseudo- | false | pseudonym | *False* name; esp., an author's pen-name |
| retro- | backward | retrospect | A looking *back* on things |
| semi- | half | semicircle | *Half* a circle |
| sub- | under | submerge | To put *under* water |
| super- | above | superfine | *Extra* fine |
| tele- | far | telescope | Seeing or viewing *afar* |
| trans- | across | transalpine | *Across* the Alps |

Although knowing the meanings of prefixes and roots can unlock the meanings of unfamiliar words, this knowledge should supplement, not replace, your dictionary use. Over the centuries, many prefixes have changed in both meaning and spelling. According to Lee Deighton, "of the 68 prominent and commonly used prefixes there are only 11 which have a single

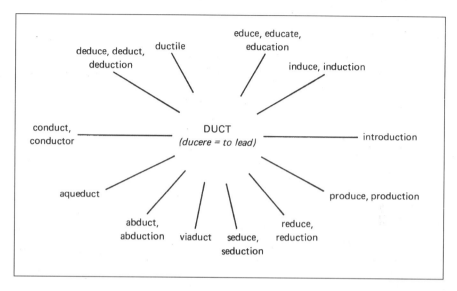

**FIGURE 6.2   A Constellation of Words from One Root**

and fairly invariant meaning."[4] The other fifty-seven prefixes have more than one meaning each.

For example, the prefix *de*-means "of" or "from"; yet the dictionary lists four different meanings for it:

1. It means "down" as in *descend,* which means to pass from a higher to a lower place.
2. It indicates separation as in *dehumidify,* which means to separate moisture from air, or in *decapitate,* which means to behead—that is, to separate the head from the rest of the body.
3. It indicates reversal as in *decode,* which means to convert from code into ordinary language, or in *depreciate,* which means to lessen in value.
4. It may be used to intensify as in *demonstrate,* which means to show or prove publicly, or in *declare,* which means to announce.

So learn as many of the common prefixes and roots as you can, but learn them for better and more precise understanding of words you already know and words that you have yet to look up in the dictionary. When you go to the dictionary, make sure that you spend some time on the prefixes and roots that make up each word. You will soon become convinced that a

---

[4]Deighton, *Vocabulary Development in the Classroom,* p. 26.

word is not an assemblage of letters put together like an anagram, but the true and natural outcome of evolution.

## MASTERING DIFFICULT WORDS

There is no quick and easy way to a powerful vocabulary. Don't fall for any advertising that claims otherwise. The only sure way is overlearning by means of recitation. All you need is a dictionary and a stack of 3 × 5 cards. On the cards write the difficult words that you find in your textbooks and hear in the classroom. These are words you need to know to understand your coursework.

When you select a word, write it on one side of a 3 × 5 card. To provide a meaningful context, write the sentence or phrase in which the word occurs and underline the word. Next, look the word up in a dictionary and write the word out in syllables, including accent and diacritical marks so that you can pronounce it correctly. On the reverse side of the card, write the definition that is most appropriate for the context. For a technical term, write the definition given in your textbook. Special terms are usually defined when first introduced or else in a glossary. If you want to pursue your study of a word in more detail, on the reverse side of the card record any information you find about its derivation; for this information you may need to consult an unabridged dictionary. Figure 6.3 shows three formats for your cards.

To study your cards, correctly pronounce the word aloud. Try to recall the definition without looking at it; then turn the card over to check your recall. If you fail, place a dot in the upper right-hand corner, on the front of the card. The next time you go through your cards, the dot will remind you that you missed on a previous try. When a card has three or more dots, it is time to give that word some special attention.

The advantage of 3 × 5 cards is that they are convenient to carry about for study at odd moments. At all times, have with you a few blank cards on which to record interesting words. Learning words that intrigue you will be immeasurably more valuable than memorizing a list made up for you by someone else.

## USING THE FRONTIER VOCABULARY SYSTEM

Consulting the dictionary or probing the histories of words can help to increase your vocabulary word by word. One highly effective way to increase your vocabulary is to use the Frontier Vocabulary System developed by

| (FRONT) (a) | (REVERSE) (a) |
|---|---|
| symbiosis<br><br>sym´bī-ō-sis | the intimate living together of two species with mutual benefit |

| (FRONT) (b) | (REVERSE) (b) |
|---|---|
| eyes like <u>chrysoprase</u><br><br>chrys´-o-prase | an apple green variety of <u>chalcedony</u><br><br>chalcedony (kăl-sĕd´-o-nĭ) = a translucent variety of quartz with waxlike luster |

| (FRONT) (c) | (REVERSE) (c) |
|---|---|
| "And I stand ready to oppose to the uttermost any group that seeks to limit or pervert the curricula of schools and colleges in order to impose upon them their own narrow and dogmatic <u>preconceptions</u> concerning matters that are properly the subject of free inquiry."<br><br>pre´con-cep´tion | pre = before; denoting before in time.<br>con = with, together, in conjunction.<br>cept = from <u>capere</u> = to take<br>    A preconceived idea; hence, a prejudice; a prepossession.<br>    preconceive = to conceive, or form opinion of, beforehand. |

**FIGURE 6.3  Vocabulary Cards in Varying Degrees of Detail** (a) A key term defined from the textbook. (b) A word in a meaningful phrase with a secondary definition given. (c) A word in full-sentence context, with information on parts and derivation and with a secondary definition.

Johnson O'Connor. The Frontier Vocabulary System is based on natural learning processes.[5] We know that a baby must crawl before it can walk and walk before it can run. We know, too, that a child can pronounce the sound $p$ at about age $3\frac{1}{2}$ but usually does not master the sound $r$ until age $7\frac{1}{2}$. Many other skills develop along with physical growth and general maturation. All learning processes have four characteristics:

1. Skills progress from the simple to the complex.
2. Each skill is developed in an orderly sequence of steps.
3. Each step is at a different level of difficulty.
4. No significant step may be skipped. Each step seems to develop the muscle or brain pattern that makes the next step possible.

From his analytical research, O'Connor concluded that learning new words is much like learning any other skill. We progress from simple words to more difficult ones in an orderly sequence. The difficulty or ease of learning a word does not depend on the length of the word, its frequency of use, its geographic origin, or its pronunciation, or on teachers, books, or parents. Instead, difficulty in learning a word depends on the complexity of the *idea* that the word stands for. Defining words with simple synonyms does not provide the learner with a background sufficient to think with the words. Because words stand for ideas, the ideas behind them must also be learned.

S.I. Hayakawa, the noted semanticist, agrees with this view. He questions the old-fashioned notion that the way to study words is to concentrate one's attention exclusively on words. Hayakawa suggests that words should be understood in relationship to other words—not only other words on the same level but also words at a higher (more abstract) level and words at a lower (more concrete) level.

## Principles Governing the Learning of Words

The following findings by O'Connor form the basis for the Frontier Vocabulary System:

1. The easiest words are learned first; then the harder ones are learned.
2. At the forward edge of the mass of all the words that have been mastered is the individual's *frontier*. Only a very few words *beyond the frontier* have already been mastered.

---

[5]Much of this discussion is based on an article by Dean Trembly, "Intellectual Abilities as Motivating Factors," *Japanese Psychological Research* 10. no. 2 (July 1968): 104–08.

3. The greatest learning takes place in the frontier area, which lies between the zone of known words and the zone of totally unknown words (see Figure 6.4).
4. The most significant characteristic of the words in the frontier area is that they are, to some extent, familiar. The maximum advancement in a person's mastery of words takes place in the frontier area, where hundreds of almost-known words need only a slight straightening out to make them familiar.
5. Learning becomes extremely inefficient and may actually break down whenever a person skips the frontier area and tries to learn totally unknown words.

Familiarity with a word in the frontier area means that you already know something about the word or its definition. You may, for example, know how to pronounce the word and know its general meaning. Or you may know one of its several meanings. The important point is this: By singling out such a frontier word and learning its specific meaning, or its several definitions, you can master the word with minimal time and effort.

---

### ZONE OF KNOWN WORDS

These are the words already mastered. They are used in reading, writing, listening, and thinking.

**The Edge of the Frontier**

---

### FRONTIER AREA

The words in this zone are the frontier words.
They are somewhat familiar.

---

### ZONE OF TOTALLY UNKNOWN WORDS

An occasional word, like an island in an unknown sea, might have been discovered and made one's own because of necessity.

---

FIGURE 6.4  **The Concept of Frontier Words**

By working continually in the frontier area, you can make rapid progress in mastering words. At the same time, you will continually be discovering new frontier words to conquer. As the process continues, the frontier area will push into the zone of totally unknown words.

## Recognizing Frontier Words

To find your own frontier words, first become aware of your daily speech, and make a list of the unusual words you use. Next, be on the lookout for words that you recognize in reading but do not use in speaking and writing. From this source choose *only* the words that appeal to you. Listen attentively while other people speak. The chances are great that you will recognize and know the general meaning of all the words you hear. Choose from this stream of speech the words that appeal to you—words that you would like to incorporate into your own speech.

Later, after writing out the definition for each of your frontier words, look for its opposite. If it interests you, learn that word too. Learning pairs of contrasting words creates the strong force of spontaneous suggestion—either word suggests the other.

## Making the Frontier System Work

Write each frontier word on a separate 3 × 5 card, underlined and in proper context. Once you have a small stack of cards, look up the words in an unabridged dictionary. Below your excerpted sentence, print the word with its syllables and diacritical markings.

On the back of the card, write the prefix and root that make up your word. Write the definition or definitions for your word and put an asterisk beside the definition that best fits the meaning of your word in its specific context.

Carry about a dozen of these completed cards in a pocket or purse so you can review them whenever you have a spare moment. Figure 6.5 shows the Frontier System format.

To master the words on the cards, do the following:

1. Always look at the front side of the card. Pronounce the word correctly; read the sentence completely; and then define the word, not necessarily in dictionary language but meaningfully in your own words. All this should be done before you look at the definition on the back.

**(FRONT) (a)**

His silence <u>implied</u> that he, at least, did not disagree with my statement.

im-ply&#x2032;        (ĭm-plī&#x2032;)
im-plied&#x2032;      (ĭm-plīd&#x2032;)

**(REVERSE) (a)**

[im = in]        [plicare = fold]
[implicare = to fold in; to entwine]

1. To express indirectly; to suggest; to hint or hint at.
2. To contain potentially.

syn.: suggest

**(FRONT) (b)**

From his silence and manner, I <u>inferred</u> that he agreed with my statement.

in-fer&#x2032;        (ĭn-fûr&#x2032;)
in-ferred&#x2032;      (ĭn-fûrd&#x2032;)
in-fer&#x2032;ring      (ĭn-fûr&#x2032;ring)

**(REVERSE) (b)**

[in = in]        [ferre = to bring (out)]

1. To derive by reasoning; to conclude from facts or premises.
2. To surmise; to guess.

syn.: deduce, conclude

**FIGURE 6.5 Frontier System Cards** These two cards (*implied* and *inferred*) show a pair of words that are opposite or complementary. Such words, studied together, are bound to take on more precise meaning. Notice that the front of each card shows the new word underlined in a complete sentence. It also shows how to pronounce the word. The reverse of each card defines prefixes and roots and gives important dictionary definitions of the word. An asterisk is placed beside the definition that most nearly matches the use of the word on the front of the card. Synonyms are also given.

2. After you have defined the word to the best of your ability, turn the card over to check on the accuracy of your definition.
3. If you are not satisfied with your definition, place a dot on the front of the card, in the upper right-hand corner. The next time you go through your cards, the dot will remind you that you missed on a previous try. When a card has three dots, it is time to give that word some special attention.
4. After the small stack of cards has been mastered, place them in a file and pick up additional ones for mastering.
5. From time to time, review the words that you have mastered.

As you master the precise meaning of each frontier word, there will be a corresponding advance in your reading, writing, speaking, and thinking.

## VOCABULARY DEVELOPMENT

The four ingredients necessary to make vocabulary building a productive adventure are a keen sense of interest, a sense of excitement, a sense of wonder, and a feeling of pleasure when you choose words and the words choose you.[6] One sure way to pick up interest, excitement, wonder, and pleasure in your adventure with words is to learn the origin of words.

Words, like facts, are difficult to remember out of context. Remembering is greatly facilitated when you have a body of information with which to associate either a word or a fact. For words, interesting origins or histories will help provide a context. For example, a *hippopotamus* is a "river horse," from the Greek *hippos*, meaning "horse," and *potamos*, meaning "river."

Indiana is called the *Hoosier state*, and its people *Hoosiers*. Why? In the early days, the pioneers were gruff in manner; when someone knocked at the front door, a pioneer's voice would often boom, "Who's yere?"

You may have wondered why runners on a cross-country track team are called *harriers*, especially by sports writers. Actually, a harrier is a swift-running dog, useful in hunting rabbits.

If you were offered a *Hobson's choice*, would you know what was meant? Thomas Hobson owned a livery stable in seventeenth-century England. He loved his horses, and to prevent any one horse from being overworked, he hired them out in turn, beginning with stall number one. Customers had to take the horses they were given. Thus *Hobson's choice* means no choice at all.

Words that are illustrated with pictures are especially memorable. Consider, for example, the word *deliberate*. Deliberation has its origins in ancient scales, the same type of scales represented in the constellation Libra. Libra means "a pair of scales" or "a balance." A deliberate decision is one made after a weighing of the consequences has occurred (see Figure 6.6). Henceforth, whenever you read or use the word *deliberate*, the picture will project itself onto the movie screen of your mind. You will be using both hemispheres of your brain: the left for reading the history of the word, and the right for absorbing the illustration of the word.

## LEARNING THE ORIGINS OF WORDS

Delving into word origins can be a pleasurable way of developing both your awareness and your understanding of words. Words take on more meaning and become more memorable when their "life stories" are unfolded.

---

[6]Deighton, *Vocabulary Development in the Classroom,* p. 59.

Deliberate

**FIGURE 6.6   "Deliberate"**

Back of almost every word in the English language there is a "life story" that will come to many as a fascinating revelation. Our words have come to us from a multitude of sources. Some of them have lived for thousands of years and have played their parts in many lands and many civilizations. They may record ancient superstitions. They may be monuments to customs dating back to classical antiquity. They may reveal our ancestors' manners and beliefs, shrouded in the mists of ancient history. Words that you use today may have been the slang of Roman soldiers twenty centuries ago or the lingo of Malay savages. They may have been used by an Athenian poet or by an Anglo-Saxon farmer.[7]

The following is an example of how memorable a word can be when its origin is learned and can be vividly pictured:[8]

Here are two lists of books that are sure to arouse your interest in words and, at the same time, increase your stock of words. The out-of-print books are worth looking for in libraries; those still in print can be obtained from their publishers.

***Books still in print***   Ciardi, John, *A Browser's Dictionary and Native's Guide to the Unknown American Language*. Published in 1980. Information and copies: Harper & Row Publishers, Inc., 10 East 53rd St. New York, NY 10022.

---

[7]By permission, from *Interesting Origins of English Words,* copyright 1959 by G, & C. Merriam Co., Publishers of the Merriam-Webster Dictionaries.
[8]From *Picturesque Word Origins,* Copyright © 1933 by Merriam-Webster, Inc. Reprinted by permission.

Funk, Charles E., *A Hog on Ice, and Other Curious Expressions.* Published in 1948. Information and copies: Harper & Row Publishers, Inc., 10 East 53rd St. New York, NY 10022.

Holt, Alfred H., *Phrase and Word Origins.* Published in 1961. Information and copies: Dover Publications, Inc., 31 E Second St., Mineola, NY 11501.

Hook, J.N., *The Grand Panjandrum.* Published in 1980. Information and copies: Macmillan Publishing Co., Inc., 866 Third Avenue, New York, NY 10022.

Maleska, Eugene T., *A Pleasure in Words.* Publsihed in 1981. Information and copies: Simon and Schuster. 1230 Avenue of the Americas, New York, NY 10020.

Mathews, Mitford M., *American Words.* Published in 1959 and again in 1976. Information and copies: Philomel Books, 200 Madison Avenue, New York, NY 10016.

*Word Mysteries & Histories.* Published in 1980. Information and copies: Houghton Mifflin Co., 222 Berkeley St., Boston, MA 02116.

**Out-of-print books**   Ernst, Margaret S., *In a Word.* Published in 1939 by Alfred A. Knopf, New York.

*Picturesque Word Origins.* Published in 1933 by G. & C. Merriam Company, Springfield, Mass.

It is good to end these few pages with a thought from the scholarly Edwin Newman:

> ". . . that learning the subtleties and nuances of our common tongue can be not only instructive and rewarding, but fun."[9]

## SUMMARY

| | |
|---|---|
| **Is there really a connection between a good vocabulary and success?** | Yes. Information is power, and the only way to send and receive information effectively is with the help of a large, wide-ranging vocabulary. |
| **What is the best way to build up my vocabulary?** | The best way to improve your vocabulary is to get into the habit of using your dictionary. When you don't know a word, look it up. |

---

[9]Edwin Newman, Foreword to *Morris Dictionary of Word and Phrase Origins.* New York: Harper & Row, Publishers, 1977. By William and Mary Morris.

**Can't I simply figure out a word's meaning from context?**

Context can give you a rough idea of a word's meaning, but it has three limitations: (1) Context provides the meaning of a word in a very specific instance. (2) It gives you a synonym rather than a bona fide definition. (3) It requires you to do guesswork, which may or may not be correct.

**What kind of dictionary should I use?**

Few students can afford to buy an unabridged dictionary; however, most libraries keep several unabridged dictionaries on hand for reference. You should buy a good abridged dictionary to use when you are studying at your desk. You might also want to buy a pocket dictionary to carry around with you.

**Is there any point in studying prefixes and word roots?**

Yes. Sixty percent of the words commonly used in English have Latin or Greek prefixes and roots. The ability to recognize and understand the meaning of these prefixes and roots can give you a real edge.

**What can be done to make vocabulary building a productive adventure?**

You need a sense of interest, a sense of excitement, a sense of wonder, and a feeling of pleasure to make vocabulary building productive. One way to gain all four is by becoming interested in the origin of words.

**How can I learn difficult words that turn up in my textbooks or in lectures?**

Mastering words takes constant practice. The most effective way to get this sort of practice is by putting difficult words encountered in your textbooks and class lectures on 3 × 5 cards.

**What's the advantage of 3 × 5 cards?**

Such cards are portable. You can easily carry a stack of cards in a pocket or purse so they'll be available whenever you have a little free time.

**What should I write on the cards?**

Put each word on a separate card. Write the word and the sentence or phrase in which it occurs on the front of the card. Look up the word in a dictionary, and write its phonetic spelling on this side as well. On the back of the card, put the word's definitions as well as its derivation.

**How do I study from the cards?**

To master the word, pronounce it; read it in context; and then define it without looking at the back of the card. Then check the back to see whether you were correct. Go through a handful of vocabulary cards until you feel secure that you have mastered them.

**What is the Frontier Vocabulary System?**

The Frontier Vocabulary System is a vocabulary-building method that focuses on words that are slightly familiar to you rather than totally unknown. If you try to learn a word that is totally unknown to you, the chances are great that you will never remember it. But if you learn a word that lies in the frontier area of your vocabulary, you are likely to hold on to its meaning. What's more, with each new word you learn you'll be pushing into the zone of unknown words.

**Should I find my own frontier words, or should I use an expert's list?**

Make up your own list. Use words that *you* are slightly familiar with, rather than words that an expert has chosen for you.

**How do I find my own frontier words?**

There are four ways to start accumulating a list of frontier words: (1) Pay attention to the words that you use routinely in conversation. Are you sure that you are clear about their meanings? (2) Look for words that you recognize in reading but never use when you speak. There's a good chance that they are frontier words. (3) Listen to the conversations of others and see whether they use words that you would like to master. (4) Learn the antonyms of the frontier words that you find. Learning words in pairs does a great deal to cement them in your memory.

**How do I master these frontier words?**

Write each frontier word on a 3 × 5 card. Treat and study these words just as you treat the difficult words encountered in your textbooks and in lectures. Master the words by reading the front of the card out loud and reciting the word's definition from memory. Then check your progress by flipping over the card.

## HAVE YOU MISSED SOMETHING?

*Sentence completion.*   Complete the following sentences with one of the three words listed below each sentence.

   **a.** There is a close relationship between a good vocabulary and _____ .
   prefixes     synonyms     success

   **b.** New vocabulary words should always be written in _____ .
   pairs     context     cursive

   **c.** Definitions in most pocket dictionaries consist mainly of _____ .
   synonyms     derivations     antonyms

*Matching.*   In each blank space in the left column, write the letter preceding the phrase in the right column that matches the left item best.

   _____ **1.** Accommodation       a. May reveal the meaning of a new word

   _____ **2.** 60                  b. Takes on a specific meaning when used in psychology

   _____ **3.** Constellation       c. Percentage of English words derived from Latin or Greek

   _____ **4.** 57                  d. Word beginning

   _____ **5.** Context             e. Zone of vocabulary used in reading, writing, speaking, and thinking

   _____ **6.** Prefix              f. Number of common prefixes that have multiple meanings

   _____ **7.** Known words         g. A group of words with a common root

   _____ **8.** Frontier area       h. Greatest learning takes place here

*True-false.*   Write *T* beside the *true* statements and *F* beside the *false* statements.

   _____ **1.** A powerful vocabulary can be acquired very quickly.

   _____ **2.** No word is ever fully defined.

   _____ **3.** Key words and terms from your courses should be mastered like frontier words.

   _____ **4.** A knowledge of prefixes and roots will eliminate any need for the dictionary.

   _____ **5.** Antonyms of words you already know can make excellent frontier words.

   _____ **6.** The words *Hobson's choice* mean *you have no choice.*

*Multiple choice.*   Choose the phrase that completes the following sentence most accurately, and circle the letter that precedes it.

**1.** Three dots on a vocabulary card indicate that the word

    a. has three different definitions.
    b. may require extra attention.
    c. has been properly mastered.
    d. consists of a common prefix and root.

**2.** Frontier words are

    a. inexhaustible in their supply.
    b. the easiest words to master.
    c. familiar in one way or another.
    d. all of the above.

*Short Answer.*   Supply a brief answer for each of the following questions.

**1.** Lee Deighton writes that an *interest in words* is the prime requirement for building a vocabulary. Do you agree? Why?
**2.** A pocket dictionary is invaluable for building vocabulary. Can you think of two reasons why it works?
**3.** The 3 × 5 vocabulary card is recommended for mastering words. Can you think of two reasons why this system works?
**4.** S. I. Hayakawa suggests that words should be understood in relationship to other words. Why?

## VOCABULARY BUILDING

DIRECTIONS: Make a light check mark (√) alongside one of the three words (choices) that most nearly expresses the meaning of the italicized word in the phrases that are in the left-hand column. (Answers are given on p. 435.)

|    |                          | 1            | 2          | 3           |
|----|--------------------------|--------------|------------|-------------|
| 1. | for *intensive* word study | quantitative | deep       | vocational  |
| 2. | *derivation* of words    | origins      | definition | synonyms    |
| 3. | dictionary is *indispensable* | convenient | unabridged | essential   |
| 4. | fairly *invariant* meanings | changeable | constant   | unreliable  |
| 5. | many humorous *anecdotes* | jokes       | incidents  | programs    |
| 6. | in a breathless *cadence* | beat        | stream     | pledge      |
| 7. | such an *aura*           | attempt      | artistry   | atmosphere  |
| 8. | he *lambasted* his opponent | attacked  | criticized | ignored     |
| 9. | for his *animated* philosophy | primitive | ancient    | lively      |

|     |                                      | **1**       | **2**        | **3**        |
| --- | ------------------------------------ | ----------- | ------------ | ------------ |
| 10. | quite so *brash*                     | aggressive  | tactless     | boastful     |
| 11. | movie of such *profundity*           | profitability | enormity   | depth        |
| 12. | was an *anomaly*                     | success     | irregularity | introduction |
| 13. | New Age *shamanism*                  | magic       | salesmanship | inventiveness |
| 14. | ominous sign of *degeneration*       | neutralism  | decline      | invention    |
| 15. | *ethereal* wealth                    | fading      | inherited    | rate         |
| 16. | *demographics* have changed          | districts   | vocations    | populations  |
| 17. | *manipulate* public concern          | regulate    | handle       | assume       |
| 18. | may *ultimately* eclipse             | immediately | seriously    | finally      |
| 19. | *justifiable* concern                | excusable   | eventual     | legal        |
| 20. | arrangement was *plausible*          | perfect     | credible     | negotiable   |
| 21. | *countenance* full of woe            | figure      | expression   | circumstance |
| 22. | the *mystic* play of shadows         | magical     | unclear      | nightly      |
| 23. | the *colloquy* of stars              | brightness  | twinkling    | conversation |
| 24. | some healthful *anodyne*             | sign        | comfort      | diagnosis    |
| 25. | let us *garlands* bring              | flowers     | bouquets     | wreaths      |

# Improving Your Reading Speed and Comprehension

*When we read too fast or too slowly, we understand nothing.*

—Blaise Pascal (1623–62), French philosopher, mathematician, and scientist

Almost anyone who reads can read faster. The way to do so, however, is to strengthen your natural way of reading and thinking—not to use some artificial method. This chapter includes information and expert research on

- Eye movements during reading
- How much the mind can see
- Vocalization while reading
- Eight ways to increase speed and comprehension

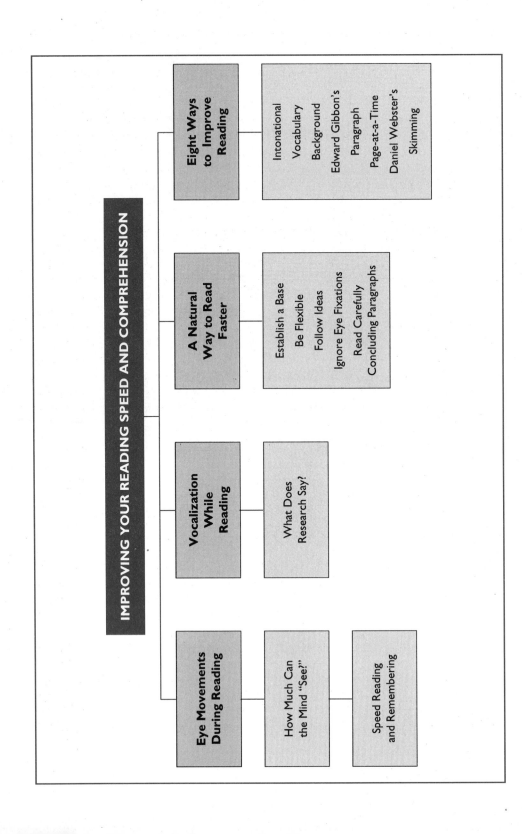

IMPROVING YOUR READING SPEED AND COMPREHENSION

Eye Movements During Reading

How Much Can the Mind "See?"

Speed Reading and Remembering

Vocalization While Reading

What Does Research Say?

A Natural Way to Read Faster

Establish a Base
Be Flexible
Follow Ideas
Ignore Eye Fixations
Read Carefully
Concluding Paragraphs

Eight Ways to Improve Reading

Intonational
Vocabulary
Background
Edward Gibbon's
Paragraph
Page-at-a-Time
Daniel Webster's
Skimming

The simple question "How can I improve my reading?" does not have a simple answer. There are many different purposes in reading, many different reading techniques that can be used, and many ways in which reading can be "improved." However, when this question is asked by a student, it usually means, "How can I *speed up* my reading so I can finish my homework in half the time with high comprehension and almost complete retention?" There is no easy way to do so, despite the numerous brochures, newspaper and magazine articles, and television programs that extol the marvels of "speed reading." Many students, as well as the general public, are convinced that speed-reading is a technique that is easy to learn and that can be used with any page of print. Unfortunately, speed-reading is virtually useless to anyone who desires to learn from the printed page.

If you desire high comprehension and almost complete retention, you must use systematic study techniques. There is no other way to master your courses. This entire book is devoted to making learning a reality through the use of efficient study skills. This chapter focuses on specific skills you can use in reading. Before examining them, however, we must discuss two aspects of reading: eye movements and vocalization. In doing so, we emphasize some negative aspects of speed-reading, for two reasons. First, academic improvement through speed-reading is just not in the cards, so don't spend your time, money, and energy on this dead end. Second, by clearing the decks of so-called easy ways to read and study, we set the stage for reading and studying systems that work.

## EYE MOVEMENTS DURING READING

### Facts about Eye Movements and Speed Reading

Newspapers have carried sensational stories about high school students who read at astronomical speeds. One student was clocked at the rate of 40,000 words per minute. Another student was timed at 50,000 words per minute! A peculiar characteristic of all such stories is that they include the statement, "with nearly 100 percent comprehension."

How fast is 40,000 words per minute? There are about 300 words on an average paperback book page. By dividing 300 into 40,000, we find that to read 40,000 words per minute, a person would have to read 133 pages per minute! The reader (or, more accurately, the page turner) would have less than half a second to spend on each page. Some students find it difficult to *turn* 133 pages in a minute, let alone see any words on those pages.

Readers who are fast page turners might be able to see a word or two on each page as it flutters by, but this would hardly lead to "nearly 100 percent comprehension." Such readers could not possibly reconstruct the ideas contained in the 133 pages.

The basic premise of speed-reading advocates is this: The eye is able to see a vast number of words in one fixation. (A *fixation* is a focusing of the eyes on an object. The eyes must pause—they must be still—to fix on the object.) Some advocates say the eye can see phrases at a glance; others say entire lines; still others say paragraphs at a time; and a few say the eye can see an entire page at a glance. Let's look at the facts.

Eye-movement photography shows that the average college student makes about four eye fixations per second. Eye-movement photography also shows that the eye sees an average of only 1.1 words during each fixation. Seldom does any person, trained or untrained, have a usable span of recognition of more than 2.5 words.[1] Recent research using computers shows that good readers take in an average of about ten usable *letters* per fixation: four letters to the left of the center of fixation and five or six letters to the right of the center of fixation.[2] Thus, a reader may take in less than one long word, such as *informational;* or one complete word, such as *basketball;* or more than one word, such as *high grade.*

These facts indicate that only a most unusual person can see 10 words per second (2.5 words per fixation × 4 fixations per second). So, in sixty seconds it is arithmetically possible for the eye to take in 600 words. This calculation does not include the time needed to return the eyes to the beginning of each line and to turn pages.

There is no evidence that anyone's eyes can see a whole line of type "at a glance." So any advice to run your eyes down the middle of a page or column, to speed-read the page, is nonsense. All you'll get is a word or two from each line—a handful of scrambled words.

Richard Feinberg[3] reported that when a reader focuses on a word, "only four to five letters immediately around the fixation point are seen with 100 percent acuity" (sharpness). The letters of words half an inch from the point of fixation are seen with only 40 percent acuity, and those one inch from the point of fixation seen with only 26 percent acuity. If the reader has less than normal vision, the fall-off in acuity is even more pronounced.

---

[1] Stanford E. Taylor, "Eye Movement in Reading: Facts and Fallacies," *American Educational Research Journal* 2, no. 4 (November 1965): 187–202.

[2] John M. Henderson and Fernanada Ferreira, "Effects of Foveal Processing Difficulty on the Perceptual Span in Reading: Implications for Attention and Eye Movement Control," *Journal of Experimental Psychology: Learning, Memory and Cognition* 16, no. 3 (1990): 417–29.

[3] Richard Feinberg, "A Study of Some Aspects of Peripheral Visual Acuity," *American Journal of Optometry and Archives of American Academy of Optometry* 26 (February–March 1949): 1–23.

## An Experiment With Eye Movements

Here's how to find out how your eyes move during reading. Use any page of print, such as the text shown in Figure 7.1, copied on a half sheet of paper. Punch a hole near the center of the page, as at the dot in Figure 7.1. Hold the page close to your own eye, with the printed side facing toward another person (the reader). As the reader silently reads the printed matter, watch his or her eyes through the peephole. You will immediately notice that the reader's eyes do not flow over the lines of print in a smooth, gliding motion. Instead, the eyes seem to jerk their way across the page, alternating fast, forward movements with momentary pauses, much like a typewriter carriage. The pauses are absolutely necessary, for they allow the eyes to focus on the type, to get a clear image of it. When the eyes are in motion, they record nothing but a blur on the retinas.

**Instructions to the Reader**   When you read the material, actually slow down your rate so that your partner will be able to count, as well as carefully observe, your eye movements. Don't try to manipulate your eyes in some unnatural way, such as by trying to focus on an entire line in one fixation; it won't work.

---

A knowledge of words, what they are and how they function, is the first and last essential of all liberal education. As Carlyle says, "If we but think of it, all that a University or final highest school can do for us is still but what the first school began doing—teach us to *read*." When a student has been trained to make the words of any page of general writing yield their full meaning, he has in his possession the primary instrument of all higher education.

•

In these days when the nation is asking that its schools produce good citizens first and specialists second, there is a marked need for a rich and wide "universal" training of the mind. This book on reading is designed to forward the process by which the whole mind, intellectual and emotional, becomes a more accurate instrument for the reception and transmission of thoughts and sensations. If our system of education does not so train the minds of its students, if it does not teach them to recognize differences, to distinguish shades of meaning, to feel as by intuition not only the hypocrisy of the demagogue and the flattery of the bootlicker but also the depth of a statesman like Lincoln and the insight of a poet like Shakespeare, it fails of its purpose.

---

**FIGURE 7.1   The Peep-Sight Experiment**
See the text discussion for instructions. *Source: From E. A. Tennev and R. C. Wardle.* Intelligent Reading *(New York: Crofts, 1943), preface.*

**Calculations**    You can make a rough calculation of the number of words perceived by the eyes by dividing the number of eye pauses into the total number of words on a line. For example, if the first line contains twelve words and the reader pauses eight times, the reader is taking in roughly one and one-half words per fixation.

## HOW MUCH THE MIND CAN SEE

Our emphasis has been on the question "How many words can the eyes see in one fixation?" A more basic question is "How does the mind process the words that are imprinted on the retina of the eyes?" Suppose the eyes take in two words at a single fixation. Does the mind impose a meaning on both words instantly and simultaneously, or must it consider each word in sequence, one at a time, to get at the meaning of each word? If the mind can handle only one word at a time, however swiftly, wouldn't it be easier for the eyes to deliver to the mind one word at a time in the first place?

### The Limitation of the Mind

Research done at the Massachusetts Institute of Technology, using M.I.T. undergraduates, gives scientific evidence that the mind can attend to only one word at a time. The researchers concluded that "even the skilled reader has considerable difficulty forming a perception of more than one word at a time."[4]

You often have the impression that you are seeing more than one word at a fixation because your eyes are moving rapidly from left to right, taking in words in rapid sequence. This process is almost like watching a movie. Although each film frame is a still picture, you "see" motion and action when the film is projected at a rate of twenty-four frames per second. Similarly, words projected on the brain at the rate of seven or eight words per second give the impression of living, moving ideas. Nevertheless, the brain is "viewing" only one word at a time.

### Speed Reading and Remembering

A final objection to speed-reading is that it does not give the mind time to consolidate new informations.[5] Even if your eyes were able to take in several

---

[4]Paul A. Kolers, "Experiments in Reading," *Scientific American* 227, no. 1 (July 1972): 84–91.
[5]R. S. Woodworth and H. Schlosberg, *Experimental Psychology* (New York: Holt, 1954), p. 773.

thousand words a minute (impossible) and your brain were able to comprehend the meaning of them all (impossible), your mind would not have time to consolidate the meaning before it was assaulted by the next batch of several thousand words. As you saw in Chapter 5, the brain requires a certain period of time in which to convert a temporary idea to a permanent one.

## VOCALIZATION WHILE READING

For many years it has been thought that vocalizing while reading is a bad habit that should be eliminated. There are four types of vocalizers: the person who whispers each word aloud; the one who pronounces each word with lip movements; the one who moves only the vocal cords; and the one who thinks the sound of each word. Those who want to eliminate vocalization claim that vocalizing slows reading speed. This claim is probably true. However, the assumption that vocalization can and should be eliminated is highly questionable because there is no research to support it. On the contrary, there is strong evidence that vocalization of one kind or another is an essential part of all reading.

### What Does Research Say?

Robert A. Hall, Jr., an internationally known linguist, has this to say about vocalization, or inner speech:

> It is commonly thought that we can read and write in complete silence, without any speech taking place. True, many people learn to suppress the movements of their organs of speech when they read, so that no sound comes forth; but nevertheless, inside the brain, the impulses for speech are still being sent forth through the nerves, and only the actualization of these impulses is being inhibited on the muscular level, as has been shown by numerous experiments. No act of reading takes place without a certain amount of subvocalization, as this kind of "silent speech" is called, and we normally subvocalize, when we write, also. Many slow readers retain the habit of reading out loud, or at least partially moving their lips as they read; fast readers learn to skip from one key point to another, and to guess at what must lie in between. The good rapid reader knows the subject-matter well enough to guess intelligently; the poor reader does not know how to choose the high spots or guess what lies between them. As the rate of reading increases, the actual muscular movements of pronunciation are reduced; but, just as soon as the going gets difficult, the rate of reading slows down and the muscular movements of pronunciation increase again, even with skilled rapid readers.

From these considerations, it is evident that the activities of speaking and reading cannot be separated. Curiously enough, literary scholars are especially under the delusion that it is possible to study "written language" in isolation, without regard to the language as it is spoken; this is because they do not realize the extent to which, as we have just pointed out, all reading and writing necessarily involve an act of speech on the part of both writer and reader.[6]

Åke Edfeldt, of the University of Stockholm Institute of Reading Research, has studied vocalization with a team of medical doctors who used electrodes to detect movement in the lips, tongues, and vocal cords of volunteer readers. After exhaustive medical tests, Edfeldt concluded:

> On the basis of the present experimental results, earlier theories concerning silent speech in reading may be judged. These theories often appear to have been constructed afterwards, in order to justify some already adopted form of remedial reading. In opposition to most of these theories, we wish to claim that silent speech occurs in the reading of all persons.
>     In any case, it seems quite clear that all kinds of training aimed at removing silent speech should be discarded.[7]

Decades ago, E. L. Thorndike (1874–1949), American psychologist and lexicographer, said that "reading is thinking." Psychologists agree that thinking is silent speech. So if reading is thinking, and thinking is silent speech, then reading must also be silent speech. It seems that if we spend our time and energy trying to knock out vocalization, we are in fact trying to knock out comprehension. Vocalization cannot and should not be eliminated, because it is part of the reading process.

## A NATURAL WAY TO READ FASTER

Speed-reading methods cannot be effective if they interfere with natural processes, or if they require that we read in a way that isn't natural to us. For example, vocalization is a natural and necessary function; methods that attempt to eliminate vocalization so as to increase reading speed cannot succeed. Methods that impose an artificial eye-fixation scheme must likewise fail.

    The only effective way to increase your reading speed is to do so naturally—to do exactly what you have been doing but do more of it or do it

---

[6]Robert A. Hall, Jr., *New Ways to Learn a Foreign Language* (New York: Bantam Books, Inc., 1966), pp. 28–29.
[7]Åke W. Edfeldt, *Silent Speech and Silent Reading* (Chicago: University of Chicago Press, 1960), p. 154.

faster. The method described in this section will help you read faster naturally. However, you must realize that it is *not* meant for textbook reading, where you must read (and often reread) slowly, to get the full meaning of each sentence and paragraph. Use the method to increase the speed at which you read novels, magazines, journals, and newspapers. To read these materials at the slow textbook rate is a waste of your time; in such cases, the mind is eager to sprint, but the textbook reading habit limits it to a deliberate pace.

## Setting the Stage for Faster Reading

Here are five things to do or to keep in mind as you practice faster reading. They are fairly general in nature, but they are important to the method. Farther on, you will see, step by step, how to practice faster reading to increase your reading speed.

**Establish a Base**    Before you begin to read a new book, take a few minutes to think about its title and to look through the table of contents. Extract as much meaning as possible from both. For example, if your book were *The Adventures of Sherlock Holmes,* you would know that you had a handful of absorbing detective stories to read. Knowing the nature of the book will create a mindset highly favorable to reading; it will be derived from the two powerful forces of anticipation and concentration.

**Be Flexible**    Match your reading speed to the material you are reading. If the book begins with introductory, "warm-up" material, move through it fast. But slow down a bit when you come to the first solid paragraph. You need to grab and hold in mind items such as names, places, and circumstances, for these are the magnetic centers around which ideas and details will cluster as you sprint through the pages. When the going gets easier, speed up again. As you read, be continually alert to slow down at paragraphs that are full of ideas and to speed up when you can. There is no reason to expect—or try—to read at a constant rate.

**Follow Ideas, Not Words**    Don't try to remember words. Simply use the words to visualize the ideas, facts, and actions that the author is presenting. Once you have done so, let the words drop out of your mind. Retain only the development of the story or the important ideas and facts.

**Ignore Your Eye Fixations**    Don't think about what your eyes are doing, for that will break both your reading rhythm and your concentration. The eye fixations will take care of themselves easily and naturally as you read along at your own pace. You don't need to think about eye fixations any more than you need to think about moving your feet while you walk. The feet take care of themselves, and so do the eyes.

**Enjoy the Concluding Paragraph**   Slow down for the last paragraph, and savor it. You will enjoy seeing how the author connects the various facts or events in an article or the various parts of a short story or novel.

    This whole process—establishing a base, being flexible in reading speed, following ideas, ignoring eye movements, and enjoying the conclusion— leads not only to faster reading but to intelligent reading as well.

## EIGHT WAYS TO IMPROVE READING

Reading comprehension cannot be improved through mechanical techniques like turning pages faster or moving the eyes in some artificial pattern. There is no magic in such actions. The magic comes only when you work at your reading skills.

    Most methods for improvement suggested in this chapter require hard work, but the rewards are great. A few of them require only the willingness to try a new way of using old knowledge, and here, too, the rewards can be great.

## THE INTONATION WAY

As we have seen at the beginning of this chapter, vocalization is part of the process of reading and comprehending. The most efficient use of vocalization, to read faster with a high degree of comprehension, is through *intonation,* which is the rise and fall of the voice in speaking. Reading with intonation means reading with expression. Intonation provides a natural means for combining individual words into meaningful mental "bites."

    To use this system, let your eyes move rapidly across the page as usual. You need not make any sound, but let your mind swing along each line with an intonational rhythm that can be heard by your "inner ear." Read with expression. In doing so, you will be replacing the important *rhythm, stress, emphasis,* and *pauses* that were taken out when the words were put into written form.

To make silent intonation a regular habit, start by reading aloud in the privacy of your room. Spend ten or fifteen minutes on one chapter from a novel. Read it with exaggerated expression, as if you were reading a part in a dramatic play. This will establish your own speech patterns in your mind, so that you will "hear" them more readily when you read silently.

## THE VOCABULARY WAY

There is probably no surer or sounder way to improve your reading permanently than by building a strong, precise vocabulary. In a precise vocabulary, every word is learned as a concept. You know its ancestry, its principal definition as well as several secondary definitions, its synonyms and the subtle differences among them, and its antonyms. Then, when you encounter it in your reading, this vast store of knowledge flashes before you, illuminating the sentence, the paragraph, and the idea the author is trying to convey.

For more on vocabulary building, refer to Chapter 6.

## THE BACKGROUND WAY

You can improve your reading tremendously by reading good books. The first reason for this is that you'll be getting a lot of practice. Even more important, you'll be storing up a stock of concepts, ideas, events, and names that will lend meaning to your later reading. This kind of information is used surprisingly often.

Psychologist David Ausubel says that the most crucial prerequisite for learning is your already established background of knowledge.[8] Ausubel means that if you are to understand what you read, then you must interpret it in the light of knowledge (background) you already have. A background is not something you are born with. You accumulate one through both direct and vicarious experiences. The vicarious experiences, of course, are those you acquire by listening, seeing films, and reading books.

---

[8]D. R. Ausubel, J. D. Novak, and H. Hanesian, *Educational Psychology: A Cognitive View,* 2nd ed. (New York: Holt, Rinehart & Winston), 1978.

Authors often make allusions to famous books, famous people, or well-known events. In many cases, you can miss these references and still understand the story. In some instances, however, an allusion will be crucial, and you will have to search for its meaning if it is not in your background. Consider this short passage by Robert Louis Stevenson (1850–94), Scottish novelist and poet:

> And not long ago I was able to lay by my lantern in content, for I found the honest man.

This sentence is composed of twenty simple words, many consisting of only two and three letters. It contains one word that is crucial to the understanding of the sentence. Go back and see whether you can pick it out before you read on.

The two words most often chosen are *honest* and *content*. Neither is the crucial word. That word is *lantern*. It is, however, no ordinary lantern to which Stevenson refers, but one that is associated with a real person in history. Whose lantern? The lantern of Diogenes. Diogenes was a fourth-century B.C. Greek cynic and critic who walked the streets of Athens during the daytime, holding a lighted lantern, peering into the faces of passers-by, and saying that he was looking for an honest man. He was dramatizing the idea that it is difficult to find an honest man, even with a lighted lantern during the day.

Obviously, without knowing the story of Diogenes you cannot fully understand Stevenson's line, and that is only one example from millions. You cannot make every fact, myth, story, and poem part of your background. But you can, through your reading, enlarge your background and thus increase the effectiveness of your reading. In other words, you can improve your reading by reading.

Read the *great* books, for it is in these books that the wisdom of the ages is passed on to posterity. These books give you the chance to "talk" with princes, kings, philosophers, travelers, playwrights, scientists, artists, and novelists. Begin with the books and subjects that interest you, and don't worry about having only narrow interests. Once you begin reading, your interests will widen naturally.

The more good books you read, the easier reading becomes, because with an expanded background, you can more easily and quickly understand the ideas and facts in other books.

But remember, you are fully responsible for initiating the process and habit of reading. Always keep in mind what Mark Twain once said, "The man who *doesn't* read good books has no advantage over the man who *can't* read them."

## EDWARD GIBBON'S WAY

The great English historian Edward Gibbon (1737–94), author of *Decline and Fall of the Roman Empire*, made constant use of the great recall technique. This is simply an organized and rather intense use of one's general background. Before starting to read a new book, or before starting to write on any subject, Gibbon would spend hours alone in his study, or he would take a long walk alone to recall everything that he knew about the subject. As he pondered some major idea, he was continually surprised by how many other ideas and fragments of ideas he would dredge up.

Gibbon's system was highly successful. His old ideas were brought to the forefront of his mind, ready for use, and they could act as magnetic centers for new ideas and new information. Great recall promotes concentration.

## THE PARAGRAPH WAY

You can improve your comprehension by stopping at the end of each textbook paragraph to summarize and condense it to a single sentence. To summarize and condense, you must understand the functions of three main types of sentences: the topic or controlling-idea sentence, the supporting sentence, and the concluding sentence. Figure 7.2 shows these three types of sentences in an actual paragraph.

The *topic* sentence announces the topic (or the portion of the topic) to be dealt with in the paragraph. Although the topic sentence may appear anywhere in the paragraph, it is usually first—and for a very good reason. This sentence provides the focus for the writer while writing and for the reader while reading. When you find the topic sentence, be sure to underline it so that it will stand out not only now but also later when you review.

The bulk of an expository paragraph is made up of *supporting* sentences, which help to explain or prove the main topic. These sentences present facts, reasons, examples, definitions, comparisons, contrasts, and other pertinent details. They are most important, because they sell the ideas.

The last sentence of a textbook paragraph is likely to be a *concluding* sentence. It is used to sum up a discussion, to emphasize a point, or to restate all or part of the topic sentence so as to bring the paragraph to a close.

Of course, the paragraphs you'll be reading will be part of some longer piece of writing—a textbook chapter, a section of a chapter, or a newspaper or magazine article. Besides expository paragraphs, in which new information

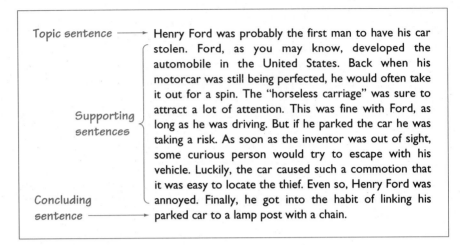

Topic sentence ⟶ Henry Ford was probably the first man to have his car stolen. Ford, as you may know, developed the automobile in the United States. Back when his motorcar was still being perfected, he would often take it out for a spin. The "horseless carriage" was sure to attract a lot of attention. This was fine with Ford, as long as he was driving. But if he parked the car he was taking a risk. As soon as the inventor was out of sight, some curious person would try to escape with his vehicle. Luckily, the car caused such a commotion that it was easy to locate the thief. Even so, Henry Ford was annoyed. Finally, he got into the habit of linking his parked car to a lamp post with a chain.

Supporting sentences

Concluding sentence ⟶

**FIGURE 7.2   The Three Elements of an Expository Paragraph**

is presented and discussed, these longer writings contain three types of paragraphs: introductory, transitional, and summarizing.

*Introductory* paragraphs tell you, in advance, such things as (1) the main idea of the chapter or section, (2) the extent or limits of the coverage, (3) how the topic is developed, and (4) the writer's attitude toward the topic. *Transitional* paragraphs are usually short; their sole function is to tie together what you have read so far and what is to come—to set the stage for succeeding paragraphs. *Summarizing* paragraphs are used to restate briefly the main ideas of the chapter or section. The writer may also draw some conclusion from these ideas, based on the evidence in the chapter, or speculate on the basis of that evidence.

All three types should *alert* you: the introductory paragraph of things to come; the transitional paragraph of a new topic; and the summarizing paragraph of main ideas that you should have gotten.

## THE PAGE-AT-A-TIME WAY

Thomas Babington Macaulay (1800–59) was an English statesman, historian, essayist, and poet. His greatest work, *The History of England*, at the time it was published outsold all other books except the Bible. Macaulay began reading adult books at the age of 3, but after consuming shelf after shelf of books, he suddenly realized that he wasn't gaining much knowledge for all his effort. He understood every word of what he read and seemed to comprehend what the writer was saying, but later he could not summarize the ideas presented or even describe, in general terms, what the writer had written. He described his solution to this problem as follows:

> At the foot of every page I read I stopped and obliged myself to give an account of what I had read on that page. At first I had to read it three or four times before I got my mind firmly fixed. But I compelled myself to comply with the plan, until now, after I have read a book through once, I can almost recite it from the beginning to the end.

There's something very basic, honest, and refreshing in the Macaulay way. There are no complicated formulas to follow. You simply stop at the bottom of a page and ask yourself, "In brief, what did the writer say on this page?" This technique will do for you what it did for Lord Macaulay. It will make you concentrate. It will also teach you to think continually while you read. Every time you pause for a brief recall, your memory will be getting stronger.

## DANIEL WEBSTER'S WAY

Daniel Webster (1782–1852), American statesman and orator, had his own special technique for building concentration. Before reading a book, he would look at the table of contents, read the preface, and turn some of the pages. Then he would make lists of (1) questions that he expected to be answered in the book, (2) the knowledge he expected to gain from his reading, and (3) where the knowledge would take him. The three lists guided him through the book; his attention and concentration were intense.

## THE SKIMMING WAY

Both students and business executives report that the workhorse of reading is skimming. Covering many speeds and uses, skimming can range from just fast reading to searching, which could hardly be classified as reading. Whether to use rapid reading or searching—or anything in between—depends on your purpose. Tailor skimming to your purpose; otherwise you'll waste time.

Here are five purposes for skimming and the techniques for each.

## Searching for a Needle in a Haystack

If you want to find specific information (name, date, word, or phrase) in a textbook or article, searching may be used because it is recognition, not comprehension, that will give you the answer. To ensure that your eyes do not overlook the word or fact you seek, concentrate on it, keeping it in mind as your eyes run over the pages. Concentration will trigger your mind to pick it out of the sea of words. Once you have located the specific word or fact, pause and read at a normal rate the sentence or paragraph surrounding it to make sure, through context, that you have found what you were looking for.

When using the searching technique, if your time is short, resist the temptation to read the whole article. What you may really be doing, subconsciously, is putting off studying. But, if you do have time, follow your curiosity and finish the article. It may not help you on the next exam, but the knowledge gained will give you an edge and contribute to your general wisdom.

## Looking for Clues

When you are seeking specific information but do not know in what words the information may appear, you must use a slower searching method. In this case, you won't be able to anticipate the exact words, so you must be alert for clues, which can appear in various forms.

In this kind of searching, you must infer the answer. For example, after reading an article about Paul Bunyan, a legendary giant lumberjack and folk hero, a student was asked a question about Paul Bunyan's birthplace. The answer was Canada, yet nowhere in the article did the word *Canada* appear. The answer had to be inferred from a sentence that stated that Paul Bunyan was born at the headwaters of the St. Lawrence River. Because the student discovered on a map that the headwaters are in Canada, she could answer the question.

When you are looking for clues, try to guess the form in which the information might appear. When you believe you have found the information you want, go back and read the paragraph to make sure, from context, that it is exactly what you seek.

## Getting the Gist

Sometimes skimming may be used to get the gist of a book or article. You can use this technique to find out whether a book pertains to the topic you are working on. To get the gist, read both introduction and summary rapidly, as well as paragraphs that have topic sentences indicating that the paragraph contains important data.

This skimming method can help when you have a term paper to write. After you have looked through the card catalogue and have made a list of books that seem related to your topic, get the books and look through them to eliminate those that are not pertinent and to keep those that are. Obviously, you would waste time and energy if you attempted to read all the books on your list. To get the main idea of each book, look at the table of contents, or select a chapter with a title related to your topic and skim it for its outstanding ideas.

## Overviewing a Textbook Chapter

An important use of skimming is discussed in Chapter 11: surveying or getting an overview of a textbook chapter before you read it thoroughly. Overviewing may be done to attain various degrees of comprehension. In most cases, this type of skimming calls for understanding captions, headings, subheadings, and portions of paragraphs well enough to locate key concepts in the chapter. Such skimming lets you see the relative importance of each part to the whole.

## Skimming to Review

Skimming also can be used to review for an examination or for a recitation. After skimming chapters that you have previously read, studied, and noted, for effective study you should pause from time to time and try to recite the main concepts in each chapter or summarize the chapter. After finishing a textbook chapter, always review to understand the chapter as a whole, like a finished jigsaw puzzle.

## SUMMARY

**How does purpose affect reading?**

Purpose determines how much time you'll spend in reading almost anything. For example, looking over a textbook chapter to gain familiarity before listening to a classroom lecture might take no more than half an hour, but reading the same chapter in preparation for a quiz might take three or four hours.

**Are eye pauses and sub-vocalization really necessary during reading?**

According to most research, eye pauses and subvocalization are absolutely necessary. The pauses allow your eyes to focus on the words; subvocalization is required for comprehension.

**Should I use the faster reading method on textbooks?**

No. Textbooks are packed with ideas and facts that cannot be understood or remembered when reading too fast. Faster reading is all right on easier novels that you read for pleasure, as well as for magazines, newspapers, and journals.

**How can I use intonation silently?**

Intonation in reading means saying the words silently—but saying them with expression or rhythm, not in a monotone. Just a little practice reading aloud will show you how it works. Reading with intonation requires close attention that will get you to concentrate. The end result will be high comprehension plus speed.

**Won't pausing to summarize each paragraph slow me down?**

Yes. But what's the sense in moving through a whole chapter without learning or remembering anything? Reading a textbook chapter straight through will yield almost no long-term remembering, so you'll have to go back and read it again anyway. Overall, you'll save time by pausing to summarize—to make sure you understand each paragraph.

**How does the paragraph way differ from the page-at-a-time way?**

The idea in both systems is to pause, think, and summarize what you have read. Do so paragraph by paragraph when the writing is packed with facts, page by page when the material is written in a more leisurely narrative style.

**Why are there various methods of skimming?**

The various methods and speed in skimming let you tailor the method to fit the job.

**What is the one rule for using skimming?**

Use skimming as a tool. Determine what the main purpose of your assignment is, and then judge whether skimming can help you achieve your purpose.

## HAVE YOU MISSED SOMETHING?

*Sentence completion.*  Complete the following sentences with one of the three words listed below each sentence.

1. Edward Gibbon learned new ideas by letting his old ones act as

   _____ .

   magnets        examples        summaries

2. A summary paragraph or sentence usually restates _____ .
   references        information        transitions

*Matching.*  In each blank space in the left column, write the letter preceding the phrase in the right column that matches the left item best.

_____ 1. Eye movement        a. Processes words one at a time

_____ 2. Fixation        b. Blurs words on a page

_____ 3. Subvocalization        c. Always accompanies reading

_____ 4. The mind        d. Should not be applied to textbooks

_____ 5. Faster reading        e. Allows the eyes to focus

_____ 6. Background        f. Helps you to understand the chapter as
         knowledge               a whole

_____ 7. Overviewing        g. Most crucial prerequisite for learning

*True-false.*  Write *T* beside the *true* statements and *F* beside the *false* statements.

_____ 1. Your eyes can see only about ten printed letters at one time.

_____ 2. Your eyes can see clearly only when they are not moving.

_____ 3. A good vocabulary is one of the best tools for effective reading.

_____ 4. Transitional paragraphs help you to follow the writer's train of thought.

_____ 5. Supporting sentences are usually placed in the middle of a paragraph.

_____ 6. You will read more effectively if you read great books.

*Multiple choice.*  Choose the phrase that completes the following sentence most accurately, and circle the letter that precedes it.

1. Reading for understanding does not require
   a. speed.
   b. fixations.

c. thinking.

d. subvocalization.

**2.** Words acquire an extra dimension when reading is done

a. Daniel Webster's way.

b. the skimming way.

c. the intonation way.

d. the vocabulary way.

*Short answer.*   Supply a brief answer for each of the following questions.

**1.** Why is vocalization a necessary part of reading for comprehension?

**2.** Why do you think the use of *intonation* helps to improve both speed and comprehension in reading?

**3.** Why do you think Thomas Babington Macaulay's "page-at-a-time way" improves your memory of what you've read?

## VOCABULARY BUILDING

DIRECTIONS: Make a light check mark (√) alongside one of the three words (choices) that most nearly expresses the meaning of the italicized word in the phrases that are in the left-hand column. (Answers are given on p. 435.)

|     |                                  | 1            | 2           | 3           |
| --- | -------------------------------- | ------------ | ----------- | ----------- |
| 1.  | under the *delusion*             | promise      | deception   | flood       |
| 2.  | the most crucial *prerequisite*  | requirement  | assumption  | compromise  |
| 3.  | *cynical* approach               | distrustful  | comical     | thoughtful  |
| 4.  | *perceptual* span in reading     | visual       | mental      | theoretical |
| 5.  | *hypocrisy* of the demagogue     | criticalness | trustfulness| fakery      |
| 6.  | the *burgeoning* operations      | heavy        | expanding   | burdensome  |
| 7.  | a *conglomerate* corporation     | diversified  | mixed       | streamlined |
| 8.  | a debt-limit *impasse*           | decision     | deadlock    | compromise  |
| 9.  | potentially more *pernicious*    | precious     | costly      | destructive |
| 10. | *exorbitant* prices              | excessive    | expensive   | ordinary    |
| 11. | familiar *miscreants*            | criminals    | creators    | messengers  |
| 12. | voters have *abdicated*          | renewed      | renounced   | transferred |
| 13. | the *stereotyped* politician     | promising    | talkative   | standardized|
| 14. | the answer, a *resounding* no    | hesitant     | regretful   | definite    |
| 15. | *platitudinous* press release    | praiseworthy | quotable    | commonplace |

|  | | **1** | **2** | **3** |
|---|---|---|---|---|
| 16. | a *plausible* argument | credible | debatable | one-sided |
| 17. | being done *covertly* | expensively | harshly | secretly |
| 18. | this whole *charade* | pretense | assemblage | arrangement |
| 19. | gone completely *unheralded* | unseen | unpublicized | unrewarded |
| 20. | recorded the *duplicity* | deception | speech | diplomat |
| 21. | in *pensive* mood | decisive | troubled | melancholy |
| 22. | with eye *serene* | calm | regretful | tearful |
| 23. | purchased *prudently* | impulsively | hastily | wisely |
| 24. | his strength had *dwindled* | increased | returned | decreased |
| 25. | in this *sequestered* nook | silent | hidden | sunny |

# 8

# Understanding and Using Key Concepts

*Ideas won't keep; something must be done about them.*

—ALFRED NORTH WHITEHEAD (1861–1947), English mathematician and philosopher

The "something" in Whitehead's epigram is *reflection*, because only through reflection can we truly and permanently weave ideas into the vital tissues of our memory. To aid you in mastering four key concepts, this chapter deals with

- The power of questions
- Gaining mastery and wisdom through reflection
- Recognizing and using signal words
- Recognizing and using organizational patterns

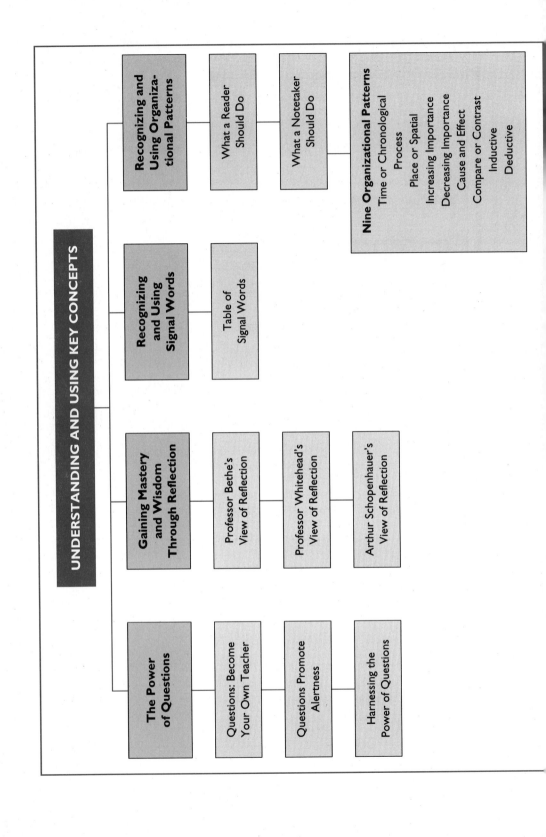

**UNDERSTANDING AND USING KEY CONCEPTS**

**The Power of Questions**

Questions: Become Your Own Teacher

Questions Promote Alertness

Harnessing the Power of Questions

**Gaining Mastery and Wisdom Through Reflection**

Professor Bethe's View of Reflection

Professor Whitehead's View of Reflection

Arthur Schopenhauer's View of Reflection

**Recognizing and Using Signal Words**

Table of Signal Words

**Recognizing and Using Organizational Patterns**

What a Reader Should Do

What a Notetaker Should Do

**Nine Organizational Patterns**
Time or Chronological
Process
Place or Spatial
Increasing Importance
Decreasing Importance
Cause and Effect
Compare or Contrast
Inductive
Deductive

T he heart of the textbook reading system and the note-taking system is the formulation of questions.

## THE POWER OF QUESTIONS

As a starting point, we will explore the power of questions through an episode in the life of Eddie Rickenbacker, World War I flying ace and later chairman of Eastern Airlines.

### Questions Help You Become Your Own Teacher

Rickenbacker left school at the age of twelve to help support his widowed mother. Later, realizing the need for further education, he took a correspondence course in mechanical engineering. Here's part of his story.

> The first lesson, I do not mind admitting, nearly finished my correspondence-school education before it began. It was tough. . . . As there was no teacher of whom I could ask a question, I had to work out the answers myself. Once I reached the answer through my own individual reasoning, my understanding was permanent and unforgettable.[1]

I can picture young Eddie Rickenbacker with paper and book spread out on a kitchen table, struggling to gain meaning from a paragraph. Doubts began to mount. Plain grit wasn't enough. He felt overwhelmed. Then, in desperation, he probably said to himself, "All right, Eddie, try it once more: What's this fellow trying to tell me?"

Right then, he created a miniature miracle. How? He asked a question! Now, with a question ringing in his ears, he focused on hearing an answer, and he heard it and understood it. Armed with this questioning technique, he became his own teacher. Previously, his eyes touched the words on the page and, in touching, expected that meaning would somehow, like a jack-in-the-box, pop up. But it didn't (and it doesn't).

We shouldn't be surprised that questions are packed with so much power. Human beings have known this for more than 2,400 years. Socrates (469–399 B.C.), the greatest of the Greek philosophers, developed what is known as the Socratic method, *the questioning method*. By a series of carefully directed questions, Socrates would lead another person, through his own step-by-step answers, to arrive at the understanding or conclusion himself.

What is it that makes a question so powerful? Maybe, as the psychologists say, questions promote concentration. If true, what a sure and easy way to

---

[1]Edward V. Rickenbacker, *Rickenbacker* (Englewood Cliffs, NJ: Prentice-Hall, Inc., 1967), pp. 31–2.

gain concentration with a technique that is available to all of us! As most of us have found out, concentration is a slippery quality.

The paradox and the slippery quality of concentration are best portrayed and explained by psychologist William James, who said that trying to seize concentration directly is "like seizing a spinning top to catch its motion, or trying to turn up the gas light quickly enough to see how the darkness looks."[2]

## Questions Promote Alertness

Questions seem to energize both body and mind. The hormone adrenalin, when released into the bloodstream, shifts the body into a state of alertness and readiness. The following story illustrates the similar effect of questions.

> Fishermen put fish into a floating tank to keep them alive until they reached port several days later. But, even so, the fish were often stale. Why? The fish just floated in one spot, gulping water and occasionally rippling a fin. One captain, however, brought back beautiful fish. They were fresh and lively. When he retired, he revealed his secret: "For every thousand live herrings, I put into the tank one big, vicious catfish. Yes, the catfish eat a few herrings, but they keep the rest moving. They keep them lively, and the herrings come back in beautiful condition."

So questions, like catfish, keep your mind from becoming stale and flabby when you read. Questions are the vital sparks that ignite the fluid powers of concentration.

## Questions Help You Master Reading and Note Taking

The question technique can be used to master the two most important academic functions that convert information into knowledge. These two functions are reading textbook assignments and understanding the notes taken of a lecture. They are each the subject of a separate chapter, but, for a glimpse of what's to come, here are two miniature examples: questions in the margins of textbooks and questions in the margins of lecture notes (see Figures 8.1 and 8.2).

There is no better way to guarantee academic success than by using the question-asking system to promote laserlike concentration.

---

[2]William James, *Psychology* (New York: Henry Holt, 1893), p. 161.

## WRITING GOOD PAPERS IN COLLEGE

*What two aspects lead to success?*

The techniques of writing a good paper are easy to follow. You should remember two important aspects that lead to success. First, start work early on the paper. Second, if you have a choice, choose a subject that you are interested in or that you can develop an interest in.

*What three elements might make up a paper?*

Much of your work in college involves absorbing knowledge; when it comes to writing papers, you have the opportunity to put down on paper what you've learned about a subject, and perhaps your opinions and conclusions on the subject.

*What's the key in choosing a topic? If not sure of a topic, do what?*

Writing is an important form of communication. To communicate well you must have something you really want to say. So if you have a choice of topics, choose one that intrigues you. If it isn't one that everyone else is writing on, all the better. If you're not sure about your choice of topic, do a little preliminary research to see what's involved in several topics before you make a final decision. Remember the caution about allowing yourself enough time? Here's where it comes into play. Take enough time to choose a topic carefully.

**FIGURE 8.1   Example of Writing Questions in the Margins of Textbooks**

## GAINING MASTERY AND WISDOM THROUGH REFLECTION

Questions provide understanding of information. Recitation (see Chapter 5) strengthens the remembering of information. *Reflection* ensures mastery of information, but, best of all, it converts information into lasting learning (and perhaps wisdom).

## What Is Reflection?

Reflection means investigating not only the ideas and facts but also their implications. It means never being satisfied but instead asking questions, noting reservations, thinking critically. Most of all, reflective thinking adds quality and creativity to our intellectual lives.

Professor Hans Bethe, Cornell University's famous nuclear physicist and Nobel Prize winner, talked about reflection as used by a scientist.

| | Sept. 10, 1997 (Wed.) – History 101 – Prof. A. Newhall |
|---|---|
| | **A. Some facts about Alaska** |
| Who purchased Alaska? When?      Cost? | 1. William H. Seward, Sec. of State – fr. Russia in 1867 – $7,200,000. |
| Rough dimensions of Mainland? | 2. Size – mainland: length = 1,500 mi. – width = 1,200 mi. |
| How long is the Yukon River? | 3. Yukon River – 1,979 mi. long |
| Name kinds of minerals? | 4. Minerals – oil, gold, silver, coal, chrome, iron, etc. |
| How are the forests? | 5. Forests – commerial timber = 85 billion board feet |
| Two most numerous fish? | 6. Fish – world's richest in salmon and halibut |
| Name several kinds of fur? | 7. Furs – seal, mink, otter, beaver, fox, etc. |
| What's the highest mt. in No. America? | 8. Mt. McKinley – 20,320 ft. – highest in No. America |
| When admitted as state? | 9. Statehood – Jan. 3, 1959 – 49th State |
| Who designed the State flag? | 10. State flag – designed by 13-year-old Benjamin Benson |

**FIGURE 8.2   Example of the Cornell Note-taking System**

> To become a good scientist one must live with the problem he's working on. The problem must follow the scientist wherever he goes. You can't be a good scientist working only eight hours a day. Science must be the consuming interest of your life. You must want to know. Nothing matters more than finding the answer to the question or the problem you are engaged in.[3]

Professor Bethe went on to say that students who go only as far as their textbooks and lectures take them can become proficient, but never creative. Creativity comes only with reflection. That is, seeing new material in the light of what you already know is the only road to original ideas, for having an idea is nothing more than discovering a relationship not seen before. And it is impossible to have ideas without reflecting.

---

[3]Interview with Professor Hans Bethe, May 19, 1960.

Professor Alred North Whitehead, famous British philosopher and mathematician, strongly advocated reflection. He, too, spoke about the knowledge that grows out of throwing ideas "into fresh combinations." He viewed reflection as taking what one already knows and projecting one's thought beyond familiar experience, considering new knowledge and ideas in the light of old, and the old in the light of the new.

The famous German philosopher Arthur Schopenhauer voiced exceptionally strong views on the importance of reflection.

> A library may be very large, but if it is in disorder, it is not so useful as one that is small but well arranged. In the same way, a man may have a great mass of knowledge, but if he has not worked it up by thinking it over for himself, it has much less value than a far smaller amount which he has thoroughly pondered. For it is only when a man looks at his knowledge from all sides, and combines the things he knows by comparing truth with truth, that he obtains a complete hold over it and gets it into his power.
>
> Reflections should not be left vague. Pursue the problem until ideas take definite shape. If you need more information, an encyclopedia or a standard book on the subject will often give you what you need to bring fuzzy ideas into focus.[4]

Reflection is a skill you can take with you wherever you go and make use of in spare moments. You can reflect while walking from one building to another, standing in line, waiting for a friend, or riding a bus. People who have made great discoveries have reported that some of their best insights came in unlikely places and at odd times.

The subconscious plays an important role in creative thinking and discovery. We have all had an exciting idea or even the solution to a problem suddenly flash upon us when we're not consciously thinking about it. The subconscious continues to work on concepts introduced deep enough into the mind through reflection.

To jump-start the process of reflection, ask yourself questions. For example, What's the significance of these facts and ideas? What principle are they based on? How can I apply them to what I already know? How do they fit? What's beyond these facts and principles?

What distinguishes learning through reflection from regular learning is your mental attitude. Knowledge gained through reflection will still be with you long after you have taken your final examinations.

The use of questions can make you an analytical person. And the continual use of reflection can hasten your becoming a person of deep understand-

---

[4]Essays of Arthur Schopenhauer, selected and translated by T. Bailey Saunders (New York: A. L. Burt, 1892), p. 321.

ing. To be communicated to others, however, the outcomes of these techniques need to be couched in *signal words* and supported by *organizational patterns*. Since we think with words, the mastery of the two literary devices below will make you a better thinker, speaker, and writer.

## RECOGNIZING AND USING SIGNAL WORDS

Words are magical messengers that can transmit ethereal thoughts from one mind to another. Furthermore, some words, which we call signal words, can indicate the direction or place of one's thoughts.

If you, as a note taker or textbook reader, know and recognize these signal words and phrases, you will be able to understand the lecturer's and writer's thoughts more rapidly and accurately. In addition, as a bonus, you can become a better writer and speaker.

In Table 8.1 you will find the most common signal words and phrases and some suggestions on how to react to them.

## RECOGNIZING AND USING ORGANIZATIONAL PATTERNS

We know for certain that patterns do what the names promise; that is, they help to organize a person's thoughts. This organization helps both the writer to write and the reader or listener to gain in understanding. Here are some specific tips for reading and listening.

### What a Reader Should Do

One way to keep your mind on your reading is to recognize and keep yourself aware of the organizational pattern that the author is using. Then you will think with the author as you read. For example, suppose you recognize that a paragraph is organized according to a chronological pattern. Then you would say to yourself, "Yes, I see what she's doing. She's describing the major events of the Great Depression as they happened, year by year." As you focused on the pattern, your mind would stay on your reading and you would be thinking about it.

**TABLE 8.1 Signal Words and Phrases**

| Categories and Examples | When you come across these words, immediately think . . . |
|---|---|
| **Example Words**<br>specifically<br>to illustrate<br>for example<br>for instance<br>that is | "Here comes an example. Must be double-checking to make sure I understood the point just made." |
| **Cause-and-Effect Words**<br>consequently<br>therefore<br>as a result<br>if . . . then<br>accordingly<br>thus, so<br>hence | "There's an effect word. Better check back when I have a chance to make sure I can find the cause now that I know what the effect is." |
| **Enumeration Words**<br>the four steps . . .<br>first, second, third<br>next, finally | "That's a lot of steps. I'd better be sure I'm keeping track of all of them and getting them in the right order." |
| **Addition Words**<br>furthermore<br>as well as<br>along with<br>in addition<br>moreover<br>also<br>not only . . . but also | "Seems there's always something else to be added. Must be worth remembering." |
| **Contrast Words**<br>on the other hand<br>in contrast<br>conversely<br>although<br>however, despite<br>whereas | "Here comes the other side of the coin. Let's see how it differs from what's been said already." |
| **Comparison Words**<br>likewise<br>similarly<br>comparatively<br>identical | "Lots of similar things, it seems." |
| **Swivel Words**<br>however<br>nevertheless<br>yet<br>but<br>still | "Looks like there's going to be a little bit of doubt or 'give back' on the point just made. Better pay attention to this qualifying remark." |

*(continued)*

**TABLE 8.1  Continued**

| Categories and Examples | When you come across these words, immediately think . . . |
| --- | --- |
| **Concession Words**<br>to be sure<br>indeed<br>though, although<br>granted<br>of course | "Okay! Here comes an argument or two from the opposing point of view." |
| **Emphasis Words**<br>more important<br>above all<br>remember<br>in other words<br>finally | "Looks as though what's coming up is going to be important." |
| **Repeat Words**<br>in other words<br>it simply means<br>that is<br>briefly<br>in essence<br>as we've seen | "Here comes another explanation. Maybe I'll understand this one a little better." |
| **Time Words**<br>before, after<br>formerly, soon<br>subsequently<br>prior, during<br>meanwhile | "Hmm! A time relationship is being established. Let's see: What came first, what came last and what came in-between?" |
| **Place Words**<br>above<br>below<br>beyond<br>adjacent to | "Okay! I'll put these ideas and facts, not only in their proper places, but also in their proper relationship." |
| **Summary Words**<br>for these reasons<br>on the whole<br>in conclusion<br>in a nutshell<br>to sum up<br>in short<br>finally | "Good. Now I'll get a simple wrap-up of the points that have been made. It's almost sure to be full of key ideas." |
| **Test Words (lectures)**<br>This is important.<br>Remember this.<br>You'll see this again.<br>Here's a pitfall. | "Sounds like a potential test item. Better be sure to pay close attention to it." |

## What a Note Taker Should Do

During a lecture, it is difficult to perceive a pattern, but if you do, then adjust your note taking to follow it. However, if you recognize no pattern during the note-taking session, read your notes back in your room. Now that you have the full lecture before you, try to see whether you can perceive a pattern. If you can, your understanding and remembering of the lecture will be greatly enhanced.

## Common Patterns

Here are brief descriptions of the most commonly used organizational patterns. Look for them when taking notes and reading your texts.

**Time or Chronological Pattern**    Events are presented in the order in which they happened. This pattern can be recognized quickly from the author's or lecturer's use of dates and such phrases as *in previous years, the next day,* and *two years later,* which denote the passage of time.

**Process Pattern**    Steps or events are presented in an orderly sequence that leads to a desired situation or product. A recipe and the instructions for assembling a bicycle provide examples of process patterns. They often include words such as *first, after this, then, next,* and *finally.* You'll often encounter this pattern in computer courses and the sciences, where the steps in a process are described in the order in which they must occur to put something together, instruct the computer, or blend ingredients.

**Place or Spatial Pattern**    Items are presented or discussed on the basis of their locations or their arrangement relative to each other. For example, an author might use this pattern to describe the geographical features of the United States from the West Coast to the East Coast. In such a case, this pattern is often called the *geographical pattern.* It is also called the *topical pattern* when it is used to describe the organization of a corporation along the lines of purchasing, manufacturing, sales, and so forth. The progression from item to item is usually orderly and easy to follow: from left to right, from high to low, from north to south.

**Increasing-Importance Pattern**    In this pattern, the most important or most dramatic item in a series is placed at the end. Each succeeding item is more important than the previous one, so a crescendo effect is created. Thus, this pattern is also called the *climactic-order pattern.*

**Decreasing-Importance Pattern**   In this pattern, the most important or most dramatic item in a series is placed at the very beginning. Such an organization grabs the reader's interest immediately, so there is a good chance the reader will stay with the writer or speaker all the way through.

**Cause-and-Effect Pattern**   This exceedingly important general pattern has such variations as the *problem-cause-solution pattern* and the *problem-effect-solution pattern*. Whatever the combination, you should be able to identify the various parts of the pattern—the problem, cause, effects, and solution. Once you hear the problem, you can generally start to anticipate the cause and the solution.

**Compare or Contrast Pattern**   Writers and speakers *compare* things, events, or people when they emphasize similarities and *contrast* them when they emphasize differences. Individual characteristics may be compared or contrasted one at a time, or lists of characteristics may be discussed as a group. In either case, the pattern can be recognized from the various similarities or differences and from the use of words such as *similarly, likewise, conversely,* and *on the other hand.*

**Inductive Pattern**   The speaker identifies a number of incidents and draws a conclusion from them. The speaker's main point will be something like this: "So, on the basis of all these facts, we come to this overriding principle, which is so-and-so."

**Deductive Pattern**   This pattern is the reverse of the inductive pattern. Here, the principle or general statement is given first and then the events or proofs are enumerated.

Recognizing these patterns will help you not only in note taking and reading but also in your own writing of reports and research papers.


## SUMMARY

| | |
|---|---|
| **What makes the question such a powerful learning device?** | The power of a question lies in its natural and inherent quality to make us *think*, and the thinking that goes into formulating an answer to a question is usually focused thinking, which, in turn, enables learning. |

| **How is wisdom gained through reflection?** | When you *reflect*, that is, look at the author's ideas to discover new relationships and new angles aided by the knowledge you already have, you add to your own creative thinking. |
| **How do signal words aid comprehension and also speed your reading?** | Signal words are the verbal equivalents of traffic signs. Both tell you what to expect ahead, thus giving you time to anticipate and adjust. |
| **How does the recognition of organizational patterns help us to comprehend better?** | Once you identify the organizational pattern used by a speaker or writer, you'll be on familiar ground. Then all you need to do is follow along the route you know they're taking. |

## HAVE YOU MISSED SOMETHING?

*Sentence completion.*   Complete the following sentences with one of the words or phrases listed below each sentence.

1. Psychologists say questions promote _____ .
   creativity      training in decision making      concentration

2. During a lecture, if you do not detect the speaker's organizational pattern, you should _____ .
   stop writing and just listen intently
   keep writing, then try to discover the pattern later
   stop writing, but later find out from other students

*Matching.*   In each blank space in the left column, write the letter preceding the phrase in the right column that matches the left item best.

_____ **1.** Questions

_____ **2.** Concentration

_____ **3.** Cognitive processing

_____ **4.** Reflection

_____ **5.** Signal words

_____ **6.** Organizational patterns

a. Depend on the arrangement of topics and ideas

b. Thinking seriously about a fact or idea

c. Gaining basic understanding

d. Writers use to guide the reader

e. Gaining undivided attention

f. Seeing relationship among ideas

*True-false.*   Write *T* beside the *true* statements and *F* beside the *false* statements.

_____ **1.** Reflection is a silent way of reciting.

_____ **2.** The main function of a question is to make a deeper impression in your memory.

_____ **3.** Concentration is as difficult as seizing a spinning top.

_____ **4.** A single key word in the margin of a textbook can serve the purpose as effectively as a question.

_____ **5.** According to Professor Bethe, creativity comes only with reflection.

_____ **6.** Signal words actually help the writer more than the reader.

_____ **7.** Selective underlining of the main ideas in a textbook serve the same purpose as writing questions in the margin.

_____ **8.** According to Schopenhauer, reflection can leave your memorized knowledge in disarray.

*Multiple choice.*   Choose the word or phrase that completes the following sentence most accurately, and circle the letter that precedes it.

**1.** The best way to formulate a question on a paragraph is to convert into a question the

   a. paragraph's caption.
   b. topic sentence.
   c. summarizing sentence.
   d. paragraph's main idea.

**2.** In a lecture or text, the words "for these reasons" most probably indicate a forthcoming

   a. summarizing statement.
   b. cause and effect explanation.
   c. comparison.
   d. concession.

**3.** In a lecture or text, the words "first, next, after this" most probably indicate a(n)

   a. chronological pattern.
   b. enumeration pattern.
   c. inductive pattern.
   d. process pattern.

   **4.** If you hear, "I've come to you with a solution," most probably the speaker
   will be using a(n)

   a. spatial pattern.
   b. increasing-importance pattern.
   c. cause-and-effect pattern.
   d. inductive pattern.

   **5.** A speaker is usually guided in his or her choice of pattern by the

   a. nature of the material.
   b. objective to be achieved.
   c. type of audience.
   d. size of audience.

*Short answer.*   Supply a brief answer for each of the following items.

   **1.** Why do questions promote better comprehension?
   **2.** Professor Bethe said, "Creativity comes only with reflection." Why is
   creativity so dependent on reflection?
   **3.** How does reflection bring about better remembering?
   **4.** How do "signal words" help you in both textbook reading and lecture
   note taking?
   **5.** Discuss why you think the recognition of an organizational pattern
   enhances understanding.

## VOCABULARY BUILDING

DIRECTIONS: Make a light check mark (√) alongside one of the three words
(choices) that most nearly expresses the meaning of the italicized word in
the phrases that are in the left-hand column. (Answers are given on p. 436.)

|  |  | 1 | 2 | 3 |
|---|---|---|---|---|
| 1. | is best *protrayed* | described | estimated | carried |
| 2. | thoroughly *pondered* | decided | discounted | considered |
| 3. | *enumeration* words | marked | numbered | emphasized |
| 4. | *concession* words | yielding | denying | factual |
| 5. | as *alluded* to | referred | permitted | engaged |
| 6. | loan portfolios *deteriorated* | improved | declined | steadied |
| 7. | to *mollify* shareholders | pacify | notify | agitate |
| 8. | *fortifying* their capital | impairing | erecting | enriching |
| 9. | it became *apparent* | evident | familiar | veiled |
| 10. | a *pending* debt-ceiling | high | unresolved | political |
| 11. | a *debilitating* disorder | renewing | feebling | costly |
| 12. | to *flaunt* a shapely figure | desire | exhibit | disguise |

|  |  | **1** | **2** | **3** |
|---|---|---|---|---|
| 13. | its great fashion *icon* | image | prize | show |
| 14. | names are *facetious* | harmonious | divisive | faceless |
| 15. | your assets are *vulnerable* | impervious | defensive | exposed |
| 16. | big lie continues *unabated* | sustained | unaltered | unanimously |
| 17. | a *bedlam* of hysteria | model | chaos | scene |
| 18. | four horsemen of the apocalypse | present | destruction | future |
| 19. | a worldwide *hysteria* | panic | uplift | message |
| 20. | to *obliterate* bacteria | propagate | eradicate | reconstruct |
| 21. | the word neither *diffident* | different | timid | confident |
| 22. | nor *ostentatious* | modest | extended | pompous |
| 23. | the formal word *precise* | indefinite | exact | proper |
| 24. | but not *pedantic* | academic | vague | ordinary |
| 25. | with patience and *deference* | defiance | respect | change |

# 9

# Listening to Take Good Notes

*Learn how to listen and you will prosper even from those who talk badly.*

—PLUTARCH (A.D. 46–120). Greek biographer and philosopher

A recent survey revealed how much time college students spend in four types of communication:

| | |
|---|---|
| Listening | 53% |
| Reading | 17% |
| Speaking | 16% |
| Writing | 14% |

Now hear this! You can't learn if you don't listen. With dozens of noises and thoughts vying for your attention, acquiring good listening skills takes hard work and practice, but the effort is worth making, and the rewards are long lasting. This chapter discusses

- Your listening habits
- Comprehensive listening
- Triple-A listening
- Ten keys to effective listening
- Listening for shifts in intonation

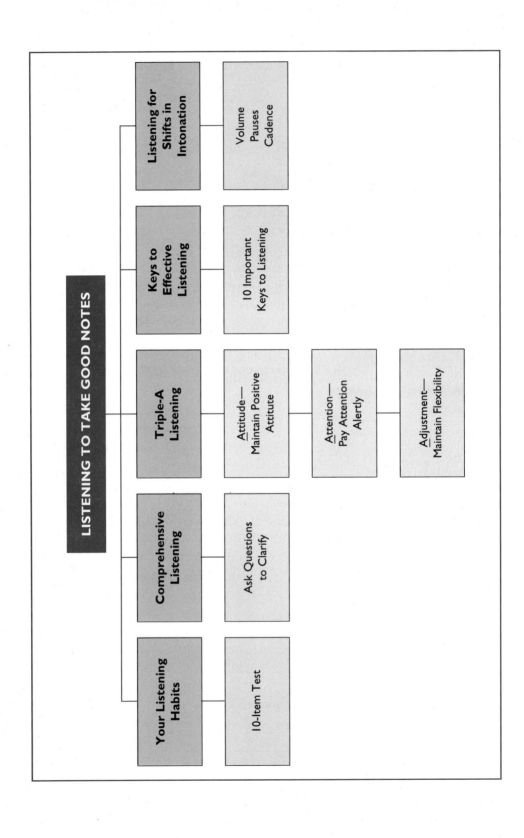

**A**lmost all the information you are responsible for in a college-level course comes from two sources: lectures and textbooks. If you can master the information from these two sources, the chances of academic success are great.

## YOUR LISTENING HABITS

This chapter focuses on procedures to help you master listening. Your goal is to get the lecturer's message. The message, however, is not always obvious, so it's necessary to listen attentively to capture on paper a series of key ideas and supporting details that you can take back to your room and piece together to achieve understanding. But first, where do you stand as a listener? Figure 9.1 presents a short quiz that will let you know.

## COMPREHENSIVE LISTENING

The following quotation illustrates the inherent difficulty of oral communication:

> I know you believe that you understand
> What you think I said, but I am not sure
> That you realize that what you heard is not what I meant.

For communication to occur, both the speaker and the listener must act responsibly. The speaker's responsibility is to make points clearly. The listener's responsibility is to understand what the speaker says. Comprehensive listening occurs when the listener encourages the speaker to fully articulate his or her message, thus enabling the speaker to be more clear. If a speaker's message is not clear and the listener asks a clarifying question, both the speaker and the listener benefit. The speaker is encouraged and gratified to know that the audience is interested. The listener can concentrate on what the speaker has to say and feel good about raising a question that was probably troubling less bold members of the audience.

A professor at the University of Virginia conducted a survey and found that 94 percent of her students had failed to understand something in at least one class lecture during the semester. Seventy percent of the students had not asked clarifying questions even though they knew they could. When asked why they had remained silent, they answered, "I was afraid I'd look stupid," "I didn't want to make myself conspicuous," "I was too proud to ask," "I was too confused to know what question to ask."

The way to dispel the fear of asking is to remember that the only dumb question is the one that was never asked. The way to dispel confusion is to

How often do you find yourself engaging in these ten bad habits of listening? Check the appropriate columns.

### Frequency

| How often do you ... | Almost always | Usually | Sometimes | Seldom | Almost never | Score |
|---|---|---|---|---|---|---|
| Decide that the topic is boring? | | | | | | |
| Criticize the speaker? | | | | | | |
| Overreact by disagreeing? | | | | | | |
| Listen only for bare facts? | | | | | | |
| Outline everything? | | | | | | |
| Fake attention? | | | | | | |
| Yield to distractions? | | | | | | |
| Avoid listening to tough technical information? | | | | | | |
| Let emotion-laden words arouse personal antagonism? | | | | | | |
| Waste thought speed by daydreaming? | | | | | | |
| Total score | | | | | | |

| Tally your score as follows: | | | Interpret your score as follows: | |
|---|---|---|---|---|
| Almost always | 2 | | Below 70 | Need training in listening |
| Usually | 4 | | 70 to 90 | You listen well |
| Sometimes | 6 | | Above 90 | Extraordinarily good listener |
| Seldom | 8 | | | |
| Almost never | 10 | | | |

**FIGURE 9.1   Listening Habits**

*Adapted from Ralph G. Nichols and Thomas R. Lewis,* Listening and Speaking, *p. 166. Originally published by Wm. C. Brown Group, 1954. Reprinted by permission of the authors.*

acknowledge it by saying, "I'm confused about the last point you made," or "I'm confused about how the example pertains to your main point." In this situation, as in most, honesty is the best policy.

Sometimes the lecturer, to create a dialogue or to see whether the class is understanding the material, will ask you a question. When this happens, a good and fair response is to begin by paraphrasing or even repeating the question. Doing this keeps you on the right track, gives you a chance to warm up your thinking on the subject, and buys you some time to compose a reasonably good opening statement and gather your thoughts.

## TRIPLE-A LISTENING

Listening is the first step in note taking. Being a good listener means being an active listener. But listening is not the same as hearing. It isn't simply a matter of acting as a human microphone and picking up the sound of the lecturer's voice. Listening is a conscious activity based on three basic skills: *a*ttitude, *a*ttention, and *a*djustment. These skills are known collectively as *triple-A listening*.

### Maintain a Positive Attitude

A positive attitude sets the stage for open-mindedness. As businessperson and author Kevin J. Murphy says in *Effective Listening*, "Minds are like parachutes; they only function when open."[1]

Although you can take many steps to improve your listening, the prerequisite to effective listening is a positive mental attitude. You must walk into the classroom convinced that the lecturer has something useful to say. If you have any doubts, take a moment to think about the kind of preparation that goes into a typical lecture. The lecturer had to do the searching, reading, selecting, discarding, and organizing of information from dozens of books and other sources—a task that can take hundreds of hours. You can reap the benefits of all that effort in a single lecture.

Maintain that positive attitude even if the lecturer makes statements you don't agree with; don't decide he or she is automatically wrong. If you hear something that rubs you the wrong way, write it down, but keep on listening. Voice your opinion by asking intelligent, clarifying questions after the lecture. In the meantime, don't let reactive interference prevent you

---

[1]Kevin J. Murphy, *Effective Listening: Hearing What People Say and Making It Work for You* (New York: Bantam Books, 1987), p. 28.

from recalling the speaker's key points. All in all, keeping a positive attitude means giving the lecturer the benefit of the doubt.

## Strive to Pay Attention

Attention is the sure path that will lead you into the wonderful state of concentration. Without concentration there is no focus, and without focus there is almost no learning.

Concentration does not mean thinking only one thought. Concentration means holding a central issue in mind while you accept or reject ideas that are related to that issue. In the words of F. Scott Fitzgerald (1896–1940), author of the novel *The Great Gatsby*, "The test of a first-rate intelligence is the ability to hold two opposed ideas in mind at the same time." If you pay attention and concentrate, you will become an active listener able to synthesize new information with facts and ideas already known.

A good way to begin concentrating is to anticipate the lecture. Before class, look over your notes from the last lecture, and take a minute to speculate about what your instructor is going to talk about today. If the lectures follow your textbook, peek ahead to see what's coming. Once the lecture starts, let your mind dart ahead (during pauses) to anticipate what's coming next. You'll be alert, engrossed in the material, and concentrating 100 percent. Another way to start the process of concentration is to look at the course syllabus.

You cannot attain concentration by concentrating on concentration. Your attention must focus on the lecture. Deep cognition, or deep thinking, is vital. When you hear a lecture, the words enter your short-term memory where they have to be swiftly processed into ideas. Active listening sets that process in motion. If your instructor's words are not processed through active listening that results from attention and concentration, they will be dumped from short-term memory and will be gone forever. If you process the words into ideas, in a flash the ideas will be stored in your long-term memory.

Research has shown that an average student remembers about 50 percent of a ten-minute lecture when tested immediately and 25 percent of the same lecture when tested forty-eight hours later. These poor results occur when students are unable to package the lecturer's ideas into easily remembered units.

## Cultivate a Capacity for Adjustment

Although some speakers clearly indicate what they intend to cover in their lectures, you need to be flexible enough to follow a lecture regardless of the direction it may take. Sometimes a speaker says, "This event had three important results" and then goes on to discuss four or five. Other times a question from the audience suddenly shifts the speaker's focus. In such cases, you can't simply tune out the parts of the lecture that don't fit with your expectations. You have to be able to "roll with the punches." That's why adjustment is such an important component of active listening. If, however, you are thoroughly lost, or if the speaker's message is not coming across and you need to ask a clarifying question, do so.

## TEN KEYS TO EFFECTIVE LISTENING

Don't compartmentalize. Use good listening skills both inside and outside the classroom.

Of the many skills a person needs to learn in this complex world, listening is just about the easiest. All you need to do is recognize the habits of a poor listener alongside the techniques used by a good listener. Then, knowing the good techniques, apply them without exception in all your daily activities.

You can make a fresh and immediate start today by referring to Figure 9.2, which lists the ten most important keys to effective listening. Then, see how the following pages amplify these skills.

### Finding Areas of Interest

In the classroom, you're a captive audience for the duration of the lecture. This time will be totally wasted if you decide not to listen. Some students try to use a lecture period to read their textbooks, but doing so is a waste of time because they will be unable to concentrate enough on either the book or the speaker.

It is best to listen intently, take notes vigorously, and show interest by your facial expression. These outward manifestations of interest will create genuine internal interest.

**Outside the Classroom** In personal listening, you have a chance to redirect an uninteresting topic. Listen intently, sincerely, and politely, but at appropriate moments ask questions about aspects of the topic that interest you most.

### Judging Content Not Delivery

Listeners are sometimes terribly rude or downright cruel when a lecturer's delivery fails to measure up to some preconceived standard. Try to approach

| Keys to Effective Listening | The Poor Listener | The Good Listener |
|---|---|---|
| 1. Find areas of interest | Tunes out dry topics. | Seizes opportunities: "What's in it for me?" |
| 2. Judge content not delivery | Tunes out if delivery is poor. | Judges content, skips over delivery errors. |
| 3. Hold your fire | Tends to enter into argument. | Doesn't judge until comprehension is complete. |
| 4. Listen for ideas | Listens for facts. | Listens for central themes. |
| 5. Be a flexible note taker | Is busy with form, misses content. | Adjusts to topic and organizational pattern. |
| 6. Work at listening | Shows no energy output, fakes attention. | Works hard; exhibits alertness. |
| 7. Resist distractions | Is distracted easily. | Fights or avoids distractions; tolerates bad habits in others; knows how to concentrate. |
| 8. Exercise your mind | Resists difficult expository material; seeks light, recreational material. | Uses heavier material as exercise for the mind. |
| 9. Keep your mind open | Reacts to emotional words. | Interprets emotional words; does not get hung up on them. |
| 10. Thought is faster than speech; use it | Tends to daydream with slow speakers. | Challenges, anticipates, mentally summarizes, weighs the evidence, listens between the lines to tone and voice. |

**FIGURE 9.2   Ten Keys to Effective Listening**
*Source: Reprinted by permission of Unisys Corporation.*

each lecture with a humane attitude. Block out negative thoughts, and determine to concentrate totally on what's being said. If you do, you'll emerge from the lecture with a positive self-image. You will also learn something.

**Outside the Classroom**   In personal listening, your kind smile and relaxed attitude can help put the speaker at ease. Don't make the speaker uncomfortable by being aloof or impatient.

## Holding Your Fire

In college you're bound to hear ideas that are different from or even contrary to those you hold. When this happens, your knee-jerk reaction may be to speak up immediately to defend your position. If you decide to attack, you will be too preoccupied to listen attentively to the rest of the lecture. You will be assessing the damage that is being done to your pet ideas, devising an embarrassing question to ask the lecturer, and fantasizing about the results once the lecturer has been "shown up." With such thoughts churning around in your mind, it's no wonder that the rest of the lecture gets tuned out.

You must learn not to get overly excited about a lecturer's point until you are certain you thoroughly understand it. Hold your fire! Do not automatically assume that you are right and someone else is wrong. Instead, listen intently to understand thoroughly the viewpoint expressed by the lecturer. Only after you have done so should you venture, not to attack, but to ask intelligent questions for clarification and explanation.

**Outside the Classroom**   When you are listening to your peers, interruption usually comes easily and quickly, and what could have been a profitable discussion often disintegrates into a shouting match. Remember: You learn much more by listening than by talking. When you talk, you're repeating what you already know. When you listen, you're open to ideas and facts that are probably new to you.

## Listening for Ideas

Don't imitate the detective who says, "The facts, ma'am, just stick to the facts." When you take notes, you do need to take down the facts, but in doing so, try to see what the facts are leading to. Try to see what principle or what idea they are supporting. Try to see how the pieces of the puzzle fit into the building of the big picture. This approach will keep you concentrating at a 100 percent level.

**Outside the Classroom**   When your peers pour out facts, try to go one step further by thinking, "What is his motivation to tell me this?" Or, "What is she leading up to?" Your aim is not to psych out anyone; instead, it is to keep your mind fully occupied and agile.

## Being a Flexible Note Taker

Flexibility in note taking depends on informed listening. Informed listening means that the listener is able to identify the organizational patterns used by the speaker. When you have detected a pattern, then you can anticipate the form of the message and adjust the way you record your notes.

Organizational patterns are easily recognizable if you know their basic structures in advance. (Nine of the most common organizational patterns are described in Chapter 8.) Now, instead of hearing just a continuous, undifferentiated outpouring of facts and ideas from a lecturer, you'll recognize the organizational pattern (the framework) that the speaker is using to present facts and ideas in a controlled, logical manner. Almost instantly, as an informed listener, you will see what the lecturer is doing; thus, you'll be able to understand more readily and, equally important, take notes more systematically and economically.

Often a lecturer will use several of the patterns in one lecture; knowing the patterns, you'll be a flexible note taker by adjusting to the changing patterns.

**Outside the Classroom**   When you are listening to any talk or conversation, try to detect the organizational pattern the speaker is using. If there is none, speculate on how the ideas or facts being poured forth could be better organized if one of the nine patterns was used.

## Working at Listening

A good listener is alert, outwardly calm but inwardly dynamic, and sits toward the front of the classroom. While taking notes the listener may nod in agreement or look quizzical when the presentation becomes unclear. Such activity promotes comprehension and learning by the listener and provides encouragement to the speaker.

**Outside the Classroom**   Active listening results in better understanding for the listener and is appreciated by the speaker.

## Resisting Distractions

There are distractions aplenty in the classroom: antics of other students, whisperings, the speaker's dress and mannerisms, outside noise, and outside views. The best way to resist distractions and maintain your concentration is to rivet your eyes on the speaker when you have a chance and focus on taking notes the rest of the time.

**Outside the Classroom**   Don't watch some other person or activity while pretending to listen to the person speaking to you. Keep your eyes on the speaker just as you would want a listener to look at you while you are speaking.

## Exercising Your Mind

More than just occasionally, sit in on lectures in fields that you know very little about. Try hard to follow the lecturer's chain of thoughts and ideas. Portions of the lecture will be unintelligible to you, but you're bound to understand parts. Such listening is hard work, but just as hard work in the gym strengthens your muscles, the hard work of listening will strengthen your will to concentrate and your power to persist.

**Outside the Classroom**   When a discussion is going on among your friends who are majoring in subjects that are foreign to you, listen and ask questions. You'll be surprised how willing they'll be to answer you.

## Keeping Your Mind Open

There are many touchy subjects of great importance in the news. You may have taken a strong position on some and a lukewarm position on others. When a lecturer uses inflammatory words to express a position contrary to yours, you are likely to harbor negative feelings toward the lecturer.

It is hard to believe that a word or phrase can cause an emotional eruption. Among poor listeners, however, that is frequently the case, and even among very good listeners fireworks occasionally go off. Words that are red flags for some listeners include *activist, liberal, conservative, evolution, creationism, feminist, abortion, pro-life,* and *free market.*

Dealing with highly charged language is similar to dealing with a fear or phobia. Often the emotional impact of the words can be decreased through a frank and open discussion. Genuinely listen to the other point of view. You might learn something that you didn't know before.

**Outside the Classroom**   Be kind and fair to your friends. Don't spring to the attack. Inform yourself of both sides of an issue and focus on facts over opinions.

## Using Your Thought Speed

One of the inherent problems with listening to lectures is that thought is faster than speech; that is, you can internalize information faster than it is spoken. When a lecturer speaks, a listener has moments of free time to dart off on mental side trips. To keep your mind from wandering as a result of this "thought speed," concentrate fully on what the speaker is saying. When you have time to think between ideas, mentally enumerate the ideas that have been expressed and then summarize them. Keep alternating in this fashion throughout the lecture.

**Outside the Classroom**   In a conversation with your peers, do the same: Listen, then enumerate; listen, then summarize.

## LISTEN FOR SHIFTS IN INTONATION

Clearly, lecturers aren't able to use different kinds of type such as bold letters for emphasis, but they do have analogous tools at their disposal: their voices. Most college lecturers speak about 120 words per minute, which means that in a fifty-minute lecture you hear roughly six thousand words. Listening for signals in a lecture is an especially helpful activity because, unlike in reading, you don't have the luxury of retracing your steps if you discover you're lost. In addition to words, intonation—variations in the lecturer's voice—is the most significant signal in spoken language. Intonation has three components: volume, pauses, and cadence.

*Volume*   In general, the introduction of a crucial idea is preceded by a change in volume; the speaker raises or lowers his or her voice.

*Pauses*   By pausing before and after main ideas, a speaker sets these ideas apart from the rest of the lecture. She or he uses pauses to achieve a dramatic effect and, on a practical level, to provide note takers with extra writing time.

*Cadence*   The rhythm of a lecturer's speaking patterns can be particularly helpful. Often, like the bulleted lists you find in textbooks, the speaker lists a series of important ideas by using a steady speaking rhythm, sometimes even beginning each idea with the same words or phrase. Whenever you detect these oral signals, your pencil should be moving steadily, adding these important points to your notes.

We need to remember that the central ingredient that makes for a good listener is concentration. The speaker's words almost always have to penetrate a thick screen of physical and psychological distractions. It is the active listener who, by concentration, parts the screen so that the message-words can reach the ears and mind.

## SUMMARY

**What is comprehensive listening?**

Comprehensive listening has to do with the feedback between speaker and listener. The speaker has an obligation to make his or her words understandable to the listener. The listener, in turn, must let the speaker know when he or she doesn't understand.

**What's the best way to let the speaker know that I don't understand?**

Ask questions. A surprising number of students are too embarrassed to ask questions. The only dumb questions, however, are the ones that go unasked.

**What should I do if the lecturer asks *me* a question?**

Simply start by paraphrasing or repeating the question. That will keep you on track, give you some time to warm up your thinking, and enable you to compose a well-focused opening statement.

**Aren't listening and hearing basically the same?**

No. Hearing is a spontaneous act. Listening, by contrast, is something you choose to do. Listening requires you not only to hear what has been said but to absorb the meaning as well.

**How do I go about being an active listener?**

By following the triple-A listening rules: go to class with a positive attitude, pay attention, and adjust to the lecturer's speed and topic.

**What is deep cognition?**

Deep cognition, or deep thinking, is the process that moves information from the uncertainty of your short-term memory to the safety of your long-term memory.

**What's the best way to concentrate?**

Start with anticipation. Look at your notes from the last lecture or peek ahead in your textbook. Either way, you'll be cultivating the mindset that is needed for 100 percent concentration during a lecture.

**What are the ten keys to effective listening?**

The ten keys are (1) finding areas of interest; (2) judging content rather than delivery; (3) holding your fire when you disagree with what's being said; (4) listening for ideas, not just facts; (5) being a flexible note taker; (6) working at listening instead of faking attention; (7) resisting outside distractions; (8) exercising your mind with challenging material; (9) keeping your mind open, even when you hear emotional words; and (10) putting new ideas to work during a lecture instead of just daydreaming.

**How do I recognize the lecturer's intonational cues?**

Listen for these three: raising or lowering of voice, pauses between ideas or facts, rhythm of lecturer's speaking pattern.

## HAVE YOU MISSED SOMETHING?

*Sentence completion.*  Complete the following sentences with one of the three words listed below each sentence.

**a.** Through listening, the meanings of words and sentences are _____ .
reflected      increased      absorbed

**b.** A good listener places great emphasis on the speaker's _____ .
delivery      appearance      facts

**c.** In listening, the most productive attitude is _____ .
combative      sympathetic      emotional

*Matching.*  In each blank space in the left column, write the letter preceding the phrase in the right column that matches the left item best.

_____ **1.** Attention

a. Percentage of students who are hesitant to ask a clarifying question

_____ **2.** Evolution

b. Sometimes faked by a poor listener

_____ **3.** Facts

c. Common pattern in science lectures

_____ **4.** 53 percent

d. Percentage of communication time devoted to listening

_____ **5.** Process

e. May be a red flag for some listeners

_____ **6.** Questions

_____ **7.** 70 percent

_____ **8.** 25 percent

f. Percentage of a lecture that is remembered after forty-eight hours

g. Can benefit both the speaker and the listener

h. Often the sole concern of a poor listener

*True-false.* Write *T* beside the *true* statements and *F* beside the *false* statements.

_____ **1.** Roughly 50 percent of a ten-minute speech is forgotten immediately.

_____ **2.** The good listener tunes out dry topics.

_____ **3.** Concentration means thinking only one thought at a time.

_____ **4.** The only dumb question is the one that is never asked.

_____ **5.** Words are processed into ideas through deep cognition.

*Multiple choice.* Choose the phrase that completes the following sentence most accurately, and circle the letter that precedes it.

**1.** Listening is
   a. strictly mechanical.
   b. the same as hearing.
   c. not automatic.
   d. all the above.

**2.** When you disagree with a lecturer's statement,
   a. begin rehearsing your rebuttal.
   b. decide he or she is automatically misinformed.
   c. take his or her stand as a bias.
   d. make a note of it, but keep on taking notes.

**3.** In active listening, you
   a. take notes of ideas as well as details.
   b. listen for the hard facts, too.
   c. convert words into ideas.
   d. do all the above.

*Short answer.* Supply a brief answer for each of the following items.

**1.** Of the ten bad habits of listening, which one habit is the most devastating? Why?

2. Why is the triple-A listening technique a good nutshell method?
3. Which of the ten effective listening skills is the most important? Why?
4. What is the main value of listening and interpreting a speaker's intonation?

## VOCABULARY BUILDING

DIRECTIONS: Make a light check mark (√) alongside one of the three words (choices) that most nearly expresses the meaning of the italicized word in the phrases that are in the left-hand column. (Answers are given on p. 436.)

|  |  | 1 | 2 | 3 |
|---|---|---|---|---|
| 1. | the *inherent* difficulty | innate | passing | alien |
| 2. | to *articulate* his message | murmur | express | write |
| 3. | less *intrepid* members | cautious | timid | brave |
| 4. | not always *obvious* | obscure | clear | independent |
| 5. | to make myself *conspicuous* | visible | trifling | modest |
| 6. | have been *reluctant* | eager | unwilling | keen |
| 7. | their *fragile* capital | delicate | durable | flexible |
| 8. | regarded as *stoic* | solid | unruffled | excitable |
| 9. | *arcane* formulas | mysterious | revealed | obvious |
| 10. | Congress's *petulant* drive | cooperative | quarrelsome | informal |
| 11. | nothing *epitomizes* the folly | represents | supplements | changes |
| 12. | an *epochal* Vermeer exhibition | assembled | momentous | selected |
| 13. | does this make them *insipid?* | dull | zestful | colorful |
| 14. | rendering *inanimate* objects | vibrant | moving | still |
| 15. | quite *vapid* compared with | dull | inspiring | vaporous |
| 16. | geographically *sequestered* | isolated | important | selected |
| 17. | sense of *immunity* | liability | safety | susceptibility |
| 18. | he *postulated* that | recalled | proposed | read |
| 19. | helping to *foster* | curb | restrain | promote |
| 20. | might become *impervious* | closed | liable | exposed |
| 21. | what is the *recompense?* | cost | reward | sacrifice |
| 22. | *recalcitrant* underling | stubborn | soldierly | obediant |
| 23. | *tumult* of the waters | serenity | uproar | constancy |
| 24. | the *nostalgia* of Spring | fragrance | warmth | remembrance |
| 25. | that *inscrutable* face | revealing | unknowable | lucid |

# 10

# Taking Good Notes

*Learn, compare, collect the facts!*

—IVAN PETROVICH PAVLOV (1849–1936), Russian
physiologist

Learning begins with information gathering. The lectures you
hear in class provide the raw material for knowledge. Because
you spend so much of your academic life accumulating information, it's unwise to do so haphazardly. To help you accumulate
information in an orderly and systematic way, this chapter focuses on

- The importance of notes
- The Cornell System
- Efficient recording
- Abbreviations and symbols
- Periodic reviews
- Types of notes
- Tips and tactics

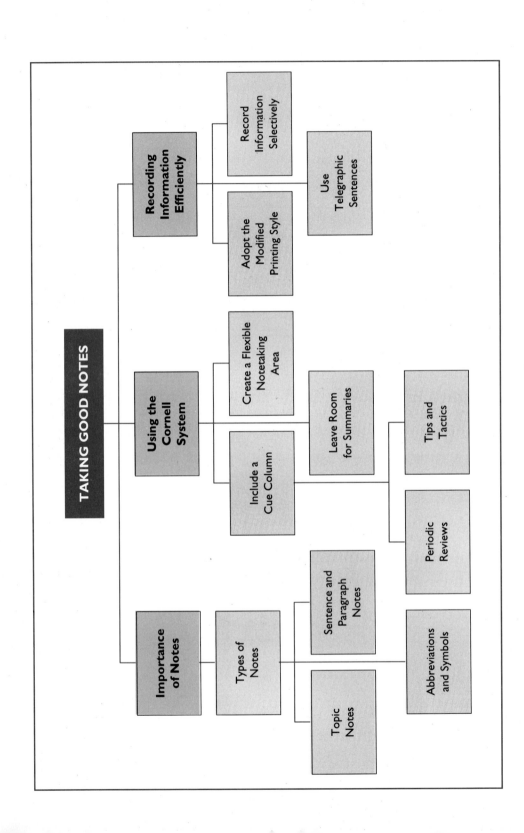

TAKING GOOD NOTES

Importance of Notes

Types of Notes

Topic Notes

Sentence and Paragraph Notes

Abbreviations and Symbols

Periodic Reviews

Tips and Tactics

Using the Cornell System

Include a Cue Column

Create a Flexible Notetaking Area

Leave Room for Summaries

Recording Information Efficiently

Adopt the Modified Printing Style

Record Information Selectively

Use Telegraphic Sentences

**W**hy take notes? Why not just sit back and listen intensively? This section answers your questions.

## THE IMPORTANCE OF NOTES

The primary goal of note taking is to provide you with a written record of what you've heard. Your short-term memory isn't equipped to retain all the ideas in a typical lecture. As a result, forgetting can be instantaneous and complete. For example, who hasn't forgotten a name only minutes after an introduction? Or had to reread a telephone number after getting a busy signal? Who would rely only on his or her memory in any academic course? Carefully controlled research further points out memory's fragility. Experiments have shown that unrehearsed information is sometimes forgotten in as little as twenty seconds.[1] In a classical experiment, Hermann Ebbinghaus examined the rate of forgetting by studying how easily he could relearn a list after different time intervals. At first, forgetting was rapid and occurred within almost the first hour, but after eight hours, further forgetting occurred at a relatively slow rate. In short, Ebbinghaus found that almost half of what is learned is forgotten within an hour.[2] Recently, psychologists carrying out experiments similar to Ebbinghaus's affirmed his findings.

The following true story further confirms the rapidity and scope of forgetting. Three professors eating lunch in the faculty lounge had this conversation:

> CLYDE: Did you hear last night's lecture?
> WALTER: No, I was busy.
> CLYDE: Well, you missed one of the best lectures in recent years.
> LEON: I agree. The four points that he developed were gems.
> CLYDE: I never heard anyone make his points so clearly.
> WALTER: I don't want you to repeat the lecture, but what were those four points?
> LEON: (Long silence) Clyde? (Passage of two or three minutes; seems like an hour.)
> LEON: Well, I'd better get back to the office.
> CLYDE: Me too!
> WALTER: Me too!

---

[1] Douglas A. Bernstein, Edward J. Roy, Thomas K. Srull, and Christopher D. Wickens, *Psychology* (Boston: Houghton Mifflin, 1988), p. 293.
[2] Alan J. Parkin, *Memory: Phenomena, Experiment and Theory* (Cambridge, MA: Blackwell, 1993); and Hermann Ebbinghaus, *Memory* (New York: Dover, 1964), p. 76.

Both Leon and Clyde were brilliant men, yet neither of them was able to recall even a fragment of any point made in the previous night's lecture. Each had forgotten the four points because neither had transferred the points from short-term memory to long-term memory by silently reciting them. Instead, they both had recited that the speaker was clear, forceful, and wise and that he had made four points—and they remembered only what they had recited. As you can surmise from the anecdote, the only sure way to overcome forgetting is by taking notes and then studying and reciting them.

## USING THE CORNELL SYSTEM

The notes you jot down can become a handwritten textbook. In fact, in many instances your notes are more practical, meaningful, and up-to-date than a textbook. If you keep them neat, complete, and well organized, they will serve you splendidly.

The best way I know of to ensure that the notes you take are useful is by adopting the Cornell note-taking system, which was developed at Cornell University more than forty years ago. Since then the Cornell System has been adopted by countless colleges and universities not only in the United States but also in other countries, including China. Although the system is far-reaching, its secret is simple: Wide margins on the left-hand side and the bottom of each page provide the keystone.

Although many office and school supply stores now sell Cornell-style note paper, you can easily use a pen and ruler to adapt standard loose-leaf paper to the task. First draw a vertical line down the left side of each page two-and-one-half inches from the edge of the paper; end the line two inches from the bottom of the sheet. This creates the *cue column*. Next draw a horizontal line two inches up from the bottom of the page. This is the border for your *summary area*. The large space to the right of the cue column and above the summary area is where your notes should be taken. Figure 10.1 shows a Cornell note sheet.

### Include a Cue Column

The cue column is a two-and-one-half-inch margin on the left-hand side of each page of your note sheets. It helps to ensure that you will actually put the notes to good use instead of simply stashing them away in a notebook until test time.

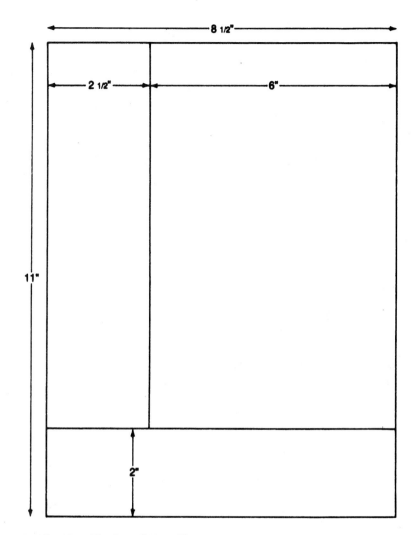

**FIGURE 10.1   The Cornell Note Sheet**
To use the Cornell System, the student writes notes in the wide (6") column. To study from the
notes, the student writes questions in the narrow column and a summary in the space at the
bottom of the note sheet.

As you're taking notes, keep the cue column empty. But when you review and recite what you've jotted down, draw questions from the ideas in your notes, and write them in the cue column. Writing questions helps clarify meanings, reveal relationships, establish continuity, and strengthen memory.

## Leave Room for Summaries

The two-inch space at the bottom of each note sheet is the summary area, in which you sum up each page of your notes in a sentence or two. The virtues of the summary area are twofold. Not only does it provide a convenient in-a-nutshell version of a page full of notes; it also helps you step back and look at the implications of what you've written down. There's always a danger that in paying close attention to the specific facts and details that make up your notes, you lose sight of their overall meaning. By encouraging you to look at "the big picture," the summary area provides perspective and helps avoid this potential note-taking pitfall.

## Create a Flexible Note-Taking Area

The information that goes in the largest space on the page varies from class to class and from student to student. Different courses come with different demands. The format you choose for taking your notes and the ideas you take down are almost entirely up to you. If you have a special way of jotting down your notes, you should be able to use it with the Cornell note sheet. Figures 10.2 and 10.3 show notes taken on a Cornell note sheet for two different subjects.

In general, however, avoid taking notes in outline form because this forces you to fit the material into a highly regimented pattern. It's fine to indent and even number your notes, but don't get so caught up in numbers, letters, and Roman numerals that you overlook content.

## THE CORNELL SYSTEM FOR TAKING NOTES IN STEPS

The Cornell note-taking system is more than a sheet of paper on which to take notes. It is a system that efficiently takes you through a completely natural learning cycle on the same sheet of paper.

Psych. 105 – Prof. Martin – Sept. 14 (Mon.)

MEMORY

Memory tricky – Can recall instantly many trivial things of childhood, yet forget things recently worked hard to learn & retain.

**How do psycholo- gists account for remembering?**

Memory Trace
— Fact that we retain information means that some change was made in the brain.
— Change called "memory trace."
— "Trace" probably a molecular arrangement similar to molecular changes in a magnetic recording tape.

**What's a "memory trace"?**

**What are the three memory systems?**

Three memory systems: sensory, short term, long term.
— Sensory (lasts one second)
Ex. Words or numbers sent to brain by sight (visual image) start to disintegrate within a few tenths of a second & gone in one full second, unless quickly transferred to S-T memory by verbal repetition.

**How long does sensory memory retain information?**

**How is information transferred to STM?**

— Short-term memory [STM] (lasts 30 seconds)
• Experiments show: a syllable of 3 letters remembered 50% of the time after 3 seconds. Totally forgotten end of 30 seconds.

**What are the reten- tion times of STM?**

**What's the capacity of the STM?**

• S-T memory — limited capacity — holds average of 7 items.
• More than 7 items — jettisons some to make room.
• To hold items in STM, must rehearse — must hear sound of words internally or externally.

**How to hold information in STM?**

**What are the reten- tion times of LTM?**

— Long-Term memory [LTM] (lasts a lifetime or short time).
• Transfer fact or idea by
(1) Associating w/information already in LTM.
(2) Organizing information into meaningful units.
(3) Understanding by comparing & making relationships.
(4) Frameworking – fit pieces in like in a jigsaw puzzle.
(5) Reorganizing – combining new & old into a new unit.
(6) Rehearsing – aloud to keep memory trace strong.

**What are the six ways to transfer infomation from STM to LTM?**

Three kinds of memory systems are sensory, which retains information for about 1 second; short-term, which retains for a maximum of 30 seconds; and long-term, which varies from a lifetime of retention to a relatively short time.

The six ways (activities) to transfer information to the long-term memory are associating, organizing, understanding, frameworking, reorganizing, and rehearsing.

**FIGURE 10.2 A Cornell Note Sheet with Jottings in the Cue Column and Summary Area**

|  |  |
|---|---|
|  | Environmental Sciences Mr. R. Evans – May 4th |
| What is the extent of grasslands? | A. Food from grasses – & attributes |
|  |   1. Grass covers 1/4 of earth – 6,000 kinds |
|  |     a. food for people & animals |
| What four purposes are served by grass? |     b. retards erosion |
|  |     c. beauty around homes & parks |
|  |     d. provides houses, tools, bowls, paper = bamboo |
| Name some foods (cereals) provided by grass. |   2. Food |
|  |     a. wheat & rye = bread fr. flour |
|  |     b. seeds as cereals = corn, rice, oats, barley |
|  |     c. sugarcane is giant grass = sugar |
| What other foods stem from grass? |   3. Grass into meat |
|  |     a. cattle, sheep, goats, etc. |
|  |     b. dairy cows = milk, cheese |
|  |     c. horses = for work & pleasure |
| How do spiders affect our food supply? | B. Relationship – spiders to food |
|  |   1. If spiders disappeared, we'd starve within few months |
|  |     – use up canned & frozen food = starve |
|  |   2. Billions of insects would devour – destroy crops & pastures |
| How many spiders per acre of grassland? |   3. Spiders eat mountains of insects day & night |
|  |   4. Density = about 2 million spiders in acre of grassland |
|  |   5. Widespread – universal |
| Where are spiders found – extent geographically? |     a. In mountains (22,000 ft.) in snow & ice |
|  |     b. In mines = 2,000 ft. down |
|  |     c. In nests of birds, squirrels, mice |
|  |   6. Spiders never eat vegetables – only insects |
| How many harmful? |   7. 50,000 different kinds – less than dozen harmful |
|  |     – harmful when feet or hands in nests (webs) |
|  |   8. Our lives depend on spiders |
|  |     – yet, we kill them |
|  |     – what a way to treat a friend! |

Grass covers 1/4 of the earth & is food – source for both man and animals. Grass produces wheat, rye, corn, rice, oats, barley, etc. Grass is the basis for producing meat, milk, cheese, etc.

    If it were not for the immense population of spiders that eat insects, the insect population would immediately zoom tremendously and consume all grasses—thus, cutting off the food supply. Starvation would result within a matter of a few months. (Own thought: The sea would be the only source of food. Also, the Eskimo would be able to survive.)

**FIGURE 10.3** **Cornell Note Sheet Showing a Simple Alphabetical and Numerical Organization But Not a Formal Outline**

First, capture the lecturer's ideas and facts in the six-inch column.

Second, at your next free period or at the latest during your evening study time, read over your notes to fill in any gaps and to make words more legible. Do this while the lecture is still relatively fresh in your mind.

Third, determine the first main idea put forth by the lecturer. Then in the cue column write a question based on the main idea.

Fourth, with a plain sheet of paper, block out the notes in the six-inch column, leaving exposed only the question in the cue column. Now glance at the question, then recite aloud, in your own words, the idea or fact needed to answer the question. After reciting, slip the plain sheet down to check your recitation. If your answer was incorrect or incomplete, cover the notes and recite again. It is important to establish an accurate, crisp, clear image in your memory at the very beginning.

Fifth, at the bottom of the sheet, write a summarizing statement—a concise, in-a-nutshell version of a page full of notes. These summaries will make the studying for your exams, especially the final one, remarkably efficient. Furthermore, by writing summaries, you will become a better thinker and writer.

Sixth, review your notes immediately so that you end up with a view of the whole rather than isolated facts and ideas. In addition to getting a global view, an immediate review impresses the fresh lecture in your memory. As you learned in Chapter 5, yesterday's knowledge interferes with today's knowledge and today's interferes with yesterday's. The battle between remembering and forgetting goes on continuously. The only way you can influence the outcome of this battle is by reviewing your notes regularly. No matter how busy you are, make it a habit, before settling down to study, to make a quick review of your previously taken notes on the subject you're about to study. Short, fast, frequent reviews will produce far better understanding and remembering than long, all-day or all-night sessions.

Last, start the process of reflection. Ask yourself: What's the significance of these facts and ideas? What principles are they based on? How can I apply them to what I already know? How do they fit? What's beyond these facts and ideas?

## RECORDING INFORMATION EFFICIENTLY

Strive to make your note taking both speedy and sparing. Of course, if you scribble down information too quickly, your notes may be illegible. And if you're too choosy about what you record, you may be left with costly gaps in your information. The way to circumvent these problems and record legible, useful notes at a reasonable speed is by adopting the modified printing style, using telegraphic sentences, and recording selectively.

## Adopt the Modified Printing Style

Poor handwriting need not keep you from taking legible notes. You can develop legible writing by adopting the *modified printing style,* a system that combines the rapidity of writing with the legibility of printing. Letters are formed smoothly, as with cursive or longhand writing, but are punctuated with the sort of stops and starts characteristic of printing. That means your words take on a cursive look, and at the same time the periodic breaks between letters prevent your writing from eroding into an unreadable blur.

What makes the modified printing style so effective and easy to learn is that it combines your style of printing with your style of cursive in a mixture that brings out the best elements of both. Here's how:

$$a\ b\ c\ d\ e\ f\ g\ h\ i\ j\ k\ l\ m\ n\ o\ p\ q\ r\ s\ t\ u\ v\ w\ x\ y\ z$$

Figure 10.4 shows how modified printing looks in a typical paragraph.

## Use Telegraphic Sentences

Long before the fax machine was invented and when telephones and E-mail were not so prevalent as they are today, important business and personal messages were sent by telegraph. The sender paid by the word; the fewer the words, the lower the cost. A three-word message such as "Arriving three pm" was much less expensive than an eleven-word message: "I will arrive home promptly at three o'clock in the afternoon."

Of course, taking notes doesn't cost money, but it does cost time. You can save time and still extract the important information from lectures by using telegraphic sentences in your notes. To do so, leave out unnecessary words such as articles (a, an, the), abbreviate words you use often (see pages 214–217 and Figures 10.10 and 10.11, pages 217–218), and streamline definitions by using a colon (":") or a dash ("—"). Two examples of this telegraphic style are shown in Figure 10.5.

## Record Information Selectively

Taking thorough notes, regardless of the format you choose, should not mean writing down everything you hear. Your emphasis should be on the

There are four advantages to using this modified printing style. First, it is faster than cursive writing; second, it is neater, permitting easy and direct comprehension; third, it saves time by precluding rewriting or typing; and fourth, it permits easy and clear reforming of letters that are ill-formed due to haste.

**FIGURE 10.4    Modified Printing Style**

ideas, not the words. And you don't want all the ideas, either, just the key ones, (as Figure 10.6 shows) along with any details or examples you need to make those ideas easier to understand.

## Sentence Notes

In most instances, sentence notes written in a telegraphic style will be the most efficient way to record a lecture. Be flexible, though, because (as Figure 10.7 shows) you might have to switch from one type of notes to another.

## Topic-Idea Notes

The topic-idea format is often useful in history, economics, and philosophy courses. The lecturer mentions a topic and then expands on it. Notice that in Figure 10.8 the "paragraph" about the law of diminishing returns is broken up by two subtopic indicators to show separate ideas.

## Paragraph Notes

If the lecturer is expounding on an idea in a straightforward fashion, don't try to impose some sort of topic and subtopic organization where there is none. Instead, write short, telegraphic sentences and end up with an almost solid paragraph, as shown in Figure 10.9.

### Lecture's words

In marketing, we try to understand customers' needs and then respond to them with the right products and services. In the past, firms often produced goods first and tried to fit the customer's needs to the goods. Today's world-class marketers pride themselves on their customer orientation. We begin with the customer and build the product or service from there. A good example is McDonald's, the fast-food chain, which tailors its menus to local tastes and customs when it opens fast-food outlets in Moscow and other international locations.

### Student's telegraphic sentences

1. Marketing understands customers' needs first.
   a. In past, firms produced goods first, then fit them to customers.
   b. World-class = having customer orientation.
   c. Ex. McDonald's in Moscow

### Lecture's words

The US Patent Office has granted numerous patents for perpetual motion machines based upon applications with complete detailed drawings. Some years ago, though, the patent office began requiring working models of such a machine before a patent would be granted. Result: no patents granted for perpetual motion machines since that time.

### Student's telegraphic sentences

Perpetual motion machine (drawings) = many patents.
Required working model = no patents since.

**FIGURE 10.5   Examples of Telegraphic Sentences**

| | Oct. 10 (Mon.) – Soc. 102 – Prof. Oxford |
|---|---|
| What's sympathetic magic?<br><br>Describe contagious magic? | A. Two kinds of magic<br> 1. Sympathetic – make model or form of a person from clay, etc.—then stick pins into object to hurt symbolized person.<br> 2. Contagious magic<br>  a. Need to possess an article belonging to another person.<br>  b. Ex. Fingernail clippings. By doing harm to these objects, feel that harm can be transmitted. |

**FIGURE 10.6   Topic-Explanation Notes**

| | Oct. 10 (Mon.) – Soc. 102 – Prof. Oxford |
|---|---|
| What's animism?<br><br><br>Describe mana!<br><br><br>How to gain mana?<br><br><br><br>Who has mana? | A. Animism<br> 1. Object has supernatural power<br> 2. Power called mana (not limited to objects)<br>  a. Objects accumulate mana<br>   Ex. Good canoe – more mana than poor one.<br>  b. Objects can lose mana<br>  c. People collect objects w/lots of mana<br>  d. Good person's objects collect mana<br>  e. People, animals, plants have mana, too.<br>   Ex. Expert canoe builder has mana – imparts mana to canoe<br>  f. Chief has lots of mana – dangerous to get too close to chief – mana around head. |

**FIGURE 10.7   Sentence Notes**

| | |
|---|---|
| | Oct. 27 (WED.) – Economics 105 – Prof. Terry |
| | <u>Some Basic Laws & Principles</u> |
| What is the Law of Diminishing Returns? | 1. Law of Diminishing Returns<br>   a. Refers to amount of extra output (production) we get when we add additional inputs, but after a point, the extra inputs yield decreasing amounts of extra output. |
| What is Malthus's Law? | b. Malthus's views depended on this law = Just so much land, but population could increase more rapidly than food supplies. |

**FIGURE 10.8   Topic-Idea Notes**

| | |
|---|---|
| | Nov. 6 (MON.) – World Lit. 106 – Prof. Warnek |
| | <u>Greece</u> |
| What is the Greek concept of a well rounded person? | 1. Unity = well rounded<br>Early Greeks vigorous. Goal was to be well rounded: unity of knowledge & activity. No separate specializations as law, literature, philosophy, etc. Believed one person should master all things equally well; not only knowledge, but be an athlete, soldier, & statesman, too. |

**FIGURE 10.9   Paragraph Notes**

## ABBREVIATIONS AND SYMBOLS

You should use only the abbreviations that fit your needs and that you will remember easily. A good idea is to introduce only a few abbreviations into your note taking at a time. Overuse may leave you with notes that are difficult to read. Here are some rules to keep in mind and examples of each.

1. Symbols are especially helpful to students in engineering and mathematics. Lists of commonly used symbols are given in most textbooks and reference books.

   | | |
   |---|---|
   | $\neq$ | does not equal |
   | f | frequency |

2. Create a family of symbols.

   | | |
   |---|---|
   | $\bigcirc$ | organism |
   | $\odot$ | individual |
   | $\circledS$ | individuals |

3. Leave out the periods in standard abbreviations.

   | | |
   |---|---|
   | cf | compare |
   | eg | for example |
   | dept | department |
   | NYC | New York City |

4. Use only the first syllable of a word.

   | | |
   |---|---|
   | pol | politics |
   | dem | democracy |
   | lib | liberal |
   | cap | capitalism |

5. Use the entire first syllable and only the first letter of a second syllable.

   | | |
   |---|---|
   | subj | subject |
   | cons | conservative |
   | tot | totalitarianism |
   | ind | individual |

6. Eliminate final letters. Use just enough of the beginning of a word to form an easily recognizable abbreviation.

   | | |
   |---|---|
   | assoc | associate, associated |
   | ach | achievement |
   | biol | biological |
   | info | information |
   | intro | introduction |
   | chem | chemistry |
   | conc | concentration |
   | max | maximum |
   | rep | repetition |

7. Omit vowels from the middle of words, and retain only enough consonants to provide a recognizable skeleton of the word.
   bkgd        background
   ppd         prepared
   prblm       problem
   estmt       estimate
   gvt         government
8. Use an apostrophe.
   gov't       government
   am't        amount
   cont'd      continued
   educat'l    educational
9. Form the plural of a symbol or abbreviated word by adding "s."
   □s          areas
   chaps       chapters
   co-ops      cooperatives
   f̲s          frequencies
   /s          ratios
10. Use "g" to represent *ing* endings.
   decrg       decreasing
   ckg         checking
   estg        establishing
   exptg       experimenting
11. Use a dot placed over a symbol or word to indicate the word *rate*.
   i̇          vibration rate
   ḟ          frequency rate
12. Generally, spell out short words such as *in, at, to, but, for,* and *key.* Symbols,
    signs, or abbreviations for short words will make the notes too dense
    with "shorthand."
13. Leave out unimportant verbs.
14. Leave out the words *a* and *the*.
15. If a term, phrase, or name is initially written out in full during the lecture,
    substitute initials whenever the term, phrase, or name is used again.
    Initial writing:   Modern Massachusetts Party
    Subsequently:   MMP
16. Use symbols for commonly recurring connective or transitional words.
   &           and
   w/          with
   w/o         without
   vs          against
   ∴           therefore

## Speed Notes for Engineers and Technicians

Many symbols and abbreviations are widely used in technical fields. They will probably cut your writing time in half. Some of the basic symbols are shown in Figure 10.10. Common technical abbreviations are given in Figure 10.11.

Other symbols and abbreviations for many different technical and nontechnical fields are often found in special sections of unabridged dictionaries. Look them up the next time you are in the library.

## TIPS AND TACTICS

If you turn the following tips and tactics into habits, your notes will be an invaluable resource to you. Use these tips and tactics until they are second nature to you.

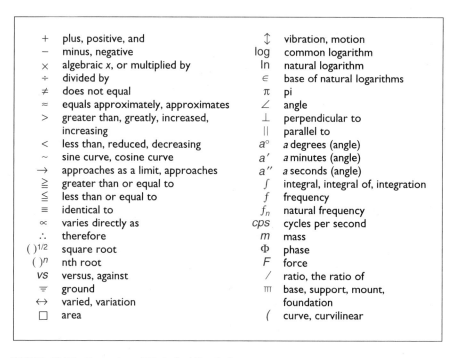

| + | plus, positive, and | $\updownarrow$ | vibration, motion |
|---|---|---|---|
| − | minus, negative | log | common logarithm |
| × | algebraic $x$, or multiplied by | ln | natural logarithm |
| ÷ | divided by | $\in$ | base of natural logarithms |
| ≠ | does not equal | π | pi |
| ≈ | equals approximately, approximates | ∠ | angle |
| > | greater than, greatly, increased, increasing | ⊥ | perpendicular to |
| | | ‖ | parallel to |
| < | less than, reduced, decreasing | $a°$ | $a$ degrees (angle) |
| ~ | sine curve, cosine curve | $a'$ | $a$ minutes (angle) |
| → | approaches as a limit, approaches | $a''$ | $a$ seconds (angle) |
| ≧ | greater than or equal to | ∫ | integral, integral of, integration |
| ≦ | less than or equal to | $f$ | frequency |
| ≡ | identical to | $f_n$ | natural frequency |
| ∝ | varies directly as | $cps$ | cycles per second |
| ∴ | therefore | $m$ | mass |
| ( )$^{1/2}$ | square root | Φ | phase |
| ( )$^n$ | nth root | $F$ | force |
| $vs$ | versus, against | / | ratio, the ratio of |
| ⏚ | ground | ⊤⊤ | base, support, mount, foundation |
| ↔ | varied, variation | | |
| □ | area | ( | curve, curvilinear |

**FIGURE 10.10   Examples of Technical Symbols**

| | | | |
|---|---|---|---|
| *anlys* | analysis | *pltg* | plotting |
| *ampltd* | amplitude | *reman* | remain |
| *asmg* | assuming | *rsnc* | resonance |
| *cald* | called | *rltnshp* | relationship |
| *cnst* | constant | *smpl* | simple |
| *dmpg* | damping | *smpfd* | simplified |
| *dmnsls* | dimensionless | *stfns* | stiffness |
| *dfln* | deflection | *systm* | system |
| *dfnd* | defined | *sgnft* | significant |
| *dstrbg* | disturbing | *ths* | this |
| *eftvns* | effectiveness | *trnsmsblty* | transmissibility |
| *frdm* | freedom | *thrtly* | theoretically |
| *frcg* | forcing | *valu* | value |
| *gvs* | gives | *wth* | with |
| *hrmc* | harmonic | *whn* | when |
| *isltr* | isolator | *xprsd* | expressed |
| *isltn* | isolation | | |

**FIGURE 10.11  Typical Technical Abbreviations**
Reprinted by permission from G. H. Logan, "Speed Notes for Engineers," *Product Engineering,*
September 30, 1963. Copyright © 1963 by Morgan-Grampian, Inc.

## Use the Two-Page System

When you need to scramble to keep up with a fast-talking lecturer, you may find this two-page system helpful. Here's the way it works: Lay your binder or notebook flat on the desk. On the left-hand page, record main ideas only. This is your primary page. On the right-hand page, record as many details as you have time for. Place the details opposite the main ideas they support. After the lecture, remain in your seat for a few minutes and fill in any gaps in your notes while the lecture is still relatively fresh in your mind.

## Don't Use Cassette or Tape

Do not use a tape or cassette recorder. If you do, you'll be wasting time and not learning very much. When a lecture is on tape, you cannot review it in five or ten minutes; you have to replay the entire lecture. Worst of all, you cannot use the technique of reciting, which is the most effective learning technique known to psychologists. Furthermore, you also lose the advantage of visual learning—that is, seeing the words and seeing the relationship between the written ideas.

Some students create written notes as they listen to the tape in the privacy of their rooms. But these notes could have been taken directly, during the live lecture.

## Acknowledge Alternative Learning Styles

There are some extraordinary circumstances when the cassette and tape recorder are a godsend for those who have real difficulty with traditional lecture note-taking methods. In such cases, the use of lecture-gathering devices is strongly encouraged.

## Avoid Shorthand

Don't take lecture notes in shorthand. Shorthand notes cannot be studied effectively while they are still in symbol form. Besides, shorthand symbols still have to be transformed into regular words. If you need a fast method to keep up with the lecturer, use the abbreviations and the symbols listed in this chapter.

## Don't Keyboard Your Notes

Write legibly the first time. Don't rationalize that you'll keyboard your notes when you return to your room. Keyboarding your notes is a waste of time, opportunity, and energy. You'll need almost a full hour to decipher and keyboard one set of scribbled lecture notes. That hour could have been extremely productive if you had spent it reciting notes taken during the lecture. Keyboarding can exhaust you physically, mentally, and emotionally, leaving you unfit for the task of learning.

Contrary to what most people think, almost no learning takes place during the keyboarding of scribbled notes. The act of deciphering and keyboarding requires almost total concentration, leaving scant concentration for comprehending the facts and ideas being keyboarded.

## Use Signal Words and Phrases

As mentioned earlier, most college lecturers speak about 120 words per minute. In a fifty-minute lecture, you hear up to six thousand words expressing ideas, facts, and details. To impose some recognizable order on those ideas, facts, and details, lecturers use signal words and phrases. (See Chapter 8.)

## Get Ready for the Final Barrage

Pay close attention to the end of the lecture. Speakers who do not pace themselves well may have to cram half the lecture into the last five or ten minutes. Record such packed finales as rapidly as you can. After class, stay in your seat for a few extra minutes to write down as much as you can remember.

## Rely on Your Own Instant Replay

As soon as you leave the lecture room, while walking to your next class, mentally recall the lecture from beginning to end. Visualize the classroom and the lecturer and any blackboard work. After mentally recalling the lecture, ask yourself some questions: What was the lecturer getting at? What really was the central point? What did I learn? How does what I learned fit in with what I already know? If you discover anything you don't quite understand, no matter how small, make a note of it and ask the instructor to explain it before the next class.

## Stick to the Basics

As awesome and novel as the idea of a laptop is, the simple basic paper-and-pencil technique is still preferred. Some disadvantages of using a laptop for taking lecture notes are (1) it's heavy to carry, (2) you still have to print out your notes, (3) it takes some expertise to copy a diagram or a calculus problem from the blackboard, and (4) if it is stolen, you might lose not only the laptop but also any lectures that you haven't yet printed.

## Arrive Early

Coming to class early enables you to find a good seat, away from distractions inside and outside the room. But best of all, you'll have a few minutes to look over the notes of the previous lecture so that you can connect them with the lecture you are about to hear. Otherwise, you are likely to have a compartmentalized view of each day's lecture. This condition might be depicted by a series of unconnected links:

On the other hand, a brief review just before class will help form a strong chain of association, helping you see the development of the lectures as a continued series:

## Don't Miss Class

If you know you'll be missing a class, supply a friend with a tape recorder and ask him or her to tape the lecture for you. Then you'll be able to take your own notes when you play it back.

## TWO DOZEN DOS AND ONE DOZEN DON'TS

The twenty-four dos and twelve don'ts that follow are the warp and woof of note taking. Weave them into a magic carpet of your own design and glide over all the rough spots of note taking.

*Dos*

1. Look over previous notes before class. (Maintains continuity.)
2. Attend *all* lectures. (It's a continuing story.)
3. Be academically aggressive. (Sit up straight with "rolled-up sleeves.")
4. Take a front seat to see and hear better. (You won't dare snooze.)
5. Use a large, loose-leaf binder. (Gives ample room.)
6. Carry lined 8½ × 11 loose-leaf sheets to class. (Insert them into a binder afterward.)
7. Write on only one side of sheet. (Spread them out for review.)

8. On top sheet, record course, lecturer, and date. (In case of spill.)
9. Begin taking notes immediately. (Don't wait for inspiration.)
10. Write in short, telegraphic sentences. (Make them meaningful.)
11. Make notes complete for later understanding. (Don't sit there puzzling.)
12. Use modified printing style. (Clear letters, not scribbles.)
13. Use lecturer's words. (Lecturers like to see their words in exams.)
14. Strive to detect main headings. (As if you peeked at the lecturer's notes.)
15. Capture ideas as well as facts. (Get the drift too.)
16. Keep your note organization simple. (Easy does it.)
17. Skip lines; leave space between main ideas. (Package the ideas.)
18. Discover the organizational pattern. (Like putting together a puzzle.)
19. If the lecture is too fast, capture fragments. (Jigsaw them together later.)
20. Leave blank spaces for words to fill in later. (Thus avoid voids.)
21. Develop your own abbreviations and symbols. (But not too many.)
22. Record lecturer's examples. (If you don't, you'll forget.)
23. Identify your own thoughts in your notes. (What's mine? What's the lecturer's?)
24. Keep separate loose-leaf binders for each course. (Don't combine notes.)

*Don'ts*

1. Don't sit near friends. (Can be distracting.)
2. Don't wait for something "important." (Record almost everything.)
3. Don't convert lecturer's words. (Takes time and invites imprecision.)
4. Don't look for facts only. (See ideas too.)
5. Don't give up if the lecturer is too fast. (Some is better than none.)
6. Don't stop to ponder. (Do so later in your room.)
7. Don't overindent. (You'll run out of right-side space.)
8. Don't doodle. (Breaks concentration and eye contact.)
9. Don't use spiral-bound notebooks. (Can't insert handouts.)
10. Don't consider any example too obvious. (Copy it!)
11. Avoid using Roman numerals. (You'll get tangled up.)
12. Avoid too many abbreviations. (Trouble deciphering later.)

## SUMMARY

**Why should I take notes?**

Forgetting wipes out information like a tornado. Taking notes provides disaster relief.

**How do I begin taking notes?**

A good way to start is with telegraphic sentences. The secret is to record only the key words.

**What's the best way to take notes—with printing or with cursive?**

Neither. Use the modified printing style. It's fast and neat, and it saves you time that you might otherwise spend recopying.

**Are there some time wasters in note taking?**

Yes. There are at least three that you should avoid: (1) Never tape a lecture. (2) Don't use shorthand. (3) Don't recopy or keyboard your notes.

**How can I use the speaker's signals to my advantage?**

Expressions such as "in contrast to" or "to sum up" act as signals and help you identify the pattern of organization the speaker is following. If you can follow the speaker's organizational pattern, you'll have little trouble fitting in the facts and ideas along the way.

**What do you mean by instant replay?**

As soon as you've left the classroom, take a moment to relive the lecture mentally from start to finish. Reflect on what the instructor has said and what it all means.

**What is the Cornell note-taking system?**

The keystone of the Cornell System is its format, a six-inch area for your lecture notes and a two-and-one-half-inch left-hand margin for cue questions.

**How do I use cue questions?**

Simply think up a question that can be answered with the information from a full fact or idea in the textbook.

**What is reflection?**

Reflection means thinking about and applying the concepts and ideas you learn.

**When should I review my notes?**

Right away if possible.

**How often should I review?**

As often as possible. If you make an effort to do a quick review of your notes every evening before you begin studying, you'll do a good job of maintaining your hard-earned knowledge.

**Are abbreviations and symbols a help in note taking?**

Used sparingly, abbreviations and symbols can be a help. If you use too many, your notes might be difficult to read easily.

## HAVE YOU MISSED SOMETHING?

*Sentence completion.*   Complete the following sentences with one of the three words listed below each sentence.

   **1.** Much of the information that a person receives is no longer available after a few _____ .
   minutes       hours       weeks

   **2.** The Leon-Clyde anecdote illustrates the problem of _____ .
   note taking       forgetting       recapitulation

*Matching.*   In each blank space in the left column, write the letter preceding the phrase in the right column that matches the left item best.

_____ **1.** Two-page system       a. Can reveal where the lecture is heading

_____ **2.** Forgetting       b. Used for cue questions

_____ **3.** Cornell System       c. Is both instant and massive

_____ **4.** 2½-inch column       d. Ideal format for coping with speedy lecturers

_____ **5.** 6-inch column       e. Is not recommended as a method of note taking

_____ **6.** Shorthand       f. Time-tested method for taking notes

_____ **7.** Signal words       g. Used for classroom lecture notes

*True-false.*   Write *T* beside the *true* statements and *F* beside the *false* statements.

_____ **1.** Notes written in the modified printing style must be keyboarded.

_____ **2.** The goal of note taking is to capture the lecturer's facts and ideas on paper.

_____ **3.** Taping the lecture is an efficient way to get all the information you need.

_____ **4.** Almost no learning takes place during the act of keyboarding.

_____ **5.** A well-written stack of notes can function as a second textbook.

_____ **6.** The last five or ten minutes of a lecture often contain the greatest concentration of information.

*Multiple choice.* Choose the phrase that completes the following sentence most accurately, and circle the letter that precedes it.

1. Telegraphic sentences provide you with

   a. verbatim notes.
   b. a secretary-style transcription.
   c. streamlined information.
   d. typed documentation.

2. The process of reflection helps you to

   a. tie facts and ideas together.
   b. bind new facts and ideas with ones you already possess.
   c. speculate beyond the facts and ideas.
   d. benefit from all the above.

3. Arriving early for class enables you to

   a. sit near friends.
   b. relax a bit before the lecture.
   c. review previous notes.
   d. have ready your notebook and pencils.

*Short answer.* Supply a brief answer for each of the following items.

1. Why take lecture notes? Discuss briefly.
2. What is the key feature of the Cornell note-taking system? Explain briefly.
3. In the cue column, why use questions instead of cue words?
4. Why a summary area at the bottom of each note sheet? Explain.
5. What is the main advantage of the modified printing style? Explain.

## VOCABULARY BUILDING

DIRECTIONS: Make a light check mark (√) alongside one of the three words (choices) that most nearly expresses the meaning of the italicized word in the phrases that are in the left-hand column. (Answers are given on p. 436.)

|   |   | 1 | 2 | 3 |
|---|---|---|---|---|
| 1. | memory's *fragility* | flexibility | weakness | tenaciousness |
| 2. | as you can *surmise* | guess | record | remember |
| 3. | from the *anecdote* | medicine | story | prescription |

|  |  | **1** | **2** | **3** |
|---|---|---|---|---|
| 4. | to *circumvent* these problems | confront | reject | bypass |
| 5. | a *compartmentalized* view | categorized | continuous | integrated |
| 6. | *ominous* political situation | encouraging | unfavorable | propitious |
| 7. | are direct *antecedents* | forerunners | consequences | results |
| 8. | *robustly* conducted | delicately | energetically | belatedly |
| 9. | an ideal *complement* | commendation | companion | denunciation |
| 10. | a *prodigious* executive | negligible | unimpressive | extraordinary |
| 11. | quiet and *profound* | imprudent | thoughtful | proud |
| 12. | Russia's *pernicious* rebellions | constant | destructive | meaningless |
| 13. | a *vibrant* person | waivering | energetic | listless |
| 14. | a *connoisseur* and collector | authority | amateur | playboy |
| 15. | a *poignant* willingness | pointed | touching | superficial |
| 16. | in this *compendium* | encyclopedia | collection | summary |
| 17. | a most *insidious* process | obvious | deceitful | candid |
| 18. | *myriad* nightmares | vivid | countless | jumbled |
| 19. | deliberately *obfuscating* report | confusing | clarifying | simplifying |
| 20. | *bolstering* research capacity | diminishing | increasing | bungling |
| 21. | *enhancing* disease surveillance | raising | minimizing | eradicating |
| 22. | a *caveat* to investors | guide | gift | warning |
| 23. | *consummate* political animal | deficient | total | crude |
| 24. | *bromide* of conventional wisdom | compound | cliché | essence |
| 25. | before I become *redundant* | trite | repetitious | terse |

# 11

# Learning from Your Textbooks

*There is a great difference between knowing a thing and understanding it.*

—CHARLES KETTERING (1876–1958), American electrical engineer and inventor

Are you going hungry? Some students devour their textbook assignments yet never learn a thing. That's because learning from a textbook involves more than just reading. It means digesting what you read. A textbook assignment needs to be read actively in order to provide food for thought. This chapter discusses

- Getting acquainted with your textbooks
- Adopting an active approach to learning
- Using the SQ3R System
- Using the Questions-in-the-Margin System

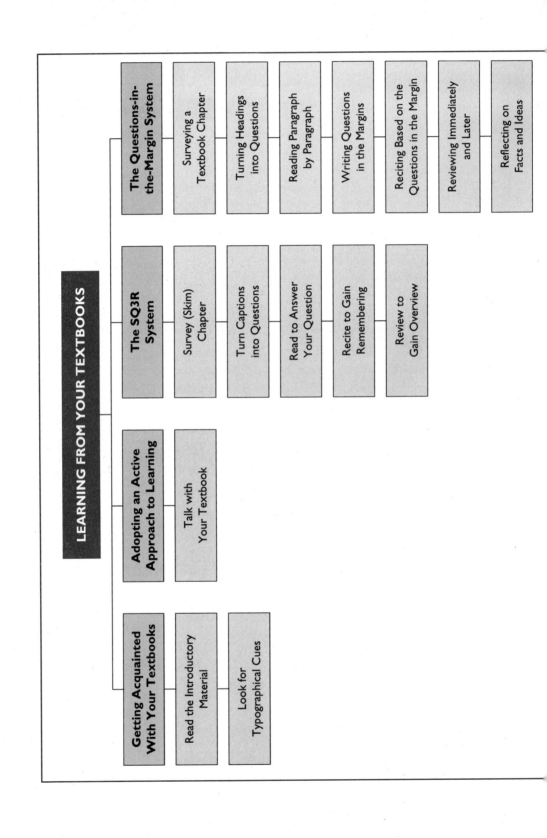

# LEARNING FROM YOUR TEXTBOOKS

**Getting Acquainted With Your Textbooks**

Read the Introductory Material

Look for Typographical Cues

**Adopting an Active Approach to Learning**

Talk with Your Textbook

**The SQ3R System**

Survey (Skim) Chapter

Turn Captions into Questions

Read to Answer Your Question

Recite to Gain Remembering

Review to Gain Overview

**The Questions-in-the-Margin System**

Surveying a Textbook Chapter

Turning Headings into Questions

Reading Paragraph by Paragraph

Writing Questions in the Margins

Reciting Based on the Questions in the Margin

Reviewing Immediately and Later

Reflecting on Facts and Ideas

**B**ecause you and your textbooks are going to spend a quarter or a semester together, you'd better become friends. How? By getting acquainted.

## GETTING ACQUAINTED WITH YOUR TEXTBOOKS

Buy all your textbooks immediately after you register. This is a wise policy even if your school allows a period in which you can attend many courses before deciding on a final few. Get a head start by reading the tables of contents, prefaces, introductions, and any other up-front material in all your books. Underline important words and sentences, and make notes in the margins. Then, while you still have the time, leaf through each of your books. Look at the pictures, tables, and diagrams; read the captions. Read chapter titles and headings and subheadings that interest you. This will give you a good idea of what the book is like and where you will be going during the semester. Later, you'll be glad you did, for you'll be able to see how the various parts of the course fit together.

### Read the Prefatory Material

Most textbooks are written in a serious, scholarly tone. In the introductory material—which may be called "Preface," "To the Student," "Introduction," or something similar—the authors often take a more personal approach to their subjects and to their readers than they do in the body of the text. In the introductory material you have a chance to meet the authors as people and to get comfortable with them. Once you do, you'll find that you can converse and even argue with them as you read the text. Now and then, you'll find yourself saying, "No, I don't agree with that statement," or "What do you mean by that?"

In the introductory material you can also find valuable information about the concepts and content of the book. For instance, one student struck pay dirt on page 54 of a ninety-page preface to *A Treatise of Human Nature* by David Hume (1711–1776), a Scottish philosopher. Hume wrote in his preface, "If I find the root of human nature, I'll be able to explain all human actions." The student accurately interpreted this sentence to mean that Hume would be using a psychological and not a traditional philosophical approach. Thus, with this proper mental set established, the student was able to read Hume's *Treatise* fairly rapidly and with clear understanding. Students who had not read the author's long preface read the book with a mental set directed at ascertaining Hume's philosophy. Most of those students never understood what David Hume was trying to explain.

In prefaces you can find valuable information such as (1) what the author's objective is, (2) what the author's objective is not, (3) the organizational plan of the book, (4) how and why the book is different from other books about the same subject, and (5) the author's qualifications for writing the book. As a practical exercise, you might find it interesting to read the preface of this book, if you have not already done so. See how much you can gain toward understanding not only the book but also the author.

**The Author's Objective**   Learning the author's objective—the purpose or goal he or she meant to achieve—enables you to read and interpret the text appropriately. For instance, the authors of *American Government* state their objectives this way:

> In preparing the fourth edition, we have thoroughly reviewed and updated all chapters, in terms of both research and current events. As a result, in this edition, we have given additional emphasis to the 1992 and 1994 elections, media and public opinion, the Supreme Court, and domestic and international policy. We have also carefully scrutinized every chapter, refining, clarifying, and tightening the text.[1]

These few sentences tell you straight off what you can expect and what particular approach the authors will be taking.

**The Organizational Plan of the Book**   Having the book's organizational plan is like having a road map. You know not only what the authors are doing but also where they are going. In the following example, you're told the title and focus of each of the book's three parts and are given examples of some of the topics that will be covered in each part:

> The text is built on a three-part framework. Part One, "Foundations of Communication," introduces basic theoretical concepts, including an overview of the communication process as well as verbal and nonverbal transactions, critical thinking, ethics, and listening.
>
> Part Two, "Personal Communication," covers intrapersonal and interpersonal communication. Personal relationships, communication apprehension, the interview, and small-group functions—among other topics—are discussed.
>
> Part Three, "Public Communication," focuses on planning, developing, structuring, and presenting successful informative, and persuasive briefings and speeches.[2]

---

[1]Alan R Gitelson, Robert L. Dudley, and Melvin J. Dubnick, *American Government*, 4th ed. (Boston: Houghton Mifflin, 1996), p. xiv.

[2]Roy M. Berko, Andrew D. Wolvin, and Darlyn R. Wolvin, *Communicating: A Social and Career Focus*, 5th ed. (Boston: Houghton Mifflin, 1992), pp. xv–xvi.

**How and Why the Book Is Different**   Recognizing what makes the textbook unique enables you to read with greater awareness and comprehension and to avoid the trap of thinking this book is just "more of the same old stuff." Notice how the specificity of the following example lets you know right away where to direct your attention: "What makes *All of Us* stand apart from other reading texts is its devotion to a curriculum of inclusion. . . . We tried to compile the richest and most ethnically diverse reading matter available."[3]

**The Author's Qualifications**   Writers usually try in some subtle way to let the reader know that their book is written by an expert on the subject and that therefore the information is trustworthy and credible. Note in the following example how the writers describe their relationship with the subject matter in a way that inspires confidence and belief in the value of their opinions:

> Economically and politically, the world has changed with the initiative of the European Community to reach economic integration (1992 initiative) and the liberalization of Eastern Europe, culminating with the dramatic events in the Soviet Union in August 1991. As authors, we have benefited enormously from being close to these changes, both through our contacts as well as our extended trips and teaching assignments in Europe. In addition, we have worked extensively with companies who are about to embark on new types of global strategies.[4]

**Supplementary Learning Aids**   Most textbook authors provide learning aids to help you understand the material. The introductory material generally names these aids and tells how they'll benefit you. In addition to these in-text features, supplementary materials such as workbooks, study guides, computer programs, and videos are often available. Reading the introductory material will alert you to the presence of these features and ancillary materials, as you can see from the following example:

> To help students understand the various topics, we include several peda-gogical features in each chapter. Each chapter opens with a highlighted myth-and-reality question, and ends with a list of definitions of key terms and concepts that have been used in that chapter. We have increased the number of key terms and concepts set off in boldface in the text in this edition. Preview outlines open each chapter and point-by-point summaries appear at the end of each chapter. The conclusion of each chapter provides a retrospective glance at the myths in light of the whole chapter discussion.

---

[3]Harvey S. Wiener and Charles Bazerman, *All of Us: A Multicultural Reading Skills Handbook,* 2nd ed. (Boston: Houghton Mifflin, 1995), p. xix.
[4]Jean Pierre Jeannet and Hubert D. Hennessey, *Global Marketing Strategies,* 2nd ed. (Boston: Houghton Mifflin, 1992), p. xix.

An updated chapter-by-chapter listing of suggested readings on topics covered throughout the text appears at the end of the book. And an appendix contains important documents, such as the Declaration of Independence, the Articles of Confederation, the Constitution, Federalist Papers Nos. 10 and 51, and a list of presidents.[5]

## Read the Introduction

The introduction is usually well written, because the writer knows that it is the book's show window—especially for prospective customers looking the book over to decide whether to buy it.

Figure 11.1 is a densely packed introduction containing information of great and immediate value for the sharper reading of textbooks. It is from a book titled *Six-Way Paragraphs.*[6] The book's sole purpose is to teach students how to spot main ideas. One hundred paragraphs are provided for practice. To prepare students for such practice, the introduction strives to explain the ins and outs of the paragraphs found in textbooks. As you read it, be aware not only of *what* the writer says but also of *how* he says it and his *purpose* for saying it.

**Preview from Front to Back**   After you've read the introductory material, survey the rest of the book. Begin by scanning the table of contents, which lists the parts, the chapters, and sometimes the major headings within each chapter. The contents shows the overall organization of the book and how the chapter topics relate to one another. It also shows whether the book contains extra material, such as appendixes, glossaries, bibliographies or references, and indexes.

Now turn to the back of the book and look at these extra sections. Appendixes contain additional information such as tables and graphs, documents, or details about a specific aspect of a subject. Glossaries are specialized dictionaries of terms common to the subject the book discusses. Bibliographies and references list the sources the authors consulted in writing the book and can point you in the direction of further readings. Indexes—alphabetical listings of significant topics, ideas, and names that appear in the text along with page references—give you a sense of the scope of the book and help you locate specific material quickly.

By familiarizing yourself with your textbook, you not only bolster your background knowledge about the subject; you also become aware of the features of the book you can use throughout the term. As a result, future

---

[5]Gitelson, Dudley, and Dubnick, *American Government,* p. xiv.
[6]Walter Pauk, *Six-Way Paragraphs* (Providence, R.I.: Jamestown Publishers, 1974).

| | | The paragraph! That's the working-unit of both writer and reader. The writer works hard to put meaning into the paragraph; the reader works hard to take meaning out of it. Though they work at opposite tasks, the work of each is closely related. Actually, to understand better the job of the reader, one must first understand better the job of the writer. So, let us look briefly at the writer's job. |

what:     *wants you to focus on the paragraph – unit*

how:      *brings you and the writer together*

purpose: *wants you to look at the paragraph through the eyes of the writer*

To make his meaning clear, a writer knows that he must follow certain basic principles. First, he knows that he must develop only one main idea per paragraph. This principle is so important that he knows it backward, too. He knows that he must not try to develop two main ideas in the same, single paragraph.

what:     *each paragraph has but one main idea*

how:      *shows you how a writer thinks*

purpose: *to convince you to look for only one idea per paragraph because writers follow this rule*

The next important principle he knows is that the topic of each main idea must be stated in a topic sentence and that such a sentence best serves its function by coming at or near the beginning of its paragraph. He knows, too, that the more clearly he can state the topic of his paragraph in an opening sentence, the more effective he will be in developing a meaningful, well-organized paragraph.

what:     *the topic of the main idea is in the topic sentence, which is usually the first one*

how:      *the writer needs to state a topic sentence to keep his own writing clear and under control*

purpose: *to instill confidence in you that the topic sentence is an important tool in a writer's kit and convince you it is there, so, look for it!*

Now, there is more to a writer's job than just writing paragraphs consisting of only bare topic sentences and main ideas. The balance of his job deals with *developing* each main idea through the use of supporting material that amplifies and clarifies the main idea and many times makes it more vivid and memorable.

what:     *developing main ideas through supporting material*

how:      *"more to a writer's job," still keeps you in the writer's shoes*

purpose: *to announce and advance the new step of supporting materials*

**FIGURE 11.1 The Content of an Introduction**

*Source: Walter Pauk, Six-Way Paragraphs (Providence, R.I.: Jamestown Publishers, 1974), pp. 7–8. Reprinted by permission of Jamestown Publishers.*

what:      (a) main ideas are often supported by examples, (b) other supporting devices listed

how:       still through the writer's eyes

purpose:   to develop the new idea of supporting materals

To support his main ideas, a writer may use a variety of forms. One of the most common forms to support a main idea is the *example*. Examples help to illustrate the main idea more vividly. Other supporting materials are anecdotes, incidents, jokes, allusions, comparisons, contrasts, analogies, definitions, exceptions, logic, and so forth.

what:      paragraph contains (a) topic sentence, (b) main idea, and (c) supporting material

how:       transfer the knowledge from the writer to you, the reader

purpose:   to summarize all the three steps

To summarize, the reader should have learned from the writer that a text-book-type paragraph usually contains these three elements: a topic sentence, a main idea, and supporting material. Knowing this, the reader should use the topic sentence to lead him to the main idea. Once he grasps the main idea, then everything else is supporting material used to illustrate, amplify, and qualify the main idea. So, in the final analysis, the reader must be able to separate the main idea from the supporting material yet see the relationship between them.

**FIGURE 11.1   The Content of an Introduction-***continued*

assignments will be easier and less time consuming, and you'll have a greater chance to master the material.

## Preview Specific Assignments

Previewing specific assignments allows you to overcome inertia, delve into the text, and get a sense of the larger picture into which you can fit specific ideas and fact. When previewing, you can use any or all of these techniques:

**Think About the Title** Take a few moments to reflect on the chapter's title. Is its meaning obvious? If not, can you guess what the chapter will discuss?

**Read the Introduction and the Summary** Although they may not be marked as such, textbook chapters frequently include an introductory paragraph, a brief summary at the end, or both. Reading these paragraphs provides advance organizers, which create a framework on which you can build the information in the chapter.

**Look over Headings and Subheadings** Flip through the pages and read the headings. Notice their hierarchy and sequence as you do.

**Take Note of Any Information Set Apart from the Rest of the Text** In general, information that is *boxed, boldfaced, bulleted* (preceded with dots or squares), *screened* (printed on a gray or colored background), or otherwise set apart is information that you won't want to miss. Take a moment to look it over now so you will already be familiar with it when you go back to read the chapter completely.

**Glance at the Visuals** Pictures and graphic materials can provide a distillation of an entire chapter's ideas in less than a page. The concept maps on the second page of each chapter in this book, for example, show the chapter at a glance. Other visuals supply vivid and easy-to-understand examples of key points.

You may want to limit the amount of time you spend surveying your book. Your primary purpose is to read and understand the chapter. If you spend too much time preparing to read, you'll run out of time and energy for the actual reading. Or as an old Chinese proverb warns, "Keep sharpening your knife and it will grow dull."

## Look for Typographical Cues

Open any textbook and you'll quickly discover that the words aren't all printed in the same size or the same style. The format may differ from text to text, but in general each book takes advantage of a variety of type sizes and styles to convey its information. By noting these typographical differences, you can pick up on signals for organization and emphasis.

**Boldface** (thick, dark type) often signals a textbook heading or subheading. It may also be used to draw your attention to a specific principle, definition, or key word within the text.

*Italics* (type that slopes to the right) places emphasis on a word or a phrase.

Underlining often performs the same functions as either boldface or italics, depending on the format of the particular textbook.

• Bullets (small markers, often circular or square) set off the items in lists.

Size, color and placement of type often call attention to headings or subheadings. Take note of words printed in larger type, in color, or on lines by themselves.

You can usually crack a book's particular typographical code simply by skimming through your text before you start reading. In addition, look for an explanation of format—especially if it is unconventional—in the book's introductory material.

## ADOPTING AN ACTIVE APPROACH TO LEARNING

Building a foundation for your learning is only the first step to knowledge. The way to make learning *last* is by acting as a full partner in the process. That means talking with your textbook, instead of just receiving its information.

### Talk With Your Textbook

Taking an active approach to reading may mean making a fundamental change in your attitude toward textbooks. Instead of approaching a textbook as a passive recipient of its information, you engage in a dialogue between your thoughts and those on the page. You do this by listening to what you read, formulating questions as you read, and following other tips for active reading.

**Listen to What You Read**  The best reading occurs when you use intonation, which is the natural rise and fall of your speaking voice. This doesn't mean reading out loud, but it does mean reading with expression. Intonation helps you combine individual words into meaningful mental "bites."

To engage in intonation, as your eyes move rapidly across the page as usual, let your mind swing along each line with an intonational rhythm that can be heard by your "inner ear." Read the line expressively. In doing so, you will be supplying the important rhythm, stress, emphasis, and pauses

> Athens and Sparta / were both Greek cities / and their people / spoke a common language. / In every other respect / they were different. / Athens rose high from the plain. / It was a city / exposed to the fresh breezes / from the sea, / willing to look / at the world / with the eyes / of a happy child. / Sparta, / on the other hand, / was built / at the bottom / of a deep valley, / and used the surrounding mountains / as a barrier / against foreign thought. / Athens / was a city of busy trade. / Sparta / was an armed camp. /

**FIGURE 11.2   Using Intonation to Hear What You Read**

*Source: Reprinted from* The Story of Mankind *by Henry B. van Loon and Gerard W. van Loon, by permission of Liveright Publishing Corporation. Copyright © 1972 by Henry B. van Loon and Gerard W. van Loon.*

that were taken out when the words were turned into written form. This will put the meaning of the words more quickly within your grasp.

To illustrate intonational reading, the passage in Figure 11.2 has been divided into "thought units." These units are separated by slash marks. (Of course, different readers would group these words into different clusters, depending on individual intonational styles.) You will probably notice how rapidly your eyes move and how easily you comprehend the meaning when you read with intonation.

To make silent intonation a regular habit, take a few minutes to read aloud in the privacy of your room. This will establish your own speech patterns in your mind so you will "hear" them more readily when you read silently.

**Formulate Questions as You Read**   Reading with intonation enables you to hear the textbook's authors as you read. You can hold up your end of the conversation by constantly formulating questions as you read, by wondering out loud about issues or aspects that concern you, and by writing out questions that help you pinpoint and remember the most important information. The latter really serves as the foundation for taking notes and mastering them.

**Follow Other Tips for Active Reading**   Engaging your book in steady conversation is the best way to encourage active reading. But there are some other ways to ensure that you stay on your toes as you move through a textbook assignment.

***Relax.***   Stress can hinder both learning and remembering, the two most important aspects of reading.[7] Before you begin reading, take a moment to

---

[7]Kenneth L. Higbee, *Your Memory: How It Works and How to Improve It,* 2nd ed. (New York: Prentice-Hall, 1988), pp. 64–65.

use one of the relaxation techniques recommended in Chapter 3. Optimal learning occurs when you are in a relaxed state. Keep in mind that being relaxed is not the same as being sluggish. A sense of relaxation makes you more, not less, alert and relieves the stress and anxiety that can make learning a chore.

***Vary your speed as you read.***    Match the speed of your reading to what you are reading. If the chapter starts out with some introductory material, move through that section quickly. When you come to the first substantial paragraph, slow down and start looking for important names, terms, and ideas. These will often serve as keys to the rest of the chapter. Once you're clear on what the chapter is going to cover and how, you can pick up the pace of your reading. But be ready to slow down when you come across a paragraph that's filled with new ideas. There is no reason to expect that you will read at a constant rate.

***Focus on the ideas, not the words.***    Memory research has shown that we remember the gist of what we've read, not the actual words. So if you get bogged down in a difficult sentence, read it through once while skipping any modifying phrases. Find the simple subject of the sentence, the verb, and the simple object to avoid getting lost in a maze of language. (Extend this process to an entire paragraph if necessary.) When the framework of this sentence shows through clearly, so that you can grasp the main idea, then go back and read the material with all its "trimmings" to get the full sense of what's being communicated.

## FINDING A TEXTBOOK READING SYSTEM

How do you cope with your textbook assignments? Are they harder to face every day? Does each day's assigned chapter become more difficult to study than the previous one? If you stop to think about the situation, it would seem that with all the practice you get, you'd become better and better at studying your textbook. If this is not the case, you probably need a system or a process that can be used over and over again, in chapter after chapter, and in book after book.

On the other hand, if you have a system, and you are still having a lot of trouble, maybe your grip is all wrong. You know that the first time you pick up a tennis racket you are likely to hold it incorrectly. When this happens, your natural grip causes unnecessary strain and weakens your stroke. Even with practice, you don't improve. So it is with a study system. A wrong one causes strain and weakens your efforts.

Most textbook reading systems are too long, too complicated, and take too much time. Furthermore, a system that is just right for your roommate may not be just right for you. You can tell when a system is the right one for you, because then your work goes along surely and easily and you get better at it day by day.

In this chapter, I'm going to present a novel approach for mastering a textbook. It has worked extremely well with the new generation of Cornell freshmen. But before I present this new system, let us start off with the venerable SQ3R System.

## THE SQ3R SYSTEM

The SQ3R System (see Figure 11.3) was devised during World War II by Francis P. Robinson, an Ohio State University psychologist. The system was designed to help military personnel enrolled in special programs at the university read faster and study better.

Robinson's imaginative, acronymic formula, SQ3R, compresses into one "word" five steps for mastering a textbook. The first step is "S," which stands for *Survey*; that is, Robinson urges students to leaf through an assigned chapter reading headings and subheadings, skimming topic sentences, and reading summary and concluding paragraphs. This initial overviewing provides students with *advance organizers*,[8] which help to make subsequent reading and learning easier.

The second step is "Q," which stands for *Question*, that is, turning headings and subheadings into questions by preceding them with *who, what, when, where,* or *how*. These types of questions help to focus a reader's concentration.

The third step is "$R_1$," which stands for *Read*. After a question is framed, students read the ensuing paragraph or section to answer the specific question.

The fourth step is "$R_2$," which stands for *Recite*. Immediately after reading, students should look away from the page and recite what they have just read in their own words.

The fifth step is "$R_3$," which stands for *Review*. After finishing the chapter, students are instructed to go back to the beginning of the chapter, glance at

---

[8]John F. Wakefield, *Educational Psychology* (Boston: Houghton Mifflin, 1996), p. 398.

*THE SQ3R SYSTEM*

| | | |
|---|---|---|
| S | *SURVEY* | *Glance through all the headings in the chapter, and read the final summary paragraph (if the chapter has one). This survey should not take more than a minute, and it will show you the three to six core ideas on which the discussion will be based. This orientation will help you organize the ideas as you read them later.* |
| Q | *QUESTION* | *Now begin to work. Turn the first heading into a question. This will arouse your curiosity and thereby increase comprehension. It will bring to mind information you already know, thus helping you understand that section more quickly. The question also will make important points stand out from explanatory details. You can turn a heading into a question as you read the heading, but it demands conscious effort on your part.* |
| $R_1$ | *READ* | *Read the paragraph or section to answer the question. Read actively.* |
| $R_2$ | *RECITE* | *After you finish reading the paragraph or section, stop, look away from the book, and try to recite the answer to your formed question. If you cannot recite the answer correctly or fully, reread the section and try again.* |
| $R_3$ | *REVIEW* | *When you have finished reading and reciting page after page, go back to the beginning of the chapter, glance at the headings and subheadings, and think briefly about the answers that you have already recited. Work your way in this manner to the end of the chapter. Now you should have ended with an integrated bird's-eye view of the entire chapter.* |

**FIGURE 11.3  The SQ3R System**
*Source: Adaptation of "Steps in the SQ3R Method" (pp. 32-33) from* Effective Study, *4th Edition, by Francis P. Robinson. Copyright 1941, 1946 by Harper & Row, Publishers, Inc. Copyright © 1961, 1970 by Francis P. Robinson. Reprinted by permission of the publisher.*

each heading and mentally note the contents, ending up with a bird's-eye view of the chapter.

SQ3R is a popular system. Although widely accepted, even SQ3R has its drawbacks. For example, it applies only to textbook assignments, it offers no guidelines for mastering lectures, and it does not use the reflection step. Despite these shortcomings, SQ3R was a valuable breakthrough in learning techniques. It demonstrated clearly that the process of mastering information could be expressed in a concrete step-by-step system.

## THE QUESTIONS-IN-THE-MARGIN SYSTEM

Though the Questions-in-the-Margin System, for purposes of instruction, is explained in seven steps, the system actually revolves around just one principal step, that is, the formulating of a question for the main idea in each paragraph. Once the question has been formulated, the rest of the steps fall in place naturally.

Employing questions provides the most effective means of activating information in a textbook chapter and bringing it to life. Without questions, even the most exciting textbook material runs the risk of remaining inert. Asking questions turns students into active readers.

The Questions-in-the-Margin System draws its questions directly from textbook paragraphs instead of from chapter headings. A textbook paragraph, after all, adheres to at least one standard. Every one contains a main idea. And if you look at it another way, every paragraph provides the answer to an unasked question. Find that question and you will have found a way of getting to the heart of the paragraph. This is the simple principle behind the Questions-in-the-Margin System.

To see how well the system enhances the comprehension, learning, and remembering processes, read the seven steps in Figure 11.4. When you finish the seventh step, you will feel as though you have put the last piece of a jigsaw puzzle in place: you will see the full picture, which will image itself indelibly in your memory.

### Step 1: Surveying a Textbook Chapter

Surveying has various uses, but its greatest use is in mastering textbook assignments. It is the grease that makes subsequent reading and studying more efficient. A good scholar would no more begin reading a chapter without first skimming it than an automotive engineer would run a car

| | |
|---|---|
| **SURVEY** | Read the title and speculate about what the chapter will be about. Read the headings to determine what ideas and facts will be presented. Read any summarizing section. |
| **QUESTION** | Turn each heading into a question by adding such words as "what," "how," or "who." Then read to answer the question. |
| **READ** | Read several paragraphs; then come back to the first paragraph and ask questions such as these: What is the main idea? How do the supporting materials support it? What do I need to know in this paragraph? |
| **QUESTIONS IN MARGINS** | Think deeply; then formulate and write a brief, telegraphic question in the margin. Next, underline very sparingly only the key words and phrases that make up the answer. The less underlining, the better. |
| **RECITE** | Counteract forgetting by reciting. Cover your textbook page, exposing only your questions in the margin. Then, in you own words, recite aloud the answers. After reciting, check for accuracy. Recite until you've completed the chapter. |
| **REVIEW** | Immediately after reciting, take a fresh look at each question; mentally glimpse and hold the answer for a few moments. In this way, work through the entire chapter. This overview of questions and answers will tend to snap the separate parts together like pieces of a jigsaw puzzle, enabling you to see the chapter as a whole. Intersperse reviews throughout the semester. |
| **REFLECT** | Manipulate the ideas and facts mentally. Turn them over, speculate on them, compare one with the other, notice where they agree and differ. Organize them under larger categories, or compress them into smaller units. Finally, free them from the chapter by weaving them into your existing knowledge. |

**FIGURE 11.4  The Questions-in-the-Margin System**

without first greasing it. The grease does not supply the power, but without it the gasoline would not be of much use.

If you skip this step, you will lose time, not save time. If you burrow directly into one paragraph after another, you'll be unearthing one compartmentalized fact after another, but you won't see how the facts relate to each other. Psychologists call this not-seeing-the-big-picture condition *tunnel vision.*

Here is how a student who had developed the technique of surveying to a fine art described this step:

I first spend two or three minutes trying to get the full meaning out of the title of the chapter. I even wonder briefly why the author picked such a title. Then I shove off by saying to myself, "Let's see what he has to say about this subject."

Next, I read the first couple of paragraphs in the regular way. If I don't do this, it's like coming into the middle of a conversation: I can't make head or tail of it.

Then I let the printer guide me. My eyes dart to the big-type headings and subheadings. I read them because I know that they are like the small headlines for newspaper items. They are little summaries. I then read a sentence or two underneath these headings. My eyes float over the rest of the material looking for other islands of information. They might be marked by clues such as italicized words, underlined words, and changes in the type.

When I first started to skim, I used to skip all the illustrations, charts, and diagrams. But after getting burned on exams, I found I could learn a lot very easily just by reading the captions and noticing what the lines on the diagrams and graphs meant. At least for me, illustrations stick in my mind better than words do; so during an exam, I take advantage of this. I close my eyes and see the illustration on the blackboard of my mind.

I'm always careful to read the last paragraph or last section marked "summary." That's where the author gathers together all the main ideas of the chapter.

Finally, I pause for a few minutes to bring all these pieces and fragments together before I begin reading and taking notes on the chapter. Sometimes to bring things together, I go back to the beginning of the chapter and leaf through the pages without reading, just looking at what I have already looked at.

There are a few other things that skimming does for me. First, I no longer put off studying. Skimming is easy, so I don't mind getting started. Second, once I get into the chapter, I find that most of the chapters contain some interesting information, so I become interested. Third, because I am interested in the material, I concentrate better. And fourth, the topics that I find by skimming somehow make good topic headings for my notes.

When you skim, don't dawdle. Move along with good comprehension, but go slowly enough to get the facts, ideas, and principles accurately. Once assimilated, a mistake is hard to eradicate.

There are four practical reasons why surveying can make a real and immediate difference in your reading.

**1.** *Surveying creates a background.* When you don't have some prior knowledge about the subject matter of an assigned chapter, you read slowly and have difficulty understanding the material. When you come to something that you recognize, your reading speed quickens and your comprehension grows. The difference is your prior knowledge. Surveying prepares you for reading by giving you some background information about a chapter.

Surveying counteracts tunnel vision. Once you have viewed the broad canvas, you will see how individual ideas fit into the complete picture.

When you skim a chapter, you spot and pick up topics by reading headings and subheadings. You pick up ideas by reading the first and last sentences of paragraphs. You become familiar with the names of people and places by skimming these names. You grasp the general objective of the chapter by reading the introductory paragraph, and you get an overview by reading the summarizing paragraph at the end of the chapter. You won't know any of these facts and ideas cold, of course. But when you meet them again during your careful reading, you will recognize them, and this familiarity will give you confidence and understanding.

**2.** *Surveying provides advance organizers.*     According to David P. Ausubel,[9] a learning-theory psychologist, a preview of the general content of a chapter creates *advance organizers,* which help students learn and remember material they later study closely. The familiar landmarks act as topics or categories under which ideas, facts, and details may be clustered. John Livingston Lowes, a professor of literature at Princeton University, characterized such familiar landmarks as *magnetic centers* around which ideas, facts, and details cluster like iron filings around a magnet.

George Katona, a psychologist, tested the effectiveness of advance organizers with two groups of students. One group was asked to read a selection in which a general principle of economics was stated in the first sentence. The second group was given the same selection, but with the first sentence deleted. When the students in the first group were tested, they not only remembered the specific content of the paragraph better than the second group, but they were able to apply the general principle to all the examples in the selection. Without the first sentence, which was an advance organizer, students in the second group viewed the examples as separate, unrelated entities and were unable to see that the examples could be clustered under the one umbrella of a common principle in economics.

**3.** *Surveying limbers the mind.*     For an athlete, a pregame warm-up limbers muscles, and it also limbers the psyche and brain. An athlete knows that success comes from the coordination of smoothly gliding muscles, a positive attitude, and a concentrating mind. The prestudy survey of a textbook achieves for the scholar what the pregame warm-up achieves for the athlete.

**4.** *Surveying overcomes mental inertia.*     How often have you said with impatience and exasperation, "Let's get started!" Getting started is hard.

---

[9]Wakefield, *Educational Psychology*, p. 368.

According to Newton's first law of motion, "A body in motion tends to remain in motion; a body at rest tends to remain at rest."

Many students find it difficult to open a textbook and begin to study. If you are one of them, use surveying to ease yourself into studying. Surveying does the job: It gets you started.

You need not always survey an entire chapter as the first step. You may begin by surveying the first part before you read it. Later, as you work your way through the chapter, you may want to skim farther ahead, page by page, as you read and study to understand.

## Step 2: Turning Headings into Questions

The people who have *answers to give* when they are finished reading are usually those who had *questions to ask* before and during their reading. Asking questions works for one main reason: The questions force you to concentrate and to observe the words keenly, directly, and selectively as you read. When you don't have a question in mind, your eyes just glide over a paragraph, and you never realize that the printed words are alive with answers. In the words of writer John Lubbock (1834–1913), "What we see depends mainly on what we look for."

As you read, you should interrogate the writer, not simply stare at the words. You must approach each paragraph like an inquiring reporter, with definite and searching questions. The better your questions, the better will be your comprehension.

How do you formulate warm-up questions as you read and study a textbook? One technique is to turn each heading into a question. For example, the main heading "Basic Aspects of Memory" could be turned into the question "What are the basic aspects of memory?" The technique is simple, but it works. Here are some additional examples:

| *Subtopic Heading* | *Question Formulated* |
|---|---|
| The Memory Trace | What is a memory trace? |
| Rate of Forgetting | How fast do we forget? |
| Organization of Recall | How is recall organized? |
| Decay Theory | What is the decay theory? |

Once you have turned a heading into a question, you read the material under the heading to answer your question. If the question is answered early in the discussion, ask another, based on what you have read.

There are general questions that you can use in reading about almost any topic. Some readers prefer to ask these general questions to uncover specific facts and ideas. Other readers just enjoy conversing with the writer through the use of a general question-and-answer technique. In either case, an active, searching attitude is created. Here are some of the general questions:

- What does this paragraph tell me?
- What are the important supporting details?
- Does this example make the main point clear?
- What evidence does the writer give?
- What is the underlying principle?
- If this fact or idea is true, then what logically follows?
- If it is true, how does it affect my existing knowledge?
- How does this paragraph fit in with this chapter?
- What questions might I be asked about this paragraph?

Some practical readers ask not only "What is the author saying?" but also "How can I use this information?" If you ask such questions, make it a rule to try to answer them. Say something. Say anything that makes sense to you. Without effort, there's no gain.

A great deal is said these days about learning how to think: Books are written; lectures are given; and teachers exhort. The subject of thinking can be summarized in this one line: Thinking at its highest level is asking the right, relevant question.

## Step 3: Reading Paragraph by Paragraph

After surveying the chapter, return to the first paragraph and read it thoroughly enough to answer only one question: What did the author say in this paragraph? If you are unable to answer this question at first, you must reread the paragraph until you can; otherwise you will not gain a functional understanding of the paragraph.

This is a crucial step. You must not move ahead to succeeding paragraphs if doing so means leaving the present paragraph unsettled. You may push on beyond a problem paragraph for the purpose of gaining context, but always with the intention of coming back to the problem paragraph. Remember that understanding a succession of paragraphs leads to comprehension of the chapter.

Guard against the habit of moving your eyes over the lines of print without grasping the writer's ideas. Read for the ideas and concepts behind the words. Pause at the end of each paragraph or at the end of a series of paragraphs, and in your own words describe the writer's main idea and the supporting details. Answer the question "What did I learn in this paragraph?" When you have described, you have understood.

**The Topic Sentence**  Use the topic sentence to help you break into the meaning of each paragraph. The topic sentence often contains the main idea or points to the main idea.

In Figure 11.5, the first sentence, the topic sentence, states the main idea. The rest of the paragraph is a long list of concrete examples supporting the main idea. The last sentence is not a continuation of the list; it rounds out or completes the paragraph. Incidentally (but importantly), notice how the writer sustains the mood of despondency from the opening sentence, through the examples, into the last clause of the last sentence.

**Textbook Troubleshooting**  As you read and study your textbook, your businesslike side should keep asking, "Am I getting it?" If the answer is, "It's getting pretty vague," you should take immediate action.

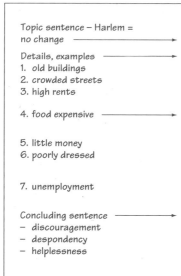

**FIGURE 11.5  The Topic Sentence**
*Source: James Baldwin,* Notes of a Native Son *(Boston: Beacon Press, 1990), p. 57.*

1. Go back a couple of paragraphs to pick up the thread of the writer's ideas again.
2. Read ahead a couple of paragraphs to see where you're going.
3. Open your dictionary and look up any words that you are not sure of and that might be holding you back.
4. Reread the troublesome paragraph aloud, using exaggerated expression and emphasis to get at the meaning of what's being said. Such reading aloud, especially with expression, brings concentration back to a 100 percent level.

**The Backdoor Technique**   While dean of the College of Engineering, Dale Corson once observed that engineers and other students in science and mathematics must often crack the meaning of an idea or concept one sentence at a time. If comprehension does not occur even at this snail's pace, then you must ask your instructor for help. "But before you do," says Dr. Corson, "ask yourself this question: What is it that I don't understand?"

Under no circumstance should you go to the instructor, open the book, and with a broad sweep of your hand say, "I don't understand this." When you go for help, you should be able to say, "I understand and follow the writer's idea up to this point and even beyond this point, but for some reason this particular section has no meaning for me." That way, the instructor knows not only what you understand and don't understand but also that you did your utmost to achieve understanding. You now have set the stage for a meaningful learning session.

The Backdoor Technique has a wonderful by-product. After analyzing and verbalizing your problem, after you have viewed it from several angles, you will most likely have solved it yourself. You may not have to discuss it with anyone else.

**Additional Reading Strategies**   When you read sentences, make full use of signal words and organizational clues. If a sentence or paragraph begins "on the one hand," watch for the inevitable "on the other hand," which introduces the other side of the argument. Innocent little everyday words such as "since," "because," and "although" are as important in relating parts of a sentence as a plus, minus, or square-root sign is in a math equation. Ignoring or misreading them can get you into serious trouble.

If you get bogged down in a difficult sentence or paragraph, try reading the material without any modifying phrases. Find the simple subject of the sentence, the verb, and the simple object, to avoid getting lost in a maze of language. When the framework shows through clearly, so that you can grasp the main idea, then go back and read the material with all its "trimmings," to get its full sense.

After you finish a paragraph and summarize it, don't plunge immediately into the next paragraph. Pause for a minute or two, to think about the meaning of the paragraph you just read. Such a thinking pause provides time for the main idea to consolidate, to sink into your memory.

Whenever you encounter a difficult, unusual, or new word or term in your textbook, look it up in a glossary or dictionary. Put these words and terms, with their definitions, on 3 × 5 cards. You can learn these words and terms by carrying the cards and looking them over whenever you have a chance.

When you feel bored, do not reward your boredom by slamming your book shut and leaving empty-minded. Above all, don't reward yourself by going to a movie. If you get bored, give yourself the limited objective of extracting one nugget of knowledge, be it ever so small. Then, with that *accomplished,* you have *earned* the right to a break or a movie.

## Step 4: Writing Questions in the Margins

The question-in-the-margin step is different in purpose from the question step of the SQ3R method. In the SQ3R method, the purpose of the question is to keep the reader alert, concentrating, and looking for an answer to the limited question that was asked. The question step of SQ3R directs the reader to turn headings and subheadings into questions. Obviously, putting "what" or "how" in front of a heading does not transform it automatically into a deep and searching question. A heading that is limited to begin with will remain limited after the addition of "what" or "how."

To be sure, this does not mean that the question step in SQ3R is not a good one. It serves a definite and valuable purpose when you are reading paragraphs or sections of the textbook for the first time. However, it is hard to imagine that you will be able to formulate a provocative question on textbook material before you have read, understood, and thought about the material. Merely asking a question before reading does not in any way guarantee that an answer will be forthcoming, regardless of how hard you read. Coming up with answers is not easy. Usually you have to dig hard for a comprehensive, accurate answer, and that is why the question-in-the-margin step comes into the system at this time—after you have read a paragraph thoroughly.

Once you have read a paragraph thoroughly and have been able to answer questions such as "What is the main idea here?" or "What are the important points made here?" you are ready to formulate and write a brief, telegraphic question in the margin of your textbook. After writing the question, you should then, for the first time, underline very sparingly only the key words and phrases that make up the answer. The less underlining you do, the better (see Chapter 12 for a detailed discussion of making notes in your textbook). Later, when you review for an exam, your eyes and mind will be directed to the words and phrases that deliver the meaning directly and efficiently. When you underline only the key words and phrases, you have to think, and thinking is what makes understanding and remembering possible.

Go through the entire chapter in this way: reading thoroughly to understand the passage; writing a brief, meaningful question; and underlining sparingly. Figure 11.6 shows the questions-in-the-margin technique applied to a textbook page.

## Step 5: Reciting Based on the Questions in the Margin

After formulating questions on the entire chapter, go back to the beginning of the chapter and cover the printed text with a blank sheet of paper, exposing

### WRITING GOOD PAPERS IN COLLEGE

**What 2 aspects lead to success?**

The techniques of writing a good paper are easy to follow. You should remember two important aspects that lead to success. First, start work early on the paper. Second, if you have a choice, choose a subject that you are interested in or that you can develop an interest in.

**What 3 elements might make up a paper?**

Much of your work in college involves absorbing knowledge; when it comes to writing papers, you have the opportunity to put down on paper what you've learned about a subject, and perhaps your opinions and conclusions on the subject.

**What's the key in choosing a topic?**

Writing is an important form of communication. To communicate well you must have something you really want to say. So if you have a choice of topics, choose one that intrigues you. If it isn't one that everyone else is writing on, all the better.

**If not sure of a topic, do what?**

If you're not sure about your choice of topic, do a little preliminary research to see what's involved in several topics before you make a final decision. Remember the caution about allowing yourself enough time? Here's where it comes into play. Take enough time to choose a topic carefully.

**FIGURE 11.6   Writing Questions in the Margin**

only the questions you've written in the margin. Read the first question aloud, and answer the question in your own words. Slide the blank sheet down to check your answer. If your answer is wrong or incomplete, recite it aloud again. Do this until you get the answer right. Go through the entire chapter in this way. Your aim is to establish in your memory an accurate, crystal-clear impression, because that's what you want to return to later during an exam. If the impression in your memory is fuzzy at this time, it will be even fuzzier three or four weeks later. (See Chapter 5.)

**Why Recite Aloud?**   Reciting aloud forces you to think, and it is this thinking that leaves behind in your memory a neural trace to come back to. Forgetting never lets up. It works continuously to expel from memory what you worked so hard—often far into the night—to put there. Don't let forgetting get the upper hand. You can bring forgetting almost to a standstill by using the power of recitation.

Reciting promotes concentration, forms a sound basis for understanding the next paragraph or the next chapter, provides time for the memory trace to consolidate, ensures that facts and ideas are remembered accurately, and provides immediate feedback on how you're doing (and when you know that you're doing well, you will make progress). Moreover, experiments have shown that the greater the proportion of reciting time to reading time, the greater is the learning. Students who spent 20 percent of their time reading and 80 percent reciting did much better than students who spent less time reciting and more time reading.

When you recite aloud, don't mumble. Express the ideas in complete sentences, using the proper signal words. For example, when you are reciting a list of ideas or facts, enumerate them by saying "first," "second," and so on. Insert words such as "furthermore," "however," and "finally." When you do so in oral practice, you will do so most naturally in writing during an exam.

**The New Way: Reciting and Visualizing**   Visualizing is a powerful new technique for increasing your learning and your remembering. As you recite, instead of just mouthing the answer, picture yourself as a scholar-orator standing by your seat in the classroom reciting your answer to the instructor. Although you are actually sitting at your desk in your room and reciting in a lively manner, in your mind's eye you are standing in the classroom speaking, explaining, and gesturing.

Many successful athletes use visualization all the time. They burn such a positive image in their minds that it becomes part of the subconscious, and they expect the performance that they visualized to be carried out in actuality. Dwight Stones, a former U.S. Olympic high jumper, is very well known for the way in which he visualizes each jump before he actually makes it. There's nothing subtle about Stones. As he stands staring at the bar, his head bobs and you can almost visualize his jump yourself. His little routine might almost be comical except for one thing: Stones has won countless gold medals in international competition, and so instead of being laughed at for his peculiar routine, he is widely imitated by younger athletes who literally and figuratively are hoping to reach the heights that Stones has achieved.

Picture yourself in a classroom writing the answer to an essay question. Visualize the entire scene: the classroom, the other students, the instructor, the exam being handed out, your reading the questions. Now look at your textbook; read the question in the margin aloud; think for a few moments how you plan to organize and deliver your answer. Then, as if you were in an exam, recite softly to yourself and at the same time write your answer as you would if the exam were real. Try to *see* yourself in the classroom, thinking and writing forcefully and successfully. In this way you'll be creating in your brain cells a deep, well-defined pattern that will be easy to come back to and follow when the real exam is given. In Chapter 13, you will learn more about how to think visually.

## Step 6: Reviewing Immediately and Later

Immediately after you have recited the whole chapter, you should finish the session with a general, relaxed overview, using the questions in the margins as cues. The purpose of the general overview is to put together all the separate questions and answers—to snap them together like the parts of a jigsaw puzzle and reveal the chapter as a whole.

This overview is made not by reciting the whole business over again—you've had enough of that for a while. Rather, look thoughtfully at each question in the margin, mentally glimpse the answer, and hold the answer in mind for a few seconds. Proceed through the entire chapter in this way. Don't make this process a chore. Actually, it could be a pleasant process, similar to taking a sweeping glance at a lawn you've finished mowing or a room you've straightened up. Take a last mental look at the questions and answers, and try to see the chapter as a whole.

The immediate review is important—very important—but it is not enough. You should review thoroughly and often. Later reviews should be conducted in the same way as the immediate review: using questions in the margins as cues, one page at a time, aloud, and in your own words. These later reviews will keep you in a state of preparedness for quizzes and exams. There will be no need to cram your head full of ideas and facts on the night before an exam. All you'll need is a refresher, in the same form—one more review.

As you review, look for ways to connect or categorize, to put like things together and to place opposite things opposite each other. Look for common characteristics, differences, or functions by which to categorize facts and ideas. This type of analysis puts you in control and gives you the chance to use your creativity—to bring the textbook to life and bring order to the mass of information you are required to learn. Categorizing also puts to practical use the Magical Number Seven Theory, described in Chapter 5—the finding that the immediate memory seems to be limited to seven categories, which can be as broad as you care to make them.

The best time for a fast review of your textbook is the half hour before going to bed. Things learned then have a way of lingering in the conscious mind during the time before sleep comes and in the subconscious mind after sleep comes.

## Step 7: Reflecting on Facts and Ideas

After you learn facts and ideas through recitation and immediate review, let your mind reflect on them. Let it speculate or play with the knowledge you've acquired. To engage in reflection is to bring creativity to your learning. Ask yourself such questions as these: What is the significance of these facts and ideas? What principle or principles are they based on? What else could they be applied to? How do they fit in with what I already know? From these facts and ideas, what else can I learn? When you reflect, you weave new facts and ideas into your existing knowledge. They then become part of your regular stock of thinking tools.

There's a huge difference between proficiency and creativity. You can become proficient by studying your textbooks and lecture notes, but you will never be creative until you try to see beyond the facts, to leap mentally beyond the given. You must reflect on the facts and ideas, because creativity comes only through reflection, not from recitation and review.

To survive academically in college, you have to recite. To grow in creativity and in wisdom, you have to reflect.

| *The Reciter . . .* | *The Reflector . . .* |
|---|---|
| • Follows strictly the ideas and facts in the textbook | • Pursues ideas and facts through additional reading in the library and goes to original works |

| *The Reciter* . . . | *The Reflector* . . . |
|---|---|
| • Is bound by the course outline | • Uses the course outline as a point of departure |
| • Is diligent and disciplined in memorizing but keeps ideas and facts at arm's length | • Is adventurous and experimental and internalizes facts and ideas |
| • Is so busy reciting that the framework of the course is vaguely seen or missed | • Is likely to see the framework of the course and to talk to the instructor because of ideas occurring during reflection |
| • Understands the literal meaning but not the implications of assignments | • Applies learning to various situations |
| • Learns and accepts facts and ideas in the sequential order of the textbook | • Thinks, hypothesizes, speculates, and then tests ideas independently |

Begin with the facts and ideas you have learned, and become curious about them. Look at them in different ways, combine them, separate them into the basics, try to find out what would happen if the opposite were true, and so on. This may be difficult at first, but it will become easier as your creativity grows. Continue your reflection until your ideas take definite shape. Don't leave them vague. If you need more information, an encyclopedia or a standard source book on the subject will often help you bring fuzzy ideas into focus.

The only type of learning that becomes a permanent part of you and increases your innate wisdom is *advantageous learning*—learning that occurs when you take a voluntary, extra step beyond the mere memorization of facts. That extra step is reflection.

## SUMMARY

**What's the best way to get the semester off to a good start?**

Buy all your books just as soon as you've registered, so that you will have time to read the table of contents, preface, introduction, and other up-front material in each textbook.

**What is meant by "talking with your textbook?"**

Reading a textbook should be like engaging in a conversation: You should listen carefully to a passage in your textbook, becoming aware of its intonation, the rises and falls in the words you would hear if the sentences were spoken.

**What does the introductory material reveal?**

In the preface, for example, you might find the author's objective, how the book is organized, how and why the book is different from other books on the same subject, and the author's qualifications for writing the book. From the introduction, you might learn the underlying principles of the book.

**What is the main value of the SQ3R method of study?**

It helps you to approach reading assignments systematically. It takes you through the five steps of survey, question, read, recite, and review, thus leading you to better understanding and better retention of facts and ideas.

**In what way is the Questions-in-the-Margin System different from the SQ3R method?**

In the SQ3R method, the question is formulated from the chapter headings and subheadings, whereas the Questions-in-the-Margin System draws its questions directly from the contents of each textbook paragraph.

**Why might a question from the Questions-in-the-Margin method be a better tool?**

In the SQ3R method, the question formulation is almost a nonthinking routine; that is, you simply put a "who," "what," "when," or "how" in front of a quite-often general caption; but, in the Questions-in-the-Margin System you have to read the paragraph, then ask yourself, "What is the main idea of this paragraph?"

**Why recite?**

If you want to remember information, there is no single more powerful technique than reciting. Reciting out loud forces you to think while you recite; also, you hear your own words, thus using listening for remembering.

**Why do an immediate review?**

Formulating the "big picture" improves the likelihood that the facts from the chapter will remain in your memory.

**Why reflect?**

Reflecting is an added dimension. You begin the process by questioning the things you learn. Wonder about their significance, the principles on which they are based, and other ideas they might be applied to. In short, try to see beyond the facts and ideas in the pages of your textbooks.

## HAVE YOU MISSED SOMETHING?

*Sentence completion.*  Complete the following sentences with one of the three words listed below each sentence.

1. Frequent and thorough reviews help to eliminate the need for _____ .
   recitation     cramming     reflection

2. When you use the Questions-in-the-Margin System, you should under-line the textbook _____ .
   sparingly     frequently     initially

3. Learning is most likely to occur when the proportion of reciting time to reading time is _____ .
   high     equal     low

*Matching.*  In each blank space in the left column, write the letter preceding the phrase in the right column that matches the left item best.

| | |
|---|---|
| _____ **1.** Reflection | a. Time-honored way to study textbooks |
| _____ **2.** Surveying | b. Pinpoints what you don't understand |
| _____ **3.** Recitation | c. Reveals author's objectives |
| _____ **4.** Intonation | d. Brings creativity to learning |
| _____ **5.** Preface | e. Replaces the rhythm, stress, emphasis, and expression often lost in writing |
| _____ **6.** SQ3R System | f. Serves as a preview for what's to come in the book |
| _____ **7.** Backdoor Technique | g. A powerful weapon for combating forgetting |
| _____ **8.** Visualization | h. Adds a new dimension to the learning process |

*True-false.* Write *T* beside the *true* statements and *F* beside the *false* statements.

_____ **1.** The first few pages of a textbook should usually be skipped.

_____ **2.** Textbook reading gives you a chance to hold a continuing conversation with the author.

_____ **3.** Surveying a chapter provides advance organizers.

_____ **4.** Visualization will weaken the power of recitation.

_____ **5.** Answers to questions in the margin may be written as well as recited.

*Multiple choice.* Choose the word or phrase that completes the following sentence most accurately, and circle the letter that precedes it.

**1.** The introductory material in a textbook does *not* include

    a. the book's purpose.
    b. the author's credentials.
    c. the book's organization.
    d. the course's objective.

**2.** The value of surveying your textbook is that it

    a. allows you merely to skim your reading assignments.
    b. motivates you to do additional reading on the subject.
    c. allows you to find the answers at the back of the book.
    d. bolsters your knowledge of the subject.

**3.** Reading with intonation means reading with

    a. a partner.
    b. a loud voice.
    c. expression.
    d. apprehension.

**4.** The Questions-in-the-Margin System ultimately aids your mind's ability to

    a. recall.
    b. recognize.
    c. reflect.
    d. rephrase.

*Short answer.* Supply a brief answer for each of the following items.

1. What are the advantages of buying your textbooks well before classes begin?
2. Why and how is "Talking with your textbook" a good idea?
3. What are the five steps of the SQ3R System?
4. Basically, how does the Questions-in-the-Margin System differ from the SQ3R System?
5. Why does the Backdoor Technique work?

## VOCABULARY BUILDING

DIRECTIONS: Make a light check mark (√) alongside one of the three words (choices) that most nearly expresses the meaning of the italicized word in the phrases that are in the left-hand column. (Answers are given on p. 437.)

|  | | 1 | 2 | 3 |
|---|---|---|---|---|
| 1. | a brief *exposition* | explanation | display | excuse |
| 2. | one or two *preconceptions* | presumptions | conclusions | predictions |
| 3. | covers *intrapersonal* dealings | individual | official | group |
| 4. | *pedagogical* features | conceptual | educational | argumentative |
| 5. | a *retrospective* glance | flashback | judgmental | critical |
| 6. | *venerable* SQ3R System | obsolete | respected | discredited |
| 7. | *innate* wisdom | inbred | acquired | fostered |
| 8. | businesslike but *affable* | haughty | friendly | brusque |
| 9. | *meticulously* organized | negligently | exactingly | imprecisely |
| 10. | to know *ultimately* | finally | uniformly | later |
| 11. | to experience *solace* | anxiety | comfort | hardship |
| 12. | victory is *ascribed* | attributed | denied | disputed |
| 13. | serious *impediments* | proposals | assessments | obstacles |
| 14. | suggests a *resurgence* | force | revival | decline |
| 15. | *rampant* corruption | widespread | restrained | secret |
| 16. | nothing *plausible* | pleasing | inconceivable | likely |
| 17. | the recent *agitation* | provocation | relaxation | pacification |
| 18. | so *obnoxious* | alluring | engaging | offensive |
| 19. | created *inadvertently* | unintentionally | deliberately | consciously |
| 20. | as the *scrutiny* increases | pressure | examination | anxiety |
| 21. | *formidable* contender | powerful | experienced | frequent |

|  |  | **1** | **2** | **3** |
|---|---|---|---|---|
| 22. | preppy *lexicon* | evaluation | appearance | vocabulary |
| 23. | *mundane* subject of profits | routine | aspiring | fascinating |
| 24. | the market's *inexorable* move | tentative | irresistible | adjusting |
| 25. | the *capitulation* of investors | surrender | victory | rejoicing |

# Noting What's Important in Readings

*A book is a very good institution! To read a book, to think it over, and to write out notes is a useful exercise; a book which will not repay some hard thought is not worth publishing.*

—MARIA MITCHELL (1818–89), astronomer, the first woman admitted as a fellow to the American Academy of Arts and Sciences

Note-taking strategies differ dramatically. When it comes to textbook assignments, some students cover each page with brightly colored ink from a highlighter pen. Other students are more cautious, marking a textbook so sparingly that from a distance the pages still seem pristine.

Which approach is the better one? Or perhaps they're both right. Or they're both wrong. One thing is certain: To remember important ideas, you must make written notes.

This chapter takes up this question and in doing so proposes a sensible, systematic note-taking method for textbook reading. It provides guidelines for

- Building on what you already know
- Using the Standard System
- Using the Questions-in-the-Margin System
- Using the Separate Notes System
- Reading and taking notes on supplemental material
- Using your notes
- Combining textbook and lecture notes

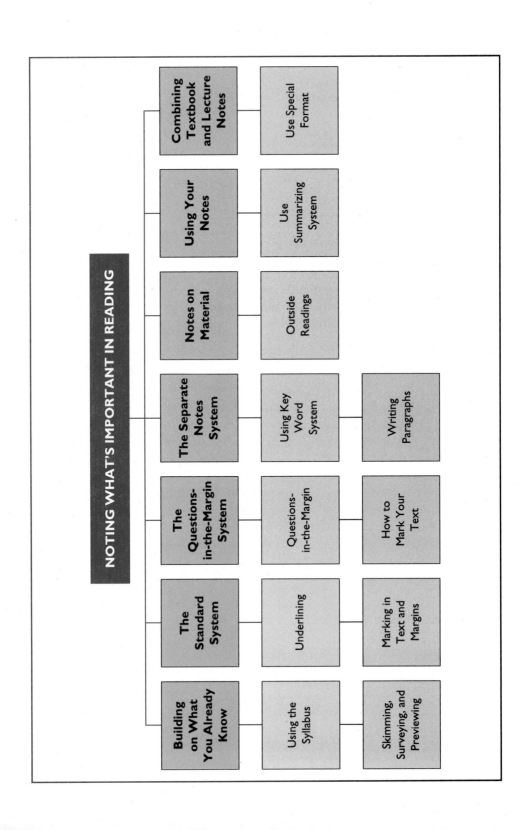

# NOTING WHAT'S IMPORTANT IN READING

**Building on What You Already Know**
- Using the Syllabus
- Skimming, Surveying, and Previewing

**The Standard System**
- Underlining
- Marking in Text and Margins

**The Questions-in-the-Margin System**
- Questions-in-the-Margin
- How to Mark Your Text

**The Separate Notes System**
- Using Key Word System
- Writing Paragraphs

**Notes on Material**
- Outside Readings

**Using Your Notes**
- Use Summarizing System

**Combining Textbook and Lecture Notes**
- Use Special Format

About one-half the information you are exposed to in a college-level course comes from textbooks. Your purpose in reading is to get to the point of what has been written. It's rare that the essence of an entire chapter will be squeezed into a single sentence. Instead, you will more likely be introduced to a series of key ideas, important points, or principles that, when pieced together, will solve the puzzle of what the author is trying to convey.

Not surprisingly, therefore, when reading an assignment you should focus your attention on ferreting out key ideas. In general, the most successful students are those who are able to track down these all-important key ideas. Luckily, the process is far more methodical than mysterious.

First, you prepare for learning by building on what you already know. Second, you adopt an active approach to learning instead of waiting for the key ideas to simply reveal themselves to you. Third, you pay attention to specific signals that indicate what material is significant. Fourth, you set about detecting organizational patterns that provide a broader view of the direction in which a reading assignment may be heading. And finally, once you've gone to the effort to extract the key ideas, you keep track of what you've been able to discern.

## BUILDING ON WHAT YOU ALREADY KNOW

Learning doesn't happen in a vacuum, and it doesn't happen all at once. For any new learning to take hold in your mind, it has to be connected to prior learning, to the knowledge you've already made your own. The process of connecting new information to old and comprehending a whole body of new information happens one step at a time.

The first place to start is with the course syllabus. A typical syllabus provides an objective or a goal for the course and an overview of the course content. Use the syllabus to activate your mind about the subject of the course. At the beginning of the term, look over the syllabus for topics you already have some familiarity with, and spend a few minutes thinking about them. Notice, too, how and where they fit into the whole, how they relate to other topics you'll be studying in the course. Consult the syllabus through-out the term for specific reading assignments, and continue building your foundation by surveying your textbook and previewing specific assignments.

There's almost no limit to the amount of work you can put into studying your textbooks. It is hard work, but it can be pleasurably rewarding if it's done right. To do it right, you must mark up the pages of your textbooks or take notes in a separate notebook. Taking notes on textbook material forces you to concentrate and makes reviewing not only easier but also more profitable. In the absence of chapter notes, reviewing for an exam is like starting from scratch, from square one. The more careful your note taking, the more knowledge you'll gain from reviewing. You have three systems to choose from:

- Standard System: underlining and jotting notes in the margins
- Questions-in-the-Margin System: writing questions in the margins and selectively underlining
- Separate Notes System: summarizing each textbook paragraph in a separate notebook

## THE STANDARD SYSTEM

Here are some guidelines for using the Standard System to mark up your textbooks.

**1.** *Finish reading before marking.*   Never mark until you have finished reading a full paragraph or a headed section and have paused to think about what you've just read. This no-marking procedure prevents you from grabbing at everything that looks important at first glance. During your initial reading, it may be difficult to tell whether the author is stating a new idea or using new words to restate an idea previously discussed. You need to understand the full context of a paragraph or section before you decide what to mark.

Read your textbook assignments a paragraph at a time. When you come to the end of a paragraph, look back at it and determine which sentence or sentences are most important. Then underline the key idea. In a different color, or with a different pen or pencil, mark any especially important secondary ideas you find. If you are marking your book with a highlighter pen, use another color or another writing instrument to mark the supporting ideas. You want to be able to pick out the key ideas easily without confusing them with ideas of lesser importance.

Remember that each paragraph generally has only one key idea, so be careful not to overmark your textbook or mark it hastily. A textbook assignment in which you have highlighted or underlined virtually every other sentence or where you have mistaken minor points for major ones will do you little good when you begin reviewing and mastering your material.

**2.** *Be extremely selective.*    Mark so that when you review later, only meaningful words, phrases, and sentences stand out. You'll appreciate your good original judgments, decisions, and discipline.

**3.** *Use your own words.*    Jottings in the margins should be in your own words. Because your own words represent your own thinking, they are powerful cues to the ideas on the page.

**4.** *Work swiftly.*    Be efficient. Don't dawdle. Read, go back for a mini-overview, make your markings and jottings. Then move on.

**5.** *Work neatly.*    Neatness is scholarly. Neatness at first takes conscious effort but not extra time. When you review, your neat jottings and markings will etch sharper, clearer, more incisive images in your mind.

**6.** *Use cross-referencing.*    If you find an idea on page 64 that has a direct bearing on an idea on page 28, draw a little arrow pointing upward and write "28" by it in the margin. Then turn back to page 28 and, alongside the idea there, draw an arrow pointing downward and write "64" by it. In this way you tie the two ideas together in your mind and in your reviewing.

**7.** *Be systematic.*    Have you ever seen a scholar's well-worn copy of a favorite book? A cherished book usually bears the owner's mark—notes that have deep significance, underlinings, papers slipped between pages, cross-references, and an array of favorite symbols. A well-marked book becomes very much your own.

Figure 12.1 contains twelve suggestions for marking textbooks. Notice especially the use of single and double underlines; the use of asterisks, circling, and boxing for important items; and the use of the top and bottom margins for long notations or summaries. If some of these ideas appeal to you, work them into your marking system. Be sure to use them consistently so that you will remember instantly what they mean.

Textbook marking can be a useful aid to study and review, but marking must be done with thought and care. Otherwise it becomes busywork. Drawing lines and boxes and inserting symbols and question marks can give you a false sense of accomplishment if you are not thinking deeply about what you read. Besides, if you overmark your book, you will defeat your purpose: quick identification of important points. When you review, you will find yourself trying to decipher a code instead of reviewing ideas. Figure 12.2 shows a page with short, crisp questions in the margin, using the question mark (?) instead of the words *what* and *why* to save precious margin-space.

Remember that the "you" who reviews the marked book will not be quite the same "you" who did the marking. As the term progresses, your knowledge grows. By the end of the term, many things that seemed so important to underscore, box, circle, star, question, comment on, or disagree

| EXPLANATION AND DESCRIPTION | SYMBOLS, MARKINGS, AND NOTATIONS |
|---|---|
| 1. Use double lines under words or phrases to signify main ideas. | Radiation can produce mutations... |
| 2. Use single lines under words or phrases to signify supporting material. | comes from cosmic rays... |
| 3. Mark small circled numbers near the initial word of an underlined group of words to indicate a series of arguments, facts, ideas—either main or supporting. | Conditions change... ① rocks rise... ② some sink... ③ the sea dashes... ④ strong winds... |
| 4. Rather than underlining a group of three or more important lines, use a vertical bracket in the margin. | had known... who gave... the time... of time... |
| 5. Use one asterisk in the margin to indicate ideas of special importance, and two for ideas of unusual importance. Reserve three asterisks for principles and high-level generalizations. | * When a nuclear blast is... ** People quite close to the... ***The main cause of mutations... |
| 6. Circle key words and terms. | The ⬭genes⬭ are the... |
| 7. Box words of enumeration and transition. | fourth, the lack of supplies... furthermore, the shortage... |
| 8. Place a question mark in the margin, opposite lines you do not understand, as a reminder to ask the instructor for clarification. | ? The lastest... cold period... about 1,000,000... Even today... |
| 9. If you disagree with a statement, indicate that in the margin. | Disagree Life became... on land only... 340 million years... |
| 10. Use the top and bottom margins of a page to record ideas of your own that are prompted by what you read. | Why not use carbon dating? .............................................................. Check on reference of fossils found in Tennessee stone quarry. |
| 11. On sheets of paper that are smaller than the pages of the book, write longer thoughts or summaries; then insert them between the pages. | Fossils Plants = 500,000,000 years old Insects = 260,000,000 " " Bees = 100,000,000 " " True Fish = 330,000,000 " " Amphibians = 300,000,000 " " Reptiles = 300,000,000 " " Birds = 150,000,000 " " |
| 12. Even though you have underlined the important ideas and supporting materials, still jot brief cues in the side margins. | Adapt – _____ fossil – _____ layer – _____ |

FIGURE 12.1  Using the Standard System to Mark Textbooks

## FOOD AND MEDICAL PRACTICE

*Why increase in population?*

The European population increased rapidly in the eighteenth century. Plague and starvation gradually disappeared, and Europeans lived longer lives.

### Diets and Nutrition

*Main food?*

*Ingredients of bread?*

*Scotland – main grain?*

*Half-cooked – why?*

At the beginning of the eighteenth century, ordinary men and women depended on grain as fully as they had in the past. Bread was quite literally the staff of life. Peasants in the Beauvais region of France ate two pounds of bread a day, washing it down with water, green wine, beer, or a little skimmed milk. Their dark bread was made from a mixture of roughly ground wheat and rye—the standard flour of the common people. The poor also ate grains in soup and gruel. In rocky northern Scotland, for example, people depended on oatmeal, which they often ate half-cooked so that it would swell in their stomachs and make them feel full.

*"Just price"?*

*Free market – explain?*

*Favored whom?*

*Poor harvests – reaction?*

*Food riots?*

*Government action?*

Not surprisingly, an adequate supply of grain and an affordable price for bread loomed in the popular imagination. Peasants, landless laborers, and urban workers all believed in the old medieval idea of the "just price"—that is, a price that was "fair" to both consumers and producers. But in the later eighteenth century, this traditional, moral view of prices and the economy clashed repeatedly with the emerging free-market philosophy of unregulated supply and demand, which government officials, large landowners, and early economists increasingly favored. In years of poor harvests and soaring prices, this clash often resulted in food riots and popular disturbances. Peasants and workers would try to stop wagons loaded with grain from leaving their region, or they would seize grain held by speculators and big merchants accused of hoarding and rigging the market. (Usually the tumultuous crowd paid what it considered to be a fair price for what it took.) Governments were keenly aware of the problem of adeqate grain supplies, and they would sometimes try to control prices to prevent unrest in crisis years.

**FIGURE 12.2   Simple Marking of a Textbook Page.**
*No need to use what & why. Use question marks. Source: Reprinted from John P. McKay, Bennett D. Hill, and John Buckler,* A History of World Societies, *p. 639. Copyright © 1996 by Houghton Mifflin Company, Boston.*

with at the beginning of the term you will be accepting as commonplace. Your early marks may hamper your review. So use the help that marking can give you, but don't go overboard.

On the following pages are examples of appropriately marked textbook pages. Figure 12.3 shows how to organize a page using enumeration; that is, encircling words such as *first* and *second*. Write in numbers to identify salient points. The underlinings should be sparse and form the answers to the questions in the margins. This type of organization not only help you to comprehend and remember the main points of the page, but also helps immensely when studying for examination when time is short.

Figure 12.4, shows how only a *few* brief questions in the margin can set up the cues for the entire page. A margin, too crowded with cue-questions, can confuse rather than clarify sequential concepts.

Figure 12.5, shows that where numerous questions in the margin are necessary, briefness keeps the margin from appearing overloaded. The judicious underlinings of the answers in the text establish an easy-to-spot relationship between question and answer.

## THE QUESTIONS-IN-THE-MARGIN SYSTEM

The guidelines for using the Questions-in-the-Margin System to mark up your textbook are surprisingly few.

1. *Survey* an entire chapter.
2. *Return* to the first paragraph and read it thoroughly to answer this question: "What's important here?"
3. *Write* a brief, telegraphic question in the margin of your textbook that requires for an answer the important point or points that you perceive in the paragraph.
4. *Underline* only the key words, phrases, and sentences that make up the answer to the question you wrote in the margin.

These four steps provide you with the essential questions and the appropriate answers. With this strong, uncomplicated system, you need nothing else (see Chapter 11 for a detailed discussion of this system).

Figure 12.6 is an example of how to formulate the questions. Your questions may be specific or general—whichever best helps you master the facts and ideas in your textbook. To add interest and variety, make up some true-false questions as well as some fill-ins. The closer your questions are

## MARITIME EXPANSION

| | |
|---|---|
| Ming period<br>Naval expeditions<br>When? Who?<br><br>Naval history<br><br><br>Relative power?<br><br>Portugal power<br>when?<br>Purpose of<br>expeditions?<br>Tribute system??<br>2 motives?<br>Contender –<br>who?<br><br><br><br><br><br><br>Admiral?<br>1st expedition<br><br>Ship's size?<br><br>Sea route?<br><br>3 consequences? | Another dramatic development of the Ming period was the series of naval expeditions sent out between 1405 and 1433 under Hong Wu's son Yong Lu and Yong Lu's successor. China had a strong maritime history stretching back to the eleventh century, and these early fifteenth-century voyages were a continuation of that tradition. The Ming expeditions established China as the greatest maritime power in the world—considerably ahead of Portugal, whose major seafaring reconnaissances began a half-century later.<br><br>    In contrast to Hong Wu, Yong Lu broadened ①diplomatic and ②commerial contacts within the tribute system. Yong Lu had two basic motives for launching overseas voyages. First, he sent them in search of Jian Wen, a serious contender for the throne whom he had defeated but who, rumor claimed, had escaped to Southeast Asia. Second, he launched the expeditions to explore, to expand trade, and to provide the imperial court with luxury objects. Led by the Muslim eunuch admiral Zheng He and navigating by compass, seven fleets sailed to East and South Asia. The first expedition (which carried 27,800 men) involved 62 major ships, the largest of which was 440 feet in length and 180 feet in the beam and had 9 masts. The expeditions crossed the Indian Ocean to Ceylon, the Persian Gulf, and the east coast of Africa.<br><br>    These voyages had important consequences. They extended the prestige of the Ming Dynasty throughout Asia.①Trade, in the form of tribute from as far as the west coast of southern India, greatly increased.②Diplomatic contacts with the distant Middle East led to the arrival in Nanjing of embassies from Egypt.③The maritime expeditions also led to the publication of geographical works. |

**FIGURE 12.3   Use of Enumeration in Textbooks**

*Use of enumerations by number and encirclements. Source: Reprinted from John P. McKay, Bennett D. Hill, and John Buckler,* A History of World Societies, *p. 711. Copyright © 1996 by Houghton Mifflin Company, Boston.*

```
5   7   3
9   0   7   6
8   5   4   0   2
0   9   1   3   5   6
8   6   0   4   8   7   2
1   7   5   4   2   4   1   9
9   6   5   8   3   0   8   0   1
5   7   3   5   1   2   0   2   8   5
3   1   7   9   2   1   5   0   6   4   2
2   1   0   1   6   7   4   1   9   8   3   5
```

Try this memory-span task. Read the top row of digits, one per second, then look away and repeat them back in order. Next, try the second row, and so on, until you make a mistake. The average person's memory span can hold seven items of information.

**FIGURE 6.4** **Memory-Span Test**

*Capacity of STM?*

*Miller's article?*

*8th or 9th item?*

*To store 7 plus — how?*

*Meaning — repackaging?*

Limited by attentional resources, short-term memory can hold only a small number of items. How small a number? To appreciate the limited capacity of STM, try the *memory-span task* presented in Figure 6.4, or test a friend. By presenting increasingly long lists of items, researchers seek to identify the point at which subjects can no longer recall without error. In tasks like this one, the average person can store seven or so list items (usually between five and nine)—regardless of whether it consists of numbers, letters, words, or names. This limit is so consistent that George Miller (1956) described the capacity of STM by the phrase, "the magical number seven, plus or minus two."

Once short-term memory is filled to capacity, the storage of new information requires that existing contents be discarded or "displaced." Thus, if you're trying to memorize historical dates, chemical elements, or a list of vocabulary words, you may find that the eighth or ninth item pushes out those earlier on the list. It's like a computer screen. As you fill the screen with new information, old material scrolls out of view. This limited capacity seems awfully disabling. But is it absolutely fixed, or can we overcome the magical number seven?

According to Miller, STM can accomodate only seven items, but there's a hitch; although an item may consist of one letter or digit, these can be grouped into *chunks* of words, sentences, and large numbers—thus enabling us to use our storage capacity more efficiently. To see the effects of chunking on short-term memory, read the following letters, pausing at each space; then look up and name as many of the letters as you can in correct order: CN NIB MMT VU SA. Since this list contains twelve discrete letters, you probably found the task quite frustrating. Now try this next list, again pausing between spaces: CNN IBM MTV USA. Better, right? This list contains the same twelve letters. But because these letters are "repackaged" in familiar groups, you had to store only four chunks, not twelve—well within the "magical" capacity (Bower, 1970).

**FIGURE 12.4  Few Notations for Descriptive Prose**
*Source: Reprinted from Saul Kassin,* Psychology, *p. 215. Copyright © 1995 by Houghton Mifflin Company, Boston.*

## FROM COLONY TO NATION

| | |
|---|---|
| When?<br>Who?<br>What?<br>Where? | On <u>February 12, 1851</u>, <u>Edward Hargraves</u>, an Australian-born prospector who had returned to Australia after unsuccessful digging in the California gold rush of 1849, <u>discovered gold</u> in a creek on the <u>western slopes of the Blue Mountains</u>. Hargraves gave the district the biblical name Ophir (Job 22:24), and the newspapers said the region was "one vast gold field." In July a |
| 2nd find where? | miner found gold at <u>Clunes, 100 miles west of Melbourne</u>, and in September gold was found in |
| 3rd find where? | what proved to be the richest field of all, <u>Ballarat, just 75 miles west of Melbourne</u>. Gold fever convulsed Australia. Although the government charged prospectors a very high license fee, men |
| Prospectors from? | and women from <u>all parts of the globe</u> flocked to Australia to share in the fabulous wealth. |
| One result? | Contemporaries agreed with explorer and politician W. C. Wentworth, who said that the gold rush opened in Australia a new era "which must in a very few years precipitate us <u>from a colony to a nation</u>." Although recent scholars have disputed Wentworth, there is much truth to his |
| Improvement<br>in what? | viewpoint. The gold rush led to an enormous improvement in <u>transportation</u> within Australia. People customarily traveled by <u>horseback</u> or on |
| Former mode? | <u>foot</u> and used two-wheel <u>ox-drawn carts</u> to bring wool from inland ranches to coastal cities. Then |
| Americans<br>introduced? | two newly arrived Americans, Freeman Cobb and James Rutherford, built sturdy <u>four-wheel coaches</u> capable of carrying heavy cargo and of negotiating the bush tracks. Carrying passengers and mail up to 80 miles a day, a week's work for ox-drawn vehicles, by 1870 Cobb and Co. coaches covered |
| Extent of coaches?<br>R.R. began<br>coverage? | <u>28,000 miles per week</u>. Railroad construction began in the <u>1870's</u>, and by <u>1890 9,000 miles of track</u> were laid. |

**FIGURE 12.5  Brief Markings in the Margins**

*Use of when, who, what, and where without additional words. Bare underlines direct eyes to facts and details. Source: Reprinted from John P. McKay, Bennett D. Hill, and John Buckler,* A History of World Societies, *p. 952. Copyright © 1996 by Houghton Mifflin Company, Boston.*

## WATCH OUT FOR QUICKSAND!

| | |
|---|---|
| What happened to Jack Pickett? | While hiking in the swamplands of Florida, Fred Stahl watched Jack Pickett <u>disappear</u> before his eyes. Pickett had stepped onto what looked like an innocent patch of dry sand and then started to sink. <u>Within fifteen minutes,</u> Pickett had disappeared completely beneath the surface. |
| How long did it take? | |
| Is quicksand real? | Pickett was a victim of quicksand. <u>If you think quicksand is something found only in adventure novels or films, you're making a big mistake.</u> And that mistake could cost you your life. |
| What did a geologist say about Q.S.? | Geologist Gerald H. Matthes, who once escaped from quicksand himself, always gave this message to hikers: "<u>Anyone who ever walks off the pavement should learn about quicksand.</u>" <u>It can be found almost anywhere.</u> |
| Where is Q.S. found? | |
| | Here are some of Matthes' tips on how to prevent being helplessly sucked under by quicksand. First of all, if you step into quicksand that is firm enough, you may be able to <u>run out. But you have to move fast.</u> If, however, the sand pulls your legs in too quickly for you to escape this way, <u>throw yourself flat on your back.</u> That's right — you can actually float in quicksand. |
| If Q.S. is firm, what to do? | |
| If Q.S. is soft, what to do? | |
| Why not raise your arms? | Don't make the common mistake of raising your arms. Resting on the surface, <u>your arms can help you to float.</u> Any movements you make should be <u>slow and deliberate.</u> <u>Quick, jerky</u> movements can cause you to be completely sucked in, just as Jack Pickett was. Try doing a <u>slow breaststroke</u> or <u>slowly rolling yourself to firm ground.</u> Above all, <u>don't panic.</u> |
| What kind of movements to make? | |
| What kind, not to make? | |
| Two ways to get out of Q.S.? | |
| Final advice? | |

**FIGURE 12.6    Questions-in-the-Margin System**

to actual test questions, the better will be your memory of the facts and ideas.

## THE SEPARATE NOTES SYSTEM

Here are some guidelines for making separate notes on the material in your textbooks.

**1.** *Use the Cornell note-taking system format.* Mark a two-and-one-half-inch margin on the left of your paper, leaving a six-inch-wide area on the right in which to make notes (see Figure 10.1, page 205). Use the narrow margin for key words. This is the ideal format for recording, reciting, and reviewing. Figures 12.7 and 12.8 illustrate this format.

| Key Words | Notes on the Chapter |
|---|---|
| Contour lines<br><br>1. Steep slope<br>2. gentle slope<br>3. cross<br>4. streams | General rules for contour lines<br><br>1. Steep slope – lines close together<br>2. Gentle slope – lines are spread<br>3. Lines never cross<br>4. Lines crossing streams – bend upstream |

**FIGURE 12.7** The Cornell Format Used for Material Emphasizing Facts

**Key Words**            **Notes on the Chapter**

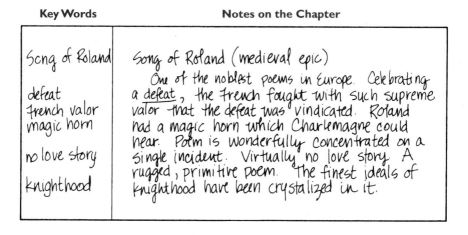

**FIGURE 12.8** Notes on Material Emphasizing Ideas and Relationships

**2.** *Finish reading before you take notes.* Never write a note until you have finished reading a full paragraph or a headed section. This prohibition will keep you from summarizing everything that looks important at first glance.

**3.** *Be extremely selective.* Pick out the essentials and write them concisely. This rule is probably the most difficult of all to follow, because to be selective you must read critically and think about what you have read. Then you'll be able to summarize each paragraph in *one sentence.* Don't try to master every idea, fact, and detail in the book; get the important ideas and the basic principles. Don't try to rewrite the textbook in longhand, for you won't be accomplishing a thing. Simply read the paragraph and reread it if necessary, decide *at that time* what is important, and write your one-sentence summary.

**4.** *Use your own words.*   After finishing the paragraph or section, ask "What is the author's main point?" Recite it, and then quickly write it in the words you just spoke. Do not mechanically transfer words from the textbook to your notebook. You will be bypassing your mind and wasting time and energy.

**5.** *Write full sentences.*   Do not make notes in outline form. Rather, write full sentences expressing full thoughts. This is what you will have to do during an exam. Also, when you review and restudy, you will be able to perceive each idea instantly. Neat writing will also be of help when you review.

**6.** *Be swift.*   You don't have all day and night for note taking. Keep alert and press for efficiency. Read, go back for a mini-overview, recite the author's idea, and write it. Then attack the next portion of the chapter.

**7.** *Don't forget visual materials.*   Important diagrams, like important facts and ideas, should be transferred to your notebook, recited, and reviewed. In biology, for example, a sure way of memorizing the structure of the amoeba is to sketch it, with all parts labeled. Take notes regarding the important aspects of maps, charts, and tables as well; they are vital parts of your text.

Figure 12.7 shows the kind of notes you might use for material that requires an orderly listing of facts, principles, or rules. Though at first glance the notes in this example may appear to be a formal outline, they are not. The facts in the wide column under "general rules for contour lines" form a simple list, and the sentences are almost complete.

Figure 12.8 shows notes on material that deals more with ideas and their relationships than with facts. Here you would be reading for concepts and theories that are likely to span many paragraphs. You would skim in your overview to get an idea of what the main concepts are and how extensively they are treated. Your task then would be to summarize and condense many paragraphs into one or two.

Slow readers often find that note taking forces them to concentrate better, and they go through each chapter faster than before. Rapid readers slow down a bit, but they learn to read with a new thoroughness.

Edward W. Fox, Cornell University's great teacher, lecturer, and historian, had this to say about note taking:

Chester G. Starr, Jr., _The Emergence of Rome_, Ch. I:
  "Geography and People of Ancient Italy"
Geography is very influential factor. Italy, long-narrow
peninsula in center of Med. Sea.

Physical Aspect :
Italy divided into 2 sections — peninsula — Med.
land imp. in ancient times, other — north of Po
R. impt. medieval and modern times. Plains in Italy
very hilly — stone villages on hillsides so more room for
farming.
Climate: Winter — westerly winds with rainstorms.
Spring — Sahara blast — drought in summer. Rome:
two months without rain. Po Valley — water from Alps.

**FIGURE 12.9  Telegraphic, Categorized Notes**

_The student will jot key words in the left margin during review. Source: Adapted from Edward W Fox,_ Syllabus for History _(Ithaca, N.Y.: Cornell University Press, 1959). Reprinted by permission of the author._

Notes are a means to an end and not the end in themselves. Some system is desirable, but a very common failing among beginning students is to develop a method so complicated and formal that it wholly defeats its purpose.

Notes taken in paragraph form on a page with a . . . left-hand margin are the most generally useful. Elaborate arrangements tend to confuse, and the traditional topical form, the use of Roman numerals, capital letters, Arabic numerals, and small letters, etc., with much indentation, has a fatal tendency to imply a logical analysis rather than elicit one.[1]

Remember, Professor Fox is talking about notes taken from books by a student who is either in his or her room or in the library. Under such unhurried conditions, he advocates making notes in _paragraph_ form, thus helping the student to express knowledge fully, in the same way you would if you were writing a short essay in an exam. This note writing is not in a lecture room where a student has to write fast and in telegraphic style. Professor Fox, too, is against making notes in the framework of a _formal outline_. (See Figure 12.9)

---

[1]Edward W. Fox, _Syllabus for History_ (Ithaca, N.Y.: Cornell University Press, 1959). Reprinted by permission of the author.

## Drawing Diagrams in Your Notebook

A word about taking notes on maps, charts, diagrams, and tables is in order. Such materials are not window-dressing; they are an important part of the text and convey information that either supplements or explains it. A map of a military campaign, a chart showing how the average dollar is spent, a diagram illustrating how distances are measured by triangulation, a table giving figures on increase in population—all these should be studied and, if important enough, sketched in your notebook. These nonverbal notes, just like your verbal notes, should be studied by the process of recall. In biology, for example, one sure way of memorizing the structure of a neuron connection is to sketch it, labeling its parts and properties, until you can easily reproduce it so that it looks something like Figure 12.10. After sketching and seeing the diagram repeatedly, you will be able to visualize it whenever you wish.

## READING AND TAKING NOTES ON SUPPLEMENTAL READING

In many undergraduate courses, assignments and lectures focus on a single textbook, but instructors often assign outside reading in other publications. Reasons for assigning the extra work include the following:

1. To amplify topics treated in the textbook or mentioned in class lectures
2. To go into greater detail—for example, by assigning original documents or primary sources
3. To expose students to another point of view or a different philosophy
4. To bring background material into discussions

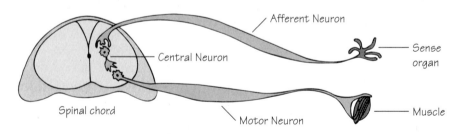

**FIGURE 12.10   Diagramming as a Study Aid**
*This sketch shows the short reflex arc from a sense organ to a reacting organ.*

Instructors generally do not expect you to master such supplementary material as thoroughly as you master your textbook. Nevertheless, once the assignment has been made, you must cope with it, in addition to the regular assignments. Clearly, you cannot spend an inordinate amount of time, but you must learn something from your supplemental reading. Here are some suggestions for doing so.

**1.** Try to figure out why the book was assigned. You might ask the instructor. If you find out, then you can skim the book looking for pertinent material, disregarding all the rest.

**2.** Read the preface. As you already know from Chapter 11, the preface provides inside information. It may tell you how this book is different from your textbook.

**3.** Study the table of contents. Notice especially the chapter titles to see whether they are like those in your textbook or different. If the chapters with similar titles contain the same information as the chapters in your textbook, then read the chapters that do not duplicate your textbook's coverage. (Do this with topics covered in your classroom lectures, too.)

**4.** If you have not yet found an "angle," read the summarizing paragraph at the end of each chapter. Make brief notes on each chapter from the information thus gained. With these notes spread out before you, try to see the overall pattern. From the overall pattern, come up with the author's central thesis, principle, problem, or solution.

**5.** Don't leave the book with only a vague notion of what it is about. You must come up with something so definite that you can talk about it the next day or write about it two weeks later. Do not waste time on details, but be ready to answer general questions: What was the author's central approach? How was it different from that of your textbook? How was it the same? Look for the central issues around which everything else is organized.

**6.** Have the courage to think big. If you lack courage, you'll waste time on minor details that you won't remember. Select the big issues and concentrate on them.

When a highly condensed summary of a book or long selection is required, you need a special approach. The introduction–thesis–body–conclusion sequence is useful in forcing you to understand the material and the way the author develops and supports it. Furthermore, a summary that follows this sequence can be highly condensed; you may be able to capture the main ideas of a collateral book in only a page or two of notes. Figure 12.11 is an example.

I. Introduction

Experiment in living close to nature.

Thoreau voluntarily withdrew from civilization which he felt was getting too complicated. He spent 2 yrs. 2 mos., and 2 days living at Walden Pond to regain the simplicity of life that comes when one lives close to the soil.

II. Thesis

Each man and woman should pause to decide just how they should spend their lives. Are they paying too dearly for unessentials?

In a complex civilization, the fast flowing current of unessentials stemming from custom, tradition, advertising, etc., somehow sweeps a person away from the genuine goals in life.

Only by temporarily cutting oneself off from civilization, could people realize that their lives need not be so complex. By getting back to nature to rethink the basic issues of life can people chart their course, and attempt to steer their lives in accordance with these standards (not expediences set up by the pressures of complex civilization).

III. Body

People should awaken and become aware of real life.

Thoreau did not wish to hold up progress or civilization; rather, he wished that people would be more contemplative and selective in their actions.

Thoreau chronicled his experiences at Walden Pond. He wanted to become familiar with nature.

a. He built his own hut.

b. Average cost of living a week was 27 cents.

c. He observed nature: trees, birds, animals, etc.

Live simply & you will live more fully.

He believed that every person ought to measure up to the best they could do. What the best is, depends upon the individual. To have a standard to measure up does not mean that all must have the same, but every one should measure up to a standard in the best way she or he is able to.

IV. Summary

Urged people to reject unessentials, and get back to fundamentals.

Thoreau wanted to demonstrate that many so-called necessities were not necessary at all. He wanted people to observe, appreciate, and evaluate what was important in life. Once people set their sights upon the good life, they should follow their sights without compromising.

**FIGURE 12.11   Notes in the Form of a Highly Condensed Summary**

## USING YOUR NOTES

When you have read and comprehended an assignment and have made notes on the central points, you are ready to practice the active recall that will convert facts and concepts into knowledge you can retain and use. Read over your notes to be sure that they say what you mean and are clear enough to mean the same thing weeks and even months later.

If you have not already done so, take the final step and summarize the notes you have made. If you have used the Cornell System for taking separate notes, study the left-hand column key words and the right-hand notes to which they pertain. Write a brief, informative summary at the bottom of the page. If you have used either the Standard System or the Questions-in-the-Margin System, you can summarize your left-hand column notes at the end of the chapter or on a separate piece of paper.

Then study one section of your notes at a time. Cover a portion of the right-hand section with a piece of paper and, from the cues, try to recall the section, reciting aloud or even writing it out. Look again at your notes to see what errors you made or what you forgot. Repeat the process until you can accurately repeat the material in your own words. (This is the same procedure recommended for effective study of lecture notes in Chapter 10.)

There is no better way to prepare for an examination than training yourself to reproduce your notes without looking at them.

## COMBINING TEXTBOOK AND LECTURE NOTES

The format shown in Figure 12.12 is ideal for lectures that mainly explain and amplify the textbook. First, in the middle column, record your notes on a previously assigned textbook chapter. Then, when you take lecture notes in the right-hand column, you can avoid repeating material you already have, while you add the lecturer's explanations, examples, and supplementary comments. When you become accustomed to the lecturer's ways, you will be able to judge how much space to leave between items in the middle column in order to keep lecture notes and textbook notes directly opposite each other. The cue words or questions that you write in the left column should pull the two sets of notes together.

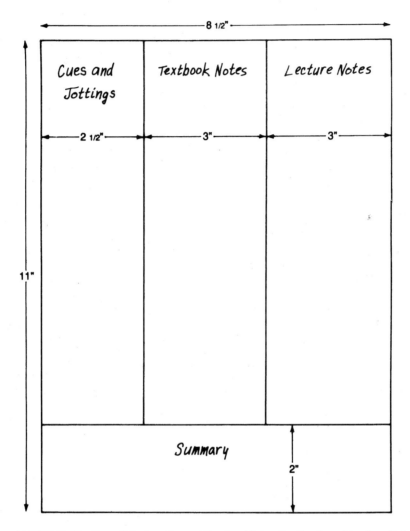

**FIGURE 12.12 Cornell System Format for Combining Textbook and Lecture Notes**

## SUMMARY

**What's the purpose of marking my textbook?**

Marking your textbook promotes concentration and thereby increases understanding. Marks both in the margin and on the text itself simplify reviewing.

**What are my options for taking notes?**

You have a choice of three systems: (1) the Standard System, (2) the Questions-in-the-Margin System, (3) the Separate Notes System.

**What steps are involved in the Standard System?**

There are seven steps: (1) Finish reading before marking. (2) Be extremely selective. (3) Use your own words. (4) Work swiftly. (5) Work neatly. (6) Use cross-referencing. (7) Be systematic.

**Are there pitfalls to textbook marking?**

The major pitfall is overmarking. Your purpose is to aid concentration and review, not to decorate your textbook with circles, underlines, and squiggles. Keep in mind that your learning increases as the semester goes on, so try not to mark too many things that will seem obvious to you in a few weeks.

**What are the guidelines for the Questions-in-the-Margin System?**

Survey the entire chapter to get a feel for it. Then read one paragraph at a time. At the end of each paragraph, take a moment to decide what's important. Once you've done this, try to formulate a question that will draw out the paragraph's main point or points. Then underline the words, terms, or phrases that make up the answer to your question.

**What are the guidelines for taking separate notes?**

Use note paper that has been ruled for the Cornell System format. Read a full paragraph before you begin taking notes. Write down only the essentials and, to ensure understanding, express them in your own words. Write complete sentences, swiftly and neatly. Don't ignore the visuals: Treat an important diagram like an important idea. Neither should be left out of your notes.

**What are supplemental readings?**

Supplemental readings, also known as outside readings, are books and articles that your instructor assigns to supplement your regular textbook in some way.

| | |
|---|---|
| **Should I approach these readings as I do assignments in my textbook?** | No. Instructors generally want you to take a broad view of supplemental readings. Your goal is to grasp the author's main thesis as well as the principles that are applied, the methodology that is used, and the problems and solutions that are mentioned. In short, concentrate on big issues rather than on details. |
| **Should I stop once I've taken notes?** | No. Capitalize on what you've learned in the note-taking process by summarizing your notes. If you've used the Cornell System, summarize in the two-inch section at the bottom of the page. If you've used the Standard System or the Questions-in-the-Margin System, summarize either at the end of the textbook chapter or on a separate sheet of paper. Then cover the right-hand material and use the key words in the left-hand column to recite your notes. |

## HAVE YOU MISSED SOMETHING?

*Sentence completion.*   Complete the following sentences with one of the three words listed below each sentence.

1. Try to summarize a textbook paragraph in a single _____ .
   word      phrase      sentence

2. Your questions in the margin should always be _____ .
   specific      general      telegraphic

3. Too much information in the margin will tend to make reciting too

   _____ .

   easy      long-winded      difficult

*Matching.*   In each blank space in the left column, write the letter preceding the phrase in the right column that matches the left item best.

| | | |
|---|---|---|
| _____ | **1.** Summarizing | a. Needed before you can mark efficiently |
| _____ | **2.** Reviewing | b. Can create a false sense of accomplishment |

_____ **3.** Overmarking

c. Can be used in understanding supplemental materials

_____ **4.** Outlines

d. Lets only meaningful words, phrases, and sentences stand out

_____ **5.** Amplification

e. Primary activity in the Separate Notes System

_____ **6.** Preface

f. Should not be used for separate note taking

_____ **7.** Context

g. One of the purposes of supplemental readings

_____ **8.** Selectivity

h. Becomes easier when textbooks are marked

*True-false.* Write *T* beside the *true* statements and *F* beside the *false* statements.

_____ **1.** The Questions-in-the-Margin System works best when used in conjunction with other note-taking methods.

_____ **2.** Marking your textbook forces you to concentrate.

_____ **3.** Marginal jottings should be expressed in your own words.

_____ **4.** True-false questions can be used with the Questions-in-the-Margin System.

_____ **5.** You can never really overmark your textbook.

_____ **6.** The "you" who marks your textbook is not the same as the "you" who reviews it.

*Multiple choice.* Choose the phrase that completes the following sentence most accurately, and circle the letter that precedes it.

1. Rapid readers who take notes
   a. read even more quickly.
   b. read with a new thoroughness.
   c. no longer need to concentrate.
   d. do all the above.

2. In both marking a textbook and taking textbook notes, you should
   a. be accurate, rather than neat.
   b. write or mark quickly to save time.
   c. use the author's words whenever possible.
   d. mark or note everything that looks important.

**3.** Underlining your textbook helps you to

   a. know that you have already studied that particular section.
   b. concentrate and understand main points.
   c. keep alert and awake.
   d. identify quickly the important points when reviewing.

*Short answer.*   Supply a brief answer for each of the following items.

   **1.** How do you combine the techniques used in the Standard System with those of the Questions-in-the-Margin System?
   **2.** When taking separate notes on your textbook, why does Professor Fox advocate writing the ideas and facts in full paragraph form?
   **3.** Why combine, on one note sheet, the notes from the textbook and the notes from lectures?

## VOCABULARY BUILDING

DIRECTIONS: Make a light check mark (√) alongside one of the three words (choices) that most nearly expresses the meaning of the italicized word in the phrases that are in the left-hand column. (Answers are given on p. 437.)

|     |                              | 1          | 2          | 3         |
|-----|------------------------------|------------|------------|-----------|
| 1.  | still seem *pristine*        | pure       | tarnished  | sparkling |
| 2.  | the course *syllabus*        | tests      | outline    | papers    |
| 3.  | *collateral* material        | identical  | negative   | additional |
| 4.  | *inordinate* amount of time  | reasonable | excessive  | moderate  |
| 5.  | don't *dawdle*               | panic      | loaf       | hurry     |
| 6.  | the *cryptic* message        | puzzling   | vaulted    | ancient   |
| 7.  | no trend appears *imminent*  | dangerous  | close      | distant   |
| 8.  | *specious* claims            | specified  | valid      | misleading |
| 9.  | *gratuitous* economic advice | groundless | free       | justified |
| 10. | speculation *titillates* the mind | tilts | satisfies  | excites   |
| 11. | like *compatible* spoons     | ill-fitting | like-minded | opposing |
| 12. | *demeaning* the human place  | degrading  | elevating  | modifying |
| 13. | such an *abyss*              | mistake    | pit        | zenith    |
| 14. | an *agnostic*                | doubter    | opponent   | pessimist |
| 15. | accidental *concatenation*   | repelling  | igniting   | linking   |
| 16. | Nature *abhors* extremes     | detests    | charishes  | abstains  |

|  | **1** | **2** | **3** |
|---|---|---|---|
| 17. this success is a *fluke* | incident | accident | reward |
| 18. your market *niche* | negative | slot | theme |
| 19. *formidable* barriers | financial | mammoth | unstable |
| 20. *classified* advertising | employment | special | categorized |
| 21. its present *dominance* | status | superiority | decline |
| 22. investing *aggressively* | boldly | conservatively | haphazardly |
| 23. *astute* investors | smart | naive | gullible |
| 24. *diversifying* internationally | specializing | spreading | concentrating |
| 25. privacy *enhanced* | minimized | elevated | compromised |

# Thinking Visually

*Man's body is faulty, his mind untrustworthy, but his imagination has made him remarkable.*

—JOHN MASEFIELD (1878–1967), English author and poet laureate

Most of us are comfortable with reading and writing in words. But the same doesn't usually hold true for pictures. This means that the entire right half of our brains, the half that processes pictures, is largely ignored or underused during a typical school day. If you can learn to read and write in pictures as comfortably as you do in words, then you will be adding a visual dimension to your studying that could dramatically affect your learning and remembering. To aid you in thinking visually, this chapter deals with

- Using your whole brain
- Making your memory stronger
- Extracting meaning from pictures
- Using the OPTIC system
- Expanding understanding with graphics
- Turning abstract ideas into maps

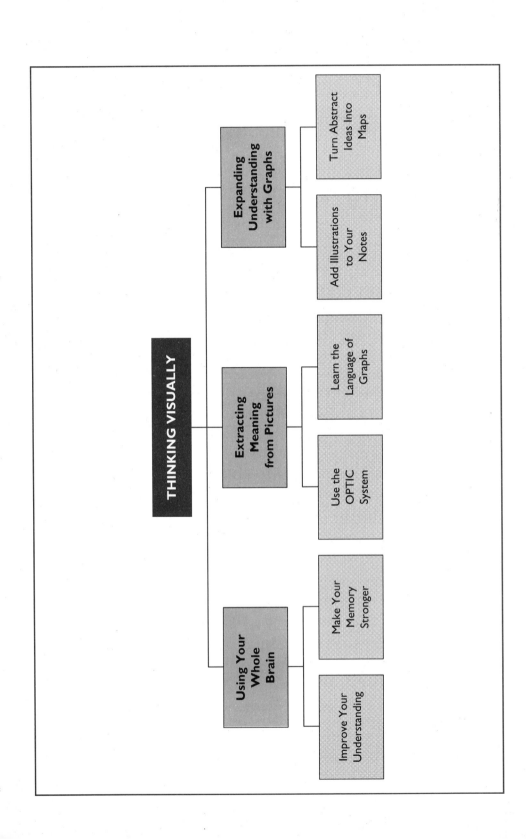

Ｗe live in a world of words, where reading and writing are crucial not only to our success but also to our survival. But words are not our only form of communication (see Figure 13.1). Think of the millions of pictures that flash on your TV screen, or consider the signs that use only pictures and shapes to convey their meanings. Although there's little danger that words will become extinct, the role of visual images appears to be increasing. Learning to think visually will broaden your mind. With your whole brain engaged, you'll be able to extract messages from pictures and use visuals to expand your understanding.

## USING YOUR WHOLE BRAIN

Although each of us has only one brain, that brain is divided into two distinct sides, or hemispheres, each with a separate set of functions. The chief function of the left side of the brain is to process written and spoken information. As you might expect, that side of the brain gets quite a workout. Although the right side does not get nearly as much use, its job is nevertheless important. One of the main functions of the brain's right side is to analyze

FIGURE 13.1 **Words are not our only form of communication**

and interpret visual information. Thinking in pictures puts the right side to work. Suddenly, instead of relying primarily on the left side of the brain, you're using both hemispheres. Your analysis of information is more balanced. This is why thinking in pictures can be said to broaden your mind. And with this broader mind, you are able to understand and remember information more easily than you could when you did the bulk of your thinking with only the left half of your brain.

## Improve Your Understanding

There is some information that the left side of the brain may be unable to understand without help. Take, for example, an elaborate set of street directions. Written out, they become the responsibility of the left side of the brain. And yet, you can read and reread all the directions and still wind up scratching your head and getting lost. But, if you put this same information into a visual form—in this case, a map—you give your right brain a chance to interpret the data. With the two sides of the brain working in concert, information that would have taken time to untangle using one-sided thinking can often be grasped in an instant.

## Make Your Memory Stronger

Thinking with your whole brain virtually doubles the odds of remembering what you've just learned. Memories that would normally be stored in only the left side of the brain are now filed in the right side as well. Indeed, Allan Paivio from the University of Western Ontario, using what he calls "dual coding," has concluded that pictures are easier to remember than words and that information is more readily recalled when it is learned as both pictures and words.[1] Thus, if you make a verbal and a visual effort to recall something you've learned, your memory will have two places to search for the information instead of just one.

## EXTRACTING MEANING FROM PICTURES

When you read a paragraph, you're cracking a code. That code is the English language, and its message is the meaning you extract from words, sentences,

---

[1] Allan Pavio, Mary Walsh, and Trudy Bons, "Concreteness Effects or Memory: When and Why?" *Journal of Experimental Psychology: Learning, Memory and Cognition* 20, no. 5 (1994): 1196–1204.

and paragraphs. Although we spend a great deal of time decoding language, most of the codes around us are visual codes. We can decode a smile, for example, and know how its meaning differs from that of a frown. Visual materials in textbooks use codes as well to supply messages that are often as important as the meanings gained from sentences and paragraphs. For that reason, they must be read every bit as carefully. And like reading a paragraph, reading a visual simply means extracting its message.

The OPTIC system enables you to extract the message from a variety of visuals. If your goal is the analysis of a graph, you will need to understand the language of that graph before you use the OPTIC system.

## Use the OPTIC System

Many students mistakenly give visuals only a quick glance or even skip over them entirely. But these graphic materials should be scrutinized as carefully and as systematically as paragraphs. The OPTIC system will help you take an organized approach to this task.

The five letters in the word OPTIC (which means "pertaining to the eye") provide you with a system for remembering the five steps for analyzing a visual.

O is for *overview.*

P is for *parts.*

T is for *title.*

I is for *interrelationships.*

C is for *conclusion.*

1. Begin by conducting a brief *overview* of the visual.
2. Then zero in on the *parts* of the visual. Read all labels, and note any elements or details that seem important.
3. Now read the *title* of the visual so you're clear on the subject it is covering.
4. Next use the title as your theory and the parts of the visual as your clues to detect and specify the *interrelationships* in the graphic.
5. Finally, try to reach a *conclusion* about the visual as a whole. What does it mean? Why was it included in the text? Sum up the message of the visual in just a sentence or two.

## Learn the Language of Graphs

You are most likely to encounter three general types of graphs: circle graphs, bar graphs, and line graphs. The purpose of a circle graph is unique, whereas bar and line graphs share the same basic function.

**Decode the Circle Graph**   The purpose of a circle graph, also known as a pie chart, is to show proportionally the relationship of parts (slices) to a whole (the pie). Although these graphs are relatively rare in highly technical books, they regularly appear in newspapers as well as in textbooks where the topic is something other than mathematics or science. The popularity of the circle graph is mainly due to its simplicity. In most cases, you can tell at a glance the proportions the graph illustrates—that is, the various-sized slices of the pie. For example, in Figure 13.2, the circle graph gives you a clear picture of the population distribution in the United States.

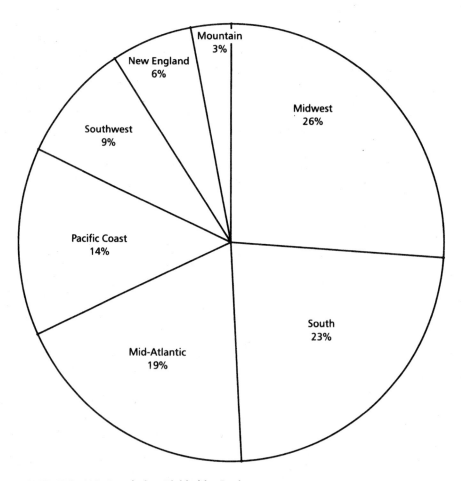

**FIGURE 13.2   U.S. Population Divided by Region**
Circle (Pie) graphs show the relationship of several parts to a whole.

**Decode Bar and Line Graphs** The purpose of bar and line graphs is to illustrate the relationship of a set of dependent variables to a set of independent variables. *Variables* are numbers that can change. For example, the number we use to refer to the year is a variable. It changes every twelve months, when it increases by one. Population is another variable. It changes when someone is born or dies, when someone becomes a citizen, or when someone leaves the country. Years and dates in general are called *independent variables* because they change on their own. The population of the United States does not influence the fact that every 365 to 366 days we begin a new year. Quantities such as population are called *dependent variables* because their change occurs in relation to another variable, such as the year. For example, we measure the changes of U.S. population every ten years when the census is taken.

Although bar and line graphs both operate in the same basic way, (showing how a dependent variable such as population increases or decreases in relation to an independent variable such as the year), each takes a slightly different approach. Bar graphs (see Figure 13.3) focus on specific changes; line graphs (Figure 13.4) illustrate long-term trends. One way to visualize this distinction is to think of bar graphs as snapshots and line graphs as movies. If you were to take successive snapshots of a long jumper, you would have a series of photographs showing successive stages of the jump. If you were to film the same jump with a movie camera, you'd have a continuous record of the entire jump. Figure 13.5 on page 294, illustrates this idea.

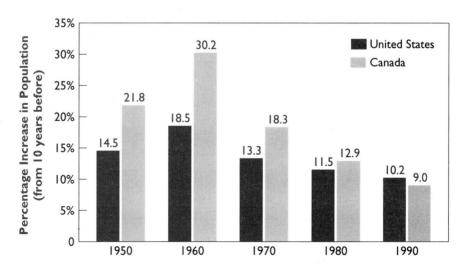

**FIGURE 13.3 Population Growth in the United States and Canada, 1950 – 1990**
Bar graphs show sizes of individual items and illustrate comparisons.

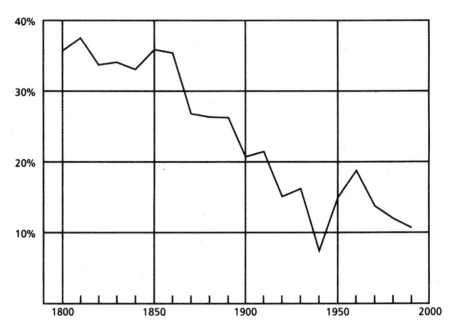

**FIGURE 13.4   Percentage Increase in U.S. Population, 1800 – 1990**
Line graphs show long-term trends in data.

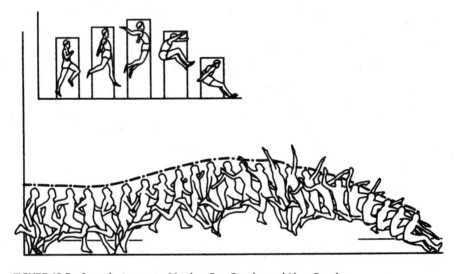

**FIGURE 13.5   Snapshots versus Movies: Bar Graphs and Line Graphs**
A bar graph can be compared to a set of snapshots, whereas a line graph is more like a movie.
*Adapted from* Track and Field Omnibook, *4th ed.,* 1985, by Ken Doherty, Tafnews Press (Track and Field News), Mountain View, CA.

Like snapshots and movies, each type of graph has its strengths. Bar graphs are good for comparing the individual sizes or amounts of items, and they provide clear comparisons of several sets of data at once. Line graphs are useful for showing changes in data over long periods of time. For instance, if you wanted to examine the country's population increase over a brief period of time or if you wanted to compare it with the population of another country, then you would probably use a bar graph. Figure 13.3 shows that the growth in U.S. population was relatively steady from 1950 through 1990, whereas Canada's population growth surged during the 1950s and 1960s. But if you wanted to show the percentage increase in U.S. population since the eighteenth century, a line graph would be a better visual. Figure 13.4 shows that the growth in U.S. population has generally slowed since 1800.

Regardless of whether the graphic is a circle, bar, or line graph, once you understand the language of the particular graph, you can methodically extract its meaning in the same way you would with a picture or diagram—by using the OPTIC system. Figure 13.6, on pages 296–297, shows a graph that has been analyzed using this system.

## EXPANDING UNDERSTANDING WITH GRAPHICS

We now know that reading a visual means studying a diagram or a graph and turning its message into a sentence or two. When you write in pictures, you simply reverse the process. You convert the sentences you've read or heard into a diagram or graph. If the information you encounter is concrete, then your task is fairly simple. For instance, you can turn a description of a computer modem into a diagram by using that description as directions for your sketch (Figure 13.7, on page 298). If, however, the ideas you read or hear are more abstract, such as information about the characteristics of amphibians, then your approach is a bit more involved. Instead of sketching the animals, which doesn't tell you much about their characteristics, you create a concept map. Although your approach to abstract ideas is different from your approach to concrete ones, your goal is the same: to turn something you can read into something you can see (see Figure 13.8, on page 299).

### Add Illustrations to Your Notes

As you read your textbook or go over your lecture notes, don't just jot down the key ideas in words; sketch some of them as well. In some subjects

**OVERVIEW**

A bar graph with a vulture in the corner and six bars moving from longest to shortest with each bar divided into plain and hatched lined sections and marked with percentages.

**PARTS**

- The six bars represent six countries: Spain, Taiwan, Singapore, Germany, Japan, and the United States.
- Percentages run horizontally at the bottom of the graph—from 0% to 12%—and represent percentage increases in salaries.
- The total length of each bar represents raises, the hatched line section stands for the rate of inflation, the plain colored part of the bar is the net raise—the raise that remains after inflation.

**TITLE**

\* "How Inflation Will Devour Raises"

The word *devour* seems to imply that inflation has a major impact on raises. The vulture is being used to make the point more dramatic and perhaps make the graph more interesting.

**INTERRELATIONSHIPS**

- Spain appears due for the largest raises, while the United States will be receiving the smallest.
- Half of the raises in Spain will be "devoured" by inflation, while roughly four-fifths of American raises will be lost to inflation.
- Of those countries listed, Spain has the highest rate of inflation (6%), while Singapore (2.5%) has the lowest rate.
- The net raises in Taiwan and Singapore are identical (5.5%), even though their rates of inflation are very different (4.5% and 2.5%).

**CONCLUSION**

With the exception of Singapore, inflation will devour a large portion—close to half and more—of anticipated raises. The United States is the hardest hit of all the countries represented in the graph, retaining only 1.2% of a 5.4% raise after inflation.

**FIGURE 13.6   Using the OPTIC System to Analyze a Graph**
*Source: Fortune,* © 1991 Time Inc. All rights reserved.

this sketching will come naturally. Science courses, for example, are full of information that can be drawn. The parts of a one-celled organism or the connections in a computer network are much easier to understand if you put little diagrams of them in your notes. Sometimes the drawing is done for you. If the instructor puts a sketch on the board or the textbook author includes diagrams in the chapter, add these pictures to your notes in the same way that you would jot down important examples. When a drawing doesn't exist, make one of your own.

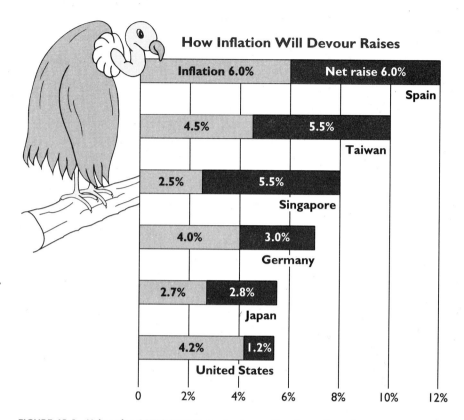

FIGURE 13.6   Using the OPTIC System to Analyze a Graph-*continued*

A history course may not feature easily drawn elements, but it does include plenty of concrete data that can be translated into picture form. A series of important dates, for example, can be turned into a time line, and individual historical facts can be visualized almost as easily.

Here is an example of how words can be converted into a picture. The following paragraph describes an experiment conducted by the English physicist and chemist Michael Faraday (1791–1867):

> In 1831, Michael Faraday, one of Britain's greatest scientists, did the experiments which completely demonstrated the close relationship between electricity and magnetism. One of his famous experiments was to take a coil of wire and connect the ends across an instrument capable of measuring tiny currents. By quickly pushing a bar magnet through the coil he was able to produce a small current in the coil and to measure that current. What he was really doing was to change the strength of the magnetic field in the coil by inserting and

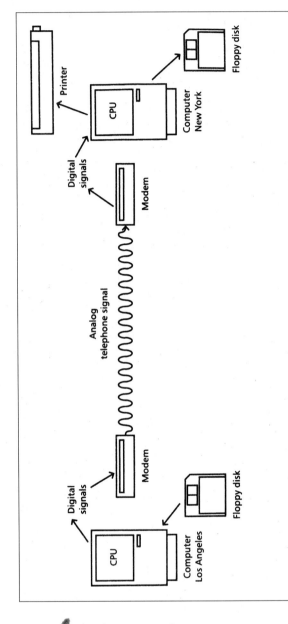

A device called a *modem* (modulator + demodulator) allows for the transference of data by telephone from one computer to another. For example, information from a floppy disk can be transferred via telephone lines from a computer in Los Angeles to a computer in New York in a matter of minutes, thereby enabling the New York user to read and even print out the information received from Los Angeles.

When the floppy disk is inserted, the information is read off the disk by the computer's central processing unit (CPU), which puts the information in a digital form that is readable by computers. For this information to be sent through the telephone lines, it must be put in an analog form, similar to the sound waves that voices produce. That is the job of the modem. Traveling across the phone lines as analog signals, the information is received by the modem at the other end of the line and is then converted back into a digital form so it will be readable by the destination computer. These digital signals go to the CPU of the New York computer, where they can be stored on a floppy disk or printed out.

**FIGURE 13.7    A Diagram Based on Text Information**

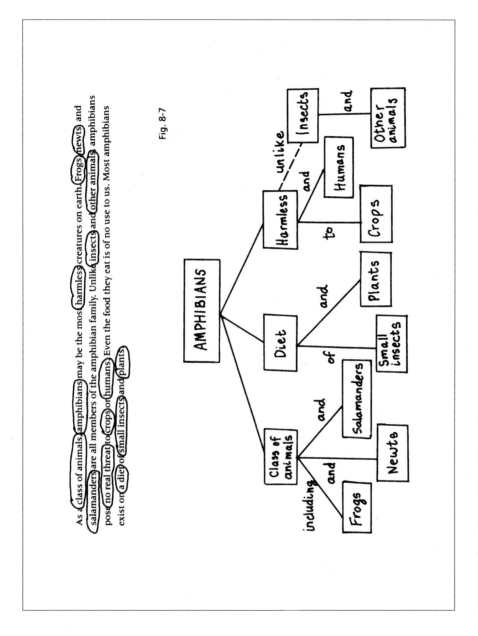

As a class of animals, amphibians may be the most harmless creatures on earth. Frogs, newts, and salamanders are all members of the amphibian family. Unlike insects and other animals, amphibians pose no real threat to crops or humans. Even the food they eat is of no use to us. Most amphibians exist on a diet of small insects and plants.

Fig. 8-7

**FIGURE 13.8   A Map of Text Information**

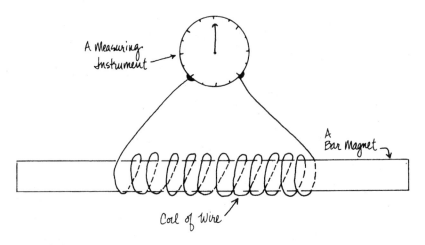

**FIGURE 13.9   A Descriptive Paragraph Made Visual**

removing the magnet. The more rapidly he changed the field the more current he could generate.[2]

Figure 13.9 is an example of how one student converted this descriptive paragraph into a diagram, which helped the student not only to understand the described process but to visualize and remember it as well. If a question about Faraday's experiment appeared on a test, it is not hard to imagine how well a student with this picture in mind would do.

You don't have to be Michelangelo or Leonardo da Vinci to draw diagrams in your notes. The important point is to tap into the right side of your brain. With your full mind at work, you'll increase your brain power, regardless of whether your drawing looks like doodling or a priceless work of art.

## Turn Abstract Ideas into Maps

Abstract ideas don't lend themselves quite as easily to diagrams as concrete ideas do. For example, you can draw a rough sketch of farmland, a field worker, and a tractor, but how would you diagram economic production, a procedure that involves all three? That's where a concept map comes in. Concept maps are used to diagram abstract processes and relationships. Drawing a concept map based on a set of abstract ideas is similar to drawing

---

[2]J. D. Jukes, *Man-Made Sun* (New York: Abelard-Schuman, 1959), p. 33.

a road map based on a set of hard-to-follow directions. And in both cases, the map that results will make the idea easier to visualize, understand, and remember. Here are the steps for mapping a text book passage:

1. Determine the topic of the passage you are planning to map. Put the topic at the top of a sheet of paper and circle it.
2. Go back to the passage and circle or list the concepts involved.
3. Find the two to five most important concepts from your list. These are the key concepts. List them on your map in a row beneath the circled topic. Circle these key concepts as well.
4. Cluster the remaining concepts under the key concepts to which they relate. Add them to your map beneath the key concepts they support, and then circle these new concepts.
5. Draw lines connecting related concepts. Along each line, you may want to specify the relationship that connects the concepts.

**Master the Map**   Drawing a concept map, like taking notes, does a great deal to help cement important ideas and concepts in your memory. And like your notes, your maps can be mastered. Although there are several systems for mastering your map, the simplest and most effective way is to look it over carefully and then, without peeking at the original passage, write a short summarizing paragraph explaining the key concepts and how they relate. The result is like writing your own textbook. You start out with the same concepts the textbook uses, but the words that result are your own instead of the author's. Figure 13.10 shows a map and its summarizing paragraph.

Concept maps are flexible study aids. They don't lock you into just one method or approach. Here are some additional ways you can use a concept map to improve your studying.

*Use the concepts for recitation.*   Take one circled concept from your map and explain out loud and without looking at the rest of the map how it relates to the map as a whole.

*Add to your map.*   New ideas frequently connect with old information. Take a moment to think about how the concepts in your map relate to ideas you already know. Add the appropriate old ideas to your map, and connect them to what you've just learned.

*Redraw your map.*   There's no right or wrong way of drawing a concept map. The same information can be mapped in a number of ways. Look over your original map and see if you can organize the concepts a little differently. Looking at the information from a different angle often makes some of the concepts a little clearer. Also, creating a second map of the same information means that the concepts will be stored in your memory an additional time.

**Textbook Passage**

There are three factors of production: land, labor and capital. Land includes all natural resources, labor all human inputs and capital all human-made items used in the production process.

**Concept Map**

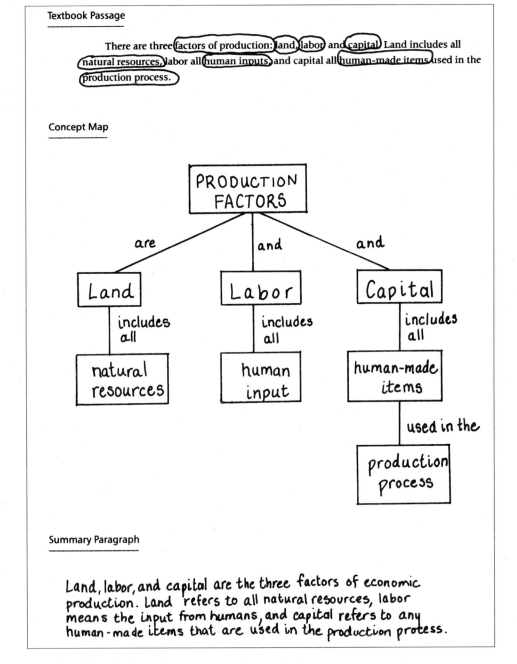

**Summary Paragraph**

Land, labor, and capital are the three factors of economic production. Land refers to all natural resources, labor means the input from humans, and capital refers to any human-made items that are used in the production process.

FIGURE 13.10   Mastering a Map

**Use Maps for Summaries** Although a map of every concept from a chapter would be huge and a concept map for even a small book would probably be the size of a billboard, you can use mapping to *summarize* the key concepts from chapters, articles, and books. The procedure for summarizing information with a concept map is identical to the one you just followed for mapping a single paragraph from your textbook or section from your notes, except that you cover more ground. Instead of containing information from one paragraph, a summary map may draw from dozens of paragraphs. For this reason, summary maps do not contain as much detail as maps created for more specific sections. The maps at the beginning of each chapter in this book provide good examples of summary maps. Notice how they include the most important concepts from the chapter they illustrate.

**Use Maps as Planning Strategies** Concept maps can be used to plan a paper or an oral report. First write the topic you've chosen at the top of a blank sheet of paper. Then after you have done a bit of preliminary research and have come up with several main concepts, add these to your map, and connect them with lines to your topic. Finally, fill out your map with any supporting ideas you've acquired, making sure to cluster them under the main concepts to which they refer. Once again, draw connecting lines to show how each piece fits into the puzzle. Here is the step-by-step procedure for mapping a paper or an oral report:

1. Do some preliminary research on your subject.
2. Write your topic at the top of a blank sheet of paper.
3. Add two to five main ideas that you plan to cover, and link them to the topic on your map.
4. Cluster any subideas under the main ideas that they support. Link them with lines.
5. Survey your map and decide whether its branches are evenly developed.
6. If your map seems lopsided, rearrange it or add information so that all its branches are balanced.
7. Use your map as a guide to do in-depth research on the concepts you plan to cover. Add to your map if necessary.

At the very least, your finished concept map can function as an outline, supplying you with all the main ideas and subideas you plan to include in your paper or oral report. In addition, the map can be used as a guide to help you do your more detailed research as systematically as possible.

Unlike a conventional outline, a map enables you to see your outline instead of just reading it. In general, a well-organized report looks fairly symmetrical when you map it. If your map has a lopsided appearance, it may mean that your report needs to be more evenly balanced. Adding some concepts or clustering your existing topics in a different arrangement should do the trick. Once you're happy with the look of your map, it can serve as a plan for further research.

## THINGS TO WATCH OUT FOR

Factual data—especially statistics—can be placed in graphic formats that distort the data. Unscrupulous people may use this device to strengthen arguments or make data appear favorable to their cause. The book *How to Lie with Statistics*[3] exposes some of the devious tricks that are used and is also fun to read. For example, you should be wary of the word *average,* and you should try to find the highest and lowest figures that went into each average. Two companies may have an average salary of $29,000. But if the range of salaries in one company is from $6,000 to $90,000, whereas in the other company the range is from $20,000 to $35,000, then the salary policies of the two companies are quite different.

Don't be overly impressed by the steepness of the lines in graphs. Look at the side of every graph to find the scale—the value of each increment. Units of $100 will make a line much steeper than units of $1,000. Always convert what you see into words; otherwise you'll remember the steepness or flatness but not the real information that is being presented.

Remember that visual relationships can be tricky. The frame around a diagram can actually change the way you see the diagram. For example, this is a diamond-shaped figure:

But notice that when the same figure is placed in a frame,

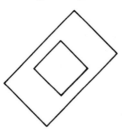

[3]Darrell Huff, *How to Lie with Statistics* (New York: Norton, paperback 1993).

it becomes a square. The size and shape of a chart or graph can also affect what you see. Data that may be quite neutral or ordinary can be made to appear startling by the form and scale of the graphic. If you read graphics carefully, you'll see them in the proper way, rather than as someone else may expect you to see them.

## SUMMARY

**How can thinking visually broaden your mind?**

Because the mind's interpretation of visual images occurs on the right side of your brain, thinking in pictures adds another dimension to thought and increases your chances of understanding and remembering information.

**What is the OPTIC system?**

The OPTIC system is a set of steps for systematically evaluating a visual. To use the system, overview the illustration, identify its constituent parts, read its title, determine the interrelationship among all these components, and arrive at a conclusion.

**What is meant by the "language of graphs"?**

The phrase indicates that graphs, like paragraphs, communicate key ideas. Although all graphs share some similarities, the most common graphs—circle, bar, and line graphs—speak their messages in slightly different ways.

**What is the purpose of a circle graph?**

The purpose of a circle graph, or pie chart, is to illustrate how a set of parts (slices) fits together to form a whole (pie). The easy readability of a circle graph makes it extremely useful for less technical articles and books.

**What is the purpose of bar and line graphs?**

Both graphs are primarily designed to illustrate the relationship between a set of dependent variables and a set of independent variables. In most cases, this illustration follows the form of cause and effect.

**How do bar and line graphs differ?**

Bar graphs usually show a few specific increases or decreases, whereas line graphs provide a broader view and are more likely to reveal an overall trend. The difference between bar graphs and line graphs is similar to that between snapshots and movies.

**How can you use visuals to expand your understanding?**

Drawing a picture or diagram to accompany written information often makes what you've read easier to understand. If the words are concrete, a picture usually helps. If they're more abstract, you may want to use a concept map instead.

**How can you master information in a concept map?**

Use each concept as a basis for recitation, explaining, or writing from memory how the concept relates to the map as a whole. You may also want to link the new ideas in your map to ones you already know or redraw your map to gain a different view of the information.

**How can concept maps be used as summaries?**

By selecting the most important concepts and arranging them in a map, you can create a convenient summary of an article, a chapter, or an entire book.

**How do maps help you in preparing for a paper or oral report?**

Arranging the important concepts you want to write or discuss in the form of a map provides you with a visual outline that makes the organization of your oral report or paper clearer. The same map can be used as a step-by-step game plan for doing your research.

## HAVE YOU MISSED SOMETHING?

*Sentence completion.* Complete the following sentences with one of the three words listed below each sentence.

1. If you commit facts and ideas to memory through words only, you are using only half of your _____ .
   wordpower    brainpower    intuition

2. The left side of the brain tends to be _____ .
   ethical    creative    logical

3. Mapping can benefit students who are visually _____ .
   impaired    oriented    deficient

*Matching.* In each blank space in the left column, write the letter preceding the phrase in the right column that matches the left item best.

_____ **1.** Memory

_____ **2.** Words

_____ **3.** Pictures

_____ **4.** OPTIC

_____ **5.** Dual coding

_____ **6.** Snapshots

_____ **7.** Movies

a. Idea of storing information as both words and pictures

b. Method for systematically analyzing graphic materials

c. Strengthened when both sides of the brain are used

d. One way to think of the function of line graphs

e. Normally fall under the jurisdiction of the brain's right side

f. Usually fall under the jurisdiction of the brain's left side

g. One way to think of the function of bar graphs

*True-false.* Write *T* beside the *true* statements and *F* beside the *false* statements.

_____ **1.** In general, bar and line graphs illustrate the same relationship.

_____ **2.** Line graphs can provide an effective illustration of long-term trends.

_____ **3.** The OPTIC system can be used with both pictures and graphs.

_____ **4.** Artistic ability isn't necessary for drawing pictures to help you study.

_____ **5.** Unlike conventional notes, concept maps cannot be recited.

*Multiple choice.* Choose the word or phrase that completes the following sentence most accurately, and circle the letter that precedes it.

**1.** Reading a paragraph or analyzing a visual can be considered

  a. left-brain thinking.
  b. cracking a code.
  c. identical endeavors.
  d. right-brain thinking.

**2.** Circle graphs are

  a. popular in newspapers.
  b. simple to understand.

   c. rare in technical books.

   d. all the above.

**3.** Independent variables include

   a. years and dates.

   b. population.

   c. words.

   d. pictures.

**4.** The subject of a concept map is usually

   a. concrete.

   b. complex.

   c. abstract.

   d. simple.

**5.** Summary maps should be drawn with

   a. less detail.

   b. black marking pen.

   c. independent variables.

   d. concrete concepts.

**6.** When used with a paper or report, a map can function as

   a. a guide for research.

   b. a visual outline.

   c. a taking-off point.

   d. all of the above.

*Short answer.*   Supply a brief answer for each of the following items.

**1.** Explain the difference between the left and right sides of the brain.

**2.** Outline the steps involved in the OPTIC system.

**3.** What is the difference between line graphs and bar graphs?

**4.** How do you master a concept map?

## VOCABULARY BUILDING

DIRECTIONS: Make a light check mark (√) alongside one of the three words (choices) that most nearly expresses the meaning of the italicized word in the phrases that are in the left-hand column. (Answers are given on p. 438.)

|  | 1 | 2 | 3 |
|---|---|---|---|
| 1. should be *scrutinized* | studied | approved | disregarded |
| 2. set of dependent *variables* | principles | rules | factors |
| 3. turn *abstract* ideas | concrete | theoretical | factual |

|  |  | **1** | **2** | **3** |
|---|---|---|---|---|
| 4. | *unscrupulos* people | smart | crooked | honorable |
| 5. | the *devious* tricks | deceitful | legal | frank |
| 6. | *frivolous* lawsuits | earnest | petty | intense |
| 7. | *outlandish* court judgments | commonplace | undeserved | preposterous |
| 8. | *plunder* retirement plans | reinstate | fleece | fix |
| 9. | amid the *tumult* | serenity | disorder | terror |
| 10. | this *pomposity* was issued | arrogance | calamity | parade |
| 11. | the situation is *ludicrous* | tragic | sad | absurd |
| 12. | whether the *largesse* | magnitude | bounty | size |
| 13. | the *benefactors* actually | supporters | recipients | charity |
| 14. | to *scuttle* any analysis | distroy | analyze | elevate |
| 15. | *braying* pack of academics | arguing | negating | noisy |
| 16. | who *propagate* aid cliches | multiply | suppress | approve |
| 17. | makes hash of *homilies* | investments | plans | sermons |
| 18. | the *corrosive* effects of aid | humanitarian | uplifting | destructive |
| 19. | with some *hyperbole* | overstatement | narrative | deceit |
| 20. | beliefs are *encapsulated* by | preserved | encased | applauded |
| 21. | to *jettison* a provision | propel | refute | discard |
| 22. | to *nullify* them | rescind | ratify | confirm |
| 23. | will *resonate* again | fail | succeed | ring |
| 24. | Congress seems *loath* | eager | reluctant | ruthless |
| 25. | back to the *unifying* themes | consolidating | divisive | uplifting |

# Managing Test Anxiety

*The will to win is nothing without the will to prepare.*

—Juma Ikangaa, *Marathoner*

A walk into an exam room can be a frightening journey into the unknown. But if you're prepared before you sit down to take your test, any fear you initially feel will evaporate, and any anxiety will subside. This chapter explains how you can manage test anxiety by

- Preparing yourself academically
- Preparing yourself mentally

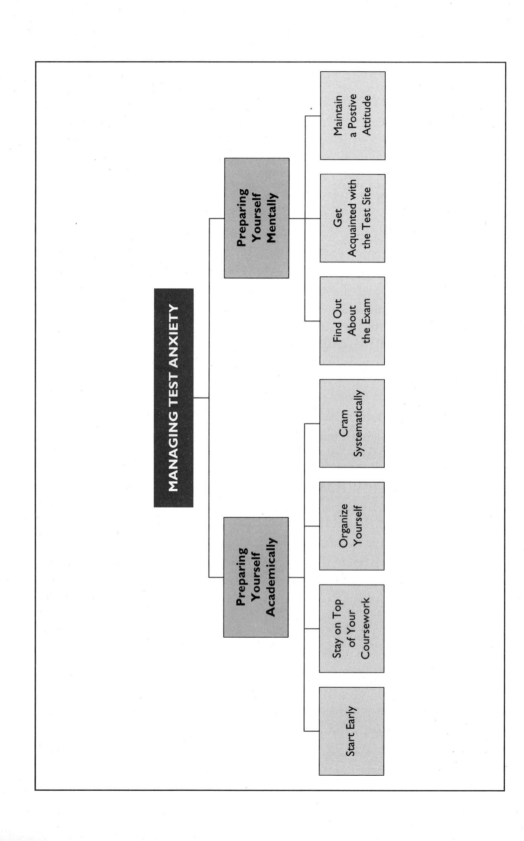

The cure for test anxiety is a simple but powerful one: preparation. Advance preparation is like a fire drill: It teaches you what to do and how to proceed, even in a high-stress situation, because you've been through the procedure so many times that you know it by heart. To manage the anxiety that often arises at test time, you can prepare yourself both academically and mentally.

## PREPARING YOURSELF ACADEMICALLY

To be prepared academically, start early, stay on top of your coursework, and organize yourself and your studying plan. Even if you're forced to cram for a test, do so as sensibly and methodically as you would if you had no time constraints.

## Start Early

The pressure's almost nonexistent at the start of a new term. Take advantage of this calm before the storm. Get a head start in a course by picking up your textbooks, looking over your syllabus, and familiarizing yourself with your school's tutoring services.

**Pick Up Your Textbooks Early**   Many students wait until the last minute, sometimes even until after the first assignment, before they pick up their textbooks. This is a common mistake. There's no reason to wait this long and every reason to buy your books as soon as you are registered for a course.

Obtaining your books in advance allows you to look leisurely through the text and get a sense of where the book and the course will be headed. Students who buy their books late in the game seldom have the opportunity to systematically go through each book, surveying the table of contents, reading the preface and the introduction, and flipping through the book as a whole. With this early start, you build a foundation of understanding.

**Read Your Syllabus**   One of the most frequently wasted resources in a college-level course is the *syllabus,* or course plan, usually handed out by the instructor during the first week of class. In the same way that surveying your textbook gives you a sense of the book as a whole, reading your syllabus from start to finish at the earliest opportunity provides you with a valuable overview of the course and makes preparing for tests much easier.

At times a syllabus can be an unexpected source of information. A few years ago, a student complained to the instructor that a paragraph-long essay question on the final exam was unreasonably difficult and totally unexpected. The instructor calmly pulled out a copy of the syllabus and pointed to the bottom of the page as the student's jaw dropped. The "unexpected" question had been printed on the last page of the syllabus and had been handed out at the beginning of the semester! The only problem was that the student hadn't bothered to read it.

**Get Help If You Need It**   As soon as you realize you're going to have trouble with one of your courses, get help. Don't struggle through a course and wait until the last minute before seeking tutoring help. By then the tutors may all have been taken.

Before the semester even begins, find out where your campus tutoring service is located and how to arrange for a tutor when you need one. New students can usually pick up this information during orientation. Keep it handy; then if you find that you are struggling with a course, you can arrange for a tutor without delay.

## Stay on Top of Your Coursework

Your preparation for exams must begin on the first day of classes and continue throughout the entire semester. To be able to focus your mind and your time on an upcoming exam, the decks must be clear—that is, your coursework must be up to date. If you have to spend valuable time getting caught up, you can seriously endanger your performance on the exam. If you stay on top of your assignments throughout the semester—by taking notes as you read or listen and by mastering those notes at the earliest possible opportunity—they won't come back to haunt you when it's time to study for finals.

**Take Notes**   In most tests you are called on either to recognize or to recall a great deal of information. You can't possibly remember everything you came across in your textbook or heard in lectures during a span of several weeks. The only way to hold onto the information that will guarantee sufficient preparation for a test or exam is by taking notes.

The Cornell note-taking format, as we've seen, provides an effective framework for recording the ideas, details, and examples gleaned from both lectures and textbook assignments. The Silver Dollar System (see Chapter 5) enables you to distill that information down to its most important ideas.

If you make a regular habit of taking notes in the Cornell format for both lectures and textbook assignments and singling out the key ideas from the notes you have taken, you'll accumulate a valuable storehouse of knowledge, and you'll have an excellent start in your preparation for upcoming exams. The next step is to master the notes you have taken.

**Master Your Material**   The key to mastery is recitation (see Chapter 5), which is the most powerful method known to psychologists for embedding facts and ideas in your memory. If you took notes using the Questions-in-the-Margin System (see Chapter 11), writing the questions in the left-hand margin enabled you to recite the information you had jotted down on your note sheet. You can then take your recitation a step further by covering your notes in the wide column and using the questions to help you recall the information. This traditional method of recitation works best when you do it out loud, from memory, and in your own words. Remember: If you can't answer the questions now, you haven't learned the material, and you won't be able to recall it later during an exam.

## Organize Yourself

The work you put into preparing yourself academically by starting early and by keeping up with your classes and assignments can be put to its best possible use if you make a point to organize both your time and your notes.

**Organize Your Time with Schedules**   Scheduling is important throughout the term. Three-part scheduling plans (explained in Chapter 2) allow you to set aside times for reviewing material, so you won't get caught off-guard by a quiz or test.

As you near the end of a term or semester, scheduling your time becomes even more crucial. If you haven't been using schedules, now's a good time to start. If you have been, you probably feel on top of things already. In either case, it's a good idea to organize your time with a homestretch schedule especially designed to help you tie any loose ends and get you through that all-important last week before exams begin. When exam week arrives, devise another schedule that specifies when each of your tests is and that enables you to schedule time for meals, sleep, and recreation, which are particularly crucial during exam week.

*Make Up a "Home-Stretch" Schedule.*    Use the format shown in Figure 14.1 to make up a home-stretch schedule. (This schedule uses the same grid discussed in Chapter 2.) Start by filling in the time blocks that will be taken up by meals, sleep, job, and recreation. Next fill in your classes. Do not miss classes for any reason; you will want to hear the instructors' answers to students' questions about exams. Finally, fill in the time you will need to complete term papers and other assignments. Make sure you get them done before exam week. You don't want unfinished business to interfere with your studying or distract your thinking during exams.

Even after you've scheduled time for all your pre-exam obligations, you will likely find that some time is available toward the end of the week. Use it to study for your exams. Fill in the exact study times and subjects. Instead of writing "Study" in the time blocks, you are wise to write exactly what

|          | M | Tu | W | Th | F | S | S |
|----------|---|----|---|----|---|---|---|
| 7:00     |   |    |   |    |   |   |   |
| 8:00     |   |    |   |    |   |   |   |
| 9:00     |   |    |   |    |   |   |   |
| 10:00    |   |    |   |    |   |   |   |
| 11:00    |   |    |   |    |   |   |   |
| 12:00    |   |    |   |    |   |   |   |
| 1:00     |   |    |   |    |   |   |   |
| 2:00     |   |    |   |    |   |   |   |
| 3:00     |   |    |   |    |   |   |   |
| 4:00     |   |    |   |    |   |   |   |
| 5:00     |   |    |   |    |   |   |   |
| 6:00     |   |    |   |    |   |   |   |
| 7:00     |   |    |   |    |   |   |   |
| 8:00     |   |    |   |    |   |   |   |
| 9:00     |   |    |   |    |   |   |   |
| 10:00    |   |    |   |    |   |   |   |

**FIGURE 14.1    Format for the "Home-Stretch" Schedule**

you plan to study: Study economics, chaps 1 to 10 or Summarize sociology notes." Make a schedule that you'll be able to follow, and then follow it.

*Use an Exam Week Schedule.* Toward the end of the week before finals, make up a schedule for exam week. Fill in the times for your exams and for your meals, rest, and recreation. Remember that you must be in tiptop shape mentally, emotionally, and physically if you are to do your best on the exams. Eating the right food, getting the right amount of sleep, and exercising regularly are all important tools not only for maintaining good health but also for managing the sort of stress all too common around exam time. Therefore, don't skip meals, sleep, or recreation in an effort to squeeze in more studying time.

By finals week, the bulk of your preparation should be completed. Leave a block of time immediately before each exam to review important information. The less time you allow between this last review and the exam, the less forgetting will take place. Review calmly and thoughtfully, and carry this calm, thoughtful behavior right into the exam room.

### Organize Your Notes with Summary Sheets

The best way to organize your notes before an exam is by consolidating them into a set of summary sheets (a highly concentrated version of your notes) and then reciting those sheets as you would your regular notes.

How can you reduce your notes so dramatically? You can do it by being selective. Although you may have been able to master the main ideas and subideas after each lecture or reading assignment, combining all this information and remembering it are not easy tasks. To recall all the lectures and readings without overloading your memory, you should limit your notes to only a handful of truly important ideas from each lecture and reading.

Why go through the process of making up summary sheets? First, it enables you to review and add to the notes you took throughout the semester and thereby increase the information you have retained. Second, it produces a superconcentrated set of notes that you can use as a refresher immediately before the exam. Finally, it helps you categorize your information under specific headings and thus improve your ability to retrieve it from your memory during the exam.

*Make Regular Summary Sheets.* If you have used the Silver Dollar System to pick out the main ideas and subideas from your notes, reducing those notes one step further should be relatively simple. Include only those notes marked with a $ in your summary sheets. If you haven't used the Silver Dollar System, you can narrow your notes all at once by employing it now, although the process will be time consuming.

Figure 14.2 provides an example of a standard summary sheet. It is indistinguishable from a regular Cornell note sheet except that this sheet

## Steps in Writing

What are four
elements of college
writing?

Writing must have: basic premise, logical development of ideas, support in paragraphs, good word choice.

### Prewriting

What are steps in
prewriting?

Brainstorm about a subject - generate ideas
Narrow to a topic - use list or concept map
Focus on a basic premise - ask a meaningful
    question that makes a point
Plot a pattern - organize points into a
    framework.

### Writing

What is the basic
Structure?

Structure - use introduction, body
    paragraphs, and conclusion.
    - write body first

What should a body
paragraph contain?

Body Paragraphs - begin each with
    topic sentence that supports basic
    premise (controlling idea)
    - support points with good examples
    and detail

What is purpose of
introduction?
What does it reveal?

Introduction - 1st paragraph-states
                        basic premise
    Reveals: - topic of essay
             - opinion about topic
             - organization pattern
                you'll use.

How do you conclude?

Conclusion - should leave reader with
    a feeling of completion
    Either: summarize basic premise
        or main points
        - state your opinion

### Revising

What are the two
main facets of
revising?

Strengthen support - data, examples, etc.
Edit for transitions, spelling, and
    grammar errors.

FIGURE 14.2  A Standard Summary Sheet

contains the most important ideas from several lectures, rather than just one, compressed into the same amount of space.

***Devise Advanced Summary Sheets.*** Although making up summary sheets of any kind gives you a chance to review your notes, devising advanced summary sheets also enables you to reflect on the information you have learned thus far. Reflection involves thinking about and applying the facts and ideas that you've learned. By rearranging your notes into categories that you've chosen yourself, you are doing just that.

Remember that "creativity comes only through reflection" (see Chapter 8). That's because reflection leads to *advantageous learning*—learning propelled by a burning desire to know something. What distinguishes advantageous learning from regular learning and advanced summary sheets from ordinary summary sheets is your mental attitude. You can't help being curious about your notes when you reorganize them for your summary sheets. The knowledge you gain from doing so not only provides excellent preparation for an exam but also remains with you long after the test is over.

Figure 14.3 shows an advanced summary sheet that represents more than ten pages of notes taken during two lectures. Notice how the points are categorized by century and are placed side by side for ease of comparison. The questions in the margin are appropriately brief; they hint at, but do not supply, each comparison.

Figure 14.4 shows an advanced summary sheet derived from textbook markings. The subcategories "Advantages" and "Disadvantages" were supplied by the student who took the notes. The material in each subcategory was originally scattered throughout the chapter.

## Cram Systematically

Academic preparation usually eliminates the need for cramming. But if you find yourself unprepared for an exam, then cramming is an unfortunate necessity. To cram systematically, limit the information that you attempt to commit to memory, and devote the bulk of your time to reciting what you've chosen to remember instead of trying to learn even more.

**Limit What You Try to Learn**  If your only chance to pass a course is to cram, then the one word to remember is *selectivity*. You must avoid falling into the trap of trying to learn too much. It will be extremely difficult to resist picking up important-looking bits of information along the way, but that is what you must do. Concentrate on essential facts, and use as much of your time as possible for remembering them.

| | Sociology 103--Dr. Lund | |
|---|---|---|
| | 19th CENTURY | 20th CENTURY |
| How is family governed? | 1. Patriarchal, Father head of family. | 1. Now, individualistic & democratic |
| Difference in stability? | 2. Family stable | 2. Family less stable |
| Status of extended family? | 3. Many children and relatives under one roof--extended family | 3. Smaller in size. Only two generations (parents & children) |
| Changes in mobility? | 4. Non-mobile. Rarely moved "Old family homestead" | 4. Mobility increased & residences changed often |
| Relationship between women & work? | 5. Women: housework and children | 5. Women: work outside & care for children after hours. |
| Attitude toward sex? | 6. Puritanical on sex | 6. Increasingly liberal |
| Variance in family types? | 7. Family types in community alike | 7. Greater variability in family type |
| Family's function? | 8. Family had many functions: political, religious, economic | 8. Now: function -- procreation and socialization |

**FIGURE 14.3    An Advanced Summary Sheet for Classroom Lecture Notes: Cornell System**

Each textbook chapter has to be skimmed and searched, and the main ideas and pertinent supporting materials must be ferreted out and written in your own words on summary sheets ruled in the Cornell format. The same must be done with your lecture notes.

**Recite Instead of Reread**    Once you've extracted the most important ideas from both your textbook and lecture notes, push aside the books and notebooks. Resist the temptation to read even more in search of important information you may have missed. It's time to admit that it's too late to try learning everything. Limit yourself to only ten or so sheets of notes from your textbook and ten sheets of notes from your classroom notes. Your hope in passing the upcoming test lies not in force-feeding yourself more and

Economics 102 – Professor Maxwell

| | |
|---|---|
| I.  Single<br>Adv:<br>  1.  freehand<br>  2.  profits–his<br>Disadv:<br>  1.  liable<br>  2.  "venture capital" | I.  Single proprietorship<br>      ADVANTAGES<br>  1.  Can do what desires<br>  2.  All profit goes to owner<br>      DISADVANTAGES<br>  1.  All losses hurt owner (unlimited liability)<br>  2.  Commerical banks ordinarily will not provide<br>     "venture capital" |
| II.  Partner–<br>Adv:<br>  1.  common pool<br>  2.  "vertical<br>    integration"<br>  3.  "horizontal<br>    integration"<br>Disadv:<br>  1.  death & change<br>  2.  liable | II.  Partnership<br>      ADVANTAGES<br>  1.  Pool wealth, profits, losses<br>  2.  "Vertical integration" = gain control of resources,<br>    become own wholesaler<br>  3.  "Horizontal integration" = buy out competitors;<br>    add products; improve products<br>      DISADVANTAGES<br>  1.  Each time a member dies or leaves, a new<br>    partnership needs to be formed<br>  2.  Unlimited liability, even if own a small share |
| III. Corporation<br>Adv:<br>  1.  legally formed<br>  2.  stock–capital<br>  3.  limited liability<br>  4.  perpetual–board<br>Adv. to society:<br>  1.  production–eff.<br>  2.  continuation<br>  3.  creates capital<br>  4.  pays taxes | III. Corporation<br>      ADVANTAGES<br>  1.  Easy to form (legal permission needed)<br>  2.  Issue stock to raise capital; banker underwrites<br>    stock issue and sells to public<br>  3.  Limited liability – Corp., distinct from its owners;<br>    can sue and be sued<br>  4.  "Perpetual succession," or existence. Board of<br>    directors<br>     ADVANTAGES TO SOCIETY<br>  1.  Technical efficiency – production of goods & services<br>  2.  Pool business risks – continuation of production<br>  3.  Creates further capital for expansion or finance new<br>  4.  It is taxed |

**FIGURE 14.4 An Advanced Summary Sheet from a Textbook Chapter**

more information at the last minute but in mastering the few facts you have in front of you.

Now recite, recite, and recite. The notes you have selected will do you no good unless you embed them in your mind so that you can mentally carry them into the examination room. To make these notes your own, read each fact you've chosen, and devise a question you can jot down in the margin of your summary sheet for which that fact is the answer. Formulating these questions will act as written recitation. Then once you have a question for every idea, cover up the answers, and test yourself by reading each question and reciting the answer from memory, again and again until you know the information cold.

By judiciously selecting the very top ideas and by using your own set of questions to help you memorize them, you will have a chance of passing the examination. You may not remember much once the test is over, but for now the objective is to survive the battle so that you can come back next term and continue the war.

Next time, through organized note taking, regular recitation, and systematic review, you can avoid the pressure and anxiety of cramming. A few days spent with your summary sheets will organize vast amounts of material in your mind—far more than you could ever learn by cramming. Moreover, you will be rested, confident, and ready for exams.

## PREPARING YOURSELF MENTALLY

When it comes to getting ready for an upcoming exam, there's no substitute for academic preparation. But even if you know your material inside and out, there's still an advantage to be gained from putting yourself in the proper mindset as well. Some students who experience test anxiety claim that even when they've studied hard, they freeze when the test is placed before them. Although academic preparation is essential, a little mental preparation can help take the sting out of an exam. If you take time to find out all you can about the exam, get yourself acquainted with the test site or a similar site, and work at maintaining a positive attitude, you're more likely to escape the test-taking anxiety that plagues unprepared students.

### Find Out About the Exam

Fear of the unknown can be a great contributor to test anxiety. If you walk into a test without knowing what to expect, you are likely to feel anxious.

Except in those rare cases when the instructor provides you with a copy of the test in advance, you can't be expected to know exactly what the exam will contain. Does this mean that anxiety is inevitable? Not at all. By asking the instructor directly and by looking at previous exams, you should be able to "guesstimate" what might be on the exam and in the process dispel some unnecessary anxiety.

**Ask the Instructor Directly** Many students overlook the most obvious method for finding out about the contents of an upcoming exam: asking the instructor directly. In many cases, instructors are not at all hesitant to discuss what the test will involve. Ask your instructor about the types of questions (objective, essay, or both) that will be asked. Find out whether your instructor will allow partial credit, how long the exam will take, and whether textbooks, notes, calculators, or other equipment will be allowed in the exam room. When you do finally sit down to take the exam, you're less apt to be knocked off balance by any surprises.

**Use Past Exams** Instructors frequently take the same approach to their exams semester after semester. Therefore, a look at an old exam can often tell you something helpful about the exam you're studying for. Try to get a copy of last semester's exam to see what kinds of questions were asked and to make sure you know the meanings of the words used in the directions. Use all this information to direct your study effort and to make sure you have the background you need to take the exam.

## Get Acquainted with the Test Site

Exams may be held in auditoriums, large lecture halls, or ordinary classrooms. To be mentally prepared for an exam, get acquainted with the site where the test will take place or with a similar location. A week or two before the exam, study for a few hours each evening at the site where you will be taking the test. Your familiarity with the room and the sense of control you feel while studying will help establish a link between working in this room and actually succeeding on the exam. If you can't study at the site of the test, you can still prepare for the atmosphere of the test.

*Study in quiet.* Some students who become anxious during a test are unnerved by the silence that is a normal part of an exam. If you take some time to study in silence, the quiet of the exam should be less disconcerting.

*Practice at a chairdesk.*   If you can't study at the actual test site, find an empty classroom that has a similar seating arrangement, and make an effort to adjust to the feel of these slightly uncomfortable accommodations.

*Use a time limit.*   So that you are not waiting until the last minute to discover how you perform with a deadline, spend some of your study time working under artificial time limits not only to get a sense of how quickly you work but also to grow accustomed to the inevitable pressure of time.

## Maintain a Positive Attitude

One of the fundamental ways of preparing yourself mentally for any sort of challenge is by cultivating a positive attitude. Test-anxious students often sabotage their own efforts by mentally preparing themselves for failure. It's better to begin with a positive attitude: Relax, use self-talk, and engage in visualization to set a successful tone to your test taking.

**Learn to Relax**   Relaxation doesn't necessarily mean taking it easy or being lazy. It means being calm enough to work efficiently. If you're an accomplished runner, you know the best races start and end with a feeling of relaxation. To improve your chances of succeeding on a test, it's a good idea to prepare yourself by relaxing. Three simple but highly effective ways of relaxing are deep breathing, progressive muscle relaxation, and visualization.

*Practice deep breathing.*   When we are anxious, we take rapid, shallow breaths from the chest. But shallow breathing can actually lead to anxiety. Countless experiments have confirmed this connection. When psychologist Dr. James Loehr[1] asked several subjects to breathe rapidly, shallowly, and irregularly for two minutes—in other words, to pant—he noticed a remarkable change in the emotional state of each subject. All found themselves feeling worried, panicked, and threatened even though nothing but their breathing patterns had changed.

Luckily, the reverse holds true as well. Deep breathing has been shown to produce a feeling of relaxation. A series of deep, slow breaths can often have a calming effect, even in the normally tense atmosphere before (or during) an exam.

If you feel tense before or during the exam, one way to cope with that feeling and to encourage relaxation is by "belly breathing"—that is, inhaling

---

[1]James E. Loehr and Peter J. McLaughlin, with Ed Quillen, *Mentally Tough* (New York: M. Evans and Company, 1986), pp. 141–142.

deeply beginning in the abdomen, instead of up in the chest. Here's how to do belly breathing:

1. Push out your stomach. That creates a pocket where the air can go.
2. With your stomach slightly puffed out, inhale slowly through your nose—one, two—filling up your abdomen with air.
3. Continue inhaling—three, four—this time sending air up into your lungs.
4. Exhale through your mouth, and reverse the process, counting—one, two—as you empty the air from your chest and then—three, four, five, six, seven, eight—as the air leaves your abdomen and your stomach deflates.
5. Repeat steps 1–4 three or four times until you're feeling relaxed.

***Practice progressive muscle relaxation.***   A technique developed in the 1930s by Dr. Edmund Jacobson, progressive muscle relaxation works by diverting your attention from your mind to your body and by slowly tensing and relaxing each of your major muscle groups. This combination defuses anxiety and relaxes the muscles, which almost without exception results in a relaxed mind as well, leaving you better prepared for tackling test problems and for recalling information from your notes.

To use progressive relaxation, deliberately tense each individual muscle group, hold that tension for five seconds, and then release it. As soon as you do, reward yourself with a deep relaxing breath. Progress systematically, beginning with your toes and moving up through your body. By the time you have tensed and released the muscles in your face, you should be feeling more relaxed and at ease throughout your entire body.

***Use visualization.***   All of us have fond memories of places where we have felt completely relaxed. Often you can evoke a feeling of relaxation no matter where you are by imagining in detail your favorite relaxing place. If it's the seashore, for example, think not only of the sight of the slowly rolling waves but also of the sound of the surf, the smell of the salt air, the sensation of the sun on your back, and the feeling of the sand between your toes. The more vivid the image you create is, the more your body will respond as it does when you are actually there—by relaxing.

**Use Self-Talk**   As we learned in Chapter 3, the idea of positive thinking is not just a starry-eyed slogan. You have an inner voice that is constantly chatting with you, either badgering you with negative thoughts or encouraging you with positive ones.

It helps to prepare yourself for an upcoming exam by listening carefully to what your inner voice is saying. If the message is self-destructive, now is the time to rewrite the script.

Psychologist S. C. Kobasa says that when you are facing a stressful situation, you can prevent overreaction and aggravation simply by *believing that you are in control and that you can find a solution to any problem or crisis.*[2] This means that if your inner voice is preaching doom and gloom, talk back to it, not necessarily out loud, but in your mind. Here are some examples of negative versus positive self-talk.

| *Negative—Don't Think This:* | *Positive—Think This:* |
| --- | --- |
| Three exams in two days is more than I can handle. | I've survived worse things than this. I'll just do the best I can. |
| This time there's no escape. | I'll just hang in there. There's always a way out. |
| I can't do these math problems. | I'll work them as far as I can and then see the TA first thing in the morning. |
| I don't know how to start this research paper. I never could write. | I'll make a list of ten titles or topics and then see the instructor in the morning for ideas. |
| I can't make heads or tails out of this chapter. I'll just forget it. | I'll go as far as I can, identify what it is I don't understand, and then see the TA or instructor immediately. |

If you can change the tone of your self-talk to make it more encouraging, you can go into the test with a constructive, rather than a destructive, attitude.

**Visualize Success**  A number of studies have shown that visualizing an action produces many of the same responses that taking the action does. For example, if you visualize yourself eating a lemon; your body will often respond by salivating the same way it would if you were actually tasting the fruit. Similarly, if you visualize yourself taking an exam and succeeding at it, when the time comes to take the test you will have already charted a course for success. Of course, taking an exam is tougher than tasting a lemon; there's no guarantee that you will automatically succeed. But by visualizing your test-taking experience in advance, you have a much greater chance of bringing it about.

---

[2]S. C. Kobasa, "Stressful Life Events, Personality, and Health: An Inquiry into Hardiness," *Journal of Personality and Social Psychology* 37 (1979): 1–11.

## SUMMARY

**How can you manage, and maybe even prevent, test anxiety?**

The way to manage test anxiety is by preparing yourself both academically and mentally for any quiz or exam.

**How can you prepare yourself academically for a test?**

Start your test preparations early, keep up with your coursework, organize yourself, and if you have to cram, do so systematically.

**What does starting early involve?**

Effective test preparation begins a few days before the first class. If you buy your textbooks as soon as you're registered for a course, read your syllabus, and ask for help at the very first sign of academic trouble, you will build a strong foundation for learning thoroughly and being able to perform well.

**How does keeping up with coursework prepare you for taking a test?**

It's not enough to actively read your assignments and carefully listen to lectures. You must take notes and thoroughly master them to retain the information you get from lectures and readings.

**What is meant by "getting yourself organized"?**

Getting organized means using your primary resources—your time and your notes—as efficiently as possible. The best way of organizing your time is by using time schedules (the home-stretch schedule and the exam week schedule) geared toward the upcoming exam. The best way of organizing your notes is by compressing and categorizing them into a handful of summary sheets, both regular and advanced.

**Is there such thing as systematic cramming?**

Yes. You can cram systematically by limiting what you try to learn, thus avoiding memory overload, and by spending most of your time reciting the limited information you've selected.

**How can you mentally prepare for an exam?**

If you find out all you can in advance about the upcoming exam, get used to the test-taking site, and make a conscientious effort to maintain a positive attitude throughout, you should be able to minimize—even eliminate—test anxiety.

**How do you find out what an exam will be like?**

You can get a pretty good idea of what the exam will contain by asking the instructor directly about the kind of exam he or she has prepared and by looking at past exams.

**What is meant by "getting acquainted with the test site"?**

This phrase means if your usual study area differs sharply from the location where you'll be taking your test, it helps to spend some time studying at the actual test site or at a place that approximates it.

**How do you maintain a positive attitude about a test?**

Think of a test as a challenge instead of a threat. You can boost your attitude by learning to relax, by using self-talk, and by visualizing success.

## HAVE YOU MISSED SOMETHING?

*Sentence completion.*   Complete the following sentences with one of the three words listed below each sentence.

1. Test grades, like the financial bottom line, are an indication of _____ .
   interest     success     anxiety

2. Experiments have shown that people do not react logically in a ____ .
   test     library     crisis

3. It is a good idea to answer the easiest test questions _____ .
   first     last     carefully

*Matching.*   In each blank space in the left column, write the letter preceding in the phrase in the right column that matches the left item best.

____ **1.** Reflection       a. Recommended cure for test anxiety

____ **2.** Cramming        b. Key to mastering your notes

____ **3.** Attitude        c. Should be done sensibly and methodically

____ **4.** Selectivity     d. Helps put a course in proper context

____ **5.** Recitation      e. Necessary to turn note sheets into summary sheets

____ **6.** Preparation     f. Bonus derived from advanced summary sheets

____ **7.** Syllabus        g. Can be improved through relaxation, self-talk, and visualization

*True-false.* Write *T* beside the *true* statements and *F* beside the *false* statements.

_____ **1.** The Silver Dollar System can be used to condense your notes into summary sheets.

_____ **2.** A regular summary sheet looks just like a Cornell note sheet.

_____ **3.** Advanced summary sheets promote advantageous learning.

_____ **4.** You should be able to predict exactly the sort of questions a test will include.

_____ **5.** Visualizing an activity can produce many of the same responses as occur when you perform that activity.

_____ **6.** Awareness of an inner voice is one more distraction that is best ignored.

_____ **7.** Relaxation provides the foundation for most mental preparation techniques.

*Multiple choice.* Choose the word or phrase that completes the following sentence most accurately, and circle the letter that precedes it.

**1.** Advance preparation for a test or exam can be compared to a(n)
  a. air raid.
  b. fire drill.
  c. road race.
  d. earthquake.

**2.** Deep breathing has been shown to produce feelings of
  a. anxiety.
  b. fatigue.
  c. relaxation.
  d. resentment.

**3.** The block of time right before an exam should be reserved for
  a. one last review session.
  b. a few moments of relaxation.
  c. a nutritious meal.
  d. rereading of a troublesome chapter.

**4.** Traditional reciting works best when it is done
  a. out loud.
  b. in your own words.
  c. from memory.
  d. in all the above ways.

**5.** Becoming acquainted with a test site means

    a. walking through the room.

    b. spending time there practicing for the test.

    c. learning the exact time and location of the test.

    d. none of the above.

**6.** You can simulate the test site by

    a. working in a quiet environment.

    b. studying at a chairdesk.

    c. using a time limit.

    d. doing all the above.

*Short answer.* Supply a brief answer for each of the following items. The number in parentheses refers to the page where the item is discussed in the text.

**1.** What is a home-stretch schedule?

**2.** How should meals, sleep, and exercise be affected by exam preparation?

**3.** What are summary sheets?

**4.** What is the difference between a regular and an advanced summary sheet?

**5.** What is the connection between progressive muscle relaxation and exam preparation?

## VOCABULARY BUILDING

DIRECTIONS: Make a light check mark (√) alongside one of the three words (choices) that most nearly expresses the meaning of the italicized word in the phrases that are in the left-hand column. (Answers are given on p. 438.)

| | | 1 | 2 | 3 |
|---|---|---|---|---|
| 1. | no time *constraints* | limits | principles | watching |
| 2. | must be *ferreted* out | transported | found | dug |
| 3. | either *badgering* | resisting | goading | helping |
| 4. | by *judiciously* selecting | inprudently | wisely | impulsively |
| 5. | *inevitable* pressure of time | unavoidable | uncertain | escapable |
| 6. | a growing *consensus* | difference | agreement | congregation |
| 7. | Taiwan's *nascent* democracy | emerging | inexperienced | new |
| 8. | they *cajoled* and pressured | extorted | threatened | coaxed |

| | | **1** | **2** | **3** |
|---|---|---|---|---|
| 9. | China's *resurrected* policy | restored | altered | rescinded |
| 10. | the government is *ossified* | exhausted | bankrupt | rigid |
| 11. | *incentives* of status | deterrents | motivations | responsibilities |
| 12. | serious *infringement* | violation | compensation | lawsuits |
| 13. | regardless of *ideology* | traits | ideals | characteristics |
| 14. | the *scourge* of violent crime | plague | fear | lawlessness |
| 15. | his *collusion* with cartels | collaboration | investments | disassociation |
| 16. | his *tirade* against business | attitude | lecture | record |
| 17. | we can *quibble* | resent | resign | argue |
| 18. | the *cumulative* experience | amassed | tentative | continuous |
| 19. | the *antiquated* systems | scientific | measured | outdated |
| 20. | the loyalty *paradigm* works | contract | example | principle |
| 21. | layoffs *obliterate* loyalty | destroy | strengthen | restore |
| 22. | the politician's *charisma* | character | magnetism | loyalty |
| 23. | the central *dilemma* | drama | circumstance | problem |
| 24. | *insatiable* demand for health | unsatisfiable | appeasable | restless |
| 25. | tax policies are *atrocious* | moderate | outrageous | one-sided |

# Mastering Objective Tests

*What is the answer? . . . In that case, what is the question?*

—GERTRUDE STEIN, *American Writer; reportedly her last words*

The real purpose of objective tests is to test your knowledge, not try your patience. Yet when faced with the prospect of answering true-false, multiple-choice, matching, or sentence-completion questions, many students would prefer to choose "none of the above." What they may not realize is that becoming an objective test expert is one of the easiest tasks to master. To show you how, this chapter looks at

- Understanding the kinds of objective questions
- Choosing effective study methods
- Moving systematically through the test
- Learning strategies for specific question types

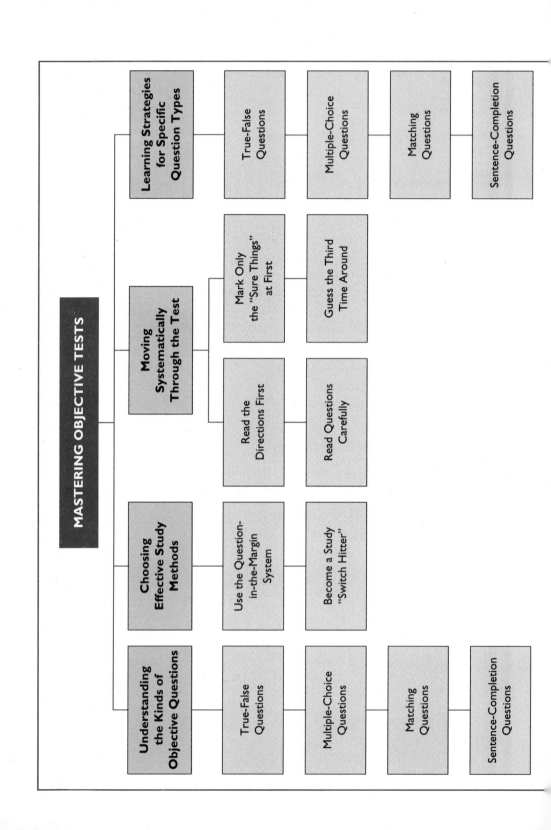

**MASTERING OBJECTIVE TESTS**

Understanding the Kinds of Objective Questions
- True-False Questions
- Multiple-Choice Questions
- Matching Questions
- Sentence-Completion Questions

Choosing Effective Study Methods
- Use the Question-in-the-Margin System
- Become a Study "Switch Hitter"

Moving Systematically Through the Test
- Read the Directions First
- Read Questions Carefully
- Mark Only the "Sure Things" at First
- Guess the Third Time Around

Learning Strategies for Specific Question Types
- True-False Questions
- Multiple-Choice Questions
- Matching Questions
- Sentence-Completion Questions

Most of the test questions you'll be expected to answer in college fall into one of two categories: essay questions and objective questions. Essay questions take a broader view of a subject and generally place an emphasis on your ability to recall and organize what you've learned and write about it. Objective questions focus more on details and on your ability to recognize, rather than recall, them. Mastering an objective test means understanding the kinds of questions that such a test will contain, choosing an effective study method for committing material to memory, moving systematically through the test itself, and learning strategies for specific question types.

## UNDERSTANDING THE KINDS OF OBJECTIVE QUESTIONS

Although they're all basically related, true-false, multiple-choice, matching, and sentence-completion questions each have qualities and quirks of their own. Awareness of these can make you a better and more confident test taker.

## True-False Questions

The basic idea behind a true-false question is simple: It consists of a single statement; your job is to decide whether it's true. What makes the choice more difficult is that to be true, this statement must be 100 percent true, not 50 percent or even 99 percent. One word is all it takes to turn a true statement into a false one. Consider, for example, the impact of a word like *always* on a true-false statement or how words like *no* or *not* radically change a statement's meaning. You have to be especially careful about reading each statement thoroughly before you answer it. Look at the following example:

    T  F  In 1787, the year the United States ratified the Constitution, Washington, D.C., became our nation's capital.

The answer to the preceding statement is false. Although it is true that the Constitution was ratified in 1787 and that the nation's capital is Washington, D.C., the United States had no federal capital until 1790, when Congress chose Philadelphia. It wasn't until ten years later, June 10, 1800, that Washington officially became the capital.

## Multiple-Choice Questions

A multiple-choice question normally begins with an incomplete sentence known as a *stem* and is followed by a series of choices, known as *options*, for completing that sentence. In most cases, your job is to find the option that best completes the stem. Here is an example:

*Stem* ———▶ In 1787, the year the United States ratified the Constitution,

 *Options*
    a.   George Washington became the country's first president.
    b.   Washington, D.C., became the nation's capital.
    c.   New Mexico was admitted to the union.
    d.   the country had no official capital.

In this question, connecting option (d) to the stem results in a true statement. Linking the stem to any other option results in a false statement.

Answering multiple-choice questions entails problems you won't encounter when you're taking a true-false test:

*Varying directions.*   Some multiple-choice directions tell you to pick more than one correct option; others ask you to mark the one option that is incorrect. Be sure to read the directions carefully and go over all the options before you mark your selection.

*Divided context.*   Because each choice in a multiple-choice question is usually divided into stem and option, you have to mentally connect the two components to determine whether an option is correct. Correct answers aren't always obvious, even when you know your material.

*Differing format.*   Most multiple-choice questions follow the incomplete stem and option format. In some cases, however, the stem may be made up of an entire sentence. A setup of this sort can take you by surprise if you're expecting a standard multiple-choice question, but in general this variation is easier because you don't have to work with a divided context.

## Matching Questions

Items in a matching test are usually divided into two columns and arranged in random order. Using a relationship that is normally explained in the directions, you systematically match the items in one column with the items in the other. Consider the following test:

Directions: Match the inventions in the right-hand column with the inventors in the left-hand column by writing the proper letter in the space provided alongside each inventor's name. Use each item in the right-hand column only once.

| Inventor | | Invention |
|---|---|---|
| _____ **1.** Eli Whitney | a. | Automobile assembly line |
| _____ **2.** James Watt | b. | Telephone |
| _____ **3.** Robert Fulton | c. | Vulcanizing of rubber |
| _____ **4.** Cyrus McCormick | d. | Six-shooter revolver |
| _____ **5.** Elias Howe | e. | Steel plow |
| _____ **6.** Henry Ford | f. | Steamboat |
| _____ **7.** James Hargreaves | g. | Motion pictures |
| _____ **8.** Richard Arkwright | h. | Cotton gin |
| _____ **9.** Samuel Colt | i. | Dynamite |
| _____ **10.** Charles Goodyear | j. | Steam engine |
| _____ **11.** Alfred Nobel | k. | Telegraph |
| _____ **12.** Thomas Edison | l. | Sewing machine |
| _____ **13.** Guglielmo Marconi | m. | Spinning frame (textiles) |
| _____ **14.** John Deere | n. | Radio |
| _____ **15.** Samuel Morse | o. | Spinning jenny |
| _____ **16.** Alexander Bell | p. | Grain-reaping machine |

Answers: 1. h   2. j   3. f   4. p   5. l   6. a   7. o   8. m   9. d   10. c   11. i   12. g
13. n   14. e   15. k   16. b

Matching tests work like multiple-choice questions with an added dimension. You're faced with a *multiple* multiple choice. Instead of one stem and several options, you have several stems and several options.

This extra dimension adds extra complications as well. Matching carelessly or guessing prematurely can sometimes lead to a chain reaction of mistakes. If you make an incorrect match, you will deprive another item of its rightful match. This can aggravate your error by increasing the chances of another bad connection, which in turn can lead to another wrong match. Avoid this potential pitfall by making your matches carefully and by pairing up the items you are sure of before you begin guessing on items you're uncertain about.

## Sentence-Completion Questions

A typical sentence-completion question consists of a partial sentence and one or more blanks. Your job in answering these kinds of questions is to read the sentences and determine what words belong in the blanks.

Sentence-completion questions work like multiple-choice questions without the choice. Unlike multiple-choice questions, sentence-completion questions can't actually be considered objective, but because the sentence is incomplete and because the answer is seldom vague or ambiguous, most sentence-completion questions can be answered following the same basic procedure you use for answering bona fide objective questions. For example:

Sentence-completion questions work like multiple choice without the _____.

# CHOOSING EFFECTIVE STUDY METHODS

As we've already discovered, your success on a test is directly related to how effectively you've studied for that test. You must master your material as efficiently as possible but in a way that will prepare you for any type of test question.

## Use the Questions-in-the-Margin System

The safest way of preparing yourself for an objective test is the safest way of preparing yourself for any kind of test—by studying to the point of recall. Although objective exams and quizzes generally test your ability to recognize, rather than recall, information, learning your notes to the point of recall gives you far greater control over what you've learned. You can tackle a question with confidence when you arrive at the answer independently of the cues that the rest of the question offers.

For that reason, the best way of studying for an objective test is by mastering your notes with the Questions-in-the-Margin System. This system (explained in Chapter 11) provides your notes with a built-in system for mastery. As you read each cue in the margin, you are compelled to recall the information to which it refers.

Another advantage that the Questions-in-the-Margin System provides has to do with the form that the marginal cues take: They're questions!

You'd be hard pressed to find a more logical way of preparing for a test filled with questions than by mastering your notes using questions as cues.

## Become a Study "Switch Hitter"

Baseball players who bat from both sides of home plate are more flexible than those who can hit only right-handed or left-handed. In the same way, you can often improve your test-taking average when you master the material in your notes from both directions instead of just one. Use the Questions-in-the-Margin System as you normally would to recall each important idea, but from time to time reverse the process by covering your questions, reading your notes, and then seeing whether you can remember the questions you wrote to accompany each important idea.

If you have time and want to make absolutely certain you know your material, write down each important idea from your notes on the front of a separate 3 × 5 card, and then jot down your cue on the back. A stack of cards, instead of a few sheets of paper, enables you to constantly rearrange your notes, ensuring that you will be able to recall important information, regardless of the order in which it's presented.

## MOVING SYSTEMATICALLY THROUGH THE TEST

Good students, those who understand what different objective questions require and have employed the most effective study methods, may still run into trouble unless they apply the same reasoned, organized approach they used in preparation to the process of taking the test. The only way to put what you know to good use is to move through the test systematically by reading the directions before anything else, by reading each question carefully, by initially marking only the "sure things," and by guessing only after you've made two sincere attempts to arrive at the answers logically. If you approach the test in this orderly fashion, you have an excellent chance of making the most of what you've learned.

## Read the Directions First

It takes just a minute or two to read a test's directions, and yet the little time that you invest can often make a drastic difference in your score.

Carelessness may do as much to torpedo a test as genuine ignorance does. If the directions for a multiple-choice test say, "Mark the two best answers," but you pass over the directions and mark only one option in each case, then most of your efforts will have been made in vain.

## Read Questions Carefully

Objective questions, no matter the type, are usually filled with information. Each word in the question is likely to be far more important than a word in an ordinary sentence. For that reason, you must read each question carefully and thoroughly to pick up important details and the complete context.

**Cope with Qualifiers**   The English language has more than a dozen common qualifiers—including *always, most, equal, good,* and *bad*—words that we use regularly in writing and conversation and that test makers often deliberately insert into objective test questions, especially true-false and multiple choice.

Qualifiers do precisely what their name implies: They complicate a simple statement or option by adding a qualification. The following two statements

It *often* rains in Seattle, Washington.

It *always* rains in Seattle, Washington.

are nearly identical. Yet one of them (the first one) is true, while the other (the second one) is false. In this case, the only thing that differentiates the two statements is their qualifiers: *often* and *always.* If you read through these statements too quickly, you may overlook their qualifiers.

Now look at a multiple-choice example:

The head of a kettle drum is

a.   struck only with wooden mallets.
b.   always made of sheepskin.
c.   often made of calfskin.
d.   tightened once a day.

In this example, option (d) is incorrect. Qualifiers indicate which of the three remaining options is correct. Without the qualifiers, all three options would be correct: Kettle drum heads *are* struck with wooden mallets, they *are* made of sheepskin, and they *are* made of calfskin. But because the qualifiers *only* and *always* overstate the case, options (a) and (b) are incorrect; while *often,* the qualifier in option (c), takes a more moderate stance and is therefore correct.

The qualifiers *only* and *always* in the first two options are both good examples of *100 percent words*. These qualifiers imply that the statements they appear in are true 100 percent of the time. Such qualifiers almost always make a statement false; very few things in this world are 100 percent one way or the other. Although it is wise to watch out for these words, don't automatically consider a statement wrong because it contains one of them. To keep you honest and alert, some instructors occasionally use 100 percent words in true statements:

*All* stars are surrounded by space.

*All* human beings need food to survive.

*No* human being can live without air.

A simple and effective strategy for coping with qualifiers is to keep careful track of them by circling each one that appears in a test question. Circling the qualifiers helps ensure that you don't ignore them. Then you can mentally substitute other words that will change the meaning of the question. This method is sometimes referred to as the *Goldilocks Technique* because you try it on several qualifiers until you find the one that's "just right." Most qualifiers are clustered in groups or "families." If you can find another family member that does a better job of completing the sentence, then the original question is probably false or, in the case of multiple choice, is probably an incorrect option. The qualifiers in the families that follow may overstate a true-false statement, understate it, or make it just right. Memorize the six families. They will help you answer true-false questions and make the right choice among multiple-choice options.

All—most—some—none (no)

Always—usually—sometimes—never

Great—much—little—no

More—equal—less

Good—bad

Is—is not

Whenever one qualifier from a set is used in a true-false statement or a multiple-choice option, substitute each of the others for it in turn. In this way, determine which of the qualifiers from the family fits best (makes the statement just right). If that is the given qualifier, the answer is true; otherwise, the answer is false.

For example, suppose you are given this question:

T  F  All birds can fly.

Substituting the other qualifiers in the "all" family gives you these four statements:

*Original Statement*      *Related Statements*

All birds can fly.        Most birds can fly.

                                                 Some birds can fly.

                                                 No birds can fly.

The statement that begins with *most* is just right, but that is not the statement you were originally given. Therefore, the original answer is false.

**Notice Negatives**  Negatives can be either words such as *no, not, none,* and *never* or prefixes such as *il,* as in illogical; *un,* as in uninterested; and *im,* as in impatient. Negatives are common in everyday speech and writing and almost as common in objective tests.

Negatives cause problems in objective questions because, like qualifiers, they can easily be overlooked, particularly negative prefixes that have a way of blending in with the words they modify. For example:

Because it is liquid at room temperature, mercury is indistinguishable from other metals.

If you read this sentence quickly, you may miss the two letters *i-n* and mark the statement true as a result. But if you read the statement carefully, you will realize that just the opposite is true.

Objective questions that contain two or more negatives can be even more troublesome. For example, you would probably be able to mark this statement "true" without much difficulty:

It is logical to assume that Thomas Edison's fame was due to his many practical inventions.

Yet you might have trouble with the sentence

It is illogical to assume that Thomas Edison's fame was not due to his many practical inventions.

even though it is also true.

When you find negatives in objective questions, circle them. Then disregard them for a moment, and try to gain the meaning of the question that remains. Finally, reread the sentence with the negatives included. Each negative you add reverses the meaning of the question. With two negatives, for example, the question's meaning should be the same as it was when the negatives were removed.

**Use Grammatical Clues** Although formats vary, all questions follow the rules of grammar. This fact can help you narrow your choices by eliminating those possible answers that don't produce grammatically correct sentences. The only way to determine whether the rules of grammar are being followed or broken is by reading the entire question so you are able to get its total context. Consider this question:

The people of Iceland

   a.  a country located just outside the Arctic Circle.
   b.  are the world's most avid readers.
   c.  claim to be descendants of the Aztecs.
   d.  the capital, Reykjavik, where arms talks have been held.

If you race through this example, you might be tempted to mark either (a) or (d) as the correct response. Indeed, Iceland is a country located just outside the Arctic Circle, and Reykjavik, the capital, has been the site of important arms negotiations. But if you take the time to read the entire question, you can see that these two responses do not complete the stem grammatically. (Response [a] is missing the predicate of the sentence, and response [d] is missing any grammatical connection to "The people of Iceland.") That leaves (b) and (c) as the only legitimate options. (The correct answer is [b].)

Grammatical clues are even more helpful in sentence-completion questions, where your response must be recalled instead of chosen from a list of possible answers. For example:

Although about 75 million meteors enter our atmosphere each day, on the average only _____ of them ever reaches the ground.

Because *reaches* is a singular verb form, the only correct answer is *one*. (Otherwise the question would have read *reach*, the plural form.)

**Choose the Best Response** Some objective questions supply more than one *good* response, but in most cases there is only one *best* response. It's difficult to tell a good response from a best response unless you have read through the question completely. If you grow impatient and mark down the first answer that sounds right, you risk missing the best answer.

Here's a multiple-choice example:

You would expect to find an aglet

   a.  on your foot.
   b.  in a nest.
   c.  in a small farming community.
   d.  at the tip of a shoelace.

An aglet is the cap, often made of plastic, at the end of a shoelace. If you read only partway through this question, you might be tempted to pick option (a). That's a good choice, but if you read the whole way through the question, you can easily see that it's not the best choice. Only with the question's entire context can you tell which option is a good answer and which is even better. (The best option is [d].)

## Mark Only the "Sure Things" at First

If a question has you stumped at first, don't feel compelled to answer it right away. And don't pick a "temporary answer" with the thought that you can come back and change it later. You may not have time, and even if you do, you may not be able to distinguish your uncertain answers from your certain ones.

On your initial pass through the test, mark only those answers you are sure of. (This is especially crucial in matching questions, where one mistake can set off a chain reaction of incorrect answers.) If an answer doesn't come to mind right away, circle any qualifiers or negatives, eliminate any choices you know are incorrect, and then move on to the next questions. These markings will provide you with a head start on your second pass.

## Guess the Third Time Around

Except when there's an extra penalty for incorrect answers, guessing is always better than simply leaving a question blank. A question unanswered guarantees a zero, whereas a guess may score some points. Furthermore, if you know something about the material and have given it some genuine thought, then you should be able to make an intelligent guess. Intelligent guesses are always superior to random ones. Consider this sentence-completion item:

> You can travel by ship from New England to Florida without ever entering the usually rough open seas by using a system of rivers and canals called the _____ .

If you don't know the official name for the system, this sentence is long enough and descriptive enough to help you come up with a good guess. You might call it the "Inland Waterway." That's not the exact name, but it is very close, and you would likely receive partial credit for it. (The answer is Intracoastal Waterway.)

## LEARNING STRATEGIES FOR SPECIFIC QUESTION TYPES

In the strictest sense, there are no tricks for taking objective tests. The requirement for taking any test is basically the same: Know your material. To select the correct answer with any degree of certainty, you must be familiar with the type of question, you must have studied effectively, and you are wise to move systematically through the test. Once you've done this, there are some other actions you can take, depending on the question type, to improve your chances of answering correctly.

### True-False Questions

Although you have a 50-50 chance of answering a single true-false statement correctly, the odds are not that high for the entire test. In fact, your chances of guessing correctly on every statement decrease geometrically with every question. In a ten-question test, the odds on guessing are against you by more than a thousand to one. If you're unsure of whether to mark "T" or "F" and you're forced to guess, adopt these two strategies to influence your decision and improve your odds.

**Mark "True" If You're Stumped**   Because instructors would rather leave true information in your mind, they tend to stack true-false tests with more true statements than false ones. You shouldn't guess right away on a true-false question, but if you're stumped and pressed for time, the odds are in your favor if you choose true over false.

**Be Suspicious of Longer Statements**   Remember the importance of context, and remember that true-false statements must be 100 percent true. Each word added to a true-false statement increases its chances of being false. All it takes is one incorrect word to make the statement false.

### Multiple-Choice Questions

You can use several more strategies to cope with multiple-choice questions.

**Pick "All the Above" If You're in Doubt**   Most multiple-choice questions present just a single fact, the option that correctly completes the stem. But with "all the above" the test maker can include several options instead of just one. Because the purpose behind a quiz or exam is not only to test but also to teach, "all the above" becomes an attractive choice for the test maker.

Here's an example of a question that uses "all the above":

Until the first half of the second millennium B.C., an army laying siege to a city had use of

a.   scaling ladders.
b.   siege towers.
c.   archery fire.
d.   all the above.

The correct answer is (d).

One way to confirm the choice "all the above" is to pick out two correct answers in the options. For instance, in the example just given, suppose you are sure that ladders and towers were used, but you aren't certain about archery fire. Unless the directions permit you to mark more than one option, you already have all the information you need to choose the correct answer. If option (a) is correct and option (b) is correct, then (d) is the only logical answer.

It would be a mistake to mark every "all the above" you run into before reading the question and carefully considering the options. But if you can't seem to come up with an answer and you're running out of time, then choosing "all the above" is usually a pretty safe bet.

**Use the True-False Technique to Change Perspective**   If you know your material but have a mental block about the multiple-choice format, you can gain a new perspective on a difficult question by using the *true-false technique.* Almost any multiple-choice question can be thought of as a series of true-false statements. Simply rethink a troublesome multiple-choice question as a set of true-false statements.

Here's an example:

Before becoming president in 1857, James Buchanan was

a.   married and divorced.
b.   secretary of defense.
c.   prime minister of Canada.
d.   secretary of state.

This question and its options can be thought of as four true-false statements:

T  Ⓕ  Before becoming president in 1857, James Buchanan was married and divorced.
T  Ⓕ  Before becoming president in 1857, James Buchanan was secretary of defense.
T  Ⓕ  Before becoming president in 1857, James Buchanan was prime minister of Canada.

Ⓣ F Before becoming president in 1857, James Buchanan was secretary of state.

Viewing the question in this way can sometimes make it easier to spot the correct answer. The true statement you find in the true-false statements you create usually contains the correct multiple-choice option.

**Discard Foolish Options** Some multiple-choice options are distractors. Whatever the reason for their inclusion, foolish options are almost always good news for students. Exactly what the foolish option says is irrelevant. The important point is that you can eliminate it right away and pick the correct answer from the options that remain. Look at this example:

According to British tradition, the queen of England is not permitted to enter

a. West London.
b. the House of Commons.
c. the Soviet Union.
d. the Indianapolis 500.

Option (d) is so silly that you can immediately cross it out. (The correct option is [b].)

**Choose the Middle Number from a Range of Numbers** Questions that use numbers as choices can be easily answered if you've memorized the correct number. But if you haven't really mastered your material or if you have a tough time with numbers in general, then this kind of question can be a nightmare.

If you have no other information to go on, you can increase your chances of guessing correctly by eliminating the highest and lowest numbers. Test writers usually include at least one number lower than the correct answer and one number higher. Using this "rule," you can eliminate half the options in a four-option question. For instance:

A water polo team has _____ players.

a. three
b. ten
c. seven
d. five

Even if you know nothing about water polo, you can use the midrange rule to eliminate two options and improve your odds from one out of four to one out of two. (The correct option in this case is [c].)

## Matching Questions

Answering matching questions effectively is mainly a matter of staying organized and saving time. You have a lot of items to read over, usually in a limited amount of time. A few strategies can increase your efficiency and reduce your confusion.

**Mark Off Matches to Avoid Redundancy**   This idea is so simple that it's often overlooked: Each time you match two items in a matching test, cross them off or mark them with a circle or an *X*. That way, when you move on to the next match, you'll have fewer items to read, and you won't be confused about which items you've chosen and which ones you haven't yet used.

**Match Shorter Items to Longer Ones**   In most matching tests, the items in one column are longer than the items in the other. For example, a typical matching test might contain a column of terms and a column of definitions. In cases like these, you can save yourself some time if you set out in search of matches for the longer items instead of the reverse. In other words, the column you keep reading and rereading contains the shorter items. That way you need to read each long item only once. It's a case of the dog wagging the tail instead of the other way around.

## Sentence-Completion Questions

Because with a sentence-completion question the answer isn't there for you to choose, there are no real tricks to help you pick out the correct answer. But there are methods that enable you to clearly define the existing context of the question. When you do this, you zero in on the answer that will fill in the blank.

**Clarify Ambiguity with a Specific Question**   Sometimes a question seems to have two or more reasonable answers. In these cases, you may need to clarify the kind of answer the question is seeking. The best strategy for coping with ambiguous questions is to raise your hand and ask a well-formulated, unambiguous question of your own to clear up the confusion. Consider this item:

> In 1901, at the age of forty-two, Republican Theodore Roosevelt became the country's _____ president.

In this example, both "youngest" and "twenty-sixth" would be reasonable answers, but it's unlikely the instructor would be looking for both. If you raised your hand and said, "I don't understand this question," you would probably get a response like "Do your best." But a well-thought-out, more specific question would probably be rewarded with a more helpful response. For example, if you asked, "Are you looking for a number?" the instructor's response would enable you to decide which of your two answers is expected.

**Disregard the Length of the Blank**    Sometimes the length of the empty line equals the length of the answer expected. But in general there's no connection between the two. Pay attention to the words that are present, rather than to those that are missing, to come up with your answer for a sentence-completion question. Don't let the blank line distract you.

**Treat Some Sentences as Two Separate Questions**    Even students who aren't influenced by the size of a single blank when answering a sentence-completion question may become flustered by one that has two blanks. If the blanks are side by side, then the question may be calling for a person's name or a place name. Paying attention to the question's context should help to confirm whether this is the case. But if the blanks in a sentence-completion question are widely separated instead of side by side, then a different strategy is called for.

The best way to treat two widely separated blanks in a sentence-completion question is as though each occurred in a separate sentence. There may or may not be a direct relationship between the missing words, so make sure that each filled-in word makes sense in its own part of the statement. Here's an example:

> Although corn is second only to _____ as the most widely grown crop in the world, no one in Europe had even heard about corn until _____ returned from the New World.

In the first portion of the sentence, the word *corn* indicates you're dealing with a grain. If you had read your textbook carefully (or if you hadn't but used your common sense), you'd know the answer is wheat. The second blank demands a person's name: Columbus.

## SUMMARY

| | |
|---|---|
| **What are the distinguishing features and pitfalls of the various kinds of objective questions?** | True-false, multiple-choice, matching, and sentence-completion questions are all related, but each has its peculiarities. A true-false statement must be 100 percent true before you can mark it as true; a single word |

can make the difference. A multiple-choice question normally asks you to complete a stem with one of four or five options. Because your choices are separated from the stem, obtaining the context can be difficult. In addition, varying directions and a differing format can complicate a multiple-choice question. A matching question operates like an expanded version of a multiple-choice question: You pair up the proper items from a column of stems and a column of options. But if you mismatch a set, you can create a chain reaction of errors. A sentence-completion question asks you to use the context of an incomplete statement to determine the word or words that are missing. The role of context is crucial because you must recall the correct answer; it isn't written out for you to choose.

**What system helps you study more efficiently for objective tests?**

The most efficient way of studying for an objective test is with the Questions-in-the-Margin System. This system not only helps you learn your material to the point of recall but also enables you to gear up for answering test questions by practicing with questions of your own.

**How can you become a study "switch hitter"?**

After you've been studying your material using the Questions-in-the-Margin System, you can increase your flexibility by switch hitting—that is, reversing the process by covering your questions and using your notes to see if you can remember the questions.

**What are the steps in moving through a test systematically?**

First read the directions. Then read each question carefully and completely. Mark only the answers you're certain about at first. Then return to those questions that stumped you. If you still draw a blank, make an intelligent guess.

**Why is it so important to read objective questions carefully?**

Reading questions thoroughly enables you to note all of a question's details, particularly any qualifiers and negatives, which modify or reverse the meaning of a statement or option. Complete reading also allows you to use grammatical clues and contextual clues to help pinpoint your answer and pick the best response instead of just a good one.

**Why should you mark only the "sure things" to start?**

Marking only the answers you are certain about at first avoids the problem of not being able to distinguish later on between your certain and uncertain answers.

**Should you guess on objective questions?**

Except in cases where you are penalized for guessing, it usually makes sense to guess if you can't answer a question after two tries.

**What strategies can you use with true-false questions?**

Become aware of the types of statements that are likely to be true and those that are apt to be false. In general a true-false test contains more true statements than false ones. If you're pressed for time and have to choose, you're safer picking true than false. But view longer true-false statements with suspicion: More words in the statement mean more chances that it is false.

**What strategies help you answer multiple-choice questions?**

If you have to guess, pick "all the above." If you know the material but have difficulties with the multiple-choice format, try converting the question into a series of true-false statements, which you'll probably find easier to handle. Also, eliminate foolish options right away, and choose one of the middle numbers in a range of numbers if you have to guess.

**What can you do to better your chances on a matching question?**

If you carefully mark each item after you've used it, you won't waste time rereading answers that you have already chosen. And if you look for matches for the column that has longer items, you'll save some time because you'll need to read each long item only once.

**What strategies can you use for answering sentence-completion questions?**

The best strategies are to clarify an ambiguous question by asking more specific clarifying questions of your own; to disregard the length of a question's blank, which may not indicate the length or size of the answer; and to treat a two-blank question as two questions instead of one.

## HAVE YOU MISSED SOMETHING?

*Sentence completion.*   Complete the following sentences with one of the three words listed below each sentence.

1. Negative and absolute words should be _____ .
   avoided    circled    defined

2. In matching questions, the fewer the remaining choices, the better are your chances of being _____ .
   incorrect    correct    alert

*Matching.*   In each blank space in the left column, write the letter preceding the phrase in the right column that matches the left item best.

_____ **1.** Negative

a. Statement that starts off a multiple-choice question

_____ **2.** Guessing

b. One of the choices that make up a multiple-choice question

_____ **3.** Context

c. Mastering possible test material from both sides

_____ **4.** Stem

d. Almost always better than leaving a question blank

_____ **5.** "Sure thing"

e. Should be marked on first pass through the test

_____ **6.** "Switch hitting"

f. Best choice when stumped by a true-false question

_____ **7.** True

g. Usually reverses meaning of a true-false statement

_____ **8.** Option

h. Provided when you read the entire question

*True-false.*  Write *T* beside the *true* statements and *F* beside the *false* statements.

_____  **1.** For a statement to be marked true, it must be entirely true.

_____  **2.** Some multiple-choice questions ask you to pick more than one answer.

_____  **3.** The stem of a multiple-choice question is always an incomplete statement.

_____  **4.** True-false tests generally contain more true statements than false ones.

_____  **5.** Qualifiers are found only in multiple-choice questions.

_____  **6.** Each word added to a true-false statement increases its chance of being false.

_____  **7.** The length of the blank dictates the size of the answer in a sentence-completion question.

*Multiple choice.*  Choose the word or phrase that completes the following sentence most accurately, and circle the letter that precedes it.

**1.** A multiple-choice question can be viewed as a series of
   a. stems.
   b. qualifiers.
   c. true-false statements.
   d. decoys or distractors.

**2.** One way to think of a matching question is as
   a. a multiple-choice question without the choice.
   b. a true-false question in two dimensions.
   c. a multiple multiple-choice question.
   d. none of the above.

**3.** Reading the entire question should help you
   a. detect grammatical clues.
   b. take advantage of context.
   c. select the best response.
   d. do all the above.

**4.** If at first a question has you stumped, you should
   a. move on to another question.
   b. ask a clarifying question.
   c. pick a temporary answer.
   d. cross out any negatives or qualifiers.

5. The greatest threat of negatives is that they can be easily
   a. replaced.
   b. overlooked.
   c. misunderstood.
   d. reversed.

6. A sentence-completion question with two widely separated blanks should be treated as
   a. a true-false question.
   b. two questions.
   c. a decoy or distractor.
   d. an essay question.

*Short answer.*   Supply a brief answer for each of the following items.

1. Compare and contrast the four basic types of objective questions.
2. What are some potential pitfalls of multiple-choice questions?
3. Explain the Goldilocks Technique.
4. What is the "chain reaction" associated with matching tests?
5. What is the purpose of the true-false technique?

## VOCABULARY BUILDING

DIRECTIONS: Make a light check mark (√) alongside one of the three words (choices) that most nearly expresses the meaning of the italicized word in the phrases that are in the left-hand column. (Answers are given on p. 438.)

|     |                             | 1            | 2           | 3              |
|-----|-----------------------------|--------------|-------------|----------------|
| 1.  | *ambiguous* questions       | unclear      | conclusive  | ambitious      |
| 2.  | answering *bona fide* questions | artificial | bogus     | genuine        |
| 3.  | chances decrease *geometrically* | in additions | in multiples | in abstractions |
| 4.  | what option is *irrelevant* | substantial  | unfitting   | related        |
| 5.  | to avoid *redundancy*       | duplication  | reflection  | indebtedness   |
| 6.  | tax system is *capricious*  | unchangeable | impulsive   | resolute       |
| 7.  | a *tortuous* path           | suffering    | straight    | winding        |
| 8.  | charges *vociferously* denied | loudly     | steadily    | innocently     |
| 9.  | much more *turbulent*       | placid       | stormy      | erratic        |
| 10. | nomination is *vilified*    | maligned     | revived     | reinstated     |
| 11. | *surreptitiously* planning  | candidly     | secretly    | strongly       |
| 12. | *lackluster* data           | drab         | brilliant   | exciting       |

| | **1** | **2** | **3** |
|---|---|---|---|
| 13. it still takes *chutzpah* | planning | nerve | courage |
| 14. people *revile* him | commend | reinstate | denounce |
| 15. a new *humility* | vanity | conceit | modesty |
| 16. presided over its *demise* | collapse | decline | demerits |
| 17. no *retinue* | revenue | receipts | staff |
| 18. a *pariah* state | emerging | strong | outcast |
| 19. the talk is *reminiscent* | similar | recent | oblivious |
| 20. provide a *forum* | foundation | policy | platform |
| 21. among political *pundits* | experts | insiders | elected |
| 22. charges of *bigotry* | tolerance | bias | faithfulness |
| 23. criticism *alienated* supporters | separated | reconciled | encouraged |
| 24. wonderful in its *candor* | diplomacy | artfulness | honesty |
| 25. the basis of *elite* status | choice | improving | aspiring |

# 16

# Tackling Essay Tests

*Omit needless words. Vigorous writing is concise.*

—William Strunk, Jr., *Professor of English; co-author of* The Elements of Style

For many students, the thought of taking an essay test, of actually writing words "from scratch" instead of marking T or F or circling an option, is a terrifying prospect. Yet what these students don't realize is that writing an essay puts them in control; they are not compelled to choose from among answers someone else has devised. With a solid strategy, any student can take the dread out of the essay test and put his or her knowledge into it. To help take the sting out of essay tests, this chapter provides advice on

- Moving through the test systematically
- Learning the basics of writing an essay exam
- Writing effectively under time constraints
- Supporting your points

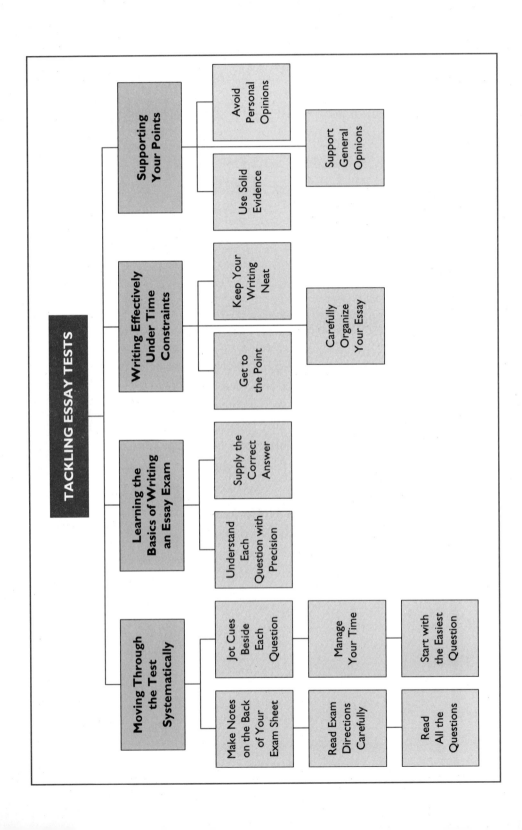

# TACKLING ESSAY TESTS

## Moving Through the Test Systematically

- Make Notes on the Back of Your Exam Sheet
  - Read Exam Directions Carefully
    - Read All the Questions
- Jot Cues Beside Each Question
  - Manage Your Time
    - Start with the Easiest Question

## Learning the Basics of Writing an Essay Exam

- Understand Each Question with Precision
- Supply the Correct Answer

## Writing Effectively Under Time Constraints

- Get to the Point
  - Carefully Organize Your Essay
- Keep Your Writing Neat

## Supporting Your Points

- Use Solid Evidence
  - Support General Opinions
- Avoid Personal Opinions

Taking an essay test requires writing anywhere from a few paragraphs to several pages on each question. Unlike objective questions, which ask you simply to recognize correct information, essay tests require you to recall ideas and facts accurately and then to organize them into thoughtful, forceful responses to the questions. You do so by moving through the test calmly and systematically, by learning the basics of writing an essay exam, by writing effectively under time constraints, and by adequately supporting your points.

## MOVING THROUGH THE TEST SYSTEMATICALLY

When an essay test is handed out, some students have difficulty resisting the temptation to jump right in and start writing. Confident students are often anxious to "get down to business" and show what they know; apprehensive test takers want to get the whole thing over with as quickly as possible. At first glance, these behaviors seem reasonable because time is limited. But if you take a few moments to plan a systematic response to the test, you'll be a lot more efficient as a result. A little preparation saves you a lot more time than it uses.

### Make Notes on the Back of Your Exam Sheet

As you walk into the exam room, your brain may be buzzing with information you want to include in your essays. Before you begin reading the test, unburden your mind by quickly jotting down on the back of the exam sheet the ideas, facts, and details you think you may forget. Almost like a summary of your summary sheets, these jottings act as cues for the Silver Dollar ideas you gleaned from your lectures and readings (see Chapter 5). Furthermore, the action of writing down these notes involves you in the exam immediately. But remember: You are graded for what you write on the *front* of the exam, so don't spend more than a minute or so jotting down reminders on the *back*.

### Read Exam Directions Carefully

Exam directions often contain specific instructions for answering the questions. They may establish the length of your answers (one paragraph, three hundred words, five pages), the approach you should take (explain, compare, contrast), the number of questions you should answer (say, four of the six presented), or time requirements (say, spend no more than fifteen minutes per question). If you miss such instructions, you will not only do a lot of needless writing and waste a great deal of time, but you may also invite criticism for carelessness.

## Read All the Questions

Before you write anything, read all the questions. If you have a choice among questions, select those for which you are best prepared. If you have to answer every question, you'll know in advance which ones will require the most attention.

## Jot Cues Beside Each Question

As you read through each question, underline or circle important words that provide clues for answering that question. Also, keep track of any key words or phrases that come to mind by jotting them in the margin. Later, when you begin writing, use these jottings and those on the back of the exam sheet to help organize your answer.

## Manage Your Time

Figure out roughly how much time you can spend on each essay to complete the test. Stick as close to your time plan as you can, but don't become overly anxious or rigid about doing so.

*If time is running out,* outline the key points you were trying to make in any unfinished essays. Instructors sometimes award partial credit when you can demonstrate that you know the material.

*If you finish early,* use the surplus time to your advantage by going over your exam, double-checking your spelling and grammar, and, if necessary, inserting words, phrases, and examples that may make your essays clearer.

## Start with the Easiest Question

Nothing inspires confidence and clear thinking more than getting off to a flying start with one question well answered. If the first question has you stumped, don't throw off your morale and your time plan. Just pick an easier question, number your answer correctly, and begin writing.

## LEARNING THE BASICS OF WRITING AN ESSAY EXAM

To write an effective essay, you need to be able to understand each question with precision and to answer that question correctly.

### Understand Each Question with Precision

A precise question requires a precise answer. Read each question carefully so you understand exactly what the question is asking. A good essay question is never vague or ambiguous. As you can see from Figure 16.1, words such as *analyze, interpret,* and *describe* have specific definitions. Therefore, if you have even the slightest uncertainty about what's being asked, don't hesitate to check with the instructor for clarification.

### Supply the Correct Answer

Although they may require some specialized skills, essays are basically no different from any other type of question. To answer any exam question, you must have mastered your material. That means attending all lectures, reading all assignments, taking thoughtful notes, and then reviewing and reciting what you've written down until you know your information cold. Students who think they can "snow" their instructors with a long but fundamentally flawed essay are sadly mistaken. If your essay is missing the correct answer, this will be obvious to even the most inexperienced teacher.

A correct answer is often a correctly phrased answer. The tone you use or the approach you take in answering the essay can have a strong influence on the grade you receive. Most instructors have favorite approaches and ways of looking at questions and are naturally, if not unconsciously, disposed to favor essays that correspond to their ways of thinking. Theoretically you shouldn't have to worry about this—the accuracy and thoroughness of your answer should be sufficient—but practically, an essay that incorporates some of the instructor's "pet ideas" is more likely to be viewed in a better light. According to respected educator Hugo Hartig, author of *The Idea of Composition.*

| Key Word | Explanation |
|---|---|
| Apply a principle | Show how a principle works, through an example. |
| Comment | Discuss briefly. |
| Compare | Emphasize similarities, but also present differences. |
| Contrast | Give differences only. |
| Criticize | Give your judgment of good points and limitations, with evidence. |
| Define | Give meanings but no details. |
| Demonstrate | Show or prove an opinion, evaluation, or judgment. |
| Describe | State the particulars in detail. |
| Diagram | Show a drawing with labels. |
| Differentiate | Show how two things are different. |
| Discuss | Give reasons pro and con, with details. |
| Distinguish | Show main differences between two things. |
| Enumerate | List the points. |
| Evaluate | Discuss advantages and disadvantages with your opinion. |
| Explain | Give reasons for happenings or situations. |
| Give cause and effect | Describe the steps that lead to an event or a situation. |
| Give an example | Give a concrete example from the textbook or from your experience. |
| Identify | List and describe. |
| Illustrate | Give an example. |
| Interpret | State the meaning in simpler terms, using your judgment. |
| Justify | Prove or give reasons. |
| List | List without details. |
| Outline | Make a short summary with headings and subheadings. |
| Prove | Give evidence and reasons. |
| Relate | Show how things interconnect. |
| Review | Show main points or events in summary form. |
| Show | List your evidence in order of time, importance, logic. |
| Solve | Come up with a solution based on given facts or your knowledge. |
| State | List main points briefly without details. |
| Summarize | Organize and bring together the main points only. |
| Support | Back up a statement with facts and proof. |
| Trace | Give main points from beginning to end of an event. |

**FIGURE 16.1  Key Words in Essay Questions**
This alphabetical list contains key words encountered in the directions for essay questions, along with brief explanations of what each word means.

An alert student can easily identify these "pet ideas" and work them out carefully in his [or her] own words. The student who does this is prepared not only to see through the instructor's questions quite readily, but he [or she] also knows exactly how to answer them, using the teacher's own methods of problem solving! Perhaps this is the very essence of grade-getting in any course that depends heavily on essay exams.[1]

## WRITING EFFECTIVELY UNDER TIME CONSTRAINTS

As in all tests, time plays a key role in essay exams. Well-supported essays will earn you superior scores. But at the very least, use the available time to make certain your essay gets to the point, is carefully organized, and is neat.

## Get to the Point

When you are writing an essay, there's no time for obscuring facts in paragraphs filled with lavish adjectives or rambling discussions. Essay exams are written in a hurry and are often read in a hurry. You have to be concise!

**Leave Off the Introduction**   A good way to guarantee that your essay will get to the point is to skip writing an introduction. Don't even start off with a high-sounding sentence such as "This is indeed a crucial question that demands a swift solution; therefore. . . ." Such a general approach scatters your ideas, thereby damaging the unity of your answer. An unfocused essay may contain all the right ideas, but if those ideas are scattered, your instructor may conclude that you don't know what you are talking about.

**Put Your Answer at the Beginning**   Begin with a strong opening sentence that both repeats the question and provides the answer. The example in Figure 16.2 shows how this principle works. The opening part of the first sentence restates but rearranges the question, while the second part supplies the answer. Such an approach keeps you honest and discourages partial or unfocused answers.

---

[1]Hugo Hartig, *The Idea of Composition* (Oshkosh, Wis: Academia, 1974), p. 32.

---

*Question:*  What does distributed practice involve?

*Answer:*  Distributed practice involves dividing an assignment into several study sessions instead of one continuous session.

---

**FIGURE 16.2   A Direct Answer**

In Figure 16.3, the student has answered the question directly in the first sentence by naming three theories of forgetting. The rest of the essay follows a logical, predictable pattern in which she explains each theory in brief and then draws a conclusion about all of them.

Although the essay in Figure 16.4 is longer than the ones in Figures 16.2 and 16.3, its basic format is no different from that of the previous examples. In the opening sentence the student answers the question directly by comparing reciting and rereading and then by contrasting the two methods. The next sentence states three reasons reciting is superior to rereading, and the paragraphs that follow develop those points.

In longer essays you don't have to include your answer in the first sentence. But you should make sure it is contained in the opening paragraph. Once your answer has been stated at the beginning, you can devote the rest

---

*Question:*  Identify three of the theories psychologists have suggested to explain forgetting.

*Answer:*  Three of the theories that psychologists have suggested to explain how forgetting occurs include fading theory, retrieval theory, and reactive interference theory. Fading theory defines memories as paths or traces in the brain. According to the theory, if these paths aren't used (recalled) regularly, they fade until they eventually disappear (are forgotten). Retrieval theory claims that memories never really disappear; they simply get lost or misfiled, like important information buried under piles of paper on a messy desk. Reactive interference theory says that your attitude or emotions can interfere with your memory. If you are bored with or bothered by information, there's a greater chance that you will forget it. In certain cases, evidence seems to support all these theories of forgetting. But they remain only theories. None of them can be proved conclusively.

---

**FIGURE 16.3   A Paragraph-Length Essay**

*Question:*  Compare and contrast reciting and rereading as methods of study.

*Answer:*  Although reciting and rereading are both common methods of study, reciting is superior to rereading as a way of mastering your material. Unlike rereading, reciting (1) gets you involved, (2) supplies motivation, and (3) provides you with feedback on your progress.

1.  Reciting gets you involved by compelling you to extract the meaning out of each paragraph you read. In contrast, it's possible to reread an assignment without understanding it.

2.  Reciting supplies motivation because it encourages you to understand what you've read. If you had trouble grasping the meaning of one paragraph, you may be determined to have an easier time with the next one. If you understood a paragraph, you'll be motivated to continue your progress. But if you simply reread your assignment, you'll have no such incentive to succeed.

3.  Because you know right away whether you've understood each paragraph, reciting provides you with immediate feedback on your progress. Potential trouble spots in your reading are brought to your attention right away. With rereading, the first real feedback you get is delayed until the test or quiz.

**FIGURE 16.4  A Longer Essay Answer**

of your essay to expanding on that answer. The ideas, facts, and details that follow all support your opening sentence or paragraph. As a result, your answer is both pertinent and unified.

Don't worry that by stating your answer so early in the essay that you are "jumping the gun." There's no advantage to keeping a grader in suspense, not even for a few sentences. If your answer is not included in the first few lines, your point may never become clear. Even worse, if time runs out before you have finished your answer, that key concept you were carefully saving could go unused.

**Avoid Wordy, Rambling Writing**  Essays that are overstuffed with big words, unnecessary adjectives, and rambling philosophical discussions will leave the reader both confused and suspicious. Complex ideas don't have to be expressed in a complicated way. According to Hartig, "Quite difficult and subtle ideas can be expressed in straightforward and simple language."[2] You don't have to use large words and flowery language to prove that you

---

[2]Ibid.

are knowledgeable. In fact, as Hartig points out, a flashy essay may even put your knowledge in question, instead of confirming it: "Any teacher who has read hundreds or thousands of papers becomes very sensitive to phoniness in student writing, because he [or she] sees so much of it."[3] Don't write answers that are deliberately difficult or disingenuous. You won't fool anybody. Strive for clarity, sincerity, and simplicity.

## Carefully Organize Your Essay

Organization comes easier when you leave off an introduction, put your answer at the beginning, and aim for simplicity and sincerity in your sentences. These elements provide a solid foundation for your essay's structure. Even so, you may want to take some extra steps to guarantee that the logic of your essay is easy to follow.

**Use a Recognizable Pattern**   Instructors don't have time to treat each essay as a puzzle in need of a solution. Take the guesswork out of your essay. Make your answer clear and obvious by following a familiar organizational pattern.

The most straightforward way of organizing your essay is by using the decreasing-importance pattern (discussed in Chapter 8). Sometimes known as the inverted pyramid, this pattern starts off with the broadest and most important information and then gradually gets narrower in scope. The advantage of this pattern is that it states the most important information at the outset so the reader can pick it up right away. It also eliminates the risk that time will run out before you've had a chance to fit in your answer.

Of course, not all essay questions are tailor-made for the decreasing-importance pattern. Key terms in the question can give you a clue as to what sort of pattern is needed. If, for example, you are asked to summarize a particular event, you'll probably want to follow the chronological pattern, progressing steadily in your description from past to present. Start off in one direction and keep moving that way until you reach the end of the essay. The same advice applies to essays that call for the spatial or the process pattern. In a descriptive essay, move systematically from one end of what you're describing to the other. Follow a process in an unbroken path from its start to its finish. And if the question asks you to compare or contrast, make sure you shift back predictably between the things you're comparing or contrasting. Whether you use the decreasing-importance pattern or some other structure, it's crucial that you move through your essay systematically and predictably.

---

[3]Ibid.

**Use Transitions** The transitions that help make textbooks and lectures easier to follow can play a similar role in your essays, letting the reader know just where you're headed. When transitions lead from the idea to the next, the reader finds the essay clear, logical, and refreshing. A number of transitional words are listed in Figure 16.5.

**End with a Summary** Summarize your essay in a final sentence or two. Finishing off your essay with a summarizing conclusion ties your points

---

The experienced essay uses "trail markers," transitional words that provide directional clues for the reader and show the relationship between sentences in a paragraph. For example, the word *furthermore* says, "Wait! I have still more to say on the subject." So the reader holds the previously read sentences in mind while reading the next few sentences. The following list suggests other words and expressions that you might find valuable.

| Transitional Words and Expressions | Intention or Relationship |
|---|---|
| For example, in other words, that is | Amplification |
| Accordingly, because, consequently, for this reason, hence, thus, therefore, if...then | Cause and effect |
| Accepting the data, granted that, of course | Concession |
| In another sense, but, conversely, despite, however, nevertheless, on the contrary, on the other hand, though, yet | Contrast or change |
| Similarly, moreover, also, too, in addition, likewise, next in importance | No change |
| Add to this, besides, in addition to this, even more, to repeat, above all, indeed, more important | Emphasis |
| At the same time, likewise, similarly | Equal value |
| Also, besides, furthermore, in addition, moreover, too | Increasing quantity |
| First, finally, last, next, second, then | Order |
| For these reasons, in brief, in conclusion, to sum up | Summary |
| Then, since then, after this, thereafter, at last, at length, from now on, afterwards, before, formerly, later, meanwhile, now, presently, previously, subsequently, ultimately, since | Time |

**FIGURE 16.5 Transitional Words and Expressions**

together and reminds the grader of the original answer that you've devoted the rest of your essay to supporting.

These suggestions for organizing your essay become even more compelling when you learn how essays are actually graded. Figure 16.6 takes a brief look behind the scenes at an essay exam grading session.

## Keep Your Writing Neat

In a carefully controlled experiment, a group of teachers was asked to grade a stack of examination papers solely on the basis of content. Unbeknownst to these instructors, several of the papers they were asked to grade were actually word-for-word duplicates, with one paper written in a good handwriting and the other in a poor one. In spite of instructions, on the average the teachers gave the neater papers the higher grades—by a full letter grade. Most instructors are unwilling to spend extra time interpreting sloppy papers.

---

**Behind the Scenes at an Essay Exam**

What happens after you finish your last essay, heave a sigh of relief, and hand in your exam? Although grading procedures may vary from school to school, here is how more than two hundred examination booklets in a popular introductory history course are graded at one college.

The day of the exam, each grader in the history department has time to scan, but not to grade, the answer booklets. Then at a meeting the next day, each grader reads aloud what he or she thinks is the one best answer for each question. A model answer for each question is then agreed on by the staff. The essential points in the model answers are noted by all the graders for use as common criteria in grading the responses.

Unfortunately, simply listing all the essential points in your essay won't automatically earn you a superior score. During the reading of the answers, one grader remarks, "Yes, this student mentioned points five and six...but I think he didn't realize what he was doing. He just happened to use the right words as he was explaining point four."

These comments reinforce the importance of crystal-clear organization in your essay. You may also want to underline the main point of the essay so it's obvious and mark off your subpoints with dark numbers. Don't forget to include transitional words to show how you got from one idea to the next. Make sure that no one thinks you just stumbled onto the correct answer.

---

**FIGURE 16.6 The Essay Grading Process**

If your paper is messy, your meaning may be lost, and your grade could suffer. Take these few precautions to ensure that your paper is neat.

**Use Ink**   Most instructors ask specifically that you write your essays in pen, not pencil, so that they are bold and clear, not faint and smeary.

**Write Legibly**   If your penmanship is less than it should be, then you should probably start using the modified printing style, explained in Chapter 10. The modified printing style is easy to learn and should enable you to write your essays quickly but neatly. Both qualities are crucial in an essay exam.

**Write on Only One Side of Each Sheet**   When you write on both sides of the paper, the writing usually shows through, resulting in an essay that looks messy and that in some cases may even be unreadable. Besides, if your essays are written in an exam booklet, writing on only one side of each page can provide you with some last-minute room. Should you need to change or add something, you can write it on the blank page and draw a neat arrow to the spot where you want it inserted on the facing page.

**Leave Plenty of Space**   A little extra space in the margins (especially the left-hand margin) and between your essays provides room for the grader to make comments and for you to add any important idea or fact that occurs to you later. These "late entries" can be blended into your original answer by using an appropriate transitional phrase, such as "An additional idea that pertains to this question is. . . ."

**Guard Against Careless Errors**   Neatness goes beyond the readability of your handwriting and the appearance of your essay on the page. It includes an essay that is free of careless spelling and grammatical errors. As Hartig observes:

> If you misspell common words, and make clumsy errors in sentence structure, or even if you write paragraphs that lack unity and coherence, many of your instructors are going to take it as a sure sign that you are sadly lacking in basic academic ability. Once a teacher thinks this about you, you will not get much credit for your ideas, even if they are brilliant.[4]

---

[4]Ibid.

## SUPPORTING YOUR POINTS

A well-supported essay goes a long way in convincing graders that they are reading the work of a superior student. You can ensure that your essay is well supported by backing your answer with solid evidence, by supporting general opinions, and by avoiding personal opinions.

## Use Solid Evidence

Obviously, whether you correctly answer an essay question is important. But because a well-written essay usually contains the answer in the first sentence (or, in longer essays, the first paragraph), the bulk of your essay should be devoted to the evidence that supports your answer.

If you've mastered your material and included your answer at the start of your essay, then providing support should be relatively easy. Every sentence that follows the first one should provide supporting ideas, facts, and details. Notice how natural this approach is. Your first sentence addresses the question directly, and the sentence that follows outlines the major points that support your answer. Then subsequent sentences—or paragraphs, if your essay is longer—will provide examples, details, and further evidence for your initial answer and its major points. When everything you write pertains to the first sentence, you cannot help but achieve unity; all your sentences will be both pertinent and cohesive.

## Support General Opinions

The evidence you supply should be factual, not opinionated. Even generally accepted opinions should be backed up with facts. According to Hartig:

> An opinion that is not supported by some kind of logical or factual evidence is not worth anything at all, even if it is absolutely correct. For example, if you make the statement: *"Huckleberry Finn* is a masterpiece of American literature," and do not give any good reason to show that the statement is true, you get a zero for the statement.[5]

In the same way, you could expect to be marked off for writing, "John F. Kennedy has been the most popular president since the end of World War II." If, however, you wrote, "Based on an average of Gallup polls conducted during his presidency, John F. Kennedy had an approval rating of 70 percent,

---

[5]Ibid., p. 31.

higher than any other president since the end of World War II," you'd be adequately supporting that opinion.

## Avoid Personal Opinions

The opinions of "experts" have a place in an essay exam, but the same can't be said for your own opinions. All of us have personal opinions, but unless a question specifically asks for yours, leave it out of your essay. The purpose of essay exams, after all, is to see what you've learned and how you can apply it.

## SUMMARY

**What's the best way of tackling an essay test?**

If you move systematically through the test, understand what writing an essay exam requires, work effectively within the time given, and substantiate your answer, you are more likely to tackle an essay test successfully.

**How do you move systematically through an essay test?**

Before you begin writing, jot down any key ideas, facts, and details you think you might forget. Then study the directions carefully, look over all the questions, and develop a rough time schedule for each question. Answer an easy question first to build your confidence and momentum.

**What are the basic skills needed to answer an essay question effectively?**

Most instructors expect your essay to demonstrate that you have understood the wording of the question and, of course, that you can arrive at the correct answer. Also, from a practical standpoint, an essay that incorporates some of the instructor's favorite ideas or approaches is more likely to be viewed in a better light.

**How do you demonstrate that you can write well under time pressure?**

If your essay makes its point quickly and is well organized and neat, you will convince most instructors that you can write well in a limited amount of time. To get to the point, omit any introduction, answer the question at the very start, and don't use any more words than are necessary to make your case. Structure your essay around a recognizable pattern, make sure that pattern is well marked with transitions, and restate your answer at the end. Finally, don't underestimate the importance of neatness. The appearance of your essays can affect your grade.

**How can you ensure that your answer is well supported?**

By answering the question at the beginning, you can devote the rest of your essay to supporting that answer. Back up every point you make with solid evidence. Support general opinions as well. Do not include personal opinions; the purpose of an essay is to show what you've learned, not what you believe.

## HAVE YOU MISSED SOMETHING?

*Sentence completion.* Complete the following sentences with one of the three words listed below each sentence.

1. In essay questions, you are graded on your _____ .
   reasoning    handwriting    decisions

2. Your answer to an essay question must demonstrate that you understand the _____ .
   facts    dates    directions

*Matching.* In each blank space in the left column, write the letter preceding the phrase in the right column that matches the left item best.

_____ **1.** Suspense      a. Often provide specifics on how each question should be answered

_____ **2.** Directions     b. The best approach to writing essay answers

_____ **3.** Simplicity     c. Narrows gradually in an essay written in the decreasing-importance pattern

_____ **4.** Space          d. Unnecessary and undesirable in essay answers

_____ **5.** Scope          e. Can be employed to make your logic more transparent

_____ **6.** Transitions        f. Allows room for late additions as well as for
                                   instructor's comments

*True-false.*   Write *T* beside the *true* statements and *F* beside the *false* statements.

_____ **1.** You should develop a time plan for taking your test and then follow
          it strictly.

_____ **2.** It's a good idea to read all the questions before you begin writing.

_____ **3.** Leftover time should be used for double-checking your answers.

_____ **4.** The appearance of your essay will have no influence on the grade
          you receive.

_____ **5.** Instructors prefer that you write in ink because it makes your
          answers easier to read.

*Multiple choice.*   Choose the word or phrase that completes the following
sentence most accurately, and circle the letter that precedes it.

**1.** Jotting down notes on the back of the test sheet
   a. gets you involved right away.
   b. is usually not permitted in an essay exam.
   c. takes time that could be better spent.
   d. will often gain you partial credit.

**2.** In an essay test, it helps to start off with the question.
   a. most difficult
   b. first
   c. last
   d. easiest

**3.** Key words in an essay question should be
   a. paraphrased.
   b. circled.
   c. discussed.
   d. replaced.

**4.** You'll help prove that you write well under time constraints if your
essay is
   a. concise.
   b. well organized.
   c. neat.
   d. all the above.

**5.** A good way to ensure that your essay gets right to the point is by

    a. leaving off the introduction.
    b. writing telegraphic sentences.
    c. avoiding complicated words.
    d. scattering your ideas.

**6.** In a sharply focused essay, a strong opening sentence

    a. restates the question.
    b. provides the answer.
    c. helps unify the answer.
    d. does all the above.

**7.** Poor handwriting can be improved through the use of

    a. the modified printing style.
    b. every other line of your exam booklet.
    c. a pencil instead of a pen.
    d. all the above.

**8.** Key points in an unfinished essay should be

    a. outlined.
    b. combined.
    c. included.
    d. deleted.

*Short answer.* Supply a brief answer for each of the following items.

  **1.** Why are some students particularly nervous about taking essay exams?
  **2.** What should you do if you are unable to finish an essay answer before time runs out?
  **3.** Explain the role of precision in taking an essay exam.
  **4.** What constitutes a "neat" essay?
  **5.** How should opinions be treated in an essay answer?

## VOCABULARY BUILDING

DIRECTIONS: Make a light check mark (√) alongside one of the three words (choices) that most nearly expresses the meaning of the italicized word in the phrases that are in the left-hand column. (Answers are given on p. 439.)

| | **1** | **2** | **3** |
|---|---|---|---|
| 1. sentences will be *cohesive* | connected | chronological | simple |
| 2. *substantiate* your answer | underscore | support | repeat |
| 3. *apprehensive* test takers | prepared | composed | worried |

|  | | 1 | 2 | 3 |
|---|---|---|---|---|
| 4. | filled with *lavish* adjectives | descriptive | fancy | limiting |
| 5. | deliberately *disingenuous* | clumsy | tricky | skillful |
| 6. | *decapitated* the season | capitalized | cut off | analyzed |
| 7. | may seek *diversity* | variety | homogeneity | familiarity |
| 8. | *spontaneous* get-togethers | instant | planned | forced |
| 9. | a *trove* of anecdotes | treasure | book | primer |
| 10. | an *impromptu* puppet show | unprepared | rehearsed | deliberate |
| 11. | a *cherished* object | bright | cheerful | treasured |
| 12. | *gregarious* teenager | solitary | shy | talkative |
| 13. | a *definitive* agreement | exact | indecisive | legal |
| 14. | Mexico is *floundering* | progressing | emerging | struggling |
| 15. | a college degree is *prestigious* | respected | progressive | regressive |
| 16. | would *dilute* earnings | divide | weaken | disperse |
| 17. | he has a *penchant* | knack | income | investment |
| 18. | there is no *allegation* | denial | judgment | accusation |
| 19. | agencies *contemplate* reduction | ignore | plan | continue |
| 20. | creating *fictitious* credits | false | fractional | future |
| 21. | crackdown is causing *tremors* | retractions | inspections | tremblings |
| 22. | eleven public *entities* | theories | structures | concepts |
| 23. | to be *shackled* | housed | released | restricted |
| 24. | *daunting* responsibilities | frightening | daring | challenging |
| 25. | *doused* expectations | drenched | revived | aroused |

# 17

# Studying Literature

*There are two worlds: the world that we can measure with line and rule, and the world we feel with our hearts and imagination.*

—LEIGH HUNT (1784–1859) English writer

Textbooks aren't literature and literature isn't text—few people would dispute that. So why read *Sons and Lovers* as though it were *Statistics and Logic?* Each of the two types of writing marches to the beat of a different drummer. This chapter deals with

- What to look for in literature
- The EVOKER system for reading imaginative prose

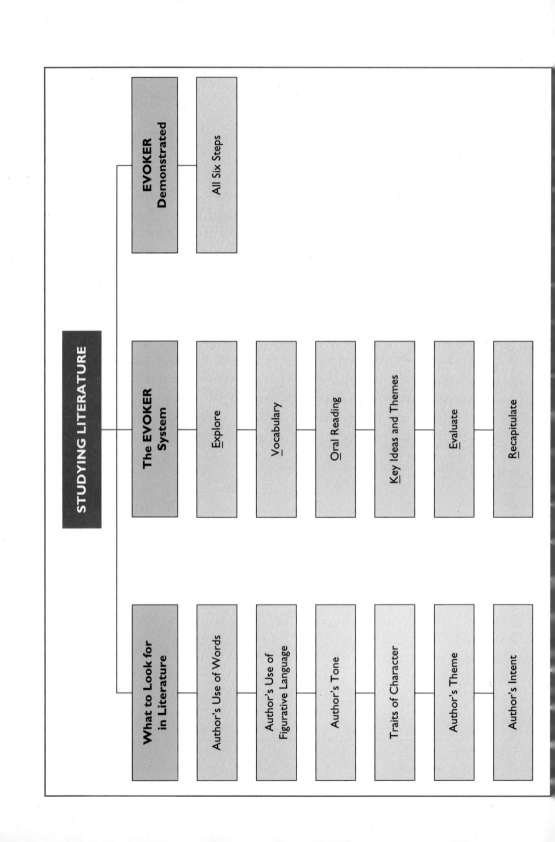

# STUDYING LITERATURE

**What to Look for in Literature**

Author's Use of Words

Author's Use of Figurative Language

Author's Tone

Traits of Character

Author's Theme

Author's Intent

**The EVOKER System**

Explore

Vocabulary

Oral Reading

Key Ideas and Themes

Evaluate

Recapitulate

**EVOKER Demonstrated**

All Six Steps

Reading literature (imaginative prose) is very much like looking at a painting. Neither reader nor viewer will learn much if he or she doesn't know what to look for.

## WHAT TO LOOK FOR IN LITERATURE

As you read literature, notice how the author uses words, figurative language, tone, and characters to present his or her stories, ideas, and themes.

### Author's Use of Words

Observe closely the way an author uses words to make a story interesting. The author may want to achieve a certain effect by choosing and arranging words in a particular way, perhaps to create a vivid picture or image, or to emphasize a point with a simple or complex sentence. For example, your idea of a person could be far different depending on whether the author says the man is *fat* or *stout, remarkable* or *odd, different* or *eccentric* and whether he *walks* or *struts.* Words also help to reveal an author's style. In sum, when you understand *what* an author does with words, and *how* the author does it, your enjoyment of the writing is bound to increase.

### Author's Use of Figurative Language

*Figures of speech* are words used in an imaginative sense to emphasize or clarify statements that otherwise would be difficult to visualize and remember. For example, "The bargain-hungry shoppers charged into the store like a herd of elephants" stirs the imagination. You can visualize the action better than if the writer had said, "The shoppers entered noisily."

### Author's Tone

Sometimes words *say* one thing but *mean* another. To find out what a writer is saying, you must know whether the writer is being serious, satiric, sarcastic, ironic, or playful. In many instances, if you miss the tone, you'll miss the intent. A classic example of a piece of writing that means something quite different from what it says is Jonathan Swift's essay, "A Modest Proposal."

Written in 1729, the "proposal" suggested that the desperate situation of the Irish people could be remedied by promoting a project for butchering and marketing surplus children as delicacies for the table, "very proper for landlords, who, as they have already devoured most of the parents, seem to have the best titles to the children." To take the essay literally, as a hideous and inhuman proposal, is of course to miss the entire point: Swift's savage indignation on behalf of the Irish people, his hatred of injustice and inhumanity. Understanding that the tone is bitterly satiric, we can appreciate this essay as a great humane statement intended to shock readers into awareness of an intolerable condition.

How do you know when to take a selection literally? There is no definite and easy way to tell. But you will acquire sensitivity to attitude, intent, and tone through reading and analyzing. Start with examples identified for you as satirical, ironic, humorous, and so on, and look for words and phrases that provide clues. With practice, you will develop an alert sense for what an author means beyond what he or she says.

## Traits of Character

Authors want their characters to be identified as real people rather than as storybook types or caricatures. Most authors create characters gradually, attributing to them a wide range of thoughts, emotions, and actions. From these materials, you build the characters in your own mind. To distinguish one character from another on the basis of traits such as pride, jealousy, shrewdness, and snobbishness, you should watch for the distinctive words and actions of each character.

## Author's Theme

Most enduring literature presents a theme or series of themes. Through their stories and characters, authors tell you what they believe and how they feel about life, humankind, truth, morality, hypocrisy, tolerance, suffering, death, love—issues of central concern to us all. In works of imaginative literature, you can see and perhaps better understand human motivation and behavior and their consequences.

## Author's Intent

As you read, keep in mind these two questions: "Why did the author write this story?" and "What did he or she try to accomplish?" Considering these questions can lead you to see the author's purpose for writing the story you're reading, which in turn can further your understanding of the story's content, meaning, and implications.

## THE EVOKER SYSTEM

A systematic approach to reading a novel takes some of the guesswork out of reading and lays a firm foundation for your continued development in reading and thinking. The EVOKER system provides you with a step-by-step procedure for approaching a piece of imaginative prose. The name is a mnemonic for Explore, Vocabulary, Oral Reading, Key Ideas and Themes, Evaluate, and Recapitulate. The steps are as follows:

1. Explore:   Read silently and quickly through the entire selection without stopping to reread a portion that you perhaps did not fully understand. By pressing on, you will frequently clarify some obscure points. And by reading the entire selection without stopping, you will gain a feeling for the whole.

2. Vocabulary:   Do not stop to look up unfamiliar words: by continuing to read, you may come across a familiar synonym. Instead, as you read, quickly underline any word that is not entirely clear to you. After you have finished the selection, look up in the dictionary definitions of words whose meanings are still vague. As you discover the meaning of each word, fit it into the context by rereading the entire paragraph in which it appears. By doing so, you will preserve the unity of the paragraph.

3. Oral Reading:   Look over the selection a second time, reading portions aloud using proper intonation (expression). Hearing not only aids comprehension but also communicates to you the stress, rhythm, and power of words and word sequences.

4. Key Ideas and Themes:   During both the silent and the oral reading in the previous two steps, you will have perceived and approximately located various key ideas. Now, in this step, locate these key ideas more precisely and underline them. This procedure will help make the key ideas stand out so you can better see and understand the author's plan of organization. The sum of these key ideas should help you formulate a general analysis of the author's main and subsidiary themes.

5. Evaluate:   Evaluate, in context, the key words, figurative language, and ideas to see how they contribute to the theme or themes. Notice, too, how the key words develop the shades of meaning, the mood, and the

tone of the selection. This detailed analysis extracts the fullest meaning of every important word, phrase, and sentence.

**6.** Recapitulate:　Having completed all these steps, you are now ready, like someone who has just fitted the last piece of a jigsaw puzzle in place, to draw back and look at the whole picture—to read the entire selection or episode slowly and completely, with insight and understanding.

## EVOKER Demonstrated[1]

The following excerpt is from D. H. Lawrence's *Sons and Lovers,* which is often assigned in English courses. Notice how each of the six steps is applied to the two short paragraphs; notice, too, how much information is gained from these fifty-two words.[2] When you are preparing to discuss an assigned novel or short story in class, this is the way to prepare for it.

> Before the younger man knew where he was he was staggering backwards from a blow across the face.
> The whole night went black. He tore off his overcoat and coat, dodging a blow, and flung the garments over Dawes. The latter swore savagely.
> Morel, in his shirtsleeves, was now alert and furious.

Now, to apply the close-reading system—The EVOKER—to the above passage, we take the following steps:

First, we read the passage silently.

Second, we make sure that all words are correctly understood. For instance, we might look up the word *staggering* to understand its full meaning.

Third, in the oral reading of the selection we unmistakably pick up the hissing sound made by the *s*'s in "swore savagely."

Fourth, we look for the author's theme or intention. In this selection the important aspect is the author's intention—to describe, in detail, a fight between two men. Next, we look for the organizational pattern—specifically, in order to find and mark off the steps taken by the author to achieve his purpose. The main steps or divisions are as follows: The author plunges the reader into the action—two men fighting; then the author describes the setting while keeping the fighting active—the time is night; next, he gives a physical description of the men; and, finally, he describes the mental states of both men.

---

[1] Two Systems for Comprehending Literature." Reprinted by permission of The College Reading Association.
[2] Reading Imaginative Prose: The EVOKER System." Reprinted by permission of The College Reading Association.

Fifth, by using the technique of detailed analysis to differentiate among shades of meaning, we find the following:

The first sentence reveals that the younger man received an unexpected blow from the older man. We know that the blow was a hard one because the word *staggered* was used. Here, *staggered* means the movement of legs not only to keep one's balance but also to keep from sinking to the ground because of the physical shock of the blow affecting the senses.

In the second sentence the author tells much with only a few words. The word *black* reveals to us not only that it is night but also that the blow to the younger man was almost a knockout.

The third sentence supplies information that helps the reader fill in the physical details more completely; at the same time, the words *overcoat* and *coat* indicate that it is quite cold.

Then, with the phrase *dodging a blow,* the author realistically keeps the fighting going while telling about the coats. In the same sentence, the words *flung the garments over Dawes* indicate that the fight is a serious one—to the finish. (In a gentlemen's fight the men would have carefully placed their coats aside with the intention of putting them on after they had gone through the motions of saving "honor.")

In the fourth sentence the word *savagely* connotes a beastlike frame of mind. We perhaps get a picture of a man who is almost fully possessed by the basic instinct of "kill or be killed." In addition to supplying the reader with a sense of Dawes's mental state, the word *savagely* conjures up the physical picture of a brutelike hulk of a man.

In the fifth sentence the author completes the picture of how Morel looks after discarding his coats but more important are the words *alert* and *furious.* The word *furious* implies a man who is geared up for a death struggle. And the word *alert* has, in this case, both a mental and physical dimension. Morel is alert physically, ready to act or react—not, however, with blind and savage instinct but under the dictates of the mind. The mind still has control over the body.

The sixth, and last, step of the EVOKER system is the recapitulation. Having used the detailed analysis to extract the fullest meaning from every word, phrase, and sentence, and now that each individual episode has been seen in the reader's mind and has contributed its bit, the reader is ready to read the entire story slowly and completely, with insight and understanding.

The EVOKER system will help you look for specific details in literature and to be fully aware of what you find. Once awareness becomes habitual, you will realize that a printed page yields up its meaning not to the eyes but, rather, to the mind, which reads and rereads, puzzles and ponders, quizzes and questions, recalls and recites, reflects and recapitulates.

## SUMMARY

**How does the author's use of words affect the meaning of his or her writing?**

Authors choose their words carefully to ensure that they convey exact shades of meaning and emphasis. The words *skinny* and *svelte*, for example, may be considered synonyms, but their effect on the reader can be entirely different. Your job as reader is to determine the author's purpose behind his or her word choice.

**What is the big question you should ask when you read literature?**

A good basis for reading any work of literature is the question "Why did the author write this story?" When you begin to understand the author's primary intent, then you will gradually see the reasons for his or her choice of words, characters, and plot.

**Why was the EVOKER system devised?**

The EVOKER system was designed to give you a procedure for comprehending and evaluating a piece of literature.

**In reading literature, isn't it best to look up new words as you encounter them?**

No. It is vital that you preserve the unity of each paragraph as you read literature. Unfamiliar words are often defined through context as you read on. If not, you can look them up in the dictionary after your first, uninterrupted reading.

**What is the purpose of reading a passage aloud?**

Oral reading adds another dimension to your understanding of literature. There is no better way to appreciate the rhythm, emphasis, and sonority of literature than by reading it aloud.

**What is the value of locating a passage's key ideas?**

Understanding the overall intent of an author's work is like doing a jigsaw puzzle. In this case, the key ideas are the individual pieces. As is not the case with a standard puzzle, however, you have to locate the pieces before you can use them. Once you find the key ideas, you can fit them together into the big picture—the author's intent or theme.

# HAVE YOU MISSED SOMETHING?

*Sentence completion.* Complete the following sentences with one of the three words or phrases listed below each sentence.

1. Authors want their characters identified as _____ .
   storybook types     real people     extreme personalities

2. The tone of a selection is developed by _____ .
   key words     actions of characters     physical setting

3. The purpose of the EVOKER system is to foster _____ .
   enjoyment     awareness     experimentation

*Matching.* In each blank space in the left column, write the letter preceding the phrase in the right column that matches the left item best.

| | |
|---|---|
| _____ **1.** Explore | a. Use intonation to help comprehension |
| _____ **2.** Vocabulary | b. Draw back and look at the whole picture |
| _____ **3.** Oral reading | c. Do it quickly and without stopping |
| _____ **4.** Key ideas | d. Use content as a powerful tool |
| _____ **5.** Evaluate | e. Underline any that you have ascertained |
| _____ **6.** Recapitulate | f. Mark it now but look it up later |

*True-false.* Write *T* beside the *true* statements and *F* beside the *false* statements.

_____ **1.** The meaning of a printed page is immediately apparent.

_____ **2.** In literature, what words say what they mean.

_____ **3.** Figures of speech can help clarify a hard-to-remember statement.

_____ **4.** You can't always be sure whether to take a passage literally.

_____ **5.** The EVOKER name is a mnemonic device.

*Multiple choice.* Choose the phrase that completes each of the following sentences most accurately, and circle the letter that precedes it.

1. Reading literature is like examining a
   a. painting.
   b. patient.
   c. prism.
   d. plant.

**2.** An author's choice of words helps to reveal his or her

    a. style.
    b. contemporaries.
    c. intelligence.
    d. research.

**3.** Figures of speech can make a statement easier to

    a. visualize.
    b. understand.
    c. remember.
    d. do all the above.

**4.** Missing a passage's tone can mean missing

    a. its rhythm.
    b. its intent.
    c. its punctuation.
    d. none of the above.

**5.** Most enduring literature has at least one

    a. satirical idea.
    b. theme.
    c. conclusion.
    d. dialogue.

**6.** During your first reading of a selection, unknown words should be

    a. underlined.
    b. looked up in a dictionary.
    c. skipped over.
    d. pronounced out loud.

**7.** Literature yields its deeper meaning to the

    a. eyes.
    b. inquisitive mind.
    c. author alone.
    d. patient.

*Short answer.*   Supply a brief answer for each of the following items.

    **1.** How do you decide whether a writing selection should be taken literally?
    **2.** Why is a theme so important in an author's work?
    **3.** What is the value of EVOKER's Recapitulate step?
    **4.** Distinguish between an author's *tone* and an author's *intent.*

## VOCABULARY BUILDING

DIRECTIONS: Make a light check mark (√) alongside one of the three words (choices) that most nearly expresses the meaning of the italicized word in the phrases that are in the left-hand column. (Answers are given on p. 439.)

|  |  | 1 | 2 | 3 |
|---|---|---|---|---|
| 1. | *intolerable* condition | unendurable | reasonable | neutral |
| 2. | take a selection *literally* | carelessly | figuratively | face value |
| 3. | identified as *satirical* | reality | ironical | theoretical |
| 4. | book types or *caricatures* | exaggerations | characters | types |
| 5. | *obscure* points | prominent | apparent | unclear |
| 6. | *dissident* shareholders | dissatisfied | similar | conforming |
| 7. | *arcane* business | understood | open | mystical |
| 8. | dissidents truly *mollified* | appeased | agitated | neutralized |
| 9. | strange genetic *mutation* | outcome | change | progression |
| 10. | *insidious* personality changes | obvious | shady | honest |
| 11. | it looks *haphazard* | deliberate | intentional | disorderly |
| 12. | at a *staid* pace | jaunty | dignified | playful |
| 13. | with astonishing *alacrity* | reluctance | nimbleness | unconcern |
| 14. | conservative and *insular* | narrow | liberal | worldly |
| 15. | an *entrepreneurial* company | traditional | established | start-up |
| 16. | it will be *relentless* | stern | compromising | compassionate |
| 17. | the more *viable* tool | vivid | thoughtful | workable |
| 18. | the *cadre* of directors | group | quality | experience |
| 19. | *complementing* their businesses | recognizing | applauding | dovetailing |
| 20. | many *culinary* classes | fashion | cooking | crafts |
| 21. | traveling to *exotic* places | native | foreign | commercial |
| 22. | spreading *skepticism* | neutralism | disbelief | faith |
| 23. | such an *innovation* | theory | improvement | practice |
| 24. | ending the *gridlock* | compromise | antagonism | jam |
| 25. | an *audacious* claim | daring | cautious | amiable |

# Studying Mathematics

*Would you have a man reason well, you must . . . exercise*
*his mind [and] nothing does this better than mathematics.*

—JOHN LOCKE,(1637–1704), English philosopher

Mathematics has always been a prerequisite for dozens of subjects. Now it seems to be a prerequisite for simple survival.
Whether you feel proficient at mathematics or not, this chapter
can be of help. It discusses

- Traditional versus contemporary mathematics instruction
- How to remedy a weak background
- How to develop good study skills
- How to develop strategies for problem solving
- How to attack nonroutine problems
- How to develop understanding and memory in mathematics

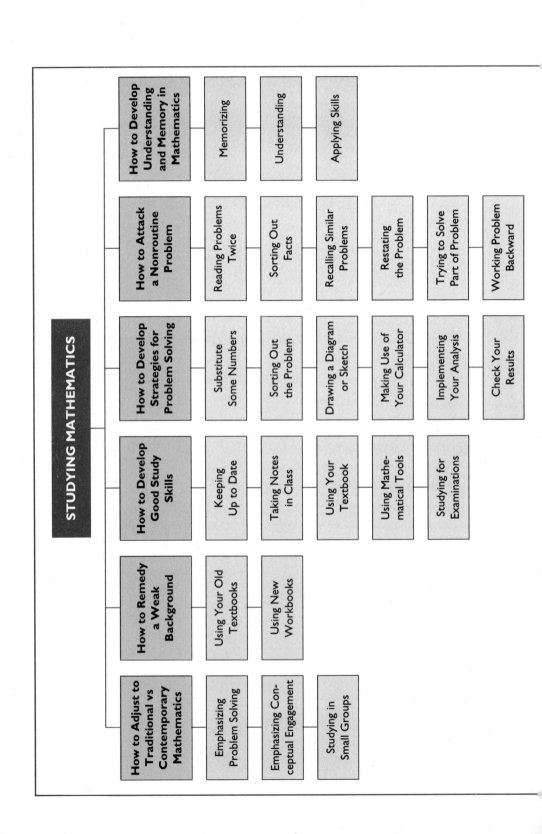

# STUDYING MATHEMATICS

**How to Adjust to Traditional vs Contemporary Mathematics**
- Emphasizing Problem Solving
- Emphasizing Conceptual Engagement
- Studying in Small Groups

**How to Remedy a Weak Background**
- Using Your Old Textbooks
- Using New Workbooks

**How to Develop Good Study Skills**
- Keeping Up to Date
- Taking Notes in Class
- Using Your Textbook
- Using Mathematical Tools
- Studying for Examinations

**How to Develop Strategies for Problem Solving**
- Substitute Some Numbers
- Sorting Out the Problem
- Drawing a Diagram or Sketch
- Making Use of Your Calculator
- Implementing Your Analysis
- Check Your Results

**How to Attack a Nonroutine Problem**
- Reading Problems Twice
- Sorting Out Facts
- Recalling Similar Problems
- Restating the Problem
- Trying to Solve Part of Problem
- Working Problem Backward

**How to Develop Understanding and Memory in Mathematics**
- Memorizing
- Understanding
- Applying Skills

Problems are intriguing, and most people enjoy solving them. Try this.

*Problem:*

At exactly 2 o'clock, two bacteria are placed in a growing medium. One minute later there are four bacteria, in another minute eight bacteria, and so on. At exactly 3 o'clock, the growing mass of bacteria measures one gallon. At what time was there one pint of bacteria?

Is this a puzzle or a mathematical problem? It's like a mathematical problem because its solution requires some analysis and some computation. But it's really more of a puzzle. You have to see, first, that the number of bacteria doubles each minute and, second, that you must compute backward from one gallon at 3 o'clock to get one-half gallon (four pints) at 2:59; two pints at 2:58; and the required one pint at 2:57.

Doing mathematics is a form of problem solving that makes use of the most efficient methods—methods that have been developed over the centuries. That's why it is applicable to so many other subject areas. Once you see the usefulness of mathematics, you'll study and learn it more surely and enthusiastically.

## TRADITIONAL VERSUS CONTEMPORARY MATHEMATICS INSTRUCTION

Compared with your prior mathematical experiences, college-level mathematics courses may present totally new demands. You may find that your previously held conceptions of what mathematics is and what it means to "do mathematics" seem out of place in the contemporary college mathematics classroom. Changing the way you have always thought about and done mathematics is essential for ensuring your future success.

Today, more than ever, mathematics instruction is emphasizing the importance of problem solving. Solving problems is different from completing exercises. The latter merely requires you to apply some previously memorized procedure to a problem that may already be familiar but uses different numbers, or different contexts. Although completing exercises involves mathematical skill, these skills are generally procedural in nature and can be applied in a somewhat rote or mechanical fashion.

In contrast, problem solving typically requires several steps, the first of which is to figure out the "problem in the problem"—that is, what it is in the problem that needs to be solved. You must solve a problem different in form and flavor from ones you have solved before and use a higher, more conceptual level of engagement. You may be required to present more than one solution to the problem, justify your solutions in writing, or present your findings to others. In short, problem solving involves much more than "finding the right answer." You may have to be more persistent.

## HOW TO REMEDY A WEAK BACKGROUND

College work in mathematics is the continuation of a learning program that began in the elementary grades with the first operations of arithmetic and continued through junior and senior high school with algebra, geometry, trigonometry, and calculus. College courses expand and extend this sequence. Each subject builds on previous subjects, and at each stage in the program you must be prepared to use all the mathematics you have studied previously. If at some point you have difficulty with mathematics, it is almost always because you have not fully mastered some earlier principle or process.

What can you do about a shaky background in mathematics? One thing you *can't* do is start all over again—at least, not on top of your regular course load. Even a thorough review would likely take too much of your time. There are, however, two practical ways to identify and strengthen weak spots or fill in gaps: spot reviewing and self-diagnosis.

First, attack each difficulty as it arises. Whenever you come to a computation process or formula or principle that you don't recognize or don't understand, clear it up so that it won't bother you again. Because you have an immediate need for that material, you have an incentive to master it. This is a good way to get the exact mathematics review that you personally need. It is also a very practical plan for someone who is experiencing only occasional difficulty with a mathematics course or with mathematics in other courses.

To do this kind of spot reviewing, you should have at hand textbooks covering all the mathematics you've learned—from arithmetic on. The best review books are those you studied from, but they may be difficult to get. Your college library or bookstore might have some texts that are similar; otherwise, your best bet is standard review books. You can also check the library or computer lab for computer-assisted programs that can help you both to diagnose those areas where you need more work and to get the practice you need. When you review, try to understand the underlying concept or principle as well as the mechanics. Note both on a 3 × 5 card (Figure 18.1); it will help you remember and will come in handy when you study for exams.

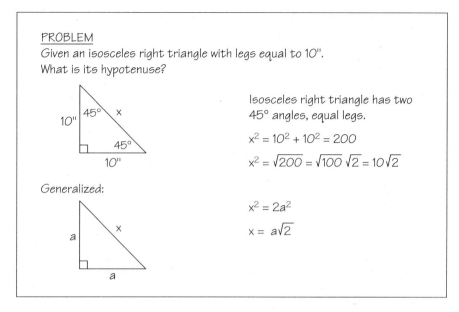

PROBLEM
Given an isosceles right triangle with legs equal to 10".
What is its hypotenuse?

Isosceles right triangle has two
45° angles, equal legs.

$x^2 = 10^2 + 10^2 = 200$

$x^2 = \sqrt{200} = \sqrt{100}\,\sqrt{2} = 10\sqrt{2}$

Generalized:

$x^2 = 2a^2$

$x = a\sqrt{2}$

**FIGURE 18.1   Card for Background Review**

The second way to strengthen weak spots in your background is by diagnosing your mathematical competence. Work your way through a self-help review book or computer program to discover what topics you need to study and practice.[1] By building your understanding in each area of difficulty, you will avoid getting into trouble at more advanced levels. But you must follow through. Attack even minor weaknesses as soon as you discover them.

In addition, remember that everyone has strengths and weaknesses. You may find it useful to have a study partner or to join a small study group. Regular meeting times during the week for reviewing or working homework problems can be very beneficial.

Many college mathematics instructors today encourage cooperative learning or require group activities or projects in their courses. If you find that your mathematics background is weaker than your partner's, don't be intimidated or let your partner take over. If you are not sure of something, say so! Be sure that you are an active and contributing participant in any group process.

---

[1]A good review workbook is M. Wiles Keller and James H. Zant, *Basic Mathematics,* in 4 volumes, 4th ed. (Boston: Houghton Mifflin, 1984). It covers arithmetic, algebra, and trigonometry and contains diagnostic tests from which you can determine your strengths and weaknesses.

# HOW TO DEVELOP GOOD STUDY SKILLS

The change from secondary school to college is greater for mathematics than for any other area of study. In college, you'll have to work exercises on your own, practicing operations and manipulations to achieve mastery and understanding. Most of this work will not be for credit: your reward will be your growing proficiency in thinking your way through the problems.

There is good reason for learning to be self-directed in mathematics. Unless you're a mathematics major, you will take college-level mathematics because it is a prerequisite for course work in your major, and/or a graduation requirement. Most college courses presume a certain level of quantitative competency on the part of their students, and it will be up to you to develop these competencies and apply them to the task at hand. To learn these competencies, you must learn to keep up to date, take notes in class, use your textbook, become proficient at the use of mathematical tools (calculators, graphing software, and the like) and study for exams. Take a course or workshop on the use of calculators if you need to.

## Keeping Up to Date

Because mathematics is a cumulative subject in which you must be prepared at any point to use anything or everything you have previously learned, and because it is a subject in which understanding of concepts is required to master essential operations, it is absolutely necessary to keep your work up to date. If you fall behind, you'll be lacking some of the background on which the newest material is based, in which case you'd have to take time from your study of current material to catch up.

## Taking Notes in Class

The general principles of note taking discussed in Chapter 10 apply to mathematics lectures and class discussion. There is, however, a major difference. You should keep your math notes to a minimum so that note taking doesn't prevent you from following the instructor's line of reasoning. Record main ideas about how to attack particular kinds of problems and jot down the individual steps in each solution. Note *how* a theorem is derived rather than its complete derivation. But do follow carefully as the instructor solves each problem and derives each theorem.

If the lectures are closely related to the textbook, read ahead before each lecture. You then can judge to what extent the lecture repeats and to what extent it supplements the text and can take notes accordingly. You might even want to keep your textbook open and write supplementary or clarifying information right on the book pages. If you do read ahead, expect to read again, more carefully, after the lecture.

If you lose the thread of a lecture or class discussion, or if you fail to understand a line of reasoning or a mathematical procedure, ask your instructor for clarification. Failure to clear up even a minor point may lead to major difficulties later. You'll have to do *your* part, though, by doing the required advance preparation and giving the instructor your full attention during the class period.

To provide maximum reinforcement for classroom learning, study your notes and the related text material and examples as soon after class as possible. Do the drill problems only when you are sure you understand the material. Working at an assignment before you are ready for it wastes time and—worse—can cause you to remember incorrect solution procedures.

## Using Your Textbook

Your textbook is a very useful learning device—if you employ it correctly. You must read mathematics with great care. Mathematical terms and symbols are defined with great precision; each word has an exact meaning and only that meaning. Each term can also imply a number of other definitions and theorems that are part of its own definition.

Consider, for example, the square, a geometric figure. No doubt you can easily imagine a square and draw a reasonable representation of one. But what would the term *square* mean to you if you saw it in your textbook? A reasonable definition of a square is "a regular polygon of four sides." To a mathematician, "regular polygon" means that all the sides are equal in length and all the angles are equal in measure; it also implies, among other things, that the diagonals are equal in length. The expression "polygon of four sides" means that the sum of the interior angles is 360°. Because each angle is equal in measure, each angle measures 90° and is a right angle. There's more, but by now you get the point: Even a simple term like *square* can stand for a wealth of information. Mathematics writers choose their terms with great care to state precisely what they mean. As a reader of mathematics, you must make sure—by reading carefully—that you understand precisely what the writer means.

Don't carry confusion along with you as you read. If you don't recall a term or concept that the author mentions, or if you can't easily define a term or concept for yourself, then stop reading. Look up the term or concept, and make sure you understand it before you go on. Review it if you have to. Do the same for operations that you're unsure of, like adding fractions or taking a particular kind of derivative. If you can't follow the author's computation, look it up.

Read with a pen and plenty of paper at hand, and do all the computations along with the author of your textbook. Do every step in each computation—including all the worked-out examples as you come to them—so that you become comfortable with the process. You can't know what a computation process is like if you read it but don't *do* it.

When you understand the material and have a feel for the mechanics, do some problem solving. Do your homework assignment if you have one or the odd-numbered exercises if you are on your own. Look up the answers if they are available, and rework any exercises you got wrong the first time around (after trying to find where you went wrong). If you can't get the listed answer after two tries, stop and make a note to ask your instructor about the problem.

## Using Mathematical Tools

Most colleges and universities today have responded in some way to the calls for reform in mathematics education. One significant aspect of these reforms is the use of intelligent "tools" in mathematics courses: scientific calculators, graphing calculators, and mathematics software for computers. As a result, the content of many courses is changing, with greater emphasis on problem solving and applications that require the use of computers or calculators.

You must be familiar with the technological tools you are required or allowed to use. Many students are unaware of the computing potential of their calculators. Read the instruction manual that came with your calculator or math software, and keep it nearby so that you can refer to it often. The more familiar you are with such tools, the more competent you will be at using them to your advantage. Make sure you know the instructor's policy on the use of calculators on examinations. Don't overrely on your calculator; know how to approach and solve problems without it. Finally, always estimate the answers to the problems you are solving, and use these estimates to judge the answer you compute with your calculator. It's all too easy to make a keystroke error when entering or manipulating data and arrive at an incorrect solution as a result.

## Studying for Examinations

The best way to study for an examination is to keep up with your daily work throughout the term. Then at examination time you can polish up what you already know.

Start early to review the problems you have had in assignments and previous tests, paying special attention to the more troublesome ones. This will give you a chance to ask your instructor for help if you are still unsure of some procedures. Review any 3 × 5 cards you made up as part of your background-repair effort.

You may also find 3 × 5 cards useful for memorizing important formulas and principles that you won't be able to look up during the examination (see Figures 18.2 and 18.3). Record one item to a card, and carry the cards around with you to study throughout the day. Be sure, however, that you understand the *meaning* of material you memorize in this way, so that you can still work the problem even if you forget the details. Consider a formula a convenience or a short cut, not an end in itself.

Whenever you get back a test or examination, rework the problems on which you made mistakes, and find out what you did wrong. Correcting your errors is one of the most valuable learning experiences you can have. You may want to draw up some review cards for these errors, to use in studying for later examinations.

## PRACTICAL SUGGESTIONS FOR PROBLEM SOLVING

Solving a mathematical problem is basically a two-part operation. First you analyze, and then you compute. If you fail to size up the problem correctly,

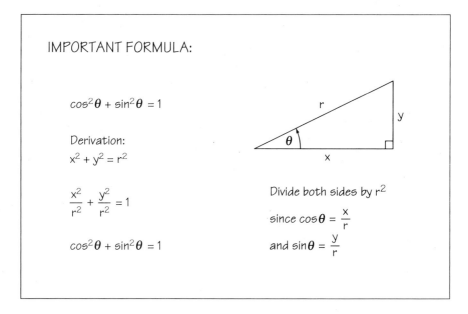

IMPORTANT FORMULA:

$$\cos^2\theta + \sin^2\theta = 1$$

Derivation:
$$x^2 + y^2 = r^2$$

$$\frac{x^2}{r^2} + \frac{y^2}{r^2} = 1$$

$$\cos^2\theta + \sin^2\theta = 1$$

Divide both sides by $r^2$

since $\cos\theta = \dfrac{x}{r}$

and $\sin\theta = \dfrac{y}{r}$

**FIGURE 18.2  Card for Memorizing Formulas**

SOLVING INEQUALITIES

If both sides of an inequality are multiplied or divided by the same positive number, the direction of the inequality is not changed. However, when multiplying or dividing by a negative number, the direction is reversed.

Ex. #1:  Since $10 > 8$, $3 \cdot 10 > 3 \cdot 8$, or $30 > 24$

Ex. #2:  $6 < 18$, but $\dfrac{6}{-3} > \dfrac{18}{-3}$ or $-2 > -6$.

**FIGURE 18.3  Card for Memorizing Principles**

you can't compute your way to the correct solution. On the other hand, an error in calculation—whether from carelessness or from inadequate understanding of the basic operations—can cancel out even a brilliant piece of analysis.

As the first step in doing any problem, read it through twice—*carefully.* This will keep you from jumping into the problem too quickly.

## Substitute Some Numbers

When the numbers involved in a problem are so large, so small, or so complicated that they interfere with your analysis of the problem, try substituting simpler numbers. This will often reveal the nature of the problem more clearly.

*Problems:*

If the mass of an electron is about $9 \times 10^{-28}$ grams, and the mass of a proton is about $1.62 \times 10^{-24}$ grams, approximately how many times the mass of an electron is the mass of a proton?

This problem can easily be sorted out, but then what? If you're unsure about which operation to perform, substitute numbers that are less difficult to work with. Here, let the proton weigh 16 grams and the electron weigh 2 grams. Then the proton obviously weighs $16/2 = 8$ times as much as the electron.

Our analysis tells us to divide proton weight by electron weight, so we calculate

$$\frac{\text{Proton weight}}{\text{Electron weight}} = \frac{1.62 \times 10^{-24} \text{ g}}{9 \times 10^{-28} \text{ g}} = 1.8 \times 10^{3}$$

## Sort Out the Problem

Begin your analysis by noting what things are given, what relationships are stated, or implied, and what is to be found or proved. Underline important points in the problem, or jot them down for easy reference.

Next, figure out how to get from the information you are given to what you need. (Don't do any calculating yet; this is a planning step.) You may find it useful to write down anything that is intermediary, that is, what you have to find in order to find what is required.

For example, suppose you were given the following problem:

A publisher of college mathematics textbooks is planning to market a new textbook. She figures the fixed costs (e.g., overhead) to publish the book are $190,000, while the variable costs (i.e., costs per book, such as materials, printing, etc.) will average $16.00 per book. The book will sell to campus bookstores for $36 per unit. Compute the number of books the publisher will need to sell in order to break even. Your analysis might look like this:

*Given:* Fixed cost ($190,000), variable costs ($16.00/book)
selling price ($36.00/book)
*Find:* Break-even point

To solve this problem, you must know what is meant by a break-even point. This is usually defined as the point at which the revenue generated by doing business is the same as the cost of doing business, that is, when revenue equals cost. Thus, you know what is needed to solve the problem:

*Need:* A cost function $C(x)$; a revenue function, $R(x)$; the break-even point will be the value of x such that $C(x) = R(x)$.

First, generate the cost function, which will be made up of the fixed cost, plus the variable, or "per book" cost. If $x =$ number of books published, then

$$C(x) = 190,000 + 16x$$

The revenue function will be $36 times the number of books sold, or

$$R(x) = 36x.$$

Finally, set $C(x) = R(x)$:

$$190,000 + 16x = 36x$$
$$190,000 = 20x$$
$$x = 9,500$$

Thus, the break-even point is 9,500; that is, the publisher needs to publish and sell 9,500 books to break even.

By analyzing what you need to find, you can often determine a plan of action and know which intermediary steps are required to solve the problem.

## Draw a Diagram

A diagram can highlight relationships and facts that are not very evident from statements alone. In the cost-revenue problem, for example, a sketch of the cost function and the revenue function may illustrate the need to find the intersection, P, of these two equations in Figure 18.4.

The diagram also shows us how to interpret our answer. Here $x = 9500$ is the $x$-coordinate of the point of intersection. Thus, the output of the cost function when $x = 9500$ is the same as the output of the revenue function when $x = 9500$: $C(9500) = 190,000 + 16(9500) = 342,000 = 36(9500) = R(9500)$. The coordinates of the point P are $(9500, 342000)$.

Sometimes a rough sketch is enough to give you insight on how to set up and solve a problem. In other cases, a more careful graph is necessary.

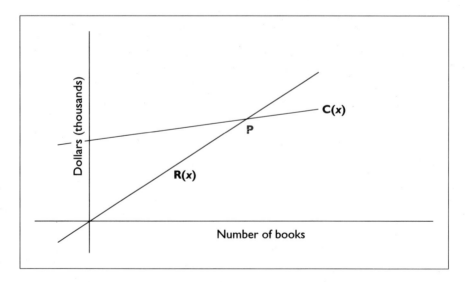

**FIGURE 18.4  Cost–Revenue Diagram**

Be sure that you have and use the necessary materials to do a careful graph: ruler, graph paper, or graphing utility. When you make a graph, be sure to label the axes, so that you (or whoever may grade your work) are clear about what the graph represents. Consider the following problem:

> A hot-air balloon is floating over a highway. To figure out their height, the balloonists measure the angle of depression to the milepost behind them to be 38°, while the angle of depression to the milepost ahead of them is 53°. What is the height of the balloon?

First sort out the problem:

*Given:* Angles of depression 38° and 53°; distance between posts = 1 mile
*Find:* Height of balloon above ground

To sketch this problem, we need to know the definition of angle of depression. We are given the measure of these angles, as well as the distance between mileposts (1 mile). The diagram might look like Figure 18.5.

The danger with this diagram is that the triangle looks nearly isosceles, which would imply that the height, h, divides the triangle into two congruent parts. If this were true, the base of the triangle would be divided in half, into segments measuring 0.5 miles each; then the problem could be easily solved by solving the equation tan 38° = h/.5 for h. However, if this were an isosceles triangle, the base angles would be equal to each other, which they are not. If we were to draw the diagram a little more accurately (as in Figure 18.6) the 53° angle would be drawn bigger than the 38° angle; then it would be clear that the base of this triangle is not bisected.

Now it is obvious from the diagram that the base is not bisected when we drop a perpendicular to the base, and the first solution path is not feasible. (To solve this problem, we could see use the Law of Sines to find a or b, then find h using this intermediary information.)

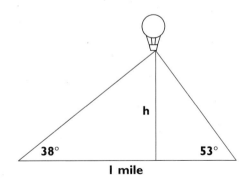

**h**

**38°**          **53°**

**l mile**

**FIGURE 18.5  Diagram for Balloon Problem 1**

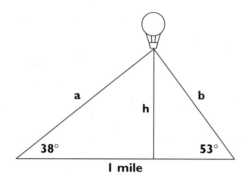

**FIGURE 18.6   Diagram for Balloon Problem 2**

Another effective technique, especially in word problems leading to equations, is to choose an answer first and use it to figure out what procedure is involved. For example, in the book-publishing example, choosing a possible number of books for the answer may aid in finding the equations for the cost and revenue functions. Imagine that the break-even point occurs when 5,000 books are published and sold. The cost to publish 5,000 books would be $190,000 + 16(5,000) = $270,000, while the revenues earned selling these books would be 36(10,000) = 180,000. From these calculations we can see that unless more books are published and sold, the publisher will lose money. Trying another possible answer, say, 10,000 books, leads to $190,000 + 16(10,000) = $350,000 in publishing costs, but 360,000 in earned revenues. By generalizing on the process of determining the costs and revenues for a particular number of books, you can derive the cost and revenue functions. Furthermore, since these are linear functions, you can see that the break-even point must lie somewhere between 5,000 and 10,000 books and must be closer to the latter number.

Substituting numbers is also helpful when you are unclear how to simplify your calculations. For example, consider the expression $\sqrt{x^2 + y^2}$. Does this expression simplify to $x + y$? To determine this, try substituting, say, 1 for x and 2 for y: $\sqrt{1^2 + 2^2} = \sqrt{5} \neq 1 + 2$. Since you have found a combination of numbers for which the statement is not true, you can conclude that, in general, $\sqrt{x^2 + y^2} \neq x + y$.

## Make Use of Your Calculator

You will use your calculator to do most of the calculations for math problems. If you don't have a calculator, you're at a disadvantage. It removes the tedium from calculations, speeds them up, and thus, gives you more time both for analysis and for doing problems. Most college math courses require you to have and know how to use a calculator.

A calculator can also be useful in the analysis stage of problem solving. In particular, it can help you test a formula or identify one that you're not sure of. Suppose you need the formula for $\cos 2\theta$ but can't remember whether it's $2 \cos^2 \theta - $ or $1 - 2 \cos^2 \theta$. To find out, simply pick a value for $\theta$ and then use your calculator to compute all three expressions. You find that the computed value for $2 \cos^2 \theta - 1$ is the same as that for $\cos 2\theta$, and you have your formula.

Although your calculator is a valuable tool, it is *only* a tool and cannot substitute for mathematical understanding. Consider the problem $y = \log_5 30$. You can solve this problem with any scientific calculator, by applying the change of base formula: $\log_5 30 = \dfrac{\log 30}{\log 5} \approx 2.113$. Therefore, to compute $\log_5 30$, you must find $\log 30$ and divide it by $\log 5$. Without the change of base formula, you can still come up with a decent approximation of $\log_5 30$ by knowing how to rewrite a logarithmic equation in exponential form. The given equation $y = \log_5 30$ can be rewritten as $5^y = 30$. Since $5^2 = 25$ and $5^3 = 125$, the power (log) that you must raise 5 to in order to get 30 will be a little more than 2. Using the $x^y$ (or $y^x$, depending on your calculator) key, substitute 5 for the base and different values around 2. _____ for the exponent until you get a result that is sufficiently close to 30.

## Implement Your Analysis

Your analysis of the problem is complete when you clearly understand how to proceed from what is given to what is required. Then do the calculations that implement the analysis as you developed it. Don't try a new idea once you've started calculating—a short cut, for example. Because you have not thought it through, it could lead you astray.

If you do want to try a different method—one that seems more elegant, perhaps, or that requires less work—do so. But do so only after you have made it part of a complete, start-to-finish analysis of the problem.

## Check Your Results

Get in the habit of checking your answer every time you complete a problem. One or more of the following checks will usually apply to every type of problem:

**1.** Substitute your answer for the unknown in the problem, to make sure it satisfies the given conditions. This check is especially applicable to word problems and problems in the form of questions.

**2.** Rework the problem by an alternative method. (You've got to know another solution method before you can use this check.)

**3.** Check the units in your solution. In the hot-balloon problem, for example, the base of the triangle in your diagram is 1 mile. Thus, your solution for the height of the balloon will be some portion of a mile. If the problem requires you to express your answer in feet, you need to multiply your answer by 5,280 (since 1 mile = 5,280 feet).

**4.** Estimate the answer before you do the computation. Then make sure the estimate and the answer are of about the same magnitude. This check, too, can be used for the majority of numerical problems.

**5.** If you work with a study partner or group, compare solutions. If your textbook comes with an optional student solutions manual, buy it; look up the solution to the given problem (or similar problem) and compare it with your solution. Often the solutions will look different, but both may be correct. The process of reconciling multiple approaches to a problem can lead to even greater understanding of the problem and to flexible thinking, which is important for the problem-solving process.

Checking can reveal errors in both analysis and computation. It will also help you understand what you are doing. Although checking might seem to be a duplication of effort, it really isn't. Rather, it is a quality control operation that can enhance your problem-solving ability and your examination grades.

## How to Attack a Nonroutine Problem

A nonroutine problem is different from the problems you may be used to solving. It can range from the slightly unusual to the unique and often is composed of many parts. Mathematics instructors ofen assign such problems to foster problem-solving skills and to test and extend your ability to apply what you have learned. To illustrate, consider the following problem, which may seem nonroutine to you:

> The relationship between air temperature T (in F°) and the altitude h (in feet above sea level) is approximately linear. When the temperature at sea level is 60°, an increase of 5000 feet in altitude lowers the air temperature about 18°.

(a) Find an equation that expresses T as a function of h (write your answer in general form);
(b) approximate the air temperature at an altitude of 13,000 feet; and
(c) approximate the altitude at which the temperature is only 10° F.

The first step is to read the problem carefully, from beginning to end. The second step? Read the problem again! You should conclude that this problem requires you to (1) write an equation that relates one variable to another, then (2) use this equation to predict the value of one variable knowing a value of the other variable. An equation written to fit observed data can be called a mathematical model. Mathematical modeling, or constructing equations that fit given data, is an important component of problem solving.

To help sort out the problem and organize the given information, it is often useful to build a table for the given data. Since you have two variables, one for temperature (T) and one for altitude (h), make a table with two columns, and enter your given information in the appropriate columns:

| T | h |
|---|---|
| 60 | 0 (the height at sea level) |
| 42 | 5000 (since 60° − 18° = 42°) |

Since you are told that the relationship will be linear, you know that you need to find an equation in the form $y = mx + b$ that will give you correct output for the given output.

Note that you are asked to find an equation that expresses T as a function of h. This means that you must be able to compute T if you are given an h value. Thus, you know that the *input* variable should be T, and the *output* variable should represent h; since the relationship is linear, this means h = mT + b. It may be useful, then, to reverse the columns, making the input the first column, and the output, the second column:

*Given* information, rearranged:

| h | T |
|---|---|
| 0 | 60 |
| 5000 | 42 |

Now that you have organized your given information, decide what you are asked to find, and what will be needed to do this:

*Find:* A linear equation through the given data points
*Need:* The slope (m), and the y intercept (b) of the line

Recall that m is defined as the slope of a straight line, and defined as $\frac{y_2 - y_1}{x_2 - x_1}$; b is defined as the y intercept, the value of y when x = 0.

We can now compute the slope and y intercept for the line through the given data:

$$m = \text{slope} = \frac{T_2 - T_1}{h_2 - h_1} = \frac{42 - 60}{5000 - 0} = \frac{-18}{5000} = -.0036$$

$$b = \text{value of T when } h = 0: 60.$$

Thus, the desired equation is $T = -.0036h + 60$. *Check* the equation by substituting the given data pairs for h and T.

Note that question (b) asks for a temperature, given a specific height, while question (c) asks for a specific height, given a specific temperature. Both (b) and (c), then, require you to use the equation you constructed in question (a) to compute specific values.

For part (b), given the altitude (h) is 2000, find T:

$$T = -.0036(13,000) + 60 = -46.8 + 60 = 13.2 \approx 13°.$$

For part (c), given the temperatures is 6° F., compute the height:

$$6 = .0036(h) + 60 \qquad \text{substract 60 from both sides}$$
$$-54 = -.0036h \qquad \text{divide both sides by } -.0036$$
$$h = 15,000 \text{ feet.}$$

Note that even without the equation, you could estimate the answers by using what you know about linear functions to extend the table. You know that each time h increases by 5000, T must decrease by 18°:

| h | T | |
|---|---|---|
| 0 | 60 | |
| 5,000 | 42 | |
| 10,000 | 24 | |
| 15,000 | 6 | |
| 20,000 | -12 | |
| 25,000 | -30 | etc. |

The solution for part (c) is thus confirmed, since (15,000, 6) is in the table. You can be confident about the solution to part (b) as well, since 13,000 is between 10,000 and 15,000, while the computed solution, 13.2, is between 24 and 6.

## UNDERSTANDING AND MEMORY IN MATHEMATICS

Most students rely too much on memory in their study and use of mathematics. Competence in mathematics is not to any great extent a matter of remembering things. It is true that a child in the early grades is encouraged to memorize the multiplication tables. But he or she is also taught that multiplication may be thought of as repeated addition. The memorization may help the child multiply more quickly; but when memory fails, the understanding that, for example, $5 \times 9 = 9 + 9 + 9 + 9 + 9$ will help the child out of difficulty.

Perhaps such early memorization leads to a habit of memorizing in high school and college math courses. Having a needed formula memorized is certainly convenient. But understanding the idea behind the formula and knowing how it comes about are critical for success in mathematics, especially as you progress beyond arithmetic and elementary algebra. In contemporary college math courses, conceptual understanding and the ability to apply those concepts are far more important than rote memorization. Many instructors supply necessary formulas or even allow their students to bring in formula sheets to written examinations.

An illustration is provided by the basic trigonometric identities. Students always seem to remember the formula $\sin^2 \theta \cos^2 \theta = 1$, but they have difficulty retaining similar formulas that relate the tangent and secant of an angle or its cotangent and cosecant. Actually, you don't have to memorize any of the identities if you understand the meanings of the trigonometric functions of angles. For example, to find the identity linking the tangent and secant of an angle, you need only draw a right triangle like that shown in Figure 18.7. Then, since $x^2 + y^2 = r^2$ (by the Pythagorean theorem), we have

$$\frac{x^2}{x^2} + \frac{y^2}{x^2} = \frac{r^2}{x^2}$$

Because $\tan \theta = y/x$ and $\sec \theta = r/x$, this becomes

$$1 + \tan^2 \theta = \sec^2 \theta$$

It's that simple, when you understand.

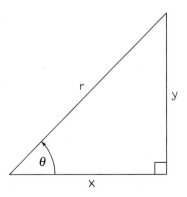

**FIGURE 18.7   Right Triangle for Use in Deriving Trigonometric Identities**

Of course, you do need skill to perform certain mathematical operations. But much of that skill comes from knowing what you are doing—from understanding what the operations are, what they produce, and what they mean. The remainder comes from practice, from doing those sometimes dreary but nonetheless useful routine problems. And you do need to memorize some facts in mathematics, as in every other subject. The proper mix of skill, memorization, and understanding, however, is one that leans heavily toward understanding.

Look at it this way: Most likely, you are studying mathematics so that later you will be able to apply it in science, engineering, business, economics, the social sciences, teaching, or some other area. You should know, then, that the usefulness of mathematics in these areas arises primarily from the application of its ideas, rather than from its formulas or processes (although all three have their uses). Memorizing and applying math formulas without understanding them is like repeating Russian words without knowing what they mean. You're not speaking the language: you're only imitating its noises.

## SUMMARY

**What makes studying mathematics so different from studying other subjects?**

Mathematics is one of the few subjects that is developed cumulatively through your school years, from grade school to college. What you didn't master years ago can keep you from progressing now.

**What can I do if my background is weak?**

You have two solutions: First, you can attack each difficulty as you discover it. Second, you can diagnose your background to find your weak areas in advance. Then beef up those areas with self-help books.

**How should note taking in math class differ from note taking in other classes?**

Math notes should be taken sparingly—covering main ideas and clarifying remarks only—so that you can concentrate on the instructor's reasoning. If the lecture follows the book fairly closely, try taking notes in the book, close to the concepts or processes that they clarify.

**How should I read my math textbook?**

Always read mathematics with great care, to make sure you extract the exact meaning of its precisely defined terms. Write out all the examples and other computations along with the author, as you read. Clear up any confusion when it arises, before you read on. Finally, do the problems only when you are sure you understand what you've read.

**How should I use my calculator?**

Be sure you know how your calculator works. Keep your instructional manual handy and refer to it often. Remember that your calculator is a tool, not a substitute for understanding. When using your calculator to solve problems, estimate your solution first to detect errors in data entry or manipulation.

**Are there any tips for preparing for math exams?**

Be sure to keep up with your assignments throughout the term. When exam time rolls around, start studying early so you'll have plenty of time to correct any problems you encounter during your review. And use 3 × 5 cards to make sure you have mastered all the important principles, processes, and formulas.

**What's the plan of attack for a standard math problem?**

First, analyze the problem. Sort out the given information, draw a diagram, and decide how you're going to find what is required. Having completed this analysis, compute the answer. Once you have an answer, check it to make sure it is *the* answer.

**How do I attack non-standard math problems?**

Begin them in much the same way you'd begin standard problems, by sorting the information and drawing a diagram. Organizing the given data into a table and looking for patterns can often provide entry into the problem. Then try to find a link with a problem you've already solved or with a simpler problem. Restating the problem could help, as might working backward from what is required to what you are given. Manipulating the diagram could also show you a path to the solution.

**Isn't memory important in studying math?**

Memorizing should be done for convenience; it is not a necessity. It is far better to base your study of mathematics on an understanding of the concepts that lie behind the processes and formulas. Then, if your memory fails, you'll still be able to solve the problems.

## HAVE YOU MISSED SOMETHING?

*Sentence completion.*   Complete the following sentences with one of the three words or phrases listed below each sentence.

1. The objective of problem solving is to train students to _____ .
   find the right answers      memorize formulas      think conceptually

2. To benefit from working with a study partner, you must be set to

   _____ .

   let your partner take over      be an active participant
   divide the work equally

3. In using computers or calculators, you _____ .
   no longer need to know how to approach the problem
   can depend on software to solve problems
   still must estimate the answers to problems

*Matching.*   In each blank space in the left column, write the letter preceding the phrase in the right column that matches the left item best.

_____ **1.** Checking

a. Involves separating and listing the problem information

_____ **2.** Mathematical terms

b. Are defined precisely to convey exact meanings

_____ **3.** Diagrams

c. Can reveal errors in analysis and computation

_____ **4.** Sorting

d. Is a firm basis for studying mathematics

_____ **5.** Understanding

e. Can reveal relationships in problems

*True-false.*   Write *T* beside the *true* statements and *F* beside the *false* statements.

_____ **1.** It is best to wait until the end of the semester to strengthen weak spots in your background.

_____ **2.** Mathematical terms are designed precisely to convey meanings.

|     |                                      | **1**    | **2**        | **3**        |
|-----|--------------------------------------|----------|--------------|--------------|
| 21. | filling narrow market *niches*       | trends   | spots        | fashions     |
| 22. | unusual *syndrome*                   | pattern  | building     | organization |
| 23. | with *vituperative* memos            | vigorous | flattering   | abusive      |
| 24. | tension became *acute*               | sharp    | noticeable   | moderate     |
| 25. | today's *atomized* business          | volatile | fragmented   | risky        |

# 19

# Learning with the Computer

*I had rather dream of the future than read a history of the past.*

—THOMAS JEFFERSON (1743–1826), third president of the United States

Does the thought of sitting down at a computer terminal leave you with high-tech anxiety? If so, you might be surprised to discover that you can learn many of the basics of computing within a few hours. Computers are not just easy to learn; they are useful. They can help you research and write papers, study, plan a schedule, and save time. This chapter covers some basic information about computing. It discusses

- Debunking myths about computers
- Identifying your school's computer resources
- Using your computer as an aid to becoming a better student
- Using the computer in the library
- Using the internet

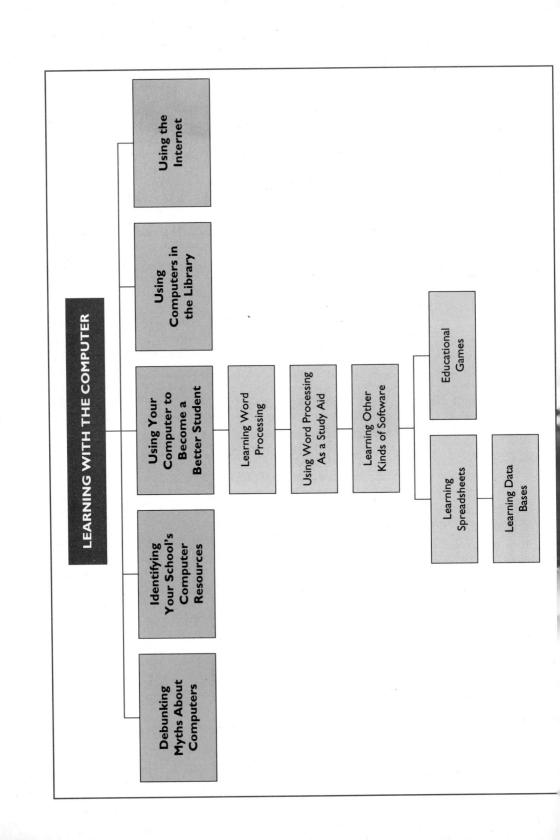

## DEBUNKING MYTHS ABOUT COMPUTERS

If you have little or no firsthand computer experience, you may be anxious about using a computer. You may believe some of the following myths.

**1.** *Everyone else knows about computers already. I'll just seem stupid.*   Most people are familiar with only a few computer applications, and they were just as apprehensive as you about facing a computer for the first time. It's natural to be anxious about new learning situations. A healthy amount of anxiety makes people mentally alert for new learning situations. Combat overanxious feelings by remembering a successful, though stressful, learning experience of your own. Recall how your initial misgivings became feelings of interest and relief once you felt in control of the situation. After learning the basics of computing, you'll wonder why you were anxious at all.

**2.** *I'm not good with machines. I could damage the equipment or lose my data.*   Computers are no more fragile than your radio. Unless you pick up the computer and throw it against the wall or spill something in it, you're not likely to damage it. A computer will not be harmed if you accidentally press the wrong keys on the keyboard. Moreover, the computer software you will use tells you what key to press to perform a particular function and double-checks whether you really want to delete material you've instructed it to delete. At worst, you may need to ask for assistance or refer to the manual that accompanies the software you're using.

**3.** *I'll have to take a computer programming course to understand computers.* Very few people need to know how to program a computer, and you don't need to know how to program one in order to use one. The word *program* refers to the internal commands that the computer reads every time it performs a task, and *programming* refers to the writing of those commands into the computer's software. *Software* refers to the instructions, written onto a disk or tape, that direct the computer to perform a particular operation. To use the computer for word processing, spreadsheet accounting, or database management, you don't need to know anything about how the software you are using was programmed, any more than you need to know how a book was written before you start reading it.

**4.** *I'll need extensive skills before I'll be able to use the computer.*   Seven or eight basic commands are usually all you'll need to begin using word-processing software. The same is true of learning to use a spreadsheet or working with a database management program. Many students can begin to use such programs within two or three hours. You'll find that after you've learned the introductory commands, you'll easily be able to learn more.

**5.** *It's a waste of time to learn on a particular computer, because they're always coming up with new models.*   There will always be a "next" model. But as the technology has continued to advance, many elements of various brands and models have been standardized, making it fairly easy to shift from one type of computer to another. Your best bet, therefore, is to identify your current computer needs and learn to use a computer and software that suit those needs. Later, if there are changes in your needs or in the technology, you'll easily be able to transfer the skills you've learned on one model to the next.

**6.** *I shouldn't try to learn computing until I can afford to own a computer.*   If you buy a computer before you learn much about computers, you may end up with equipment not well suited to your needs. There's nothing wrong with buying your own computer eventually. But if you're still learning about computers, it's best to gain some experience before you spend your money. Use a friend's computer or learn in a workshop or computer lab. Computers in college labs are set up and ready to go, and the lab operators should be able to answer your questions.

## IDENTIFYING YOUR SCHOOL'S COMPUTER RESOURCES

Because the use of computers will be a valuable learning and organizing tool for you to use during your college career, if a computer course is required for graduation, you should take it at first opportunity—your first semester if possible. Not only will you build your computer skills, you will also learn about computer resources available on campus. If such a course is not required, you may want to take a course or a workshop for specific computer applications such as word processing, spreadsheets, or database management.

Take the initiative the first week of school, or even during campus orientation before school begins, to find out about computer facilities. If you are already well into the semester, do it now! Don't be shy about asking questions: Where are computers located that students can use? What kind are they, and what do I need to do in order to use them? If I'm not familiar with computers, what help is available?

In addition you need to know:

**1.** *How many computers or computer terminals are available?*   Depending on the facilities of your campus computer lab, you will have access to computers, computer terminals, or both. A *computer* is any electronic device that can accept, process, store, display, and print information or data. Microcomputers such as the Apple Macintosh or the IBM personal computer (PC) are two well-known examples. The term computer can also apply to powerful main-frames, capable of supporting many computer terminals. A *computer terminal* normally consists only of a keyboard and a screen. You input data with the keyboard and see the data displayed on the screen. Unlike a microcomputer, a computer terminal doesn't process, store, or output information. Those tasks are performed by the mainframe to which the terminal is connected.

**2.** *What types of computers and computer software are available?* You are likely to have access to a number of different computers. Initially, you may feel most comfortable by picking one type and learning on it. As you become experienced, you can experiment with others. The same applies to software. At the outset, it's usually a good idea to master only one type of software. Once you become comfortable with that type, you can learn another. If possible, start with software that is widely used. More people will be able to help you if you have questions about well-known software. In addition, such software is often the most flexible and is more likely to be compatible with several types of computers. Microsoft Word and WordPerfect, two examples of popular word-processing software, come in versions for both IBM and Apple computers.

**3.** *How many and what kinds of printers are available?* A printer is the device that gives you a printed version (the hard copy) of your work. Several kinds of printers are available, and each kind gives you a different quality of print on the page. The highest quality of print comes from a laser printer. Laser printers produce letter-quality results—the printed characters are good enough for professional correspondence and other documents. Dot matrix printers use a series of pins that strike the printer ribbon to produce characters. As the name implies, each character is composed of small dots. Ink jet printers also use small dots to produce characters, but they do so by shooting ink through tiny holes. Most dot matrix and ink jet printers generate quite readable print, and some can produce letter-quality print. In addition, both printers are relatively inexpensive to buy and operate, and the computer lab is most likely to have more of them than other more expensive printers. They are excellent for printing drafts and final copy for college papers and projects.

**4.** *What are the general rules for using the computer lab?* Find out first whether the lab uses personal computers or terminals. If it uses PCs, you may be required to furnish your own disks and perhaps even some software. If the lab uses terminals, you will probably be assigned a password—a word or series of nonsense characters—that you use to log in to the mainframe computer. Passwords protect the material in your files from being used by any other user. Determine whether you need to sign up in advance to use a computer or a terminal. This may be necessary, especially during periods of heavy use such as the end of the term, when many students are completing term projects and research papers.

You may also want to determine whether the Internet and electronic mail are available to students through your school, and to learn how to use the library computer catalog and databases as soon as possible.

## USING YOUR COMPUTER AS AN AID TO BECOMING A BETTER STUDENT

The kind of work a student undertakes in college makes the use of the computer invaluable. When you take courses in humanities or social sciences, you will benefit from word processing. If you study math, any of the sciences, or a technical field, learning how to store and retrieve information in a database will improve your ability to generate useful reports. You will find spreadsheets invaluable in business, economics, and accounting courses. But you will also find them useful in tracking your courses or grades. In addition, many fields of study make use of educational software to supplement or reinforce learning.

### Learning Word Processing

If you've ever labored over several drafts of a research paper, writing and rewriting through piles of paper, you want to learn word processing. Word processing is a simple as typing: you type into the computer, and your text is displayed on the screen. A simple command stores that information, probably on a floppy disk that you have inserted into the computer or on the hard drive of your personal computer. You can print the text at any time or retrieve it for further work.

If you don't know the keyboard, word processing is a skill you need to learn. The less you have to think about finding letters, the more you can think about what you are writing. Don't be intimidated by the keyboard; you will only get better with practice, and mistakes are easy to fix. The computer lab may have a typing tutorial program to help you get started.

Once you get comfortable using the keyboard and a few basic editing functions, you will find yourself thinking and composing at the computer, rather than using it just to type. Writing is a process. The final product doesn't magically flow from your pen or keyboard. Many times you need to actually see something in writing to know what you think of it or to develop an idea further. Most students say composing on computers is more fun. The use of the keyboard allows you an easy way to brainstorm.

Once you've input the text, you can use a few simple commands to edit it quickly and efficiently. You can move a word, a line, or a large block of text from one place in the document to another. You can delete text from, or add text to, any place you like. In short, you can edit and rewrite with a few keystrokes, instead of retyping the entire paper. Of course, the storage system on the computer allows you to keep all your drafts. You can do several versions and keep the best.

Other features of word-processing software include spelling checkers, an electronic thesaurus, and style checkers. A spelling checker scans your manuscript, highlights the misspelled words it finds, and allows you to correct them. An electronic thesaurus provides on-screen lists of synonyms and antonyms, helpful if you're stuck trying to think of a word. Style checkers point out awkward or grammatically incorrect language and punctuation errors. These features don't guarantee you'll write a great paper, but they'll help you check and edit your work, thus giving you more time for improving the quality of your work. In addition, the appearance of your work is enhanced by using a quality printer.

You will want to remember some basic computer common sense. Get in the habit of saving your work into your computer file about every five minutes or so. When you save it the first time, you will be asked to name your document. Choose a name that identifies what is on the document. If you are saving to a disk, carefully label what is on that disk, or you'll find yourself spending hours going through disks looking for something.

You will also want to make sure that you back up your work. Make two copies of important documents so that if one is lost or damaged, you still have your information.

Keep in mind that a disk is magnetic. Magnets will erase the contents of your disk. Although disks are sturdy, use caution when transporting them from place to place. Avoid moisture and temperature extremes (don't leave disks on your dashboard, for instance).

## Using Word Processing as a Study Aid

Once you can think and compose at the computer rather than just using it to type finished products, you can expand the scope of your study skills. In addition to generating, composing, and typing the final draft of papers and assignments, you will find that you can also use word-processing programs to study more efficiently.

Kinesthetic and visual learners are particularly helped by using the computer. Kinesthetic learners prefer and actually learn better when they touch and are physically involved in what they are studying. They find that when they physically do something, they understand it and remember it. Using the computer gets you physically involved and does more than just studying your notes would do. Visual learners need to see what they are learning and often the appearance of the printed product will stay longer in memory than their own written notes.

The Cornell System and the Questions-in-the-Margin System use the principle of selectivity. When preparing for final exams or a major test, you may want to carry selectivity one step further by taking your Cornell notes from class and the questions-in-the-margin notes in your text and making study guides combining the important ideas from both. Summarizing and selecting what is important to include in your guide is a very powerful part of the learning and review process. You may also want to use your computer to keep a list of vocabulary words in each course you know you will need for tests.

One of the most effective ways of using your computer to learn is to compose practice tests. Use selectivity to narrow the amount of material to a manageable amount. After putting the material to be learned into a test form, the actual test will be easier because you have thought of the information in a test format rather than memorizing facts. And because you have already practiced taking your test, maybe even more than once, you reduce test anxiety for the real thing.

## Learning Other Kinds of Software

In addition to using word processing as a way to learn on your computer, you may also use tutorial software, problem-solving software, and simulations. Many textbooks are sold with software bound inside. Or you may ask your professor if such software is available for your course. In its simplest form, sometimes called programmed instruction, it resembles flash cards on the screen. In the typical program, a problem, accompanying question, and possible answers are simultaneously displayed on the screen. The software allows you to choose the correct answer and immediately receive feedback about your response. Because the questions are usually matching or multiple-choice questions, this kind of software is most useful for review of basic concepts in mathematics, the sciences, and languages. For instance, you could use a chemistry program to review the elements in the Periodic Table. A mathematics program could display a problem and ask you to select the correct solution. Using this program and others like it requires only that you have simple word-processing skills.

Tutorial programs are similar; however, they are constructed so that all necessary instructions appear on the screen. No other supplemental instructions are required. You may want to use tutorial programs to learn typing or other computer skills. Problem-solving software can help teach problem-solving skills in the context of a particular discipline such as math, the sciences, or social sciences. Problem-solving software typically asks you to recognize a problem, formulate a hypothesis or possible solution to that problem, gather information, test potential solutions, and arrive at a viable solution.

The popular computer-based flight simulators, available at both computer stores and toy stores, are an entertaining example of an invaluable category of computer programs: simulation software. Simulation software is a program that uses data to model a real-life event. The software allows you to change certain conditions so that you can test various hypotheses and predict different outcomes. Like mathematics software, simulation software provides immediate feedback about situations that would take days or weeks to calculate using conventional methods. It also teaches and reinforces principles about complex phenomena that might otherwise exist only as abstractions. A simulation program could allow you to predict and then simulate certain chemical reactions, and it then would display the results of your simulation either in text or in graphics. Another type of simulation software allows you to forecast the economic results of certain stock market transactions and other economic events.

**Educational Games**  Educational games teach strategizing, logical skills, and concept skills. Depending on the game, you can compete against yourself, the computer, or a friend. Playing an educational game can lower your anxiety about using the computer in the first place, or it can sharpen your skills and relax you during a particularly intense studying session. Keep in mind that the level at which you learn is related to the demands of the game. Games in which you shoot aliens are not too likely to increase your problem-solving skills.

## Learning Spreadsheets

An electronic spreadsheet takes the place of the conventional spreadsheet used by accountants and financial analysts. Like conventional spreadsheets, electronic spreadsheets are composed of horizontal rows and vertical columns that intersect and allow you to insert data at the cells. You can enter numbers, words, or formulas into each cell, store what you've entered, and then manipulate the stored information. The software is programmed so that you can quickly and easily perform a variety of calculations with the data. The functions you are likely to encounter if you work with a spreadsheet are similar to those used in word processing. You can see how becoming proficient with one type of software helps you with another type.

Spreadsheets are used in business, economics, and accounting courses in which students work with case studies, problem sets, and statistical models. You can make personal use of spreadsheets as well. Spreadsheets simplify managing a personal budget or keeping financial records for an organization or social club. They also allow for quick and efficient personal tax planning.

One of the best things you can do as a student is to set up your course of study on a spreadsheet. List all the courses you will need to graduate in categories as listed in your catalog. As you take a course, mark the grade you achieve and keep up with your average for a class or chart your GPA.

## Learning Databases

You've probably called the telephone operator, asked for someone's phone number, and been given it by an electronic recording. This was accomplished by means of a database management program. A database management program allows you to enter data into a database (the place where it is stored) and retrieve it quickly and easily. The cross-reference filing in the system allows you to retrieve and manipulate the information in a number of ways.

Think of a database as you would think of a conventional filing cabinet. The item that holds the largest group of information in the filing cabinet is the file drawer. Each drawer is capable of holding several small file folders. Each folder holds numerous pieces of information, such as letters and numbers. In an electronic database, the file drawer is called the *file;* the folders it holds are called *records;* the pieces of information contained in the records are called *fields.* Individual numbers, letters, and symbols called *characters* are inserted into the fields. Although spreadsheets and database management can make accounting, bibliographies, and statistical and other tasks quick and easy, the library and the Internet are the most likely places you will be using databases.

## Using Computers in the Library

The card catalog is an organized inventory of the library's holding. Most colleges now have this catalog computerized or on-line. On-line or computer catalogs vary greatly from library to library. Most are user-friendly and have "help" screens. The on-line catalogs are searched from computer terminals centrally located in the library. You may be able to access the catalog through the academic computing system or remotely with a microcomputer and modem.

Most systems offer a flexible approach to searching for library materials. Items may be located by author, title, author/title combination, Library of Congress subject headings, or key terms. In addition, you can usually limit search results by language, publication date, publication format, and other simple constraints.

You will want to take time at the beginning of the semester to learn how to operate the computer catalog so that when you need it, you won't have to stop and learn. Sometimes there is a library orientation. There will probably be handouts and instructions printed near the computer, or you can ask the librarians to help you. Do not hesitate to ask. You are certainly not the only student who needs help.

In addition to on-line catalogs, many libraries will have various electronic databases such as CD/ROM. Specialized databases should be available in most subjects across the curriculum. Some of the better-known databases on CD/ROM are ABI/inform; Business NewsBank PLUS; ERIC; America: History and Life on Disc; Historical Abstracts on Disc; Index to American Periodicals; MLA International Bibliography, Contemporary Authors on CD-ROM, The Music Index on CD-ROM; Comprehensive MEDLINE/EBSCO; HEALTH Planning and Administration; PsycLIT; Dissertation Abstracts Ondisc and numerous U.S. government publications such as the U.S. Census. Ask your major instructors or librarian which is the best database to use for each subject you need to research.

Larger libraries will have expanded academic indexes. Instead of using print indexes such as *Readers Guide,* you may be able to access this information on a computer database. One such index, Infotrac, indexes and abstracts approximately 1,600 scholarly and general interest periodicals covering the humanities, communications studies, the social sciences, the arts, science, and technology. Some articles are available in full-text in this electronic information resource. Again, it is important for you to know what computer services the library offers and how to use them. They will save you valuable time in your search for information.

## Using the Internet

In addition to the electronic resources in the library, you will have literally hundreds of thousands of resources available to you on the Internet. The Internet is more than a medium for electronic mail; it is a repository for information from all over the world. Ask whether the Internet is available to students at your school and how you can subscribe to it. In fact, some professors may require that you have an E-mail account.

Many universities use a Campus-Wide Information System or CWIS to consolidate campus information and computing services in one place. These CWISs will usually be available on the Internet. You will find things like the school catalog, course offerings, campus services, and the library on-line catalog. You should also be able to keep up to date with campus events. Tools such as Usenet News or Revised Listserv organize discussion groups ranging from very specific to very general and can be local or worldwide. Individuals and institutions also have collections of papers or databases available on the Internet. By using tools such as Gopher, World Wide Web, and Wide Area Information Servers (WAIS), users can retrieve information about such subjects as art, business and the economy, computers, education, entertainment, government, health, news, recreation, reference, science, social science, society and culture, and weather. Many periodicals such as *USA Today,* the *New York Times,* the *Los Angeles Times,* and *Forbes* are available on the Internet. In addition, classical works of literature such as Shakespeare, the Bible, and *Moby Dick* are available. You can find audio documents as well as video. In short, the Internet is a virtual reference desk on almost any subject and it all can be downloaded to your computer.

If you are unable to get on your institution's Internet line, you may want to subscribe to a commercial information service such as CompuServe, America Online, Prodigy, Genie, or Delphi. These perform many of the same functions as the Internet Services and are as easy to access.

Whichever system you choose, be aware that some on-line information may be more detailed than you need. Be selective.

## SUMMARY

| | |
|---|---|
| **What are some myths about computers?** | (1) Everyone else already knows how to use a computer. (2) I may damage the equipment. (3) I need to know computer programming to use a computer. (4) I'll need extensive training. (5) Computers become outdated so quickly, I'd waste my time learning on one. (6) I really have to own a computer. |
| **What questions should I ask as I check my college's computer facilities?** | (1) How many computer terminals are available? (2) What types of computers and computer software are available? (3) How many and what type of printers are available? (4) What are the general rules for |

using the computer labs? (5) Do I need to sign up in advance to use the facilities?

**How is word processing helpful to students?**

Word processing makes it easier to write and edit once the material is input. Features such as spelling checkers, thesauruses, and style checkers are available.

**What are some common-sense basics to apply to using a computer?**

Save files often, file and label logically, handle disks with care.

**Why are computers beneficial to kinesthetic and visual learners?**

Kinesthetic learners need to be physically involved in what they are learning and visual learners need to see the material. The computer allows for both.

**How can I use the computer to learn?**

By making study guides and by processing notes from lectures and textbooks, vocabulary words, and practice tests.

**What types of learning software are available?**

Tutorial, problem-solving, and simulation software aid in learning. Educational games may also help.

**What do spreadsheet and database management programs do?**

Spreadsheet accounting software allows you to enter, store, retrieve, and manipulate data for accounting and other purposes. You can perform a variety of calculations with speed and accuracy. Database management software allows you to retrieve and manipulate data that have been entered into a database.

**What are some uses of the computer in the library?**

You will use the on-line card catalog and databases such as those on CD/ROM or academic indexes such as Infotrac.

**What are two uses of the Internet?**

The Internet can be used for electronic mail (E-mail) and for reference and research.

## HAVE YOU MISSED SOMETHING?

*Sentence completion.* Complete the following sentences with one of the three words or phrases listed below each sentence.

1. One of the most important uses of a computer in college is for _____ .
   typing term papers    storing lecture notes    keeping you organized

 2. The word processor's main function is to _____ .
    indicate misspelled words        save you time and energy
    offer a list of synonyms
 3. One skill that a computer user doesn't need to know is _____ .
    typing      programming      filing

*Matching.*   In each blank space in the left column, write the letter preceding the phrase in the right column that matches the left item best.

_____ **1.** The Internet          a. Programmed instruction

_____ **2.** Infotrack             b. Composed of horizontal and vertical col-
                                        umns that intersect and allow you to
                                        insert data at the cells

_____ **3.** Spreadsheets          c. Expanded academic index that indexes
                                        and abstracts over 1,600 periodicals

_____ **4.** Databases             d. Software programmed for specific learn-
                                        ing situations

_____ **5.** Educational           e. Electronic medium for personal com-
            games                       munication as well as a repository for
                                        information from all over the world

_____ **6.** Simulation  soft-     f. Holds information arranged for easy ac-
            ware                        cess

_____ **7.** Tutorial software     g. Uses data to model a real-life event

*True-false.*   Write *T* beside the *true* statements and *F* beside the *false* statements.

_____ **1.** Learning to program a computer and learning to use different
           kinds of software are basically the same.

_____ **2.** A college student will probably use a computer only to type papers
           and assignments.

_____ **3.** One advantage of word processing over typing is the ease of
           editing.

_____ **4.** There is no need to learn how to use a computer; it will be
           outdated before you can really use it.

_____ **5.** Computers can help visual and audio learners learn better.

_____ **6.** You really need to be able to type well in order to use a computer.

_____ **7.** Creating practice tests on the computer may actually reduce test
           anxiety.

_____ **8.** Most word-processing programs are simple enough that you can learn one while you are typing your first paper.

_____ **9.** You will probably have to get on the Internet to use your library's on-line card catalog.

_____ **10.** The printed version of a paper is usually referred to as a "hard copy."

*Multiple choice.* Choose the phrase that completes each of the following sentences most accurately and circle the letter that precedes it.

**1.** Using a word-processing program is likely to increase your

   a. productivity.
   b. alternatives.
   c. preparation.
   d. labor.

**2.** Probably the biggest advantage to becoming computer literate is that you

   a. understand programming languages.
   b. can take advantage of new ways of learning.
   c. know complex terminology.
   d. know which computer to buy for yourself.

**3.** Most people who use computers are familiar only with computer

   a. programming.
   b. applications.
   c. terminology.
   d. engineering.

**4.** Database management programs use

   a. files.
   b. records.
   c. fields.
   d. all the above.

**5.** In computing, *program* refers to

   a. an electronic connection.
   b. internal commands the computer reads.
   c. a system that simplifies accounting.
   d. none of the above.

6. Word processing is nearly the same as
   a. editing.
   b. arithmetic.
   c. illustrating.
   d. typing.

*Short answer.*   Supply a brief answer for each of the following items.

1. Name three strategies to enhance your learning with the computer.
2. Name three commonsense basics to word processing.
3. List the computer labs available on your campus. Include the hours available.
4. What must you do to use the computers in each lab?
5. What word-processing programs are available to use? Which will you try?
6. Name three people who know how to use this program.
7. Make a practice test for the next test you know you will have.
8. Ask in each course you are taking what software is available to supplement your learning with either drill and practice, tutorial, simulation, problem solving, or educational games.

   Course                                    Software

   _____       _____
   _____       _____
   _____       _____
   _____       _____
   _____       _____

9. Use the on-line computer catalog in your library to answer the following.
   What command do you type to perform an author search? _____
   What command do you type to perform a title search? _____
   What command do you type to perform a subject search? _____
   What command do you type if you know only part of the title? _____
   How many entries does the catalog have for *learning styles?* _____
   What are the titles of three books by Mark Twain?

   _____
   _____
   _____

   Name three books in your library about using the Internet.

   _____
   _____
   _____

10. What databases are available in your library? Name three.

_____

_____

_____

11. Considering your major, which databases are you likely to use most often? (You may need to ask a professor in your major.)

_____

_____

12. How can a student on your campus get on the Internet?

_____

_____

_____

13. Name three people on your campus who use the Internet and who might help you if you ask.

_____

_____

_____

14. Use the Internet to find information about your campus. List four things you found out.

_____

_____

_____

_____

*Practice using the internet*

1. Register for three newsgroups, read at least five messages on different topics, and report on each in a few sentences.
   *Hint:* Type *news at $*
          Type *set PROFILE/DIRECTORY = REGISTER*

2. Go into Gopher or Netscape. Find and report on
   (a) a part time student job listing
   (b) four other interesting things you found using Gopher or Netscape
       *Hint: $ Gopher*

3. Use FINGER in E-Mail to look up the address of someone in your class and send them a message. Copy it to your instructor.

4. Explore one of the following WWW addresses and write a paragraph about what you found.

http://www.duke.edu/~rwal (that's one, not L)
http://www.cfn.cs.da1.ca
http://www.timeinc.com/vg
http://www.secap1.com/cgi-bin/qs
http://enigma.phys.utk.edu/syost/nepal.html (L)
http://drum. ncsc.org/~okolo

## VOCABULARY BUILDING

DIRECTIONS: Make a light check mark (√) alongside one of the three words (choices) that most nearly expresses the meaning of the italicized word in the phrases that are in the left-hand column. (Answers are given on p. 440.)

|  | | 1 | 2 | 3 |
|---|---|---|---|---|
| 1. | to *delete* material | remove | emphasize | italicize |
| 2. | an electronic *thesaurus* | instrument | collection | dictionary |
| 3. | *kinesthetic* learners | mental | muscular | visual |
| 4. | *viable* solution | workable | moderate | impractical |
| 5. | flight *simulations* | solutions | imitations | experience |
| 6. | disputes with *colleagues* | associates | competitors | management |
| 7. | listing a dozen *infractions* | examples | violations | models |
| 8. | officially *apprised* | informed | inspected | estimated |
| 9. | just as *ludicrous* | melancholy | tragic | ridiculous |
| 10. | after that *debacle* | triumph | achievement | disaster |
| 11. | to *provoke* a discussion | gratify | cause | ease |
| 12. | America's *clandestine* history | candid | political | undercover |
| 13. | he is a *gullible* servant | suspicious | naive | sophisticated |
| 14. | its *moribund* economy | dying | modest | improving |
| 15. | with the *ostensible* aim | actual | apparent | genuine |
| 16. | *deterrents* to investments | problems | restraints | rules |
| 17. | the *sanctions* have impact | incentives | approvals | prohibitions |
| 18. | such a *quandry* | collection | dilemma | assortment |
| 19. | a *listless* audience | sluggish | attentive | unnumbered |
| 20. | this natural *incredulity* | trustfulness | suspicion | investment |
| 21. | money *diverted* safely | deflected | invested | apportioned |
| 22. | a *stellar* manager | youthful | creative | outstanding |
| 23. | given it's *mandate* | vote | request | approval |
| 24. | finally *succumbed* to pressure | submitted | resisted | diverted |
| 25. | the *tenuous* negotiations | legal | substantial | flimsy |

# Appendix:   Answers _____

## Chapter 1   Setting Goals

### Have You Missed Something?

Sentence completion:     1. focused     2. destinations

Matching:     1. e     2. f     3. b     4. h     5. a     6. c     7. d     8. g

True-false:     1. F     2. F     3. T     4. F     5. T     6. F     7. T     8. F
9. F     10. T

Multiple choice:     1. c     2. d

### Vocabulary Building

| | | | | | | | | |
|---|---|---|---|---|---|---|---|---|
| 1. 2 | 2. 3 | 3. 1 | 4. 1 | 5. 2 | 6. 3 | 7. 1 | 8. 3 | 9. 3 |
| 10. 1 | 11. 1 | 12. 2 | 13. 3 | 14. 1 | 15. 3 | 16. 1 | 17. 2 | |
| 18. 3 | 19. 1 | 20. 1 | 21. 1 | 22. 1 | 23. 1 | 24. 2 | 25. 1 | |

## Chapter 2   Managing Your Time

### Have You Missed Something?

Sentence completion:     1. time     2. habit

Matching:     1. g     2. f     3. d     4. b     5. h     6. c     7. a
8. e

True-false:     1. F     2. T     3. T     4. F     5. T     6. T

Multiple choice:     1. b     2. a     3. c     4. b     5. c     6. b     7. d
8. c

### Vocabulary Building

| | | | | | | | | |
|---|---|---|---|---|---|---|---|---|
| 1. 2 | 2. 3 | 3. 1 | 4. 2 | 5. 3 | 6. 2 | 7. 1 | 8. 2 | 9. 2 |
| 10. 1 | 11. 2 | 12. 3 | 13. 1 | 14. 2 | 15. 1 | 16. 3 | 17. 1 | |
| 18. 3 | 19. 2 | 20. 3 | 21. 1 | 22. 3 | 23. 2 | 24. 2 | 25. 3 | |

## Chapter 3   Managing Stress

*Have You Missed Something?*

Sentence completion:     1. stress     2. failure

Matching:     1. b     2. f     3. e     4. c     5. a     6. d

True-false:     1. T     2. T     3. T     4. F     5. F     6. T

Multiple choice:     1. c     2. d     3. b     4. d     5. b     6. c     7. b

*Vocabulary Building*

1. 2     2. 1     3. 3     4. 2     5. 3     6. 2     7. 3     8. 1     9. 2

10. 1     11. 1     12. 3     13. 1     14. 2     15. 1     16. 3     17. 1

18. 2     19. 3     20. 2     21. 3     22. 2     23. 3     24. 1     25. 2

## Chapter 4   Concentrating and Focusing

*Have You Missed Something?*

Sentence completion:     1. broken     2. the library     3. self-discipline

Matching:     1. g     2. h     3. a     4. f     5. b     6. d     7. e     8. c

True-false:     1. T     2. F     3. T     4. F     5. F     6. F     7. T

Multiple choice:     1. a     2. d     3. c     4. a     5. b     6. c

*Vocabulary Building*

1. 2     2. 3     3. 2     4. 1     5. 3     6. 2     7. 1     8. 3     9. 1

10. 2     11. 1     12. 3     13. 2     14. 1     15. 3     16. 2     17. 1

18. 3     19. 3     20. 2     21. 2     22. 1     23. 3     24. 1     25. 2

## Chapter 5   Forgetting and Remembering

*Have You Missed Something?*

Sentence completion:     1. middle     2. disliked

Matching:     1. c     2. h     3. g     4. e     5. a     6. b     7. d     8. f

True-false:     1. T     2. T     3. T     4. F     5. F

Multiple choice:     1. b     2. a     3. c     4. b     5. a

*Vocabulary Building*

| | | | | | | | | |
|---|---|---|---|---|---|---|---|---|
| 1. 2 | 2. 1 | 3. 3 | 4. 1 | 5. 2 | 6. 3 | 7. 2 | 8. 3 | 9. 1 |
| 10. 3 | 11. 1 | 12. 1 | 13. 3 | 14. 2 | 15. 1 | 16. 3 | 17. 3 | |
| 18. 1 | 19. 3 | 20. 2 | 21. 3 | 22. 1 | 23. 2 | 24. 3 | 25. 3 | |

## Chapter 6   Improving Your Vocabulary

*Have You Missed Something?*

Sentence completion:    1. success    2. context    3. synonyms

Matching:    1. b    2. c    3. g    4. f    5. a    6. d    7. e    8. h

True-false:    1. F    2. T    3. T    4. F    5. T    6. T

Multiple choice:    1. b    2. d

*Vocabulary Building*

| | | | | | | | | |
|---|---|---|---|---|---|---|---|---|
| 1. 2 | 2. 1 | 3. 3 | 4. 2 | 5. 2 | 6. 1 | 7. 3 | 8. 2 | 9. 3 |
| 10. 2 | 11. 3 | 12. 2 | 13. 1 | 14. 2 | 15. 3 | 16. 3 | 17. 2 | |
| 18. 3 | 19. 1 | 20. 2 | 21. 2 | 22. 1 | 23. 3 | 24. 2 | 25. 3 | |

## Chapter 7   Improving Your Reading Speed and Comprehension

*Have You Missed Something?*

Sentence completion:    1. magnets    2. information

Matching:    1. c    2. e    3. d    4. g    5. a    6. b    7. f

True-false:    1. F    2. T    3. T    4. T    5. T    6. F

Multiple choice:    1. a    2. c

*Vocabulary Building*

| | | | | | | | | |
|---|---|---|---|---|---|---|---|---|
| 1. 2 | 2. 1 | 3. 1 | 4. 1 | 5. 3 | 6. 2 | 7. 2 | 8. 2 | 9. 3 |
| 10. 1 | 11. 1 | 12. 2 | 13. 3 | 14. 3 | 15. 3 | 16. 1 | 17. 3 | |
| 18. 1 | 19. 2 | 20. 1 | 21. 3 | 22. 1 | 23. 3 | 24. 3 | 25. 2 | |

## Chapter 8   Understanding and Using Key Concepts

*Have You Missed Something?*

Sentence completion:     1. concentration

2. keep writing, then try to discover the pattern later

Matching:      1. c      2. e      3. b      4. f      5. d      6. a

True-false:      1. F      2. F      3. F      4. F      5. T      6. F      7. F      8. F

Multiple choice:      1. d      2. a      3. a      4. c      5. a

*Vocabulary Building*

1. 1      2. 3      3. 2      4. 1      5. 1      6. 2      7. 1      8. 3      9. 1

10. 2      11. 2      12. 2      13. 1      14. 2      15. 3      16. 2      17. 2

18. 2      19. 1      20. 2      21. 2      22. 3      23. 2      24. 1      25. 2

## Chapter 9   Listening to Take Good Notes

*Have You Missed Something?*

Sentence completion:      1. absorbed      2. facts      3. sympathetic

Matching:      1. b      2. e      3. h      4. d      5. c      6. g      7. a      8. f

True-false:      1. T      2. F      3. F      4. T      5. T

Multiple choice:      1. c      2. d      3. d

*Vocabulary Building*

1. 1      2. 2      3. 3      4. 2      5. 1      6. 2      7. 1      8. 2      9. 1

10. 2      11. 1      12. 2      13. 1      14. 3      15. 1      16. 1      17. 2

18. 2      19. 3      20. 1      21. 2      22. 1      23. 2      24. 3      25. 2

## Chapter 10   Taking Good Notes

*Have You Missed Something?*

Sentence completion:      1. minutes      2. forgetting

Matching:      1. d      2. c      3. f      4. b      5. g      6. e      7. a

True-false:      1. F      2. T      3. F      4. T      5. T      6. T

Multiple choice:      1. c      2. d      3. c

*Vocabulary Building*

1. 2    2. 1    3. 2    4. 3    5. 1    6. 2    7. 1    8. 2    9. 2

10. 3    11. 2    12. 2    13. 2    14. 1    15. 2    16. 3    17. 2

18. 2    19. 1    20. 2    21. 1    22. 3    23. 2    24. 2    25. 2

## Chapter 11    Learning from Your Textbook

*Have You Missed Something?*

Sentence completion:    1. cramming    2. sparingly    3. high

Matching:    1. d    2. f    3. g    4. e    5. c    6. a    7. b    8. h

True-false:    1. F    2. T    3. T    4. F    5. T

Multiple choice:    1. d    2. b    3. c    4. a

*Vocabulary Building*

1. 1    2. 1    3. 1    4. 2    5. 1    6. 2    7. 1    8. 2    9. 2

10. 1    11. 2    12. 1    13. 3    14. 2    15. 1    16. 3    17. 1

18. 3    19. 1    20. 2    21. 1    22. 3    23. 1    24. 2    25. 1

## Chapter 12    Noting What's Important in Readings

*Have You Missed Something?*

Sentence completion:    1. sentence    2. telegraphic    3. easy

Matching:    1. e    2. h    3. b    4. f    5. g    6. c    7. a    8. d

True-false:    1. F    2. T    3. T    4. T    5. F    6. T

Multiple choice:    1. b    2. b    3. d

*Vocabulary Building*

1. 1    2. 2    3. 3    4. 2    5. 2    6. 1    7. 2    8. 3    9. 2

10. 3    11. 2    12. 1    13. 2    14. 1    15. 3    16. 1    17. 2

18. 2    19. 2    20. 3    21. 2    22. 1    23. 1    24. 2    25. 2

## Chapter 13    Thinking Visually

### *Have You Missed Something?*

Sentence completion:    1. brainpower    2. logical    3. oriented

Matching:    1. c    2. f    3. e    4. b    5. a    6. g    7. d

True-false:    1. T    2. T    3. T    4. T    5. F

Multiple choice:    1. b    2. d    3. a    4. c    5. a    6. d

### *Vocabulary Building*

1. 1    2. 3    3. 2    4. 2    5. 1    6. 2    7. 3    8. 2    9. 2

10. 1    11. 3    12. 2    13. 1    14. 1    15. 3    16. 1    17. 3

18. 3    19. 1    20. 2    21. 3    22. 1    23. 3    24. 2    25. 1

## Chapter 14    Managing Test Anxiety

### *Have You Missed Something?*

Sentence completion:    1. success    2. crisis    3. first

Matching:    1. f    2. c    3. g    4. e    5. b    6. a    7. d

True-false:    1. T    2. T    3. T    4. F    5. T    6. F    7. T

Multiple choice:    1. b    2. c    3. a    4. d    5. b    6. d

### *Vocabulary Building*

1. 1    2. 3    3. 2    4. 2    5. 1    6. 2    7. 3    8. 3    9. 1

10. 3    11. 2    12. 1    13. 2    14. 1    15. 1    16. 2    17. 3

18. 1    19. 3    20. 2    21. 1    22. 2    23. 3    24. 1    25. 2

## Chapter 15    Mastering Objective Tests

### *Have You Missed Something?*

Sentence completion:    1. circled    2. correct

Matching:    1. g    2. d    3. h    4. a    5. e    6. c    7. f    8. b

True-false:    1. T    2. T    3. F    4. T    5. F    6. T    7. F

Multiple choice:    1. c    2. c    3. d    4. a    5. b    6. b

*Vocabulary Building*

| 1. 1 | 2. 3 | 3. 2 | 4. 2 | 5. 1 | 6. 2 | 7. 3 | 8. 1 | 9. 2 |
|------|------|------|------|------|------|------|------|------|
| 10. 1 | 11. 2 | 12. 1 | 13. 2 | 14. 3 | 15. 3 | 16. 1 | 17. 3 | |
| 18. 3 | 19. 1 | 20. 3 | 21. 1 | 22. 2 | 23. 1 | 24. 3 | 25. 1 | |

## Chapter 16  Tackling Essay Tests

*Have You Missed Something?*

Sentence completion:  1. reasoning  2. facts

Matching:  1. d  2. a  3. b  4. f  5. c  6. e

True-false:  1. F  2. T  3. T  4. F  5. T

Multiple choice:  1. a  2. d  3. b  4. d  5. a  6. d  7. a  8. a

*Vocabulary Building*

| 1. 1 | 2. 2 | 3. 3 | 4. 2 | 5. 2 | 6. 2 | 7. 1 | 8. 1 | 9. 1 |
|------|------|------|------|------|------|------|------|------|
| 10. 1 | 11. 3 | 12. 3 | 13. 1 | 14. 3 | 15. 1 | 16. 2 | 17. 1 | |
| 18. 3 | 19. 2 | 20. 1 | 21. 3 | 22. 2 | 23. 3 | 24. 1 | 25. 1 | |

## Chapter 17  Studying Literature

*Have You Missed Something?*

Sentence completion:  1. real people  2. key words  3. awareness

Matching:  1. c  2. f  3. a  4. e  5. d  6. b

True-false:  1. F  2. F  3. T  4. T  5. T

Multiple choice:  1. a  2. a  3. d  4. b  5. b  6. a  7. b

*Vocabulary Building*

| 1. 1 | 2. 3 | 3. 2 | 4. 1 | 5. 3 | 6. 1 | 7. 3 | 8. 1 | 9. 2 |
|------|------|------|------|------|------|------|------|------|
| 10. 2 | 11. 3 | 12. 2 | 13. 2 | 14. 1 | 15. 3 | 16. 1 | 17. 3 | |
| 18. 1 | 19. 3 | 20. 2 | 21. 2 | 22. 2 | 23. 2 | 24. 3 | 25. 1 | |

## Chapter 18   Studying Mathematics

*Have You Missed Something?*

Sentence completion:     1. think conceptually     2. be an active participant

3. still must estimate the answers to problems

Matching:     1. c     2. b     3. e     4. a     5. d

True-false:     1. F     2. T     3. T     4. T     5. F     6. T

Multiple choice:     1. b     2. d     3. d     4. c     5. d     6. a

*Vocabulary Building*

1. 1     2. 3     3. 2     4. 2     5. 1     6. 1     7. 2     8. 1     9. 1

10. 2     11. 1     12. 3     13. 2     14. 1     15. 2     16. 1     17. 2

18. 3     19. 2     20. 2     21. 2     22. 1     23. 3     24. 1     25. 2


## Chapter 19   Learning with the Computer

*Have You Missed Something?*

Sentence completion:     1. keeping you organized

2. save you time and energy     3. programming

Matching:     1. e     2. c     3. b     4. f     5. d     6. g     7. a

True-false:     1. F     2. F     3. T     4. F     5. T     6. F     7. T

8. F     9. F     10. T

Multiple choice:     1. a     2. b     3. b     4. d     5. b     6. d

*Vocabulary Building*

1. 1     2. 3     3. 2     4. 1     5. 2     6. 1     7. 2     8. 1     9. 3

10. 3     11. 2     12. 3     13. 2     14. 1     15. 2     16. 2     17. 2

18. 2     19. 1     20. 2     21. 1     22. 3     23. 3     24. 1     25. 3

# Index

Abbreviations
    for note taking, 215–217
    technical, 217, 218
Action, for goal achievement, 4, 5, 9–10,
    11–12 *see also* Procrastination
Active reading, of textbooks, 236–238
Addition words, 177
Adjustment, for listening, 190–191
Advanced summary sheets, 319, 320, 321
Advance organizers, surveying textbooks
    and, 244
Advantageous learning, 319
Aerobic exercise, 66–67
Alarm clock
    sleep deprivation and, 54
    time management and, 23
Alcohol, sleep and, 59
Answers, recitation and, 112–113
Artificial connections, memory and,
    106–110
Assignment-oriented weekly schedule,
    34–36
Assignments, completing, 13–14
Association, memory and, 103–111
Attention, for listening, 190
    *see also* Concentration
Attitude, *see* Positive attitude
Audiocassettes, hidden time use and, 24
Ausubel, David P., 157, 244

Backdoor Technique, for reading text-
    books, 248
Background
    memory and, 105–106
    reading improved with, 157–158
    surveying textbooks and, 243–244
Bar graphs, 293–295
Bed, as workspace, 59, 68, 81
Bethe, Hans, 173–174
Biology, mnemonic devices for, 108
Boldface, in textbooks, 235
Bookstand, for concentration, 83
Breakfast, importance of, 61
Breaks, from studying, 23, 85, 114–115
Breathing, for relaxation, 47–48

Brody, Jane, 60–61
Bullets, in textbooks, 236

Caffeine, sleep and, 59, 60
Calculator, for mathematics, 396, 402
Campus-Wide Information System
    (CWIS), 426
Carbohydrates, 62–63
Carskadon, Mary, 55
Cassette recorder, for lecture notes, 219
Category and cluster organization system,
    102–103, 104
Cause-and-effect pattern, for notes, 180
Cause-and-effect words, 177
Character traits, in literature, 380
Charlesworth, Edward A., 47
Cholesterol, 62
Chronological pattern
    for essay tests, 366
    for notes, 179
Circadian rhythms, 56, 57
Circle graph, 292
Climactic-order pattern, for notes, 179
Coffee, effects of, 59, 60
Compare or contrast pattern
    for essay tests, 366
    for notes, 180
Comparison words, 177
Complex carbohydrates, 64
Comprehensive listening, 187, 189
Computers, 415–432
    course on, 418
    databases and, 424–426
    definition of, 418
    Internet and, 425–426
    in library, 424–425
    myths about, 417–418
    school's resources for, 418–420
    software and, 420–423
    spreadsheets and, 420, 423–424
    word processing and, 420–422
Concentration, 77–92
    balance between goal and skills for,
        85–86
    bookstand for, 83